INDIA'S CONSTITUTION

INDIA'S
CONSTITUTION

by

M. V. PYLEE

ASIA PUBLISHING HOUSE (P.) LTD.
BOMBAY . CALCUTTA . NEW DELHI . MADRAS
LUCKNOW . NEW YORK

© 1962, 1967, 1979 M. V. P Y L E E

First Published by Asia Publishing House: 1962
Reprinted: 1963
Reprinted: 1965
Second Revised Edition: 1967
Reprinted: 1967
Reprinted: 1968
Reprinted: 1974
Third Revised Edition Published by Asia Publishing House (P.) Ltd: 1979

ISBN: 0.210.33709.5

PRINTED IN INDIA

BY G. G. PATHARE AT POPULAR PRESS (BOM.) PVT. LTD., BOMBAY AND PUBLISHED BY ANANDA JAISINGH, ASIA PUBLISHING HOUSE (P.) LTD., BOMBAY.

PREFACE TO THE THIRD EDITION

TWELVE YEARS have passed since the second edition of this book
was published in 1967. It is a rather long interval. During that
period, however, three reprints of the book were brought out to
meet the public demand.

The last decade was remarkable from the point of view
of constitutional changes. Many significant amendments to the
Constitution have been passed during this period. In fact, the
country has witnessed, during these years, the most momentous
period from the point of view of debates and discussions and
controversies on the different aspects of the Constitution and its
working. The Forty-second Amendment was the most controversial in this context.

Apart from these amendments of far reaching importance, there
were several judicial pronouncements, especially those of the
Supreme Court of India which played a significant role in the
development of the Constitution. Some of these decisions have
also been equally controversial.

The legislative and administrative machinery both at the Centre
and the States (the Parliament and the Government of India and
the legislatures and the Governments in the States) have also contributed in substantial measure towards the growth of the Constitution during this period. Many important legislative enactments have been passed; also many important administrative
decisions have been made and implemented.

All these have been included in this revised edition making the
book uptodate in all respects.

It is a matter of great satisfaction to the author that this book
has been very widely in demand ever since it was first published
in 1962. The several reprints of both the previous editions bear
testimony to this. At the international book exhibition in Delhi
in 1972 it was acknowledged as one of the best-sellers among
the non-fiction series of books. The work has now also appeared
in Indian language editions. This goes to show its popularity
and wide acceptance by those interested in the subject. The
author is indeed greatly encouraged by the favourable reader reac-

tion.   He is therefore very happy that the new edition is now ready for release.

The author would like to take this opportunity to express his deep sense of gratitude to all those who encouraged him to bring out this new edition.   He would also like to thank all those who conveyed to him their comments, critical or otherwise, with a view to improving the contents of the book.

M. V. PYLEE

PREFACE TO THE SECOND EDITION

THE SECOND edition of the book is brought out nearly four years after it was first published. The first edition, however, had two reprints. Since 1962 there have been several constitutional changes of far reaching importance. A new edition has become necessary to incorporate these changes as well as for analysing their impact on the working of the Constitution. As a result, almost every chapter of the original work, except the one which deals with the Historical Background, has undergone change in varying degrees. The main basis of these changes has been fourfold: constitutional amendments, legislative enactments, judicial pronouncements and administrative practices and procedures.

The fact that the first edition had two reprints during the last two years shows the very generous welcome this book has received from those who are interested in the subject. Nothing is more encouraging to an author.

A Hindi edition of the book was brought out two years ago and a Tamil edition is expected to be out soon. These are, again heartening indications of the increasing interest in the book and the wider acceptance that it is receiving.

I would like to take this opportunity to express my deep sense of gratitude to all those who gave their views, critical or otherwise, on the first edition of the book either directly to me or through their valued reviews which appeared in many journals both in India and abroad. Due regard has been shown to these while the work on the present edition was undertaken.

M. V. PYLEE

PREFACE TO THE FIRST EDITION

THE FIRST major achievement of Independent India was the framing of a new constitution based on the ideals of justice, liberty, equality and fraternity. But the Constitution has been criticised for being unusually long and complex. In one or two respects there is some justification in this criticism. But by and large, the alleged over-elaboration and complexity are more apparent than real.

No other constitution-making body had ever faced a task so difficult as the Constituent Assembly of India. Any constitution that is designed to provide for the governmental machinery of a vast country like India with 360 million people was bound to be complicated. But with India it was not merely a matter of number or size. There was a perplexing diversity—of language, race, religion and culture.

Prior to 1947, there were two Indias politically, British India and Indian India. The former was under the direct rule of Britain for two centuries. The latter was a political medley, composed of hundreds of heterogeneous Princely States, some big but most of them small, some modern but most of them feudal, some liberal but most of them autocratic, and all equally under the paramountcy of the British Crown.

Economically, although impoverished in general as a result of colonial exploitation, India nevertheless provided a paradox—certain areas were comparatively advanced and prosperous while others were unbelievably backward; certain classes fabulously rich, others living in abject poverty. Socially, the evils of a degenerated caste-system, the curse of untouchability and the canker of communalism, based upon religious differences, were destroying the very vitals of the once dynamic Indian society.

Despite all the artificial barriers, political, economic and social, there had still been a cultural unity pervading the entire country. But that too was fast disappearing under the influence of fissiparous forces. On top of it all, there came the partition of the country into India and Pakistan, with all the pangs of that painful process.

It was difficult to find a more baffling political entity with such complex social and economic problems, than the India of 1947. To evolve out of the weltering chaos a compact, well-knit nation was the task that confronted the constitution-makers.

The Constitution of India attempts to tackle this by laying down the fundamental law of the new nation. It is not merely a document dealing with the governmental machinery for running the administration of the country, but is in fact, an embodiment of the ideals and aspirations of the people of India. At the same time, it is also the product of the pattern of social forces that obtained in India in the wake of her winning political independence.

Naturally, such a document is bound to be long, complicated and, at least in parts, beyond the comprehension of the layman. But such complexity was not the result of deliberate intent, nor the product of loose thinking and poor drafting. Every part of it has a history behind it; every part of it has a definite purpose to serve; every part of it is the result of a sustained effort by the best intellects in India that got together in the Constituent Assembly. It has, nevertheless, some imperfections, like all things human.

Almost every modern constitution is a complicated document. This is mainly because of the complications involved in the mechanism of modern government, which is no longer the simple thing that it was in the past. It is no longer an embodiment of the traditional concept of 'a hindrance to hindrances to the good life'. Today it has to play a positive role. It has to lead and guide human beings in many of their activities.

The layman is comparatively ignorant of the working of the complicated mechanism of modern government just as he is incapable of understanding the complicated mechanism of a technological device. It is a field for the expert and even experts do not know all about it. Yet, the ordinary man is capable of judging whether that mechanism works well or ill on the basis of the benefits that he enjoys through it.

It is not the simplicity or the complexity of the Constitution that matters. What matters is how it works; whether or not its objectives are being realised in practice. The text may be long or short, simple or obscure. But if it works well and produces good results, it is a good constitution. This is the test that we should apply to the Constitution of India.

A little over a decade is too short a period for this purpose. Yet, during the last eleven years, the Constitution has more or less been meeting the requirements of a country that has embarked upon a programme of revolutionary but peaceful change. How it has actually been working in the circumstances is a matter that calls for careful study.

This book attempts to make such a study, not in a very detailed way, yet, in a fairly comprehensive manner. It seeks to focus the attention of those interested in the subject on the way the different aspects of the Constitution have been in operation, on their proved merits and drawbacks. The impact of a reasonably successful system of constitutional government in India will not be confined to the four hundred million people of India; it will in fact affect the destiny of many nations of Asia and Africa who have recently achieved or are in the process of achieving their political independence.

I wish to express my sincere gratitude to all those from many parts of the country who have encouraged me in writing this book ever since the publication of my earlier work *Constitutional Government in India* (1960). I would like to recommend that work to those who wish to have more detailed comments on the different aspects covered by this book.

M. V. PYLEE

CONTENTS

PART VII
MISCELLANEOUS PROVISIONS

MAPS

Facing Page

"I feel that it is workable, it is flexible and it is strong enough to hold the country together both in peace-time and in war-time. Indeed, if I may say so, if things go wrong under the new Constitution, the reason will not be that we had a bad constitution. What we will have to say is that Man was vile."

B. R. AMBEDKAR
Chairman, Drafting Committee
of the Constituent Assembly

PART I

INTRODUCTORY

CHAPTER 1

THE DAWN OF A NEW ERA

THE TWENTY-SIXTH January, 1950, marked a great event in the long and chequered history of India. For, on that day, was brought into force the present Constitution of India, which announced to the world the birth of a new republic. It was in fact the re-birth of an ancient country, after centuries of dire vicissitudes.

The struggle for national independence was over by August 15, 1947. On that day the two-hundred-year-old British rule in India was brought to an end by the transfer of political authority to Indian hands. However, the attainment of independence was not an end in itself. It was only the beginning of a new struggle, the struggle to live as an independent nation and, at the same time, to establish a democracy based upon the ideals of justice, liberty, equality and fraternity. The need of a new constitution forming the basic law of the land for the realisation of these ideals was paramount. Therefore, one of the first tasks undertaken by independent India was the framing of a new constitution. The present Constitution of India is its result. It represents the political, economic and social ideals and aspirations of the vast majority of the Indian people.

A constitution is a set of laws and rules setting up the machinery of the government of a State and which defines and determines the relations between the different institutions and areas of government, the executive, the legislature and the judiciary, the central, the regional and the local governments. The first well-known instance of a written constitution was that of the United States of America which set up an original pattern, and which for its "brevity, restraint and simplicity" is universally hailed as a remarkable document. The makers of the Indian Constitution drew much from the American Constitution though not its brevity, and added to that the experience of later constitutions in different parts of the world, especially much from the British-made Government of India Act of 1935. Thus, the Constitution of India is the result of considerable imitation and adaptation rather than of originality.

Napoleon once told Talleyrand, his leading political adviser,

3

that a "constitution ought to be short and clear." But the latter countered, "No Sire, it ought to be long and obscure!" Of the two qualities prescribed by the ingenious Frenchman, there can be no doubt that the Indian Constitution possesses the first; it is debatable, however, whether we have achieved the second quality. The Constitution in XXII Parts,[1] with its 395 Articles;[2] many of which contain a number of exceptions, limitations and qualifications, and nine Schedules and forty-three Amendments (so far), runs into some three-hundred pages making it the longest in the history of constitutions.

The Elephantine Size of the Constitution

What made the Constitution so "bulky" is perhaps the first question which anyone who glances over it might ask. To begin with, therefore, we may deal with this question. The size of the Constitution is the result of many contributory factors. The most important of these are as follows:

(1) India has a federal constitution. Normally, a federal constitution because of the detailed provisions that it embodies with respect to the division of powers between the federation and the States, is longer than the constitution of a unitary State. In the case of India, the federal system established under the Constitution is dealt with in greater detail than normally done elsewhere. Further, the Constitution of India is not merely that of a federation. Unlike most federal constitutions it prescribes not only a constitution for the Union but also for the States. The framers of the Constitution were eager to avoid as much legal conflict as possible arising out of the division of powers between the Union and the States. They were of the opinion that a clear-cut and well-defined division of powers between the Union and the States would ensure such a result. Hence they went into elaborate details which were embodied in separate chapters such as legislative relations, administrative relations, financial relations and inter-state trade and commerce.

(2) Part III of the Constitution embodies the Fundamental

[1] The Forty-second Amendment added a new Part to the Constitution, Part IV-A, which contains Fundamental Duties.

[2] The total number of Articles also has gone up as a result of the many amendments of the Constitution.

Rights and consists of 29 Articles. Most of the modern constitutions have a chapter on fundamental rights. But seldom has any constitution attempted to set out these rights in such details. Because of the peculiar conditions and circumstances prevailing in India, the framers of the Constitution were compelled not only to incorporate rights which are unknown to other constitutions such as the abolition of "Untouchability" but also details which may be considered unnecessary elsewhere.

(3) The Constituent Assembly thought fit to include also a chapter on "Directive Principles of State Policy". Part IV contains these Directives which, although, according to the Constitution, not "enforceable by any court of law", are nevertheless fundamental in the governance of the country.

(4) There are problems peculiar to India which, in the opinion of the Constituent Assembly, required special treatment in the Constitution itself. These include the "Services under the Union, and the States", Special Provisions relating to classes such as the Scheduled Castes, Scheduled Tribes and Anglo-Indians, Official Language, and the Emergency Provisions. The Constitution has also a chapter on "Elections", another on "Miscellaneous Provisions", and a third on "Temporary and Transitional Provisions". Almost three-fourth of the Constitution is covered by the items mentioned above, and that explains the size of the Constitution.

(5) The justification for the inclusion of provisions for what would otherwise be regulated by ordinary legislation is to be found in the constitutional history of India under the British rule. The Constitution derives directly from the Government of India Act, 1935, many of its provisions almost verbatim. That Act was the largest ever passed by the British Parliament and its main purpose was to transfer power, subject to numerous so-called safeguards, from British officials to Indian politicians. The Constitution had to create a new federal legislature and, at the same time, reform the governments of the former Indian Princely States. Hence, the Constitution Act of 1935 was full of compromises designed to meet this double objective resulting in an extremely elaborate and complex document. Although the Government of India Act of 1935 was not fully put into operation, an important part of it was implemented in 1937 and, in any case, Indians had become familiar with its provisions ever since. The same Act was suitably

modified to become the Constitution of the Dominion of India
between 15 August 1947 and 26 January 1950, the date of commencement of the present Constitution. It was only natural, therefore, that the fathers of the Constitution should borrow provisions
of the Act of 1935 and make them part of the new constitution
they were framing. Making a specific reference to this aspect of
the Constitution, Ambedkar, the Chairman of the Drafting Committee, said in the Constituent Assembly:

> "As to the accusation that the Draft Constitution has repro-
> duced a good part of the provisions of the Government of India
> Act, 1935, I make no apologies. There is nothing to be ashamed
> of in borrowing. It involves no plagiarism. *Nobody holds any*
> *patent rights in the fundamental ideas of a Constitution.* What
> I am sorry about is that the provisions taken from the Govern-
> ment of India Act, 1935, relate mostly to the details of admi-
> nistration."[3]

This he justified on the ground that in India democratic traditions
had yet to develop and in the absence of such traditions it was
too much of a risk to leave the constitution in general terms.

(6)   Another consideration that influenced the founding fathers
of the Constitution was the existence of certain factors which were
peculiar to India. Most of the members of the Constituent Assembly, particularly the leading lights, had the unpleasant experience of having undergone varying terms of imprisonment while
non-violently fighting against the British rule. Very often, it was
an arbitrary Government decision that sent them to jail. This convinced them of the necessity to limit, rigidly by law, the powers
of government. Consequently, they made a special effort to go into
as much detail as possible in every part of the Constitution.

(7)   India is a land of immense diversity. From a religious
point of view, Hinduism and Islam are the leading faiths. But there
are considerable numbers of adherents of other religions like Chris-
tianity, Sikhism, Buddhism, Jainism, Zoroastrianism and Judaism.
Among the Hindus, who are traditionally divided into different
castes, are a large number of the so-called "Untouchables". There
are also the tribal people who occupy certain isolated pockets in

[3] C.A.D. VII, p. 38.

different parts of the country, almost cut-off from the rest of the people. From a racial point of view there are at least three major groups, the Indo-Aryans, the Dravidians and the Mongolo-Aryans. There are not less than a dozen well-developed major languages spoken in different parts of the country. Some of these have a literature as old as 3000 years. From a cultural point of view also, great differences can be noticed between different areas within the Indian sub-continent. The Constitution-makers were called upon to draw up a document which adequately protected the interests of these various minorities and yet safeguarded the essential unity of the nation. This again tended to enlarge the size of the Constitution.

(8) One can easily notice the spirit of not only political democracy but also economic democracy that breathes through the entire body of the Constitution. This is the result of an ardent desire of the framers to effect a rapid modernisation of economic and social institutions. It was impossible to think of a constitution of 1950 creating the framework of a "laissez faire" State rather than a welfare State. Particularly, a country like India after two centuries of foreign rule and with a huge population, could not leave this matter to either legislative discretion or judicial interpretation.

(9) The exercise of both judicial and administrative functions by the same officer was one of the controversies of British India. The Collector, the head of a District, was more often than not, a local dictator. This was due to the combination of executive and judicial functions in his office. Agitation for the separation of these functions has a century-old history in India. Hence, it was no surprise that the Constitution-makers should have dealt with this problem in detail. As a result, the doctrine of the separation of powers has received a new interpretation in India. Such separation calls for not merely the independence of the superior courts but also a differentiation of local functions. Judicial administration, even at the lower levels, has become a subject of constitutional importance. The Articles of the Constitution dealing with the judiciary are based on the theory that the subject is of such great importance that it should be dealt with in detail by constitutional law and not by ordinary law.

(10) All these special problems and circumstances have made their conspicuous contribution to making the Constitution a bulky

and even complex document. The predominance of the lawyer-element in the making of the Constitution may have been an additional factor.[4] It must also be remembered that the Indian Constitution-makers were not framing a constitution anew after a "bloody" revolution as in some other countries. Political power was transferred in a peaceful manner in India. Hence, the framers did not and could not altogether ignore, in the new framework, the administrative structure which was in existence and had been working for a long time.

The Alleged Paradise of the Lawyers

One of the most frequently heard complaints against the Constitution, both in the Constituent Assembly during the discussion on the Draft Constitution and outside it, was that it was "a lawyer's paradise". Making a general comment on the Constitution, a member said that "the Draft tends to make people more litigious, more inclined to go to law courts, less truthful and less likely to follow the methods of truth and non-violence. If I may say so, the Draft is really a lawyer's paradise. It opens up vast avenues of litigation and will give our able and ingenious lawyers plenty of work to do".[5]

It is true that the Constitution is a complex document. The complexity, as we have noted above, is mainly due to the difficult problems which the framers confronted at the time of its making and their attempt to embody solutions for them in the Constitution itself. It is also because of the elaborate and detailed language in which the provisions of the Constitution are worded. Further, the language in which it was drafted is that which is familiar only in courts of law. A striking feature of the Constitution in this context is the numerous exceptions, qualifications and explanations that one finds along with almost every provision. Whatever might be the reasons for their inclusion, their presence makes the understanding of the Constitution extremely difficult for the ordinary reader. Only an experienced lawyer, well-versed in constitu-

---

[4] Five members of the seven-member Drafting Committee, including its Chairman were leading legal luminaries of the time. They were : B. R. Ambedkar (Chairman), Alladi Krishnaswami Aiyar, K. M. Munshi, M. Saadulla and Madhava Rao. The two others were N. Gopalaswami Ayyangar and T. T. Krishnamachari.

[5] H. K. Maheswari, C.A.D. VII, p. 293.

tional law, can understand the implications of the legal language in which most of these provisions are couched. This would seem to justify the description of the Constitution as a lawyer's paradise.

On a closer examination, however, it will be seen that such a description is the result of misunderstanding and a misplaced apprehension. The fact that the Constitution is a complex document need not necessarily mean that it should become a fertile source of litigation. Neither the length nor complexity of a legal document has in itself a direct relation to litigation. An apparently simple and easily understood provision might provide a rich field for prolonged legal battles. A classic example is the "Commerce Clause" of the American Constitution which provides that "the Congress shall have power to regulate commerce with foreign Nations, and among the several States, and with the Indian Tribes". It is almost impossible to think of simpler terms to describe the idea embodied in this clause. Apparently, no legal assistance is required for anyone to understand its meaning. And yet, the commerce clause has been a rich source of unending litigation throughout the history of the American Republic. This is true of several other apparently simple and easily understood provisions of the American Constitution. The "General Welfare" clause is another example. Such examples can be cited from other constitutions as well. Section 92 of the Australian Constitution which deals with inter-state trade and commerce is one in point. The history of the section is a conspicuous example of the pitfalls likely to be encountered by a rigid Constitution in a changing world. No section in the Australian Constitution, in the opinion of an Australian critic, has given rise to so much litigation or difference of judicial opinion.

As has already been pointed out, the American Constitution, compared to the Indian Constitution, is a marvel of brevity and simplicity. But this has not in any way cut down litigation. On an average, the Supreme Court of the United States is called upon to decide over thirteen hundred cases a year. In contrast, the Supreme Court of India in its constitutional field has yet to reach even half that figure a year in its career so far. The number of cases that come before the Supreme Court compares favourably with that which come before other federal Supreme Courts such as the Canadian Supreme Court and the Australian High Court.

The elaborate nature of the Indian Constitution, instead of enhancing the scope of litigation, has in fact helped to reduce it considerably. The best example of this is provided by those chapters of the Constitution which deal with the relations between the Union and the States. Under any federal system, one of the major sources of litigation is provided by that part of the constitution which deals with the division of powers between the Union and the States. This has been the case in the United States, in Canada and Australia. But in India, over a quarter century of the working of the Constitution, there has been a proportionately small number of cases in this field. The credit for this should go largely to the detailed character of the provisions of the Constitution.

If there is any part of the Constitution which can be called a lawyer's paradise on the basis of the extent of litigation that it has caused so far, it is the chapter which embodies the Fundamental Rights. Even a casual glance over the pages of the Supreme Court reports will show that there have been more cases in this area than in any other. Critics of the Constitution were severe on these provisions at the time of their adoption and predicted that they would beat all records as a source of litigation. But it stands to the credit of the Constitution that even in this field, the number of cases has not been too large. Normally, fundamental rights, by their very nature provide a continuously rich source of litigation. The conflict between man and the State is a perennial problem. As such, any constitution that guarantees fundamental rights and makes the judiciary its protector makes also an invitation to litigation. The Bill of Rights under the American Constitution is the best example. The fact that the American Bill of Rights is couched in the simplest language imaginable did not in any way reduce litigation. On the contrary, the American Supreme Court, again and again, in thousands of cases, was called upon to adjudicate the competing claims of individual freedom and social control. It is not a fact that in India, the litigation arising out of the provisions of the chapter on fundamental rights has been due to the detailed nature of the provisions or because of the numerous exceptions and qualifications. Such litigation is an inevitable expression of the democratic vigilance in regard to the freedom of the individual. It is a sign of health, and not necessarily the result of any defects in the law.

Constitutional litigation is generally a product of verbal defects such as ambiguity, vagueness of the expressions used and the lack of precision and certainty. Viewed from this point, one could find several provisions in the Constitution of India, as originally passed, which were far from satisfactory. This is one of the reasons for the comparatively large number of amendments of the Constitution. Article 31 which dealt with the right to property which caused, perhaps, the largest amount of litigation on any single article, provides one of the best illustrations of such provisions.

In an unusually long constitutional document like the Constitution of India, which attempts to provide almost a panacea for the many political, social and economic ills which the country had been suffering from at the time of its independence, it is not impossible to find provisions that may be vague or ambiguous. But to denigrate the Constitution as a lawyer's paradise on account of its detailed provisions or of its complex nature is not justified. On the contrary, the Constitution has so far not yielded any abundant opportunities for legal wrangles only on account of its length, and it is improbable that it will ever do so in future. It was certainly no conspiracy of the lawyer constitution-makers that made the Constitution complex. The problems which India faced in the wake of freedom were many and complex. No Constituent Assembly charged with the task of framing a democratic document ever faced such diverse and difficult problems. Simplicity in itself is not a virtue. Adequacy is a more essential quality in a legal document. And the virtue of the Constitution is finally to be judged from the results it produces.

Some Further Points of Criticism

Apart from the bulkiness and the complexity which made the critics of the Constitution assail it as a lawyer's paradise, there were also other serious criticisms which deserve at least a mention.

(1) One of the most important of these criticisms has been that no part of the Constitution represents the ancient polity of India, its genius and the spirit of its hallowed and glorious traditions. Many members in the Constituent Assembly drew the attention of the House and the country to this omission. Some of them

also pointed out that the Constitution did not embody the principles for which "Gandhism" stood or the ideology of the Indian National Congress. Others thought that it should have been "raised and built upon village panchayats and district panchayats". A few extremists even advocated the abolition of the Central and the Provincial Governments. They just wanted an India full of village governments!

Answering these criticisms, Ambedkar said in the Constituent Assembly:

"The love of the intellectual Indian for the village community is of course infinite if not pathetic [*Laughter*]. It is largely due to the fulsome praise bestowed upon it by Metcalfe who described them as little republics having nearly everything that they want within themselves, and almost independent of any foreign relations. The existence of these village communities each one forming a separate little State in itself has, according to Metcalfe, contributed more than any other cause to the preservation of the people of India, through all the revolutions and changes which they have suffered, and is in a high degree conducive to their happiness and to the enjoyment of a great portion of freedom and independence. No doubt the village communities do not care to consider what little part they have played in the affairs and the destiny of the country; and why? Their part in the destiny of the country has been well described by Metcalfe himself who says: 'Dynasty after dynasty tumbles down. Revolution succeeds to revolution. Hindoo, Pathan, Moghul, Maratha, Sikh, English are all masters in turn but the village communities remain the same. In times of trouble they arm and fortify themselves. A hostile army passes through the country. The village communities collect their little cattle within their walls, and let the enemy pass unprovoked'.

"Such is the part the village communities have played in the history of their country. Knowing this, what pride can one feel in them? That they have survived through all vicissitudes may be a fact. But mere survival has no value. The question is on what plane they have survived. Surely on a low, on a selfish level. I hold that these village republics have been the ruination of India. I am therefore surprised that those who condemn provincialism and communalism should come forward as champions of the village. What is the village but a sink of localism, a den of ignorance, narrow-mindedness and communalism? I am glad that the Draft Constitution has discarded the village and adopted the individual as its unit."[6]

Ambedkar's criticism has been largely justified in the light of the performance of village panchayats wherever they have been established in the country. There can be no doubt that the stability and security of Indian democracy depend largely on the successful functioning of the village panchayats which have to become its real backbone. But the fact is that the village panchayats, today, are nowhere near that position. And it is doubtful whether they would in the near future develop themselves to assume such a role. Nothing but all-round education and the cultivation of civic virtues and responsibilities at the village level can build, over a period of years, a sound foundation for a democratic system to flourish in the country. If the Constitution had attempted to establish straightway "village republics" in mid-twentieth century on the plea that such institutions flourished in the country in the remote past, ignoring the conditions of the modern technological age, there would have been nothing but confusion and anarchy, and the unity that was established as a result of so much sacrifice would have been lost in no time once again, perhaps for ever.

(2) Critics of the federal provisions can be divided into two categories. According to most of them, the Centre has been made too strong. But some of them wanted it to be made stronger. The Constitution has struck a balance. As Ambedkar said:

"However much you may deny powers to the Centre, it is difficult to prevent the Centre from becoming strong. Conditions in the modern world are such that centralisation of powers is inevitable. One has only to consider the growth of the Federal Government in the U.S.A. which, notwithstanding the very limited powers given to it by the Constitution, has outgrown its former self and has overshadowed and eclipsed the State Governments. This is due to modern conditions. The same conditions are sure to operate on the Government of India and

[6] C.A.D. VII, p. 38.

nothing that one can do will help to prevent it from being strong. On the other hand, we must resist the tendency to make it stronger. It cannot chew more than it can digest. Its strength must be commensurate with its weight. It would be a folly to make it so strong that it may fall by its own weight."[7]

The experience of a quarter century and more shows that the federal system has, on the whole, worked remarkably well. The apprehensions of the critics that the Centre being too strong would devour the States, and that they would be reduced to the status of administrative units of the Union, have not materialised. On the contrary, the States have been holding their own and maintaining their individuality and autonomy within the framework of the Constitution. Litigation in the field of Centre-State relationship has been conspicuous by its negligible size rather than its enormity which is one of the common defects of the older federations. Although there had been seventeen Amendments to the Constitution within fifteen years after its inauguration none of these seriously affected the field of Centre-State relationship except for minor changes. The later amendments, except the Forty-second, also showed the same trend. The fear that the existence of a long Concurrent List, instead of reducing litigation, might lead to an increase of it, has been falsified. In fact, the success of the federal system is largely the result, while distributing and allocating legislative powers, of taking into account the political and economic conditions obtaining in the country, rather than of relying on *a priori* theories of federalism.

Perhaps, the most criticised part of the Constitution is that which deals with the Fundamental Rights. It has been alleged that every fundamental right embodied in the Constitution is riddled with so many exceptions and qualifications that these have eaten up the rights altogether. Further, it is pointed out that the life and liberty of the subject has been placed at the mercy of the executive Government and there is hardly any protection against tyrannical laws.

Dealing with the exceptions and qualifications, Ambedkar said:

"In the opinion of the critics, fundamental rights are not

[7] C.A.D. VII p. 42.

fundamental rights unless they are also absolute rights. The critics rely on the Constitution of the United States and the Bill of Rights embodied in the first ten Amendments to that Constitution in support of their contention. It is said that the fundamental rights in the American Bill of Rights are real because they are not subjected to limitations or exceptions.

"I am sorry to say that the whole of the criticism about fundamental rights is based upon a misconception. In the first place, the criticism insofar as it seeks to distinguish fundamental rights from non-fundamental rights is not sound. It is incorrect to say that fundamental rights are absolute while non-fundamental rights are created by agreement between parties while fundamental rights are the gift of the law. Because fundamental rights are the gift of the State it does not follow that the State cannot qualify them.

"In the second place, it is wrong to say that fundamental rights in America are absolute. The difference between the position under the American Constitution and the Draft Constitution is one of form and not of substance. That the fundamental rights in America are not absolute rights is beyond dispute. In support of every exception to the Fundamental Rights set out in the Draft Constitution one can refer to at least one judgement of the United States Supreme Court".[8]

(3) The criticism that the protection against tyrannical laws and the arbitrary conduct of the executive against the life and liberty of the subject is too slender, has a good deal of force in it. For, under Article 21, life and liberty can be taken away so long as it is done in accordance with the procedure established by law. Similarly, private property can be compulsorily acquired by the State for a public purpose and the legislature may at its will fix the quantum of compensation. In both these cases, the ultimate power is vested in the legislature to fix the limits and the citizen has no remedy against an oppressive legislative majority, a serious drawback from the point of view of fundamental rights. The existence of a provision which permits "preventive detention" for the purposes of the State leaves in the hands of the executive an extraordinary power to curb individual freedom. These are

[8] C.A.D. VII, p. 40.

serious limitations on the scope of fundamental rights and, as such, they form a weighty criticism of an important part of the Constitution.

(4) The inclusion of a set of non-justiciable rights—the Directive Principles of State Policy—in the Constitution has been criticised as the inclusion of a set of pious declarations which have no binding force. According to Ambedkar, this criticism is super-fluous. "The Constitution itself says so in so many words. If it is said that the Directive Priciples have no legal force behind them, I am prepared to admit it. But I am not prepared to admit that they have no sort of binding force at all. Nor am I prepared to concede that they are useless because they have no binding force in law".

Apart from the fact that the Directive Principles form a code of conduct both for legislators and administrators and set before the country a socio-economic objective that is to be realised as early as possible, they help the people to assess in the light of a clearly laid-down standard, the achievements of each government in office at the time of every general election. Further, the separa-tion of non-justiciable rights from justiciable ones has a special advantage. It avoids the necessity of bringing under the same category, rights of varying value.

(5) The Constitution has been criticised by some for the special safeguards that it provides for minorities and certain classes who are socially and educationally backward. Commending the wisdom underlying these provisions, Ambedkar said: "Speaking for myself, I have no doubt that the Constituent Assembly has done wisely in providing such safeguards for minorities as it has done. In this country both the minorities and the majorities have followed a wrong path. It is wrong for the majority to deny the existence of minorities. It is equally wrong for the minorities to perpetuate themselves. A solution must be found which will serve a double purpose. It must recognise the existence of the minorities to start with. It must also be such that it will enable majorities and minorities to merge some day into one. The solution proposed by the Constituent Assembly is to be welcomed because it is a solution which serves this two-fold purpose. To diehards who have developed a kind of fanaticism against minority protection I would like to say two things. One is that minorities are an explosive force

which, if it erupts, can blow up the whole fabric of the State. The history of Europe bears ample and appalling testimony to this fact. The other is that the minorities in India have agreed to place their existence in the hands of the majority. In the history of negotiations for preventing the partition of Ireland, Redmond said to Carson, "Ask for any safeguard you like for the Protestant minority but let us have a United Ireland". Carson's reply was, "Damn your safeguards, we don't want to be ruled by you". No minority in India has taken this stand. They have loyally accepted the rule of the majority which is basically a communal majority and not a political majority. It is for the majority to realise its duty not to discriminate against minorities. Whether the minorities will continue or will vanish must depend upon this habit of the majority. The moment the majority loses the habit of discriminating against the minority, the minorites can have no ground to exist. They will vanish".[9]

The Draft Constitution was discussed in most of the Provincial Assemblies even before it was considered in detail by the Constituent Assembly. A remarkable trend to these discussions was the general consensus of opinion on the soundness of its fundamentals, and the firm hope that the Constitution would prove a working document for a new India that was taking shape. The only serious criticism voiced was about the Centre-State financial provisions which, it was feared, placed the States at the mercy of the Centre in the financial field. It is significant to note that no section of the people, however advanced or backward their views were, denounced the Constitution in toto. In fact, two political parties, the Socialist Party of India and the Hindu Maha Sabha, had prepared their own constitutions for free India. And the most striking feature of these constitutional drafts was that both of them were in agreement with the main features of the Constitution adopted by the Constituent Assembly.

No constitution is perfect and the Constitution of India is no exception to this universal rule. There can however be no doubt that it is a workable document. It is a blend of idealism and realism. In hammering it out, the framers traversed all the processes of "democratic manufactory" and ranged through the whole gamut of democratic factors. There have been careful

[9] C.A.D. VII, p. 39.

2

thought, close analysis, argument and counter-argument. There was even fierce controversy, so fierce that, as Frank Anthony observed, it was apprehended at times that the members might reach the stage of what the Romans called *argumentum ad baculum,* i.e. settling it by actual physical force. But in the final analysis, a real sense of accommodation prevailed and a real sense of forbearance. As a result, the Constitution emerged as a basis for all the people of India to work in co-operation and collaboration in a mighty endeavour to build a new, free India. As Ambedkar said:

"I feel that it is workable, it is flexible and it is strong enough to hold the country together both in peacetime and in wartime. Indeed, if I may say so, if things go wrong under the new Constitution, the reason will not be that we had a bad Constitution. What we will have to say is that Man was vile".[10]

[10] C.A.D. VII, p. 44.

CHAPTER 2

BASIC PRINCIPLES

IF THE division of power is the basis of civilised government, a constitution is the best device by which such division could be facilitated. Constitutionalism is an achievement of the modern world. But it is a comparatively recent achievement. As such, it has not become fully stabilised. Meanwhile, every constitution aims to build up a governmental structure based upon certain basic principles. And these principles are more or less well-established. Although some of these principles are common to most constitutions, there are others which vary from constitution to constitution. Such variations are the product of the varying conditions and circumstances that determine the principles of the constitution. The Constitution of India is not an exception to this rule and it has its own basic principles. We shall, therefore, begin by a study of the basic principles of the Constitution, which form the foundations of democratic government in India.

A careful study of the Constitution will show that there are at least seven basic principles which are embodied in it and which form the foundations of democracy in India. These are: (1) popular sovereignty, (2) secularism, (3) fundamental rights, (4) directive principles of State policy, (5) judicial independence, (6) federalism and (7) cabinet government. We may examine briefly the scope of each of these principles.

Popular Sovereignty

The Constitution proclaims the sovereignty of the people in its opening words. The Preamble begins with the words, "We the people of India, having solemnly resolved to constitute India into a sovereign... republic". The idea is reaffirmed in several places in the Constitution, particularly in the chapter dealing with elections. Article 326 declares that "the elections to the House of People and to the Legislative Assembly of every State shall be on the basis of adult suffrage". As a result, the Government at the Centre and in the States derive their authority from the people who choose their representatives for Parliament and the State Legislatures at regular intervals. Further, those who wield the executive power of the government are responsible to the legislature and through them to the people. Thus, in the affairs of the State, it is the will of the people that prevails ultimately and not the will of a few selfish individuals. This is the principle of popular sovereignty.

There have been kings, revolutions, constitutions and vast bureaucracies since time immemorial. But the idea of adult suffrage and the common man as elector are of very recent origin. To Aristotle the ideal form of democracy meant that the vital decisions affecting the community made by the assembly of the whole citizenry in the market place. Today, it means that every adult citizen—man and woman alike—goes to the polling booth and casts his (or her) vote in favour of those who, in his opinion are the best persons to represent him in the management of the affairs of his Government. Elections are not the only possible method for securing representatives. But they are considered the most democratic method. They are democratic because every adult citizen gets a chance at regular intervals to participate in the selection of those who will rule over him. It is impossible, therefore, to over-emphasise the importance of free popular elections to ensure a democratic government based upon the consent of the governed.

In spite of the ignorance and illiteracy of large sections of the Indian people, the Constituent Assembly adopted the principle of adult franchise with faith in the common man and the ultimate success of democratic rule. The Assembly was of the opinion that democratic Government on the basis of adult suffrage would alone "bring enlightenment and promote well-being, the standard of life, the comfort and decent living of the common man".

The principle of popular sovereignty has not been a mere ideal embodied in the Constitution but has been a living reality during the last three decades during which the Constitution has been in operation. The six general elections the country has had so far (1951 52, 1957, 1962, 1967, 1971 and 1977) have demonstrated that the illiterate and presumably ignorant masses of India are not altogether incapable of independently exercising the right of franchise. In fact, this precious right in their hands, which ensures the democratic ideal of "one man, one vote, one value", irrespective of his wealth, education, social status and "importance", has, in fact, enchanced their self-respect as citizens of a democratic India. It has instilled in them the belief that they are no more mere "hewers of wood and drawers of water", but are important enough as members of a vast new human society engaged in the great co-operative enterprise of building up a new nation. The awareness that the strength of the State is the aggregate strength of its individual citizens is fast dawning upon them. They are also fast realising that suffrage is the link that binds, in a bond of mutual interest and responsibility, the fortunes of the citizens to the fortunes of the State. It is this realisation and its increasing impact in successive elections in the future that will prove the strongest and the most enduring base on which the superstructure of democratic government in India is to flourish.

Free elections are, perhaps, the greatest forum of mass education. The dangers inherent in adult suffrage among an illiterate people can be mitigated only by the blessings of universal education. In a country like India, the large majority of whose population is illiterate,[1] the attainment of universal education is a goal still a long way off. But this need not necessarily mean that until a certain minimum standard of universal education is realised, the Indian masses are incapable of properly exercising their right of franchise. Illiteracy is not quite the same thing as ignorance. A free election, which ensures the free exchange of ideas and free canvassing by contending parties who stand for differing programmes of social organisation for the realisation of the common welfare, offers the best medium for the political education of the illiterate masses. It is this that the Constitution guarantees. The constitution-makers were not satisfied by merely providing for adult suffrage. They wanted to ensure free elections by creating an independent constitutional authority to be in charge of everything connected with elections. Free election is a reality in India. It ensures for the electors both the freedom of choice and the secrecy of the ballot. The six general elections have demonstrated that the ordinary man, in spite of his so-called ignorance, has been able to exercise his robust commonsense in electing candi-

[1] According to the 1971 Census, only 28 per cent of the population of India was literate.

dates of his choice. Neither money nor social status nor official position has been powerful enough to make him a convenient tool in the hands of self-seeking politicians. This perhaps is the surest and the most welcome guarantee that popular sovereignty will remain a living reality in India despite the fact that most of its people are steeped in ignorance, poverty and social backwardness.

Secularism

The Constitution aims to establish a secular State. And a secular State means in essence that the State will not make any discrimination whatsoever on the ground of religion or community against any person professing any particular forms of religious faith. No particular religion in the State will be identified as State religion nor will it receive any State patronage or preferential status. The State will not establish any State religion; nor will the State accord any preferential treatment to any citizen or discriminate against him simply on the ground that he professes a particular form of religion. The fact that a person professes a particular religion will not be taken into consideration in his relationship with the State or its agencies.

This does not mean that the State in India is anti-religious. Secularism in its original, historical sense was an anti-God and anti-religious concept. But in the Indian context that concept has no relevance. In the words of Ambedkar, secular State does not mean that we shall not take into consideration the religious sentiments of the people. "All that a secular State means is that this Parliament shall not be competent to impose any particular religion upon the rest of the people".

Thus the distinguishing features of a secular democracy as contemplated by the Constitution of India are (i) that the State will not identify itself with or be controlled by any religion; (ii) that while the State guarantees to every one the right to profess whatever religion one chooses to follow (which includes also the right to be an agnostic or an athiest), it will not accord any preferential treatment to any of them; (iii) that no discrimination will be shown by the State against any person on account of his religion or faith; and (iv) that the right of every citizen, subject to any general condition, to enter any office under the State will be equal to that of his fellow citizens. Political equality which entitles any Indian citizen to seek the highest office under the State is the heart and soul of secularism as envisaged by the Constitution.

Fundamental Rights

Discussing the implications of democracy in his, *Liberty in the Modern State,* Harold Laksi says, that first, it involves a frame of government in which men are given the chance of making the government under which they live, at stated intervals. We have seen above how this principle is safeguarded under the Constitution. Secondly, he says, it involves the securing to the citizens certain fundamental human rights and the maintenance of those rights by the separation of the judicial from the executive powers. Thirdly, it involves the bringing into existence of a Bill of Rights for safeguarding the fundamental human rights, such as freedom of speech, protection from arbitrary arrest and the like. According to Laski, the supremacy of the "rule of law" is essential for the working of a democracy. Only where the rule of law prevails, true democracy can function and the success or failure of a democracy depends largely on the extent to which civil liberties are enjoyed by the citizens in general.

Liberty, however, is not an easy word to define. "The world has never had a good definition of the word liberty" said Abraham Lincoln on 18 April 1864, soon after the American civil war on the question of slavery, "and the American people, just now, are much in want of one. We all declare for liberty; but in using the same *word* we do not all mean the same *thing*. With some the word liberty may mean for each man to do as he pleases with himself, and the product of his labour; while with others the same word may mean for some men to do as they please with other men, and the product of other men's labour. Here are two, not only different, but incompatible things, called by the same name, liberty. And it follows that each of the things is, by the respective parties, called by two different and incompatible names—liberty and tyranny".

Genuine democracy must forever guard against the temptation to transform itself into a system under which the ruling majority claims infallibility for itself. While democracy requires that the will of the people limit the freedom of the Government, it also requires that the freedom of the popular will be limited. A popular will not so limited becomes the tyranny of the majority which destroys the freedom of political competition and thus uses the powers of the government to entrench itself permanently in the seat of power and to prevent a new majority from forming. Further, it will tend to think and act as if it will provide the ultimate standard of thought and action and there is no higher law to limit its freedom. As Laski has put it, "If in any State there is a body of men who possess unlimited political power, those over whom they rule can never be free." The emergence of such a state of affairs will result in the disappearance of certain vital characteristics of democracy, the spirit of questioning and individual initiative. Their place will be taken up by unquestioned submissiveness and conformity, the most distinguishing characteristics of a totalitarian system. This is perhaps the most serious danger inherent in the dynamics of modern democracy which is to be strongly guarded against.

There are two possible alternative safeguards which a constitution can provide to remedy the situation. First, it can guarantee certain basic rights to the individual citizen against all encroachment by the State. Secondly, it may so divide the powers of the State and entrust them to separate agencies that no body of men possesses unlimited power. The Constitution of India has chosen the first alternative and tries to achieve the objective by embodying in it a set of fundamental rights and guaranteeing them through an independent judiciary. These rights impose limitations both on legislative and executive powers. On the one hand, the legislature is prohibited from passing certain laws which would curtail the individual's freedom. On the other, the executive is compelled to adhere to certain formalities and procedures when it deals with the citizens. Thus, in an attempt to secure fundamental freedoms, the Constitution delimits the respective spheres of activity of the State and the individual and erects a wall, as it were, between the government and the people.

The Constitution affirms the basic principle that every individual is entitled to enjoy certain rights as a human being and the enjoyment of such rights does not depend upon the will of any majority or minority. No majority has the right to abrogate such rights.

In fact, the legitimacy of the majority to rule is derived from the existence of these rights. These rights include all the basic liberties such as freedom of speech, movement and association, equality before law and equal protection of laws, freedom of religious belief, and cultural and educational freedoms. The Constitution has classified these rights into seven categories and one of them is the right to constitutional remedies which entitles every aggrieved person to approach even the Supreme Court of India to restore to him any fundamental right that may have been violated.

It is, thus, a basic affirmation of the Constitution that the political system that it establishes should provide conditions favourable for the maximum development of the individual's personality. The framers of the Constitution were conscious of the fact that in the absence of the enjoyment of the above-mentioned rights, such development of the personality was impossible and democracy would sound an empty word. Having spent most of their lives under a foreign rule and having fought relentlessly for the enjoyment of these rights by themselves, it was only natural that they should have wanted to embody them in the Constitution they framed for the establishment of a democratic political order. They hoped to build this political order on the firm foundation of the freedom of political competition. The prime importance of these rights is that while the will of the majority decides how these freedoms are to be implemented, the existence of the freedoms themselves is not subject to that will. On the contrary, these freedoms set the conditions under which the will of the majority is to be formed and exercised. They establish the framework of "democratic legitimacy" for the rule of the majority.

It must be stressed, however, that the fundamental freedoms guaranteed to the individual under the Constitution are not absolute. Individual rights, however basic they are, cannot override national security and general welfare. For, in the absence of national security and general welfare, individual rights themselves are not secure. Freedom of speech does not mean freedom to abuse another; freedom of movement does not mean freedom of physical attack on others. The Constitution has made express provisions dealing with such limitations of fundamental rights so that those who seek to enjoy the rights may also realise the obligations attending them.

Directive Principles

The wall of separation which the fundamental rights erect between the government and the people is indeed one of the greatest and surest safeguards of the life, liberty and the pursuit of happiness of the individual.   But conditions of absolute and unhindered growth of private power, like absolute governmental power, are capable of destroying individual freedom.   Concentration of private power, mainly in the form of economic controls, in the hands of a few individuals is equally destructive of the dynamic qualities of a democratic society as a dictatorial government could be.   In a highly capitalist society, a few giants in the industrial and financial world, who concentrate in themselves the bulk of economic power, can easily subject the rest of the community to the travails of a new feudalistic order.   After having provided against the emergence of a totalitarian system through the constitutional guarantees of fundamental rights, the framers turned their attention to deal with the possible future menace of a private capitalist concentration of economic power and to ensure the establishment and sustenance of a society which provided for the diffusion of economic power among the different sections of the people.   The methods they sought to provide for the purpose are embodied in the chapter on Directive Principles of State Policy, which embodies another basic principle of the Constitution.

Writing about post-war constitutions which are estimated to number over fifty, a thoughtful critic has observed:

"Liberty the constitutions could and did promise, but not bread and the modicum of economic security the little man yearns for. To him it is the plain and unadorned truth that the political decisions which are vital for the well-being of all no longer occur' within the frame of the constitution. The social forces move and battle extra-constitutionally, because the constitutions did not even attempt the required solutions".[2]

Critics of the Constitution of India cannot accuse the framers of any lack of awareness of this problem or of not attempting to provide solutions for it.

[2] Loewenstein, *Reflections on the value of constitutions and constitutional trends since World War II*, 1951, p. 191.

While many of the older constitutions including that of the United States adopted the second method, namely the separation of powers for avoiding the evil and largely failed in their attempt, the Constitution of India adopts a different method, following the example of the Constitution of the Irish Republic. According to this method, the State and every one of its agencies are commanded to follow certain fundamental principles while they frame their policies regarding the various fields of state activity. These principles, on the one hand, are assurances to the people as to what they can expect from the State and, on the other, are directives to the Government, Central and State, to establish and maintain a new "social order in which justice, social, economic and political, shall inform all the institutions of national life". The State shall in particular, direct its policy towards securing:

(*a*) that the citizens, men and women equally, have the right to an adequate means of livelihood;

(*b*) that the ownership and control of the material resources of the community are so distributed as best to subserve the common good;

(*c*) that the operation of the economic system does not result in the concentration of wealth and the means of production to the common detriment;

(*d*) that there is equal pay for equal work for both men and women;

(*e*) that the health and strength of workers, men and women, and the tender age of children are not abused and that citizens are not forced by economic necessity to enter avocations unsuited to their age or strength;

(*f*) that childhood and youth are protected against exploitation and against moral and material abandonment.

In short, these and other Directive Principles form a new Magna Carta, a charter of economic freedoms, to the under-privileged, ordinary man in Indian society.

Speaking about the value of their inclusion in the Constitution, Ambedkar said in the Constituent Assembly:

"The Draft Constitution as framed only provides a machinery

for the government of the country. It is not a contrivance to install any particular party in power, as has been done in some countries. Who should be in power is left to be determined by the people, as it must be, if the system is to satisfy the test of democracy. But whoever captures power will not be free to do what he likes with it. In the exercise of it, he will have to respect these instruments of instructions which are called Directive Principles. He cannot ignore them. He may not have to answer for their breach in a Court of Law. But he will certainly have to answer for them before the electorate at election time. What great value these directive principles possess will be realized better when the forces of right contrive to capture power".[3]

Judicial Independence

"Justice is the end of government", said *The Federalist*. "It ever has been and ever will be pursued until it be obtained, or until liberty is lost in the pursuit". No wonder, therefore, if justice has been often characterised as the primary, or even the only *ideal* purpose of government.

The judicial function is indeed a delicate and difficult one. It involves the process of deciding what is just in a controversy between two or more contending parties. If the parties have no confidence in the impartiality of the judiciary, justice becomes an empty word. Man's long struggle has been to live under a government of laws, not of men. Equal justice under law has for long been his cherished ideal, a system under which the same law is applicable to all alike. Man has in all ages been striving to escape the regime that dispenses justice according to the political or religious ideology of the litigant or the whim or caprice of those who run the Government. As a consequence of this struggle, there was established a principle of abiding value, that no judiciary can be impartial unless it is independent. In fact, the judicial process ceases to be judicial the moment those who seek to judge cease to be independent of every form of external influence. Hence the importance of judicial independence.

As Lord Hewart has pointed out, the independence of the

[3] C.A.D. VII, p. 41.

judiciary is essential because many of the significant victories for freedom and justice have been won in the law courts and the liberties of the citizen are closely bound up with the complete independence of the judges. Obviously, the men who are to administer justice in the courts, the methods by which they are to be chosen, the way in which they are to perform their function, the terms upon which they shall hold power, these and their related problems become inseparably bound up with the ideal of judicial independence.   Judicial independence acts as a safeguard, not merely against the manipulations of the law for political purposes at the behest of the government in power, but also against the corruption of judicial organs of the State by bribery and intimidation by powerful outside interests which threaten the impartial administration of justice from time to time.

The framers of the Constitution were aware that democratic freedoms were meaningless in the absence of an independent machinery to safeguard them. No subordinate or agent of the Government could be trusted to be just and impartial in judging the merits of a conflict in which the Government itself was a party. Similarly, a judiciary subordinate either to the Centre or the States could not be trusted as an impartial arbiter of conflicts and controversies between the Centre and the States. These were the compelling reasons for the creation of an independent judiciary as an integral part of the Constitution and for the adoption of judicial independence as a basic principle of the Constitution.

In its bid to establish complete independence of the judiciary, the Constitution has first erected a wall of separation between the executive and the judiciary. After effecting such separation, it has created conditions that are conducive to making the judiciary independent. Thus, rigid qualifications are laid down for the appointment of judges and provision has been made for compulsory consultation of the Chief Justice of India in the appointment of every judge of the Supreme Court and the High Courts. The Judges are appointed almost for life[4] and their conditions of service cannot be altered to their disadvantage, once they are appointed. They are given high salaries and their conduct is made a subject beyond the scope of discussion in the legislature. They can be removed

[4] The retiring age for judges of the Supreme Court of India is sixty-five years, the highest for any service in the country.

from office only for proved misbehaviour. For this purpose, both the Houses of Parliament will have to pass resolutions against a judge supported by a two-third majority of those who sit and vote and at least an absolute majority of the total membership of the House.

The judiciary in India, even under the British rule, was noted for its integrity and independence. Under the Constitution, its position has been made doubly secure so that it can become in reality the most impartial arbiter of the conflicts and controversies which fall within its jurisdiction. Anyone can approach it to secure the restoration of a fundamental right whenever it is violated. Even a casual analysis of the hundreds of decisions which the Supreme Court and the High Courts have given so far will easily prove that the judiciary in India is working in a spirit of impartiality and in an atmosphere of independence.

Federalism

Federalism is one of the most important aspects of modern constitutionalism. It is established all over the world perhaps, as the only form of political organisation suited to communities with a diversified pattern of objectives, interests and traditions, who seek to join together in the pursuit of common objectives and interests and the cultivation of common traditions. The basic objective of federalism is thus unity in diversity, devolution in authority and decentralisation in administration. Its fundamental characteristic is the division of powers between two sets of governments—a Central Government and Local or State Governments—each independent of the other in its own sphere of activity. The framers of the Constitution turned to federalism as a solution of a number of problems they confronted in their attempt to frame a constitution for a new, united India. Particularly, they wanted to preserve both the "infinite variety and the innate unity" that animated the length and breadth of India.

The choice of federalism as a constitutional form and as the basis of a national government in India was not a sudden development upon the transfer of power on 15 August 1947. It was there for many years and, in a limited form, it was already in operation in British India. For the solution of the constitutional problem of a multi-racial, multi-lingual and multi-communal country like India with a vast area and a huge population, federalism was only a natural choice. Nevertheless, the framers were cautious to ensure that the unity they sought to establish through federalism was of an abiding nature, and in case of a future conflict between that unity and the diversity preserved under the Constitution, the former should prevail over the latter. In other words, it was their intention to create an indestructible Union and the supremacy of the Union over the States in a number of matters vitally affecting the interests of the nation.

Cabinet Government

The most distinctive characteristic of a Cabinet System of Government is the complete and continuous responsibility of the executive to the legislature. The Cabinet is composed of the Prime Minister, who is the chief of the executive, and his senior colleagues who share the responsibility with him for the formulation and execution of the policies of the government. In contrast to a system of checks and balances as obtains under the Presidential system of the United States, the Cabinet System embodies the principle of concentrated authority under strict control. The Cabinet is the central shaft to which all the other agencies of government are geared. Individual members of the Cabinet are the heads of the different departments of the administration. Collectively, the Cabinet shapes the programme of legislation which is submitted to Parliament and from it emanate the broad and general policies. The Parliament also checks and controls the performance of the administration. Thus, the Cabinet system facilitates, on the one hand, the intimate co-operation between the executive and the legislature and, on the other, ensures the responsibility of the executive to the legislature, the representative of the people.

Under the Cabinet system, the Head of the State occupies a position of great dignity, but practically all authority, nominally vested in him, is exercised by the Cabinet or the Ministry which assumes full responsibility for acts performed in his name. The unity and collective responsibility of the Cabinet are achieved through the Prime Minister, who is the key-stone of the Cabinet arch. His colleagues in the Cabinet are appointed on his recommendation and they always go out of office along with him. He is thus central both to the formation and the dissolution of the Cabinet.

The real merit of a Cabinet system is that the executive being responsible to the legislature is always being watched. The moment it proves unequal to the task, or it goes off the track or flouts the will of the legislature, it can be removed from office by a successful vote of no-confidence. Under the modern party system, if the Party in office has a stable majority in the legislature, the Cabinet may wield overwhelming power, so long as the members of the Party are solidly behind it. Under such conditions, as Herman Finer put it, the Cabinet although a creature of Parliament becomes a creature which leads its creator. But under different conditions, Parliament will assert and no Cabinet will be able to dominate. If instability of Cabinet does not become chronic as was the case under the Fourth Republic of France, a Parliamentary executive is preferable to a Presidential executive whose main merit is the stability of the executive for a fixed period.

The Constitution of India has adopted as a basic principle the British Cabinet system almost in its entirety. The only special feature of the Indian Constitution which deserves special mention in this context is the position of the Prime Minister. The Constitution expressly gives him a distinctly superior position by making him the head of the Council of Ministers. In Britain, although in practice the Prime Minister holds a superior position, he is, at least in theory, described as first among equals. In India, the Cabinet system of government under the Constitution is established not only at the Central level, but also in the States. In every State there is a Council of Ministers headed by a Chief Minister, just like the Prime Minister who heads the Central Cabinet.

CHAPTER 3

HISTORICAL BACKGROUND

The East India Company

THE ORIGINS of the Constitution of the Indian Republic, to a great extent, are rooted in the history of India under the British rule. That history began with the incorporation in England of the East India Company in 1600, although the British had not become a ruling power of India until the second half of the 18th century. The essentially commercial character of the Company in the beginning gradually underwent a complete change in the course of a century and a half. The downfall of the Mughal Empire—which was the main unifying force in the country—by the end of the 18th century, the consequent disintegration of a centralised administration, and the rise of innumerable local rulers who rivalled among themselves, provided the Company with an opportunity to enter the field of Indian politics. The victory of the Company's forces in the battle of Plassey in 1757 against Suraj-ud-Doula, the Nawab of Bengal, had laid the foundation of the British Empire in India.

As the Company began to transform itself from a commercial concern into a territorial power, there was a corresponding change in the attitude of the British Parliament toward it. Through a series of enactments the Parliament increased its control over the affairs of the Company in India. The Regulating Act, 1773, Pitt's India Act, 1784, and a series of Charter Acts that followed them are important in this connection. The net result of these enactments was the emergence of a highly centralised British administration in India.

The Revolution of 1857

The revolution of 1857 which had been characterised by the British as the "Sepoy Mutiny" was, on the one hand, an abortive attempt to oust the foreign ruler, and, on the other, a valiant protest against the autocratic and irresponsible character of the government that prevailed in India. It also exposed the utter

33

3

incapacity of the Company to handle the government of a vast territory, in spite of a certain amount of control by the British Parliament. There was an uproar in England against the continuance of the Company's rule in India any further. As a result, in 1858, the Government of British India was transferred from the Company to the British Crown. This, indeed, was a landmark in the political evolution of India.

The Emergence of Bureaucratic Government

When the Crown assumed direct responsibility for the Government of India in 1858, all powers—legislative, administrative and financial—came to be centralised in the Secretary of State for India and his Council on behalf of the Crown. As a necessary consequence, in India, also, power came to reside in the hands of the Governor-General in Council and it was exercised through a vast network of officials spread over the whole country. The resulting form of administration has been called "Bureaucratic Government".

In this form, the administration was carried on by a hierarchy or gradation of officers, the lower officers being the agents of and, therefore, entirely responsible to those superior to them. At the top of this bureaucratic hierarchy stood the Secretary of State for India and his Council responsible to the British Parliament for the administration of India. Below him was the Viceroy and Governor-General of India who was at the head of the Indian administration and the "man on the spot". Then came a number of Governors, Lieutenant-Governors and Chief Commissioners who were at the head of various classes of Provinces into which the country was divided and who were the agents of and, therefore, responsible to the Governor-General in Council. Finally, within the Provinces a more or less uniform system of administration came to be established, the unit of which was the District. The chief executive officer of the District was the Collector-Magistrate or the Deputy Commissioner. Thus, the whole system from top to bottom was well-knit and, therefore, highly centralised and behaved like an unbreakable steel-frame with all the characteristics of a full-fledged autocracy.

Movement toward Decentralisation

The defects of this highly centralised system of administration had become obvious even before the process of centralisation itself was complete. The realisation of this provided an impetus to give a start to an opposite process—a process of decentralisation as between the Central and the Provincial Governments. The rapid growth of communications, the introduction and spread of English education, the assimilation of western ideas of Parliamentary Government by Indians and the consequent modernisation of their outlook, all these must have been contributory forces for the introduction of this new process of decentralisation and the gradual change in the tone and character of the British Indian Government. If one word could summarise the most striking characteristic of the British administration in India prior to 1858, that was "centralisation". Similarly, if one word could sum up the post-1858 administration of the British in India, it was "decentralisation" which gradually led the way for the introduction of a federal system of Government as embodied, first, in the Constitution Act of 1935, and then in the Constitution of the Indian Republic in 1950.

The Stages of Decentralisation

The process began with the passing of the Indian Councils Act in 1861 which, for the first time, introduced the principle of consultation in the Indian political scene by the British rulers. However indirect and unsatisfactory the nature of that consultation might have been, it sought, for the first time, the co-operation of the Indian people in the administration of the country. It was a movement in the right direction.

The Minto-Morley Reforms of 1909 tried to mitigate the evils of bureaucracy in two ways: first, by further decentralising the existing authority through encouragement of local self-government and giving wider powers to the Provincial governments and, secondly, by enhancing the powers of the Legislative Councils and increasing Indian representation in them. The Act of 1909 was essentially of an evolutionary character extending the application of the principle already enunciated. It was only a mild response to the moderate character of the political demands made during the pre-1909 period by Indian nationalism. However, when put to the test, it created only disillusionment. The extent of decentralisation embodied in the Act was not sufficient enough to modify the character of British Indian bureaucracy to the extent demanded by public opinion. The agitation for greater share in the administration continued unabated.

A series of developments, both in India and abroad soon after created a favourable situation to the Indian cause. Of these, the outbreak of the First World War was the most important. Britain was anxious to enlist Indian support in the war effort. Consequently, the British Government announced its new policy toward India. That policy envisaged the increasing association of Indians in every branch of the administration with a view to the gradual development of self-governing institutions. Closely following upon the announcement, Montagu, the then Secretary of State, visited India and in consultation with Lord Chelmsford, the Governor-General, drew up a report on Indian Constitutional Reforms, popularly known as the Mont-Ford Report. On the basis of the Report, a new Act was passed by the British Parliament—the Act of 1919.

The Government of India Act of 1919 and Dyarchy

The Act was based on the principles set forth in the above Report. It had two important features. First, it envisaged the maximum amount of decentralisation through the division of authority between the Central and the Provincial Governments in the various fields of administration and, secondly, the introduction of "Dyarchy" in the Provinces, a division of the executive power between the Indian representatives and the British advisers of the Governor.

The principle of division of authority between the Centre and the Provinces was that subjects of all-India importance were to be allotted to the Central Government and matters which were of predominantly local interest to the Provincial Governments. It must be noted, however, that the division was not as rigid as it is in a federation. This is clear from the fact that the Central Legislature was competent to legislate on Provincial subjects. In other words, there was still no federal principle in operation and the Government of India still remained essentially unitary in form and substance. Nevertheless, the powers that were given to the Provinces in matters of legislation, finance and administration were substantial.

In spite of all the decentralisation and some democratisation brought about by the Act of 1919, the results, as evidenced through its working, did not enthuse the people. Instead, there was widespread dissatisfaction and all-round disappointment. The chief reason for this was the failure of dyarchy as a constitutional experiment. The most important feature of the Act of 1919 was the introduction of dyarchy in the Provinces. When put to the test of practice, it was found that there was no substantial transfer of power to the representatives of the people. The entire scheme of the Act was bound to fail in the absence of co-operation from the "Swarajists" who formed the majority group in most of the Provincial Legislatures. But even those optimists like the "Liberals" who gave a fair trial to the Act, found it wanting in the essentials of a responsible government and were, therefore, terribly disappointed.

Demand for Complete Transfer of Power

The result was the emergence of a new spirit, zeal and unity of the educated classes under the leadership of the Indian National Congress. The non-violent non-co-operation movement started by Gandhiji gathered momentum and assumed the shape of a full-fledged agitation for complete transfer of power to Indian hands. Every one felt the need of a new constitution which would suit the needs and conditions of India. The only difference of opinion was as to the nature of the new Constitution, whether it should be federal or unitary in structure.

The Simon Commission, which was appointed by the British Government in 1927 to report on constitutional reforms in India, had recommended against an all-India federation. The Nehru Committee, an Indian parallel to the Simon Commission, and appointed by the Indian National Congress, on the other hand, had recommended the formation of such a federation. Powerful spokesmen of the Indian Princes, too, had expressed themselves in favour of an all-India federation. The British Government, who were undecided for a time, discarded the Report of the Simon Commission and expressed themselves also in favour of establishing a federation for India as a solution to the constitutional problem. To facilitate the formation of the federation by drawing up a constitution, a series of conferences were held in London known as the Round Table Conferences.

The Indian National Congress, on account of serious differences with the British Government with regard to the nature of self-government that was to be established in India under the proposed constitution, withdrew itself from these deliberations. But the British Government was bent upon imposing a new constitution on India. With this object in view, they introduced a new Bill in the Parliament which, after prolonged discussions and deliberations, was finally passed in 1935 and became the Government of India Act, 1935.

The Constitution Act of 1935

There were two very important provisions in the Government of India Act, 1935, which deserve special mention. They were (1) the introduction of a federal polity in India, and (2) the establishment of Provincial autonomy in the British Indian Provinces. Both these were radical changes. In place of the old unitary form of government the new federal form was to bring in both the British Indian Provinces and the Indian States into one organic union embracing the entire country. Both the Provinces and the States were to function as constituent units of the federation, the former self-governing and the latter self-acting.

The all-India federation that was contemplated by the Act did not, however materialise during the period of its operation. All that was effected by the Act was only a semi-federation of the British Indian Provinces. Still the change was of great significance. In the words of the first Chief Justice of India, Sir Maurice Gwyer, "there came into being in place of the pre-existing Provinces which were under the tutelage of the Central Government, eleven autonomous States, pulsating with a vigorous life of their own and dividing with the Government of India the legislative and executive powers of government, that is to say, a federation of the eleven British Indian Provinces associated together in an organic union".

Provincial Autonomy

1 April 1937 marked a historic event when constitutional progress in India recorded the beginning of a new chapter. General

elections under the Constitution Act were already over in all the eleven Provinces and responsible governments were installed in every one of them by that date. The Congress Party which secured overwhelming majority in seven Provinces was entrusted with the administration in those Provinces and in the remaining ones coalition governments controlled the administration.

Despite all the misgivings expressed about the new set-up, it must be admitted that the Ministries in the Provinces functioned with remarkable success. There was a spirit of accommodation both on the part of the British Government in the Provinces who were at the head of the administration and the Indian leaders who accepted office and wanted to give a trial to the new experiment in constitutionalism. The result was a smooth and efficient functioning of governments in the Provinces according to the well-known principles of parliamentary democracy. However, this was destined to be a shortlived experiment as events with far-reaching consequences were developing in the horizon of international politics with their inevitable impact on India.

The Impact of the Second World War

The outbreak of the Second World War in September 1939, created a first class constitutional crisis in India threatening the very foundation of the existing responsible government in the Provinces. The crisis was precipitated by the short-sighted policy of the British authorities who were then at the helm of affairs in the country. The Governor-General, Lord Linlithgow, made an automatic declaration of war on Germany following a similar one in the British Parliament by the Prime Minister of Great Britain. The high-handed behaviour on the part of the Governor-General gave an unexpectedly rude shock to the popular Ministries in the British Indian Provinces. It was not the declaration of war as such that shocked them, but the manner in which it was done. The British bureaucracy never thought that it was necessary for them even to consult the popular political forces in India before committing the country to a world war. The importance of this action can be fully realised if we consider the cases of British Dominions like Canada, Australia and South Africa which, instead of making automatic declaration of war, submitted the matter to their respective Parliaments for decision. It was only at the will of their Parliaments that they could commit themselves to the war.

The Governor-General's autocratic action led the Indian leaders to the inevitable conclusion that Britain still considered India only as one of her colonies. It was their duty to fight that disgraceful position and establish the complete independence of the country. In a statement issued by the Working Committee of the Indian National Congress on 14 September 1939, it said among other things: "If Great Britain fights for the maintenance and extension of democracy, then she must necessarily end imperialism in her possessions and establish full democracy in India and the Indian people must have the right of self-determination by framing their own constitution through a Constituent Assembly. A free democratic India will gladly associate herself with other free nations for mutual defence against aggression." Therefore, it was only a natural consequence of their renewed determination to fight for their independence that they tendered the resignation of their offices in the Provincial administration. But the Governor-General and his henchmen in India wanted to impose their dictatorial will on the people of India even against their will. An emergency was declared all over India and the administration of the whole country was concentrated into the hands of the Governor-General through the Governors and the Indian Civil Service. A series of new emergency Ordinances were passed to meet any opposition from the popular forces in the country. Most of the national leaders had been arrested and sent to jail. Provincial autonomy, which was the foundation of the limited federal system that existed under the Constitution Act was no more a living constitutional feature but only a dream of the past. Indian administration, once again, was pressured into the all-India steel-frame of the old centralised bureaucracy.

The Cripps Mission

The first two years of the war were the most disastrous for Great Britain during the whole of her history as a world power. Not only that Britain was fighting for her life at home against German air attacks but she was also losing her colonies in the East to Japan which was almost at the doorstep of the Indian Empire.

These set-backs compelled her to revise the British policy towards India. With this end in view, Sir Stafford Cripps was sent to India on a special mission for finding a "just and final solution" of the constitutional crisis.

The Cripps Mission envisaged complete transfer of power to Indians after the war, and partial transfer during the war. In return for this, Britain wanted the Indian leaders to support and work wholeheartedly for the prosecution of the war. The Indian National Congress declining the "Cripps Offer" declared that the essential condition was the freedom of India without the realisation of which the hearts of millions of Indians could not be illumined nor could they be moved into action. This the British Government was not prepared for and, therefore, the Cripps Mission failed.

The Quit India Resolution

Soon after the failure of the Cripps Mission the All India Congress Committee met at Bombay in August 1942, and adopted the famous "Quit India" Resolution for the immediate ending of the British rule in India. Gandhiji was the pilot who led the Congress Committee in adopting this resolution. Among other things, the Resolution said:

" . . . The Committee is of opinion that the immediate ending of British rule in India is an urgent necessity, both for the sake of India and for the success of the cause of the United Nations. The continuation of that rule is degrading and enfeebling India and making her progressively less capable of defending herself and of contributing to the cause of world freedom. . . .

"The freedom of India must be the symbol of and the prelude to the freedom of all other Asian nations under foreign domination. Burma, Malaya, Indo-China, the Dutch Indies, Iran and Iraq must also attain their complete freedom.

"The Committee is of opinion that the future peace, security and orderly progress of the world demand a world-federation of free nations and on no other basis can the problems of the modern world be solved. . . . An independent India would gladly join such a federation and co-operate on an equal basis with other countries in the solution of international problems."

The British Government in reply at once arrested all the Congress leaders and banned all Congress organisations throughout India. The arrest of the leaders of the nation provoked a widespread revolution in India, known as the August Revolution. Thousands became prey to the onslaughts of the British Police forces in India and the war-efforts of the Government were seriously hampered by the apathy of the public. However, the August Revolution was suppressed with an iron hand.

The Simla Conference

Victory for the Allies came in Europe in May, 1945. Three years had passed since the Cripps Mission. All this time the national leaders were in jail. In June 1945, the Governor-General announced the release of the Congress leaders as a preparatory measure for negotiations with them. A conference was called, soon after, at Simla where all the leading political parties took part. But it could not arrive at any agreed solution. Immediately after this, Lord Wavell, the then Governor-General, visited England where there had taken place tremendous political changes due to the defeat of the Conservative Party in the general elections and the formation of the Labour Government. On his return to India in September 1945, Lord Wavell announced the determination of the British Government to go ahead with the hope of bringing India to self-government speedily.

Parliamentary Delegation

In February, 1946, the British Prime Minister, Clement Attlee announced in the House of Commons that a Parliamentary Delegation would visit India with a view to meeting the national leaders and discuss the various problems connected with self-government in India. The Delegation, consisting of members of Parliament belonging to all important parties, visited India soon after and spent over four weeks in the country. This paved the way of further progress in Indo-British understanding regarding India's constitutional problem. By this time, the Labour Government was convinced of the imperative necessity to grant India complete self-government. Prime Minister Attlee declared in the House of Commons on March 14, 1945, that while he hoped that the Indian people might elect to remain in the Commonwealth, they had a right to elect for independence. He recognised the obligation of Britain to help to make the transition as smooth and easy as possible. To translate this promise into reality a Cabinet Mission was sent to India immediately following the above announcement.

Proposals of the Cabinet Mission

The Cabinet Mission consisted of three members of the British Government—Sir Stafford Cripps, Lord Pethic Lawrence and Mr. A. V. Alexander. From the third week of March to the middle of June the three British Ministers had a series of conferences with all the important political leaders of India representing every important party. Toward the end of their stay in India they announced their plan regarding the future political set-up of India, known as the Cabinet Mission Plan. The Plan, while rejecting the demand of the All India Muslim League for partition of the country and establishment of a fully sovereign Pakistan, envisaged a confederation consisting of three groups of autonomous states vesting the powers of three departments—Defence, External Affairs and Communications—in a Central Government and all the remaining powers with the groups themselves. Each of the groups was free to have a separate constitution of its own choice, thus giving ample scope for both the leading religious groups, Hindus and Muslims, to live unitedly but, at the same time, to enjoy complete autonomy in areas where they were in a majority. The Plan had two parts, namely, a long-term programme and a short-term one. While the former was concerned with the future political set-up on a permanent basis, the latter was intended to establish an immediate Indian Interim Government.

The Muslim League accepted both parts of the Plan while the Indian National Congress decided that it would unreservedly accept only the long-term programme. As a result, later on, the Muslim League rejected the Plan as a whole and declared that it would resort to direct action to achieve its own demands. Meanwhile, elections in the British Indian Provinces were completed and the Provincial autonomy scheme of the Constitution Act of 1935 was given effect to by forming popular Ministries in all the Provinces. But the question of forming an interim Cabinet at the Centre still remained unsolved. As a temporary measure, a Caretaker Government of senior Civil Service officials was formed by the Governor-General toward the end of June, 1946.

Formation of the Interim Government

While Lord Wavell was exploring the possibilities of bringing the rival parties to some agreement, the announcement of the Muslim League to start direct action had serious and far-reaching repercussions all over India. Communal tension was mounting up day after day, resulting in the outbreak of communal disturbances, starting first at Bombay on July 1, 1946, and spreading to other parts like a violent conflagration. On August 12, 1946, Lord Wavell invited Pandit Jawaharlal Nehru to consider proposals for the formation of an interim Government at the Centre. The discussions bore fruit by the Interim Government coming into being on the 2nd of September.

But in the meantime, resort to direct action by the Muslim League had already resulted in widespread communal disturbances of a magnitude unprecedented in India. Even the Muslim League nominees joining the Interim Government, a few weeks later, did not bring the situation to normalcy.

The Mountbatten Plan

It was felt all over the country and in England that events in India were moving so fast and in so dangerous a direction that a catastrophe was imminent if immediate action was not forthcoming. The British Government thought that Lord Wavell was not equal to the situation and, therefore, they appointed Lord Louis Mountbatten to succeed him as the Governor-General. On February 20, 1947, the British Government made a historic announcement declaring their intention to transfer power to responsible Indian hands not later than June, 1948. Lord Mountbatten, immediately after assumption of office, plunged himself into prolonged negotiations with party leaders. He found that the only solution to bring to an end the orgy of communal violence and bloodshed lay in the immediate transfer of power to Indian hands. With a view to facilitating this transfer, and at the same time to accommodate the rival claims of the two leading communities, he devised the plan of partition of the country into India and Pakistan. It was according to this Plan that the Punjab and the Bengal Provinces were partitioned between the two new Nations.

The Indian Independence Act, 1947

The Mountbatten Plan was finally accepted by the two leading parties in India and also the British Government. The decision to effect the transfer of power earlier than June 1948, was announced in the British Parliament in June 1947. Accordingly, the Indian Independence Act was passed providing for the setting up of a Dominion of India and a Dominion of Pakistan on August 15, 1947. Thus on that historic day, August 15, 1947, at zero hour, the two new Dominions of India and Pakistan were born restoring the political freedom of four hundred millions constituting one-fifth of the human race.

Position of the Indian States

When the British left India in August, 1947, politically, India was divided between British India and Indian India. The former consisted of nine Governors' Provinces, five Chief Commissioners' Provinces and certain other areas like the tribal areas, the frontier regions and the Andaman and Nicobar islands. The latter consisted of over 500 Indian States. Of these, over a hundred were major States. They included States like Hyderabad, Kashmir, Mysore, Travancore and Baroda. Barring a few exceptions, the Governments of these States were autocratic. Some of them resembled the feudal principalities of medieval Europe. A large number of them could not be really called States as they were too small in size and too poor in resources. Yet they all became "sovereign" States on the 15th of August, 1947, as the paramountcy of the British Crown over them lapsed on that date. According to the British Prime Minister, these States were completely independent and were free to join either of the two Dominions, India or Pakistan, as they chose.

It was inconceivable of these States remaining separate, independent entities. Their choice lay in joining and becoming an integral part of either of the two new Dominions. Geographical and political considerations had much to do with their choice.

The wishes of the people of these States also had great influence in deciding this issue. Except for a few which acceded to Pakistan, all the Indian States joined the Dominion of India and helped the unification of the country for the first time in several hundred years.

Accession of the States and Territorial Readjustment

The accession of these States to the Indian Dominion set in motion a new movement for territorial readjustment. It was a twofold operation, integration and merger. By the process of integration two or more States joined together to form one viable administrative unit. Such States as Rajasthan, Travancore-Cochin and Saurashtra of the Indian Union of 1950 are the result of the process of integration. By the process of merger, many small States merged themselves in the neighbouring Provinces to become their integral parts. The merger of Seraikella and Kasravan States in Bihar, Orissa Feudatory States in Orissa and Pudukkotah in Madras are examples of this.

The process of integration and merger had remarkably good results. First, the number of State units in the Indian Union was brought to sixteen from about six hundred. Of these sixteen, nine were called Part B States under the original Constitution in 1950 and the remaining seven as Part C States. Secondly, the process helped the introduction of representative and responsible governments in these areas. Thirdly, even though India had been partitioned into India and Pakistan, the new India became a well-knit Union providing for the formation of a federal constitution with a strong Central Government.[1] This magnificent achievement was the result of the vision and constructive statesmanship of Sardar Vallabhbhai Patel who had been one of the chief architects of Republican India.

Decision to Become a Republic

India did not remain a Dominion of the British Commonwealth of Nations for long. The Constituent Assembly decided in May, 1949, that India should become a Republic. It was also decided

[1] Further reorganisation of the States leading to the present set-up is dealt with in the next chapter.

that she should continue to remain a member of the Commonwealth of Nations (no more British Commonwealth) and recognise the monarch of England as the symbolic head of the Commonwealth. It is interesting to note that this decision is not embodied in the Republican Constitution of India but rests merely on an understanding between India and other members of the Commonwealth.

The Constituent Assembly

Even before the complete transfer of power that was effected by the Indian Independence Act, 1947, a Constituent Assembly had been set up in order to draw up the new constitution for India. This was done on the basis of the agreement between the Cabinet Mission and the major Indian political parties in 1946. It was also decided that elections to the proposed Constituent Assembly should be indirect, so that all possible delay in the convening of the Assembly could be avoided. Accordingly, members to the Constituent Assembly were elected by the elected Legislative Assemblies of the Provinces. A total of 292 seats were allotted to the British Indian Provinces and 93 seats, in addition, were set apart for the Indian States' representatives in the Assembly. Thus, the total membership of the Constituent Assembly was 385. It was this body that was entrusted with the framing of the new Constitution.

At the time it was first convened, the Constituent Assembly was not a sovereign body. This was because it was subject to the final authority of the British Parliament. But the Indian independence Act of 1947 brought about a complete change in its character and made it a sovereign body. On August 14, 1947, it reassembled to assume power on behalf of the Government of India.

The members of the Constituent Assembly were not selected purely on a party basis, but were drawn from all walks of life and represented almost every section of the Indian people. They included some of the most leading personalities of Indian public life. The moving spirit of the Assembly was Jawaharlal Nehru, the first Prime Minister of free India. Rajendra Prasad was its President. Vallabhbhai Patel was one of the most important among the leading lights. While these leaders had contributed more than all others for the formulation of the basic principles of the

Constitution, it was the Drafting Committee, headed by B. R. Ambedkar, which was in charge of its drafting. Ambedkar was ably assisted in the task of constitution-making by the other members of the Drafting Committee among whom Alladi Krishnaswami Aiyar, N. Gopalaswami Ayyangar, K. M. Munshi and T. T. Krishnamachari were the most prominent.

The brick and mortar of the structure were provided by the reports of the Union Powers Committee, the Union Constitution Committee, the Provincial Constitution Committee, the Advisory Committee on Minorities and Fundamental Rights, the Committee on Chief Commissioners' Provinces, the Committee on Financial Provisions of the Union Constitution and the Advisory Committee on Tribal Areas. But the final shape and form were given by Dr. Ambedkar and his colleagues in the Drafting Committee.

It took two years, eleven months and seventeen days for the Constituent Assembly to finalise the Constitution since its first meeting on the 9th of December, 1946. During this period, it had eleven sessions and 165 days of actual work. The Draft Constitution had 315 Articles and 13 Schedules. The final form of the Constitution, as it was originally passed in 1949, had 395 Articles and 8 Schedules. This shows that the original draft had undergone considerable changes. In fact, there were notices for over 7,000 amendments to the Draft Constitution. Of these 2,473 were actually moved, debated and disposed of. This alone should show the manner in which the Assembly conducted its business. To anyone who goes through the proceedings of the Assembly, it will be abundantly clear that it was indeed a great democratic exercise. Discussion was encouraged to the maximum. There was great tolerance of criticism and no impatience with long drawn-out debates, no attempt to hustle through, no endeavour at imposition. It was a full-fledged democratic procedure of which Indians can be proud.

In its final form, the Constitution was passed and adopted by the Assembly on the 26th of November, 1949. However, the Constitution was inaugurated only on the 26th of January, 1950, which was the twentieth anniversary of the day on which the Indian National Congress adopted the Resolution on *Purna Swaraj* (complete independence) and which has ever since become the Republic Day of India.

PART II

PREAMBLE, TERRITORY AND CITIZENSHIP

CHAPTER 4

THE PREAMBLE

EVERY CONSTITUTION has a Preamble with which it begins and which embodies its objectives or basic purposes. The framers of the Constitution in this respect were in a most happy position. For, here was an opportunity for them to give expression to the dreams of a new order they had been dreaming of for years. Naturally, they were eager to draw up a Preamble which embodied the fundamental principles of that new order.

From a strictly legal point of view, the importance of a preamble is limited. It cannot qualify the provisions of the enactment so long as its text is clear and unambiguous. But if the statute is ambiguous, the preamble can be referred to in order to explain and elucidate it as "it is a key to open the mind of the makers of the Act and, the mischiefs they intended to redress". The Supreme Court of India is substantially in agreement with this position.

The Preamble of the Constitution of India reads as follows:

"We, THE PEOPLE OF INDIA,
having solemnly resolved to constitute India into a SOVEREIGN, SOCIALIST, SECULAR DEMOCRATIC REPUBLIC and to secure to all its citizens:
JUSTICE, social, economic and political;
LIBERTY of thought, expression, belief, faith and worship;
EQUALITY of status and of opportunity;
   and to promote among them all
FRATERNITY assuring the dignity of the individual and the
   unity and integrity of the nation;
IN OUR CONSTITUENT ASSEMBLY this twenty-sixth day
   of November 1949
do HEREBY ADOPT, ENACT, AND GIVE TO OUR-
   SELVES THIS CONSTITUTION."

The sentiments expressed in the Preamble were those described by Jawaharlal Nehru in the Objectives Resolution which he moved in the Constituent Assembly in its first session and which the Assembly adopted unanimously. But Nehru's resolution itself had

51

taken shape out of what had been already said many times by Mahatma Gandhi. In 1931 when Gandhiji was standing on the deck of a ship taking him to London, as the spokesman and representative of nationalist India to the second Round Table Conference, he was asked by a newspaper correspondent as to what constitution he would bring back if he could help it. Gandhiji's reply is worth reproducing here:

"I shall strive for a Constitution, which will release India from all thraldom and patronage, and give her, if need be, the right to sin. I shall work for an India, in which the poorest shall feel that it is their country in whose making they have an effective voice; an India in which there shall be no high class and low class of people; an India in which all communities shall live in perfect harmony. There can be no room in such an India for the curse of un-touchability or the curse of intoxicating drinks and drugs. Women shall enjoy the same rights as men. Since we shall be at peace with all the rest of the world, neither exploiting nor being exploited, we should have the smallest army imaginable. All interests not in conflict with the interests of the dumb millions will be scrupulously respected, whether foreign or indigenous. Personally, I hate distinction between foreign and indigenous. This is the India of my dreams."

It is not an exaggeration to say that not only in the Preamble but throughout the Constitution, there is a perceptible vibration of the Gandhian concept of independent India.

Reading through the Preamble, one can see the purposes that it serves, namely, the declaration of (1) the source of the Constitution, (2) a statement of its objectives and (3) the date of its adoption.

The opening words of the Preamble emphasise the ultimate authority of the People from whose will the Constitution emerges. Most of the modern constitutions emphasise the same principle. Since the Constituent Assembly "enacted and adopted" the Constitution in the name of the people of India, the question has been asked whether the Assembly was really representative of the people of India. "Does the Constitution reflect the will of the people of India?" This question was raised both within and outside the Assembly. Notice of a motion to this effect was given by a member of the Assembly who asked the House to adjourn the discussion on the Draft Constitution altogether and called for a new House on the basis of adult franchise to be elected, claiming that such a House alone should deal with the framing of the Constitution. The motion was, however, rejected by the Assembly as there was no one to support it.

The circumstances under which the Constituent Assembly came into being will show that it was impracticable to constitute such a body in 1946 with adult suffrage as its basis. No part of the country had the experience of adult suffrage. To prepare an electoral roll on the basis of adult suffrage for the country and to hold elections on that basis would have certainly taken a number of years. It was rightly thought unwise to postpone the task of constitution making until such an election was held. At the same time the necessity for having a new Constitution made by Indians to suit the conditions and circumstances in the country was keenly felt. This was the main justification for accepting the Cabinet Mission Plan for constituting the Assembly through indirect election.

If the time factor was the main consideration in 1946, one might ask the question: "What prevented the Constitution being referred to the people through a referendum in 1950 for their approval?" Such a procedure would have established the popular character of the Constitution despite the fact that the Assembly was not elected on a popular basis. Here again, the answer is simple. To conduct a nation-wide referendum involving some 180 million voters was indeed a task which involved elaborate preparation and enormous expense. But the effect of such a referendum was soon provided by the First General Elections of 1951-52 conducted under the new Constitution on the basis of adult suffrage. In that election some of the leading Opposition Parties had declared that if they returned to power, they would scrap the present Constitution and write an altogether new one. But the results of the election proved beyond any doubt that the Constituent Assembly although elected indirectly, was a fully representative body and the Constitution was an instrument of the popular will. For, not only were those Parties who opposed the Constitution severely defeated at the polls, but almost every member of the Constituent Assembly who stood for election was returned to the new Parliament of India or a State Legislature with convincing majorities. The talk of scrapping the Constitution has not been heard since then, and today, every political party in the country is wedded to the principle of supporting and upholding the Constitution and to working within its four corners if elected to power. No one will seriously challenge today what Ambedkar said on the floor of the Constituent Assembly in 1949: "I say that this Preamble embodies what is the desire of every member of the House, that this Constitution should have its root, its authority, its sovereignty from the people. That it has".[1]

The Preamble as it was originally passed, proclaimed the solemn resolution of the people of India "to constitute India into a sovereign, democratic republic". The Forty-second Amendment (1976 added the terms Socialist and Secular after the term Sovereign. India had already ceased to be a dependency of the British Empire by the passing of the Indian Independence Act, 1947. From the 15th of August, 1947, to the 26th January, 1950, her political status was that of a Dominion in the British Commonwealth of Nations. But with the inauguration of the present Constitution, India became "a Sovereign Republic" like the United States of America or the Swiss Republic. However, India is still a member of the Commonwealth of Nations. This peculiar position is the result of an agreement reached at the Commonwealth Prime Ministers' Conference in London in April 1949. There, India made a declaration to the effect that notwithstanding her becoming a sovereign independent Republic, she would continue "her full membership of the Commonwealth of Nations and her acceptance of the King (of England) as the symbol of the free association of the Commonwealth". But it is to be noted in this connection that this declaration was extra-legal. There is no mention of it in the Constitution of India. It is a voluntary declaration which indicates a free association with no legal obligation. Its acceptance of the King (or Queen) of England as a symbolic head of the Commonwealth does not create any allegiance of the citizens of India to the King of England. Hence this voluntary association of India with the Commonwealth does not affect her sovereignty in any manner

[1] C.A.D. X, p. 456.

and India could cut off that association as easily as it had been declared.

The concepts of socialism and secularism were implicit in the Constitution as it was originally passed. A number of provisions in Part IV of the Constitution dealing with the Directive principles of State Policy (Articles 38, 39, 40 and 41 are examples) are intended to bring about a socialist order of society. These objectives had been later summed up in the phrase "Socialistic pattern of society" and has been explained at length in the Five Year Plan documents. Similarly Articles 14, 15, 16 and 25 to 28 are intended to ensure the establishment and maintenance of a Secular State in India.

The term "democratic" is comprehensive. In a narrow political sense it refers only to the form of Government, a representative and responsible system under which those who administer the affairs of the State are chosen by the electorate and accountable to them. But in its broadest sense, it embraces, in addition to political democracy, also social and economic democracy. The term "democratic" is used in this sense in the Preamble.

The term "republic" implies an elected head of the State. A democratic State may have an elected or a hereditary head. Britain is perhaps the best example of the latter type. There, the monarch, a hereditary ruler, is no hindrance to democratic government as the real power of the State is in the hands of the representatives of the electorate. Under a republican form, on the contrary, the head of the State, single or collective, is always elected for a prescribed period. For example, in the United States the head of the State and Chief Executive—the President—is elected for a fixed period of four years. In Switzerland, on the other hand, a collegium of seven members is elected for a period of seven years to constitute the Executive. By deciding to become a republic, India has chosen the system of electing one of its citizens as its President—the head of the State—at regular intervals.

The Preamble proceeds further to define the objectives of the Indian Republic. These objectives are four in number: Justice, Liberty, Equality and Fraternity. Justice implies a "harmonious reconcilement of individual conduct with the general welfare of society". The essence of justice is the attainment of the common good. It embraces, as the Preamble proclaims, the entire social, economic and political spheres of human activity.

The term "liberty" is used in the Preamble not merely in a negative but also in a positive sense. It signifies not only the absence of any arbitrary restraint on the freedom of individual action but also the creation of conditions which provide the essential ingredients necessary for the fullest development of the personality of the individual. Since society is constituted of individuals, social progress depends on the progress of the individual. Hence it is in the interest of society to ensure the maximum liberty of thought and action of the individual commensurate with social conditions and circumstances.

Liberty and equality are complementary. Equality does not mean that all human beings are equal mentally and physically. It signifies equality of status, the status of free individuals, and equality of opportunity. As the French Revolutionaries proclaimed: "Men are born and remain free and equal in rights. Social distinctions are based only upon public utility". Equality of opportunity implies the availability of opportunity to every one to develop his or her potential capacities. The declaration of the Rights of Man and Citizen said: "Law is the expression of the public will. It must be same for all, whether it protects or punishes. . . . All citizens being equal in its eyes, are equally eligible for all public dignities, places and employments according to their capacities and without distinction of their virtues and talents". The concept of equality that is envisaged in the Preamble as it embraces both equality of status and of opportunity, is the widest in scope.

Finally, the Preamble emphasises the objective of Fraternity in order to ensure both the dignity of the individual and the unity and integrity of the nation. The necessity of the spirit of brotherhood among the citizens was first emphasised by the French Revolution which adopted it along with liberty and equality as the foundations of the new order that it aimed to establish. Ever since the French Declaration it has become a slogan of universal application. In its Declaration of Human Rights, the United Nations proclaims: "All human beings are born free and equal in dignity and rights. They are endowed with reason and conscience and should act towards one another in a spirit of brotherhood". It is this spirit of brotherhood that is emphasised by the use of the term "fraternity" in the Preamble. In a country like India with many disruptive social forces, communal and caste, sectional and denominational, local and regional, linguistic and cultural, the unity and integrity of the nation can be preserved, only through a spirit of brotherhood that pervades the entire country, among all its citizens irrespective of their differences. Through the establishment of a new nation based upon justice, liberty and equality, all must feel that they are the children of the same soil, of the same motherland and members of the same Fraternity.

The Preamble of the Constitution of India is one of the best of its kind ever drafted. A glance over the preambles of constitutions all the world over will show that both in ideas and ideals and in expression, ours is unrivalled. It embodies the spirit of the Constitution, the determination of the Indian people to unite themselves in a common adventure of building up a new and independent nation which will ensure the triumph of justice, liberty, equality and fraternity. Commending the beautiful form in which the Preamble is couched, one of the members in the Constituent Assembly rose to poetic heights when he said: "The Preamble is the most precious part of the Constitution. It is the soul of the Constitution. It is a key to the Constitution".

CHAPTER 5

THE UNION AND ITS TERRITORY

THE FIRST Article of the Constitution declares that India is a Union of States. Explaining the significance of the term "Union of States", Ambedkar said that it implied two things: First, the Indian Federation was not the result of an agreement among the units. Secondly, the component units had no freedom to secede from the Union. Those who were not happy with the term Union contended in the Constituent Assembly that it did not sufficiently emphasise the federal nature of the Constitution. They wanted the adoption of the term "Federation of States".

An important feature of the States in the Indian Union, which may be mentioned in this context is that none of them was a sovereign entity at the time of the formation of the Constitution. The British Indian Provinces, under the Constitution Act of 1935 were at best only autonomous units. The Indian States, until August 15, 1947, were under the paramountcy of the British Crown not only in the field of external affairs but even in respect of internal administration. Perhaps, in a technical sense, they all became sovereign on August 15, 1947, as a result of the Indian Independence Act and the consequent lapse of British paramountcy. But whatever the content of the sovereignty of the Rulers, it was surrendered by them to the Government of India during the 1947-50 period on a negotiated basis.

Thus, none of the constituent units of India was sovereign in the sense the thirteen American Colonies after the Declaration of Independence or the Swiss Cantons were before they decided to enter into federal compacts by pooling their sovereignty. Nor was the Constituent Assembly a representative of the units. It derived its power from the sovereign people, and, therefore, was entirely unfettered by any previous commitment in evolving a constitutional pattern suitable to the genius and requirements of the Indian people as a whole. Thus, the significance of the provision, "India is a Union of States", is that although it establishes a federal polity, the units have no right to secede from the Union as the federal system is the result of an expression of the will of the people through the Constituent Assembly.

Under Article 2, the Parliament of India is empowered to admit into the Union, or establish, new States on terms and conditions it thinks fit. Thus, it may form a new State by separation of territory from any State or by uniting two or more States or parts of States or by uniting any territory to a part of any State. In the process, it can increase or decrease the area of any State, or alter the boundaries, or change the name of any State (Art. 3). Although the power of Parliament in this respect is exclusive, the Constitution provides for a procedure which enables the legislatures of the States concerned to express their opinion in the matter. According to this, every bill contemplating any of the above changes can be introduced in Parliament only on the recommendation of the President and after prior reference by the President to the Legislature of the State concerned for its opinion. The procedure thus helps Parliament to have in view the sentiments of the people of the State concerned before taking a final decision. Any such change made by Parliament and the consequent alterations effected in the Constitution will not amount to an amendment of the Constitution (Art. 4).

Is Parliament competent, under Article 3, to make a law with a view to transferring a part of the territory of the Indian Union to another country? This question came up for detailed examination by the Supreme Court on a reference made to it by the President in 1960. The reference was necessitated by the controversy that arose from a decision of the Government to transfer part of a territory known as Berubari Union (West-Bengal) to Pakistan in exchange of Pakistani territory in pursuance of the agreement between the Governments of India and Pakistan in 1958. The Court held that Parliament was not competent to make a law under Article 3 for the implementation of the agreement. The implementation could only be effected by an amendment of the Constitution under Article 368. Subsequently the Constitution (Ninth Amendment) Act, 1960, was passed to give effect to the transfer of the territory concerned.

At present, the Union of India is composed of twenty-two States which are the units of the federal Union and nine Territories which are under the direct administration of the Central Government. As such, the political map of India today presents a comparatively simple picture in contrast to what it was in 1947 when India became independent and in 1950 when the present Constitution was inaugurated. But this was the result of the successful execution of a gigantic task of integration and reorganisation during the first ten years of Independent India. The process was indeed a difficult and even painful one and it cannot yet be said with certainty that the pattern which emerged and which exists at present is the final one. An attempt is made here to give a short account of the story of this integration and reorganisation.

In 1947 when the British left India, the organisation of Provinces remained in the same form in which it was operating under the Constitution Act, 1935, except for the changes that resulted from the partition of the country into India and Pakistan. We have pointed out earlier the consequences of the lapse of British Paramountcy over the Indian States in August 1947. But even while the Indian Independence Bill was being drafted negotiations were started with a number of Indian Rulers with a view to bringing their States into the Indian Union through accession. Several Rulers at once reacted favourably to the idea of accession and their example compelled others soon to follow suit. The policy of accession ensured the fundamental unity of the country. India had become one federation, with the Provinces and the States as its integral parts. Further, the Standstill Agreements between the Rulers of the States and the Government of India provided the basis for retaining intact the many agreements and administrative arrangements which had been built up over a century for safeguarding all-India interests and which, with the termination of paramountcy, had threatened to disappear and in the process throw the whole country into a State of chaos and confusion.

In his address to the Constituent Assembly on August 15, 1947, Lord Mountbatten referred to the success of the accession policy and paid a tribute to Sardar Patel as a far-sighted statesman who played the most important role of bringing about such a satisfactory situation.

The period immediately following the transfer of power to India saw a revolutionary change come over the Indian States with dramatic speed. Once the States had acceded to India, it was impossible for them to resist such a change, however much they had disliked it. Two strikingly novel devices were made use of to bring about this change, "integration" and "merger". Integra-

THE UNION AND ITS TERRITORY 61

tion represented the joining of two or more contiguous States in order to form a new viable unit of the Union. By merger was meant the outright disappearance of a State unit by its incorporation into a Province within which it was situated. As a result of this process of integration and merger, the number of State units in the Indian Union was brought down to a very small one from a number which stood around five hundred. Only three of the former States survived this process of integration and merger, namely, Hyderabad, Mysore and Jammu and Kashmir.

Side by side with the development of integration, there was also the extension of the authority of the Central Government. Further, under the initiative of the Centre, federal financial integration with the States was also realised. The movement for democratisation of the administrative set-up in the States had already made considerable progress and in many States or States-Unions, full-fledged responsible Government had already taken over the reins of administration. Thus, the Provinces and the States became equal partners in the Union.

While factors such as linguistic and ethnic homogeneity or historical tradition were taken into consideration to the extent practicable in the process of integration and merger, the compulsion of the dynamic urges of the time necessitated prompt decisions. A number of settlements, therefore, made in respect of these States had to be in the nature of transitional expedients. Hence, it was inevitable that some of the features of the old order should be incorporated in the Constitution. The result of all these had been the emergence of a peculiar State-system established under the Constitution as it was originally passed in 1949. Under this system, the constituent units of the Union had no uniform status. Instead, they were recognised under three separate categories, Part A, Part B and Part C States.

There were ten Part A States which were, generally speaking, the Provinces that constituted the bulk of former British India which formed part of the Indian Union. Some of these had become larger in size, as a result of the merger of some former Indian States in their territory, while others had become smaller owing to the partition of the country. All the Part A States were full-fledged members of the Union and their status was based on the concept of federalism.

There were eight Part B States. These were mostly the products of integration. They too enjoyed a status similar to that of Part A States as members of the federal Union. Yet, they were a step below the Part A States in political progress and, as such, were not entitled to enjoy the fullest measure of autonomy as defined by the Constitution. This was embodied in Article 371 of the Constitution, according to which the Government of every Part B State was to be under the general control of, and comply with such particular directions of the Central Government. Another distinguishing feature of the Part B States was that they were headed by *Rajapramukhs* and not Governors as in the case of Part A States.

The Part C States, although they were called as such, were not really States in the federal Union, for, they were territories directly administered by the Centre on a unitary basis. They were in all ten in number. Some of these were the former Chief Commissioners' Provinces under the British. Although some of them had been allowed from 1952 to have Legislative Assemblies of their own and Ministers responsible to them, the powers of these Assemblies were subject to the direct control of Parliament and the Union Executive was responsible to Parliament for their administration.

Apart from these three categories of States in the Union, there were also territories under Part D which formed part of the country. The only territories under Part D were the islands of the Bay of Bengal—Andaman and Nicobar Islands—which were under the direct and full control of the Central Government. The names of the different States under Part A, B, and C and the territories under Part D, as well as the area and population of each in 1950, at the time of the inauguration of the Constitution are given in table 1 (p 64).*

The constitutional provisions establishing the three-tier State-system were the product of expediency. No one was happy with this arrangement and desired to end it at the earliest opportunity. But the situation underwent an unexpected change in 1952 when the Central Government took a sudden decision to create a separate

* This table is a modified one and includes the new Andhra State which came into being in 1953.

State of Andhra out of certain parts of the former undivided Part A State of Madras, on account of the compelling demands of the Telugu-speaking people of Madras State. The State of Andhra came into existence on October 1, 1953. The inauguration of the new State was not, however, an isolated incident. Formation of new States on a linguistic basis and the consequent reorganisation of the entire State-system became almost a militant demand all over the country. Political leadership found it no longer possible to stem the tide of this surging demand. The result was the appointment of the States Reorganisation Commission in December 1953, to go into the entire question of reorganisation "objectively and dispassionately" and make its recommendations with a view to settling this tangled problem.

The Commission was headed by a former Justice of the Supreme Court of India, Fazl Ali, and had, in addition, two distinguished public men, H. N. Kunzru and K. M. Panikkar, as Members. The Commission took over a year and a half for their work and submitted their report on September 30, 1955.

After considering fully all the aspects of the problem of reorganisation, the Commission arrived at four major principles which were to be given the highest importance in any scheme of reorganisation of States. These are:

(1) Preservation and strengthening of the unity and security of India;
(2) Linguistic and cultural homogeneity;
(3) Financial, economic and administrative considerations; and
(4) Successful working of the national development plans.

In addition to these major principles, the Commission thought that there were others which ought to be given due weight although they came only next to these in importance. Among these were a common historical tradition which fosters a sense of kinship and oneness, geographical contiguity, administrative considerations and the wishes of the people to the extent that they were objectively ascertainable and did not come into conflict with larger national interests. Despite the enunciation and enumeration of these principles, the Commission recognised that the problems of reorganisation varied from region to region.

TABLE 1

State	Area (sq. miles)	Population
P A R T　A		
1. Andhra	63,608	20,801,792
2. Assam	85,012	9,043,707
3. Bihar	70,330	40,225,947
4. Bombay	111,434	35,956,150
5. Madhya Pradesh	130,272	21,247,533
6. Madras	60,263	35,736,489
7. Orissa	60,136	14,645,946
8. Punjab	37,378	12,641,205
9. Uttar Pradesh	113,409	63,215,742
10. West Bengal	30,775	24,810,308
P A R T　B		
1. Hyderabad	82,168	18,655,108
2. Jammu & Kashmir	92,780	4,410,000
3. Madhya Bharat	46,478	7,954,254
4. Mysore	29,489	9,074,972
5. P E P S U	10,078	3,493,685
6. Rajasthan	130,207	15,290,797
7. Saurashtra	21,431	4,137,359
8. Travancore-Cochin	9,144	9,280,425
P A R T　C		
1. Ajmer	2,417	693,372
2. Bilaspur	453	126,099
3. Bhopal	8,878	836,474
4. Coorg	1,586	229,405
5. Delhi	578	1,744,072
6. Himachal Pradesh	10,451	983,367
7. Kutch	16,742	567,606
8. Manipur	8,628	577,635
9. Tripura	4,032	639,029
10. Vindhya Pradesh	23,603	3,574,690
P A R T　D		
The Andamans and the Nicobar Islands	3,215	30,971

"It has to be kept in mind that the interplay for centuries of historical, linguistic, geographical, economic and other factors has produced peculiar patterns in different regions. Each case, therefore, has its own background. Besides, the problems of reorganisation are so complex that it would be unrealistic to determine any case by a single test alone. We have, accordingly, examined each case on its own merits and in its own context and arrived at conclusions after taking into consideration the totality of circumstances and on an overall assessment of the solutions proposed".

In making their recommendations, the Commission dealt with not only territorial readjustments but also other matters such as financial implications, administrative changes, integration of services, etc. Taking these as a whole, the following recommendations deserve special mention:

(1) Abolition of the classification of States into three categories, Part A, B and C, which was essentially a temporary expedient and the constitution of States enjoying a uniform status.

(2) Abolition of the special agreements entered into with the Union in consequence of the financial integration of Part B States. Also, abolition of the general control vested in the Government of India by Article 371 as well as the abolition of the institution of *Rajapramukhs*.

(3) Since there was no adequate recompense for all the financial, administrative and constitutional difficulties which the Part C States presented, they, with the exception of three (Delhi, the federal capital, Manipur and the Andaman and Nicobar Islands) to be centrally administered, should be merged with the adjoining states.

(4) On the basis of these changes, the Commission recommended the creation of 16 States and 3 centrally administered territories as shown in table 2 (p. 66).

The publication of the S.R.C. Report precipitated disturbances in many parts of the country. Where wholesale changes in the existing system were recommended, it was only natural that many interests should be adversely affected. Further, where sentiments could be aroused and tempers frayed on account of these, the results could never be happy. And where people imagined that political pressure and agitation could possibly dictate the course of action on the part of those who were in power, anything could happen. This was what happened after the publication of the Report. No one could claim that the recommendations of the

5

	Area (In sq. miles) (approximately)	Population (In millions) (approximately)
STATES		
Madras	50,170	30.0
Kerala	14,980	13.6
Karnataka	72,730	19.0
Hyderabad	45,300	11.3
Andhra	64,950	20.9
Bombay	151,360	40.2
Vidarbha	36,880	7.6
Madhya Pradesh	171,200	26.1
Rajasthan	232,300	16.0
Punjab	58,140	17.2
Uttar Pradesh	113,410	63.2
Bihar	66,520	38.5
West Bengal	34,590	26.5
Assam	89,040	9.7
Orissa	60,140	14.6
Jammu and Kashmir	92,780	4.4
TERRITORIES		
Delhi	578	1,744,072
Manipur	8,628	577,635
The Andaman and Nicobar Islands	3,215	30,971

Commission were flawless. For one thing, despite all the major principles, to which the Commission gave due weight in the scheme of reorganisation, the pattern that emerged from their recommendations consisted of practically unilingual States only. But that was perhaps inevitable in the context of prevailing conditions and circumstances in the country.

The Report was placed before Parliament and the State Legislatures which discussed it at length. After prolonged discussions both inside the legislatures and outside, and after protracted negotiations between the Union Cabinet and the interested parties, the Government announced its decision which was embodied in a Bill called the States Reorganisation Bill. The Constitution also needed amendment at many places as a result of the proposed reorganisation. Both the amendment of the Constitution (the Seventh Amendment) and the Reorganisation Bills were passed in 1956 and were put into effect on 1 November 1956.

The Provisions of both the Amendment and the Act are based upon the recommendations of the S.R.C. except in a few instances. The most important of these were the decisions with respect to the formation of the Bombay State and the immediate creation of a United Telugu-speaking State of Andhra Pradesh. The number of the centrally administered areas also was increased from the recommended three to six. Table 3 (p. 69) shows the reorganised States as they emerged from the States Reorganisation Act, 1956.

As may be seen from this table, the Union of India then consisted of fourteen States and six centrally administered territories.

That position, however, did not last long. The pattern underwent a further change in 1960 when on account of intense and persistent popular demand, Bombay was divided on a linguistic basis to form two new States, a Marathi-speaking State of Maharashtra and a Gujarati-speaking State of Gujarat.

In 1961 yet another new State was created when the Nagaland (Territorial Provisions) Regulations were promulgated by the President. The areas comprising Naga Hills and Tuensang Area assumed the name of Nagaland and was given the status of the sixteenth State of the Indian Union.

During the next ten years between 1961 to 1971 five more new States were formed. The first of these was Haryana by reorganising Punjab to form two States, Punjab and Haryana, in 1966. In 1970 the Union Territory of Himachal Pradesh was made a full-fledged State. Manipur and Tripura were also given the status of States, in 1971. In the same year yet another State was created and that was Meghalaya which was part of Assam until then.

In 1975 Sikhim acceded to India and was given the status of a State, thus raising the total number of States to twenty-two.

The number of Union Territories also has registered an increase since 1956. In August 1961 Dadra and Nagar Haveli were integrated with the Union of India at the request of the Varishta Panchayat and the people of Free Dadra and Nagar Haveli. Similarly, Goa, Daman and Diu were also united with India in December 1961 and thus the remnants of Portuguese colonialism, which was the last to disappear, were brought to an end. Pondicherry, a former French Colony, became a Union Territory in 1962 along with other French settlements in India. In 1966 as a result of the reorganisation of the Punjab, Chandigarh became a Union Territory. In 1971 two more Union Territories came into being, Mizoram and Arunachal Pradesh. Table 4 (p. 71) will show the picture of the Union and its territory as it exists at present.

Before the reorganisation of States, Madhya Pradesh was the largest among the States, with an area of 130,272 square miles, as big in size, as two-thirds of France. But as a result of the reorganisation Bombay became first with an area of 190,668 square miles, almost as large as France. But with the division of Bombay into Maharashtra and Gujarat, Madhya Pradesh once again got back its place as the largest State in India. Sikhim is the smallest of the States.

From a population point of view, Uttar Pradesh comes first, with more than 95 million people which is more than the population of the Federal Republic of West Germany and the German Democratic Republic together. Sikhim has also the smallest population, approximately a little more than 300,000. But if density of population per square mile is taken into consideration, Kerala comes first with about 1,125 people per square mile, perhaps the most densely populated state in the world.

A comparison between a country like India and a continent like Europe makes an interesting study from many points of view, such as area, population, language and races. India is two-thirds of the whole of Europe in size. The population of India is even more than that of Europe. From a linguistic point of view, while Europe has a score of main languages, India too has a linguistic diversity which is not less pronounced. From a racial point of view, the people of India present a greater diversity than the whole of Europe presents. But while India is today a single political entity, Europe has over a score of sovereign States. How difficult a problem it would be if an attempt is made to weld together Europe minus Russia into a single political entity. The efforts to form a Western European Federation are yet to find fruition. It is well to remember these facts while dealing with the problems of India, a sub-continent which presents both perplexing diversity and immensity.

TABLE 3

REORGANISED STATES

Sl. No.	Name of State	Area sq. miles	Population	Capital	Principal Language
1	2	3	4	5	6
1.	Andhra Pradesh	105,963	31,260,333	Hyderabad	Telugu
2.	Assam	50,043	9,043,707	Shillong	Assamese
3.	Bihar	67,164	38,784,172	Patna	Hindi
4.	Bombay	190,919	48,265,221	Bombay	Marathi & Gujarati
5.	Jammu and Kashmir	85,861	4,021,615	Srinagar	Kashmiri & Urdu
6.	Kerala	15,035	13,549,118	Trivandrum	Malayalam
7.	Madhya Pradesh	171,201	26,071,637	Bhopal	Hindi
8.	Madras	50,110	29,974,936	Madras	Tamil
9.	Mysore	74,326	19,401,193	Bangalore	Kannada
10.	Orissa	60,136	14,645,946	Bhuvaneshwar	Oriya
11.	Punjab	47,456	16,134,890	Chandigarh	Punjabi and Hindi

TABLE 3—(*Contd.*)

1	2	3	4	5	6
12.	Rajasthan	132,077	15,970,774	Jaipur	Rajasthani and Hindi
13.	Uttar Pradesh	113,409	63,215,742	Lucknow	Hindi
14.	West Bengal	34,945	26,310,992	Calcutta	Bengali
	Centrally Administered Territories				
1.	Delhi	578	1,744,072	Delhi (Union Capital)	Hindi, Urdu, Punjabi
2.	Himachal Pradesh	10,904	1,109,466	Simla	Hindi and Pahari
3.	Manipur	8,628	577,635	Imphal	Manipuri
4.	Tripura	4,032	639,029	Agartala	Bengali and Tripuri
5.	Andaman and Nicobar Islands	3,215	30,971	Port Blair	Bengali
6.	Laccadive, Minicoy and Amindivi Islands	10	21,035	Kozhikode	Malayalam

TABLE 4

AREA, POPULATION, CAPITAL CITY AND PRINCIPAL LANGUAGE OF THE COMPONENT STATES AND UNION TERRITORIES*

	Area in sq. miles	Population 1971	Capital	Principal language
1	2	3	4	5

STATES

Andhra Pradesh	2,76,814	4,35,02,708	Hyderabad	Telugu
Assam†	78,523	1,46,25,152	Shillong	Assamese
Bihar	1,73,876	5,63,53,369	Patna	Hindi
Gujarat	1,95,984	2,66,97,475	Ahmedabad	Gujarati
Haryana	44,222	1,00,36,808	Chandigarh	Hindi
Himachal Pradesh	55,673	34,60,434	Simla	Hindi, Pahari
Jammu & Kashmir	2,22,236††	46,16,632	Srinagar	Kashmiri
Karnataka	1,91,773	2,92,99,014	Bangalore	Kannada
Kerala	38,864	2,13,47,375	Trivandrum	Malayalam
Madhya Pradesh	4,42,841	4,16,54,119	Bhopal	Hindi
Maharashtra	3,07,762	5,04,12,235	Bombay	Marathi
Manipur	22,356	10,72,753	Imphal	Manipuri
Meghalaya	22,489	10,11,699	Shillong	Assamese
Nagaland	16,527	5,16,449	Kohima	Naga
Orissa	1,55,782	2,19,44,615	Bubaneswar	Oriya
Punjab	50,362	1,35,51,060	Chandigarh	Punjabi, Hindi

TABLE 4—(Contd.)

1	2	3	4	5
Rajasthan	3,42,214	2,57,65,806	Jaipur	Rajasthani
S.khim	7,300	1,97,000	Gangtok	
Tamil Nadu	1,30,069	4,11,99,168	Madras	Tamil
Tripura	10,477	15,56,342	Agartala	Bengali, Tripuri
Uttar Pradesh	2,94,413	8,83,41,144	Lucknow	Hindi
West Bengal	84,853	4,43,12,011	Calcutta	Bengali
UNION TERRITORIES				
Andaman & Nicobar Islands	8,293@	1,15,133	Port Blair	Bengali
Arunachal Pradesh	83,578	4,67,511	Itanagar	
Chandigarh	114	2,57,251	Chandighar	Panjabi and Hindi
Dadra & Nagar Haveli	491	74,170	N. A.	Gujarati
Delhi	1,485	40,65,698	Delhi	Hindi, Urdu, Panjabi
Goa, Daman & Diu	3,813	8,57,771	Panjim	Marathi
Lakshadweep	32	31,810	Kozhikode	Malayalam
Mizoram	21,087	3,32,390	Aizwal	
Pondicherry	480	4,71,707	Pondicherry	French

* Provisional, as on 1 July 1971. @ As on 1 January 1966.

† As reorganised on 21 January 1972 according to North-Eastern Areas (Reorganisation) Act, 1971.

†† Includes area under illegal occupation of Pakistan and China.

CHAPTER 6

CITIZENSHIP

THE CONSTITUENT ASSEMBLY took more than two years to arrive at a final decision with respect to the provisions dealing with citizenship. This was mainly due to some special problems created by the partition of India as well as the presence of a large number of Indians abroad. Between 1947 and 1949, millions of people had crossed and recrossed the frontiers that separate India from Pakistan, in order to make final choice of their nationality. On the one hand, Hindus and Sikhs who were born and domiciled in that part of India which became Pakistan and who migrated to India, had to be given the citizenship of new India; on the other, Muslims who left India to become citizens of Pakistan had to be excluded. There was also the case of persons of Indian origin living abroad, in many countries and for many years, and who might now prefer to reside in India permanently as she had become a free nation. Several drafts were prepared and destroyed by the Drafting Committee in its effort to cover all the cases which it was thought necessary and desirable to cover. Even so, the final draft that it placed before the Assembly had to face a large number of amendments, as many as 140, thereby indicating how difficult it was to reach a solution of this complicated problem. The provisions as finally passed are covered by Articles 5 to 11 and are embodied in Part II of the Constitution.

Article 5 refers to citizenship not in any general sense but to citizenship on the date of the commencement of the Constitution. It is not the object of this Article to lay down a permanent law of citizenship for the country. That business is left to the Parliament of India. Accordingly, at the commencement of the Constitution, every person who had his domicile in the territory of India and (*a*) who was born in India, or (*b*) either of whose parents was born in India, or (*c*) who had been ordinarily resident in India for not less than five years immediately preceding the commencement of the Constitution, was to be considered a citizen of India. Persons of Indian origin who had been residing outside India at the commencement of the Constitution were given the free choice of becoming Indian citizens under the above provisions if they so desired. The only condition that they had to fulfil in this connection was to get themselves registered as Indian citizens by the diplomatic or consular representatives of India in the country where they were residing (Art. 8).

Articles 6 and 7 deal with two categories of persons, namely, those who were residents in India but had migrated to Pakistan and those who were residents in Pakistan but had migrated to India. Those who migrated from Pakistan to India were divided into two categories: (a) those who came before July 19, 1948 and (b) those who came after that date. According to Article 6 those who came before July 19, would automatically become citizens on the commencement of the Constitution, and those who came after July 19 would become such provided they had been registered in the form and manner prescribed for this purpose by the Government of India. These two articles thus provided for all cases of mass migration from Pakistan to India without making any distinction between one community and another, although the partition of the country itself was based upon such a distinction.

Article 7 provides for those who had migrated to Pakistan but who had returned to India from Pakistan with the intention of permanently residing in India. Such a provision had to be made because the Government of India, in dealing with persons who left India for Pakistan and who subsequently returned from Pakistan to India, allowed them to come and settle permanently under what is called a "permit system". This permit system was introduced from July 19, 1948. Under this system, every person who desired to return to India and permanently reside in India was required to get a separate permit.

It is clear from the nature of these provisions that their object was not to place before the Constituent Assembly anything like a code of nationality laws. In fact, there is hardly any constitution in which an attempt has been made to embody a detailed nationality law. But since India's Constitution is of a republican character and provision is made throughout the Constitution for election to various offices under the State by and from among the citizens, it was thought essential to have some provisions which precisely determined who was an Indian citizen at the commencement of the Constitution. Otherwise, there could have arisen difficulties in connection with the holding of particular offices and even with the starting of representative institutions in the country under the republican Constitution. This is why Parliament has been given plenary power to deal with the question of nationality and enact any law in this connection that it deems suited to the conditions of the country. Such Parliamentary power embraces not only the question of acquisition of citizenship but also its termination as well as any other matter relating to citizenship (Art. 11). Also under Article 9 of the Constitution, any person who voluntarily acquires the citizenship of any foreign State, even if qualified for Indian citizenship under any provision of the Constitution, may not be a citizen of India.

The Citizenship Act, 1955

A comprehensive law dealing with citizenship was passed by Parliament in 1955 in accordance with the powers vested in it by Article 11 of the Constitution. The provisions of the Act may be broadly divided into three parts, acquisition of citizenship, termination of citizenship and supplemental provisions. The Act provides five modes of acquiring the citizenship of India. These are:

(1) *By Birth*: Every person born in India on or after January 26, 1950, shall be a citizen of India by birth. There are two exceptions, however, to this rule, namely, children born to foreign diplomatic personnel in India and those of enemy aliens whose birth occurs in a place then under occupation by the enemy.

(2) *By Descent*: A person born outside India on or after January 26, 1950, shall be a citizen of India by descent if his father is a citizen of India at the time of his birth. Children of those who are citizens of India by descent, as also children of non-citizens who are in service under a government in India, may also take advantage of this provision and become Indian citizens by descent, if they so desire, through registration.

(3) *By Registration*: Any person who is not already an Indian citizen by virtue of the provisions of the Constitution or those of this Act can acquire citizenship by registration if that person belongs to any one of the following five categories:

(*a*) persons of Indian origin who are ordinarily resident in

India and who have been so resident for at least six months immediately before making an application for registration;

(*b*)   persons of Indian origin who are ordinarily resident in any country or place outside undivided India;

(*c*)   women who are, or have been, married to citizens of India;

(*d*)   minor children of persons who are citizens of India; and

(*e*)   Persons of full age and capacity who are citizens of the Commonwealth countries or the Republic of Ireland.

(4) *By Naturalisation*: Any person who does not come under any of the categories mentioned above can acquire Indian citizenship by naturalisation if his application for the same has been acceded to by the Government of India and a certificate is granted to him to that effect. An applicant for a naturalisation certificate has to satisfy the following conditions: (*a*) He is not a citizen of a country which prohibits Indians becoming citizens of that country by naturalisation; (*b*) He has renounced the citizenship of the country to which he belonged; (c) He has either resided in India or has been in the service of a government in India, normally, for one year immediately prior to the date of application; (*d*) During the seven years preceding the above mentioned one year, he has resided in India or been in the service of a government in India for a period amounting in the aggregate to not less than four years; (*e*) He is of good character; (*f*) He has an adequate knowledge of a language specified in the Constitution; (*g*) If granted a certificate, he intends to reside in India or enter into, or continue in, service under a government in India. The Act provides, however, for a conspicuous exemption under which any or all of the above conditions may be waived in favour of a person who has rendered distinguished service to the cause of science, philosophy, art, literature, world peace or human progress generally. Every person to whom a certificate of naturalisation is granted has to take an oath of allegiance solemnly affirming that he will bear true faith and allegiance to the Constitution of India as by law established, and that he will faithfully observe the laws of India and fulfil his duties as a citizen of India.

(5) *By Incorporation of Territory*: If any territory becomes part of India, the Government of India, by order, may specify the

persons who shall be citizens of India by reason of their connection with that territory.

The Act envisages three situations under which a citizen of India may lose his Indian nationality. These are:

(1) *By Renunciation*: If any citizen of India who is also a national of another country renounces his Indian citizenship through a declaration in the prescribed manner, he ceases to be an Indian citizen on registration of such declaration. When a male person ceases to be a citizen of India, every minor child of his also ceases to be a citizen of India. However, such a child may within one year after attaining full age, become an Indian citizen by making a declaration of his intention to resume Indian citizenship.

(2) *By Termination*: Any person who acquired Indian citizenship by naturalisation, registration or otherwise, if he or she voluntarily acquired the citizenship of another country at any time between January 26, 1950, the date of commencement of the Constitution, and December 30, 1955, the date of commencement of this Act, shall have ceased to be a citizen of India from the date of such acquisition.

(3) *By Deprivation*: The Central Government is empowered to deprive a citizen of his citizenship by issuing an order under section 10 of the Act. But this power of the Government may not be used in case of every citizen; it applies only to those who acquired Indian citizenship by naturalisation or by virtue only of clause (c) of Article 5 of the Constitution or by registration. The possible grounds of such deprivation are: the obtaining of a citizenship certificate by means of fraud, false representation, concealment of any material fact; disloyalty or disaffection towards the Constitution shown by act or speech; assisting an enemy with whom India is at war; sentence to imprisonment in any country for a term of not less than two years within the first five years after the acquisition of Indian citizenship and continuous residence outside India for a period of seven years without expressing in a prescribed manner his intention to retain his Indian citizenship. The Act also provides for reasonable safeguards in order to see that a proper procedure is followed in every case of deprivation of citizenship.

Commonwealth Citizenship

India's Commonwealth tie is reflected in the Citizenship Act by providing for the status of a Commonwealth citizen. According to this, every person who is a citizen of a Commonwealth country, by virtue of that citizenship, has been given the status of a commonwealth citizen in India. Further, the Central Government is empowered to make provisions on a basis of reciprocity for the conferment of any of the rights of a citizen of India on the citizens of Commonwealth countries. During the discussion on the Citizenship Bill in Parliament, it was stressed on behalf of the Government that the privileges extended to Commonwealth citizens would be available only to the citizens of those Commonwealth countries which extended to Indians the same privileges.

The Citizenship Act, on the whole, is one of the most liberal enactments of its kind anywhere. Not only does it provide for the acquisition of Indian citizenship in a comparatively simple and easy manner, but it even recognises dual nationality under certain circumstances. The attacks on the provisions dealing with Commonwealth citizenship and the criticism that Indian citizenship has been made very cheap do not stand serious examination in the light of India's relationship with the Commonwealth, and the modern conditions and circumstances which facilitate social mobility on an international basis.

Single Citizenship

The most important aspect of the Constitutional provisions dealing with citizenship is that it has established a uniform or single system of citizenship law for the whole country. A citizen of India is accepted legally as a citizen in every part of the territory of India with almost all the benefits and privileges that attend such a status. This is in striking contrast to the system of double citizenship that prevails in some federal States.[1] Before the inauguration of the Constitution, there were two broad divisions among Indian citizens, British Indian subjects and State subjects. Since there were over 500 Indian States, the state subjects them-

---

[1] For example, in the United States of America, a citizen of the United States is at the same time also a citizen of one of the States.

selves were further subdivided into as many groups of citizens as there were States. Thus, the term Indian citizenship had little precise legal significance except that the Indian people as a whole, came under the overall jurisdiction of the British Government that ruled India. The abolition of such distinctions makes the essential unity of the nation a reality. A single citizenship for the entire country removes much of the artificial State barriers that prevailed in pre-Independence days and facilitates the freedom of trade and commerce throughout the territory of India.

There is, however, one barrier still that hinders that full realisation of the ideal of a single citizenship established under the Constitution. This is the existence of what are known as "domiciliary rules" in the different States in India. The term "domicile" is difficult to define. According to the rules prevailing today in the different States in India, domicile requirements vary from three to fifteen years' continuous residence within the State in addition to other conditions. Thus, the status of domicile is given only to a permanent resident of the State. On the basis of such a distinction, there exist practices in different States which amount to gross discrimination as between citizen and citizen. They also engender provincialism and parochialism which tend to disrupt the unity of the nation. Domiciliary rules which govern eligibility to public services in most of the States illustrate this point. Such rules are applied in some States not only to determine eligibility for appointment to public services but also to regulate the awards of contracts and rights in respect of fisheries, ferries, toll-bridges, forests and excise shops. The conditions to be satisfied for acquiring a domicile in some of the States are of such an extremely rigorous nature that it is almost impossible for any person to satisfy them.

It is unnecessary to emphasise that such stipulations are not only inconsistent with the Fundamental Rights of equality before law, equal protection of laws, equality of opportunity in matters of public employment and freedom to practise any profession or carry on any occupation, trade or business, but strike at the very root of the conception of an Indian citizenship. Until and unless the artificial restrictions arising out of the still existing domiciliary laws are removed and the citizens are respected and accepted in practice wherever they go within the territory of India, the intention with which the Constituent Assembly passed Part II of the Constitution, and Parliament enacted the citizenship law, will remain only half-fulfilled. The remedy is the passing of appropriate Parliamentary legislation as contemplated under Article 35 of the Constitution and the strict enforcement thereof. Parliament has already attended to this in so far as it concerns opportunities of public employment. It has to go a step further and see that the domiciliary rules prevailing in different States do not stand in the way of establishing a truly single citizenship for the country as a whole.

PART III

FUNDAMENTAL RIGHTS AND THE DIRECTIVE PRINCIPLES

CHAPTER 7

FUNDAMENTAL RIGHTS:
GENERAL NATURE

THE CONFLICT between man and the State is as old as human history. Although attempts have been made for centuries to bring about a proper adjustment between the competing claims of the State and the individual, the solution seems to be still far off. This is primarily because of the dynamic nature of human society where old values, ideas and forces constantly yield place to new ones. It is obvious that if individuals are allowed to have absolute freedom of speech and action, the result would be chaos, ruin and anarchy. On the other hand, if the State has absolute power to determine the extent of personal liberty, the result would be tyranny. Hence, the eternal problem that faced statesmen and political scientists was how to make a fitting adjustment between individual independence and social control, the need for protecting personal liberty against governmental power and that of limiting personal liberty by governmental power.

This problem assumes extreme difficulty only under a democratic system of government. For, the success or failure of a democracy depends largely on the extent to which civil liberties are enjoyed by the citizens in general. A democracy aims at the maximum development of the individual's personality; and the personality of the individual is inseparably bound with his liberty. Only a free society can ensure the all-round progress of its members which ultimately helps the advancement of human welfare. Therefore, every democracy pays special attention to securing this bare objective to the maximum extent without, at the same time, endangering the security of the state itself. A common device that is adopted by most of them for this purpose is to incorporate a list of fundamental rights in their constitutions and guarantee them from violation by executive and legislative authorities.

The British Position

Almost every modern constitution has followed this pattern.

83

The only exception to this almost universal rule is the case of the British Parliament as a constitution-making body. This is why the written constitutions of British Dominions like Canada and Australia embody no fundamental rights. British politicians and constitutionalists are generally of the view that written rights are not of much practical value. Abstract declarations, according to them, are useless unless there exists the will and the means to make them effective. The real guarantee of liberty lies in an effective public opinion and the existence of a government that is amenable to such public opinion.

Fundamentally, this is a sound position. It is true that in Great Britain today there is perhaps more individual freedom than in most of the countries in the world. Yet, the British attitude towards written rights is not unimpeachable. For, one might ask the simple question: "How long has it taken Britain to reach the present position? And at what price?" One can easily point out at least two revolutions in the process, one "bloody" and the other "bloodless". For establishing the liberties which the present generation of Englishmen enjoy, thousands of their ancestors paid a heavy price with their life, liberty and property. Further, no one can ignore the stupendous importance of documents like the Magna Carta, the Bill of Rights, the Petition of Rights, etc. in establishing the basic rights which a citizen ought to enjoy both as a human being and as a member of a given political society, and safeguarding them against all encroachments by the executive authority of the State. The most striking feature of the fight of the British people for civil liberties was that it was always directed against the arbitrary power of the Executive but seldom against the Legislature. This was because the despotic power of the King stood in the way of Parliament, the representative of the people. Hence, the British were always anxious to cut down the power of the executive and correspondingly increase that of the legislature. This is why the great charters like the Magna Carta speak only of limiting the powers of the King. The British never accepted the idea that a legislature could also become a tyrannous body and that hence the individual's liberties are to be safeguarded against legislative majorities too. The doctrine of Parliamentary sovereignty is the product of such an attitude.

The American Position

In contrast, the framers of the American Constitution, although most of them were educated in the British tradition, were unwilling to accept the British position. They did not believe in the sovereignty of the legislature however popular that body might be. True, the original constitution had not included in it a Bill of Rights. But within two years of the inauguration of the Constitution, a series of amendments were enacted in order to constitute such a Bill of Rights. The task of enforcing and protecting these rights was entrusted to the judiciary, particularly to the Supreme Court of the United States. The American concept, as one can see from the nature of these rights as well as the manner in which they are safeguarded, is that fundamental rights are not matters to be drawn into the vortex of political controversy or to be placed at the mercy of legislative majorities. They are to be definitely recognised in the constitution and protected against any violation either by the authority of the executive or by the legislature through an independent and impartial judiciary.

Why Guaranteed Rights

What is the purpose of guaranteed fundamental rights? Their very purpose is to withdraw certain subjects from the changing pattern of political controversy, to place them beyond the reach of a majority in a legislature and officials in the government and to establish them as legal principles to be applied by the Courts. For, if the danger of personal rule by despotic rulers has more or less disappeared as a result of representative institutions coming into their own, that from legislative interference has correspondingly increased because of the high-handed manner in which majorities might manage affairs in the legislature. A dominant group of legislators could pass any discriminatory or unjust legislation and prejudice the interests of considerable sections of the people. This meant in reality the substitution of one kind of tyranny by another, replacement of personal rule of the monarch by the tyranny of a legislative majority. One's right to life, liberty and property, to free speech and free expression, freedom of worship and assembly, and other fundamental rights are not subjects to be submitted to vote. They should not depend on the outcome of elections.

When legislatures were prohibited from encroaching upon certain rights through constitutional safeguards, the protection of these rights was achieved against the arbitrary conduct of both the executive and the legislature. When an independent judiciary was made the guardian of these rights by the constitution itself, the process of the protection of fundamental rights was complete and the enjoyment of these rights by all irrespective of wealth or social status, race or religious belief, was fully ensured. Herein lies the importance of fundamental rights. The United States has led many countries in this respect. Today, the idea of a list of written rights as an integral part of a new constitution has been generally accepted. Even the British do not seriously contest the wisdom of this arrangement and are prepared to concede its value at least to a limited extent.

The Indian Demand for Fundamental Rights

The idea of incorporating a list of fundamental rights in a new constitution of India had excited the imagination of almost all political thinkers and constitutionalists in India from the time the idea of the transfer of power from Britain to Indian hands had taken shape. The American Bill of Rights had a tremendous impact on Indian thinking on this subject. The Indian National Congress, the Liberals, moderates of all shades and the religious minorities like the Muslims, the Christians and the Sikhs, all considered it not only desirable but essential, both for the protection of the rights of minorities and for infusing confidence in the majority community. The British Government, however, never agreed with this idea and, therefore, none of the constitution acts passed by the British Parliament contained any fundamental rights.

The absence of guaranteed fundamental rights showed how free the Government of India was to do whatever it liked however illegal it was. During the war years, civil liberties lost all their meaning in India and the Courts including the Federal Court of India found it impossible to safeguard them. A series of ordinances by the Governor-General replaced legislative enactments in this field. Special Courts were set up to try persons for all types of political activities. Such courts ignored even the provisions of the Code of Criminal Procedure. Their decisions were placed beyond any review by High Courts. When the Federal Court declared the Ordinance which established these Courts invalid, thereby rendering the imprisonment of thousands of persons illegal, the Governor-General promulgated another Ordinance in identical terms the very next day! Hundreds of cases were brought before the various High Courts seeking protection from wanton conduct on the part of the Executive, but the Courts could not help, for there was no constitutional guarantee under which they could act. A decade of the working of the Constitution Act of 1935 amply demonstrated the imperative necessity of incorporating a list of fundamental rights in the Constitution of independent India.

As a result, the British Cabinet Mission agreed upon the necessity of the incorporation of a separate chapter of fundamental rights in the future Constitution of India.

Attitude of the Constituent Assembly

When the Constituent Assembly met for the first time in 1946, no member opposed the idea of a chapter of fundamental rights as an integral part of the Constitution. In fact, it was unreservedly supported by all sections of opinion in the Assembly. Over the Special Committee appointed for the purpose, Sardar Patel presided and it included prominent members of the various minority communities. The Committee made a detailed study of the whole problem and recommended a number of measures. On the basis of this report, the Drafting Committee of the Constituent Assembly prepared the provisions on Fundamental Rights as embodied in the Draft Constitution.

Even a rapid glance over the two chapters of the Constitution —Fundamental Rights and Directive Principles—will satisfy any impartial observer that the one desire that was dominant in the framers of the Constitution was for the rapid modernisation of the country's political, social and economic institutions. That desire has found its expressions in the chapter on Fundamental Rights along with that on Directive Principles. In this regard, they were primarily guided by the ideals of the American and French Revolutions. Intellectually, the leaders of contemporary India are the children of the West, that region of the world where modernism had its birth and growth. Hence it was no wonder that in the constitution they framed, an important place was given to these rights with a view to modernising their political, social and economic institutions.

The rights which were thus selected fell broadly into two categories—public and private—but both had the same purpose in view, namely, to put an end to arbitrary rule. Among the public or political rights were the right of men to choose their rulers, the right to hold them responsible for their conduct, the right to a share in law-making and the right to bear arms. Among the private rights were the right to personal freedom, the right to freedom of religious belief, the right to freedom of thought and expression, the right to equality and to the possession and use of property. Political thinkers of the age gave a philosophical explanation for these rights being regarded as fundamental. Assuming that happiness is the goal of human life, they pointed out, that man had, independently of his government, a right to the enjoyment of all those conditions which are essential for the pursuit of happiness. To such conditions, the term 'Rights' was applied and this meaning of Rights has, on the whole, come to stay although political thinkers of more recent times refer to the goal of human life as the development of personality. From their point of view, rights are those conditions which a person should possess if he is to develop his personality and become the best that he is capable of becoming. The two views do not however make much of a difference so far as enunciation of fundamental rights is concerned. By about the beginning of the nineteenth century, philosophers as well as statesmen were able to evolve a formula of fundamental rights and those who framed new constitutions in the subsequent period had not much difficulty in selecting the rights to be safeguarded as fundamental for incorporation in their own constitution.

The fathers of the Indian Constitution were, therefore, in a happy position to examine the experience of a variety of constitutions from different parts of the world. Of these, the Bill of Rights of the American Constitution, the French Declaration of the Rights of Man and the Irish Constitution of 1935—all of the era preceding the Second World War—were the most important which influenced them. Among the post-war constitutions, those of Japan (which was American-inspired) and Burma (which had many problems similar to those of India) were the two which attracted them most. There was also the influence of the Universal Human Rights Charter which was almost at its final stage of adoption by the United Nations. It must be emphasised, however, that the Indian Constitution-makers were not content with merely borrowing from experience abroad. They were profoundly influenced in the selection of these rights by at least three other factors peculiar to the situation in India. First, there were the special disabilities from which they suffered during the British rule, the disabilities which were similar to those to which the peoples of the West were subject in the days of despotism, but with the added circumstance of alien domination. The second was the institution of caste which was the dominant feature of the Indian social system as a consequence of which a large section of the people came to be treated as "Untouchables". The third was the existence of a number of religious, linguistic and racial minorities in the country whose cultural rights had to be safeguarded. Some of the rights included in the Constitution, therefore, owe their origin to one or other of these three factors.

The real problem that confronted the framers, however, was how to limit their selection of rights to certain categories only. What rights were fundamental and what were not, and why? If the rights to life, liberty and property were fundamental, what about right to employment and education? Has not the traditional concept of fundamental rights in its individualistic setting undergone a change in the modern era of the Welfare State? The framers had no doubt about the answers to these questions. They were quite conscious of the change in the character of the modern State. They knew that the age of the American Bill of Rights which believed in the "perfectibility of man and the malignancy of government" had gone for ever. And yet, it was a task of utmost difficulty. This was because the State in India was not yet in a position to guarantee the right to employment or education. It was a matter of physical impossibility, not the lack of will. Hence, they divided these rights into two categories, justiciable and non-justiciable. Justiciable rights are those which can be enforced by a court of law. Part III of the Constitution which is entitled "Fundamental Rights" contains justiciable rights like the right to life, liberty and property. Part IV, "The Directive Principles of State

Policy", contains non-justiciable rights such as right to employment and education. The citizen has no judicial remedy if he is denied the enjoyment of these rights.

We may now consider in detail the various provisions relating to Fundamental Rights.

General Provisions

Article 12 defines the term "State" as it applies to the provisions of this chapter. According to it, State includes the Government (Executive) and Parliament of India and the Government and the Legislature of each of the States and all local and other authorities within the territory of India or under the control of the Government of India. The definition is made so comprehensive that it includes every governmental authority, legislative or executive, Central, State or Local and the rights are guaranteed against violation by every one of those authorities.

Article 13 has two important aspects. On the one hand, it invalidates all laws which were in force at the commencement of the Constitution in so far as they were inconsistent with the Fundamental Rights and to the extent of their inconsistency with those rights. On the other, it imposes a prohibition upon the State not to make any law which takes away or abridges the rights conferred by this chapter. In case any law is made in contravention of this provision, such law would be invalid to the extent of its inconsistency with any of the rights guaranteed. The importance of this provision is that it makes express provision for judicial review of legislative enactments as to their conformity with the Constitution.

In addition to Articles 12 and 13, Articles 33, 34 and 35 in the chapter on Fundamental Rights also contain certain general provisions. Article 33 gives the power to Parliament to suitably modify the Fundamental Rights so as to apply them to the Armed Forces with a view to ensuring the proper discharge of their duties and the maintenance of discipline among them. Article 34 deals with the restriction of Fundamental Rights while martial law is in force in any area. If the right to life and personal liberty cannot be violated except according to procedure established by law, the application of martial law might become impossible in the country and it would be impossible for the State to restore order quickly in an area which has become rebellious, riotous or in any other way violently disorderly. Therefore, it was thought necessary to make a special provision to permit any act proclaimed by the Commander-in-Chief of the area where martial law prevails, as an offence to be reckoned as an offence under the established law. Similarly, the procedure prescribed by him shall be procedure deemed to have been established by law. Further Parliament is empowered to indemnify any person in respect of any act done by him in connection with the restoration and maintenance of order in any area where martial law was in force. Thus, Article 34 makes the operation of martial law and the consequent restoration of peace possible.

Article 35 deals with legislation intended to give effect to some of the provisions dealing with Fundamental Rights. Under this, Parliament has been given exclusive power to make laws with respect to the following matters: Right to Constitutional remedies; prescribing residence qualifications required for public employment; Armed Forces and martial law. Parliament is given exclusive power also for prescribing punishment for those acts which are declared to be offences under the chapter on Fundamental Rights. The Constitution in express terms prohibits the States from passing any law with respect to these items. The purpose of these provisions is clearly to establish uniform standards for the whole country as these are subjects which if handled by the States would create different standards which would be detrimental to the ideals of single citizenship and national unity which the Constitution aims to establish.

CHAPTER 8

RIGHT TO EQUALITY

(*Arts.* 14, 15, 16, 17 *and* 18)

ARTICLE 14 declares that "the State shall not deny to any person equality before the law or equal protection of the laws within the territory of India." The phrase "equality before the law" occurs in almost all written constitutions that guarantee fundamental rights. Equality before the law is an expression of English Common Law while "equal protection of laws" owes its origin to the American Constitution. Both the phrases aim to establish what is called the "equality of status and of opportunity" as embodied in the Preamble of the Constitution. While equality before the law is a somewhat negative concept implying the absence of any special privilege in favour of any individual and the equal subjection of all classes to the ordinary law, equal protection of laws is a more positive concept implying equality of treatment under equal circumstances. Thus, Article 14 stands for the establishment of a situation under which there is complete absence of any arbitrary discrimination by the laws themselves or in their administration.

Interpreting the scope of the Article, the Supreme Court of India held in Chiranjit Lal Choudhury *vs.* The Union of India that: (*a*) Equal protection means equal protection under equal circumstances; (*b*) The State can make reasonable classification for purposes of legislation; (*c*) Presumption of reasonableness is in favour of the legislation; (*d*) The burden of proof is on those who challenge the legislation. Explaining the scope of reasonable classification, the Court held that "even one corporation or a group of persons can be taken to be a class by itself for the purpose of legislation, provided there is sufficient basis or reason for it. The onus of proving that there were also other companies similarly situated and this company alone has been discriminated against, was on the petitioner."

In its struggle for social and political freedom mankind has always tried to move towards the ideal of equality for all. The urge for equality and liberty has been the motive force of many revolutions. The charter of the United Nations records the determination of the member nations to reaffirm their faith in the equal rights of men and women. Indeed, real and effective democracy cannot be achieved unless equality in all spheres is realised in a full measure. However, complete equality among men and women in all spheres of life is a distant ideal to be realised only by the march of humanity along the long and difficult path of economic, social and political progress. The constitution and laws of a country can at best assure to its citizens only a limited measure of equality. The framers of the Indian Constitution were fully conscious of this. This is why while they gave political and legal equality the status of a fundamental right, economic and social equality was largely left within the scope of Directive Principles of State policy.

The Right to Equality affords protection not only against discriminatory laws passed by legislatures but also prevents arbitrary discretion being vested in the executive. In the modern State, the executive is armed with vast powers, in the matter of enforcing by-laws, rules and regulations as well as in the performance of a number of other functions. The equality clause prevents such power being exercised in a discriminatory manner. For example, the issue of licences regulating various trades and business activities cannot be left to the unqualified discretion of the licensing authority. The law regulating such activities should lay down the principles under which the licensing authority has to act in the grant of these licences.

Article 14 prevents discriminatory practices only by the State and not by individuals. For instance, if a private employer like the owner of a private business concern discriminates in choosing his employees or treats his employees unequally, the person discriminated against will have no judicial remedy. One might ask here, why should the Constitution not extend the scope of this right to private individuals also. There is good reason for not doing so. For, such extension to individual action may result in serious interference with the liberty of the individual and, in the process, fundamental rights themselves may become meaningless. After all, real democracy can be achieved only by a proper balance between the freedom of the individual and the restrictions imposed on him in the interests of the community. Yet, even individual action in certain spheres has been restricted by the Constitution, as for example, the abolition of untouchability, and its practice in any form by any one being made an offence. Altogether, Article 14 lays down an important fundamental right which has to be closely and vigilantly guarded.

There is a related matter that deserves consideration here. The right to equality and equal protection of laws loses its reality if all the citizens do not have equal facilities of access to the courts for the protection of their fundamental rights. The fact that these rights are guaranteed in the Constitution does not make them real unless legal assistance is available for all on reasonable terms. There cannot be any real equality in the right "to sue and be sued" unless the poorer sections of the community have equal access to courts as the richer sections. There is evidence that this point is widely appreciated in the country as a whole and the Government of India in particular and that is why steps are now being taken to establish a system of legal aid to those who cannot afford the prohibitive legal cost that prevails in all parts of the country.

Prohibition of Discrimination on Certain Grounds (*Art.* 15)

Not content with a mere general declaration of the right to equality, and fully conscious of the types of discrimination prevalent in the country, the framers went a step further in Article 15, which is more illustrative in character than introducing anything substantially new. Yet, there is one striking feature in it which brings within its scope, although in a limited way, the actions of private individuals. According to the Article, "the State shall not discriminate against any citizen on grounds only of religion, race, caste, sex, place of birth or any of them. Further, on the basis of any of these grounds a citizen cannot be denied access to shops, public restaurants or the use of wells, tanks, bathing ghats, roads and places of public resort maintained wholly or partly out of State funds or dedicated to the use of the general public."

Interpreting the scope of the Article, the Supreme Court held that "it is plain that the fundamental rights conferred by Article 15(1) is conferred on a citizen as an individual and is a guarantee against his being subjected to discrimination in the matter of rights, privileges and immunities pertaining to him as a citizen generally." In another decision the Court rejected the plea that residence in the State was equivalent to place of birth and held that these are two distinct conceptions with different connotations both in law and in fact, and when Article 15(1) prohibits discrimination based on the place of birth, it cannot be read as prohibiting discrimination based on residence. Residence as a qualification for certain purposes such as employment may not be classed with discrimination based on caste and place of birth. The significance of the Article is that it is a guarantee against every form of discrimination by the State on the basis of religion, race, caste or sex. It also strikes at the root of provincialism by prohibiting discrimination based upon one's place of birth. It also goes well with the ideal of a single citizenship which the Constitution establishes for the entire country. By including within its scope certain discriminatory actions of private individuals, the Article anticipates Article 17 which abolishes untouchability and facilitates the removal of discriminatory practices indulged in by the higher castes against the lower castes and helps in a substantial measure the progress of social equality.

Article 15 has, however, two notable exceptions in its application. The first of these permits the State to make special provision for the benefit of women and children. The second allows the State to make any special provision for the advancement of any socially and educationally backward classes of citizens or for the Scheduled Castes and the Scheduled Tribes. The special treatment meted out to women and children is in the larger and the long-range interest of the community itself. It also recognises the social customs and background of the country as a whole. The second exception was not in the original constitution but was later on added to it as a result of the First Amendment of the Constitution in 1951.

Equality of Opportunity in Matters of Public Employment
(Art. 16)

Article 16 guarantees equality of opportunity in matters of public employment. In the first part of the Article, the general rule is laid down that there shall be equal opportunity for all citizens, wherever they are living, in matters of employment under the State; thereby the universality of Indian citizenship is emphasised. In the next section, the general principle is explained in detail. According to this, the State is prohibited from showing any discrimination against any citizen on grounds of religion, caste, race, sex, descent, place of birth or residence. The next clauses are in the nature of exceptions. According to the first, residence qualifications may be made necessary in the case of appointments under the State for particular positions. But instead of leaving it to individual States to make any rules they like in this regard, the power is vested in Parliament to prescribe the requirement as to residence within the State. This is intended to make the qualifying test uniform throughout India. The second exception is in favour of reservation of positions in public employment for any backward class of citizens. This is meant to help those who have had very little share so far in public employment. The determination of a backward community is a matter that is left to each State Government. The third exception seeks to take out of the scope of the general principle the management of the affairs of any religious or denominational institution under any special law providing for the same.

Although Article 16 guarantees equality of opportunity in matters of public employment for all citizens and is expected to provide a bulwark against considerations of caste, community and religion, the result so far has been far from satisfactory. This has been fully brought out in judicial decisions as well as reports and findings. The States Reorganisation Commission observed:

"Recruitment to the services is a prolific source of discontent among linguistic minorities. The main complaint is that a number of States confine entry to their services to permanent residents of the State, 'permanent residents' being defined in varying ways. These domicile tests, it is contended, have been so devised as to exclude the minority groups from the services.

"The residence required under these rules varies from three years in certain cases to fifteen years. These rules are, strictly speaking, in contravention of Article 16(1) of the Constitution. They have apparently been allowed to continue in terms of Article 36(b) pending a general review of the position."

In Venkataramana's case, the Supreme Court declared invalid the Communal G.O. of the Madras Government reserving posts in the public services for various communities on the principle of communal representation. According to the Court, the ineligibility of the petitioner for appointment to the Madras Provincial Service created by the Communal G.O. was not sanctioned in spite of the exception that permitted the State to provide for reservation of appointments in favour of backward class citizens and, therefore, it was an infringement of the fundamental rights guaranteed to him as an individual citizen under Article 16(1). The Communal G.O. was repugnant to the provisions of the article and, as such, void and illegal.

Hardly any other constitution has gone into such details in regard to the question of equality in public services. Yet, the operation of these provisions has not been in accordance with their spirit, and has been a source of discontent among large sections of people. Provincialism, communalism and "casteism" have been making serious inroads into the arena of the public services. The real problem that confronts the State today is how, on the one hand, it can ensure the building up and maintenance of a public service which is not torn by dissensions and sundered by divisions based on caste and group, community and religion, and which evinces social cohesion and civic solidarity, and has its foundation in merit, while, on the other hand, it also provides an opportunity for those who have been the victims of a petrified social system to come forward and become equal partners of their more fortunate brethren sharing the responsibilities of office in a common national endeavour. It is indeed a difficult problem and it still awaits a satisfactory solution.

Abolition of domicile tests for eligibility to state services is sought in a new Act that has been passed by Parliament seven years after the inauguration of the Constitution. The measure, the Public Employment (Requirement as to Residence) Act, 1957, seeks to repeal all existing domiciliary laws in the country which prescribe a period of residence within a particular State or Union Territory for any public employment there. This is one of the safeguards for linguistic minorities suggested by the States Reorganisation Commission in regard to employment in public services. The Central Government as a result is empowered to draft service rules with due regard to the requirements of different areas. The implementation of this Act,[1] which aims at the control of this field by the Central Government should indeed go a long way in translating into reality the fundamental right of equality in public employment.[2]

The Central Government has been taking several measures to translate the ideal embodied in Article 16 into practice. It convenes, on a regular basis, a conference of State Ministers of Backward Classes with a view to assessing the measures already taken and suggesting necessary modifications to existing practices in order to produce better results. It also advises the State Governments from time to time on specific actions, such as, the deletion of references to caste from official records and application forms for admission to educational institutions and issuing warnings against the practice of untouchability to all Government servants, etc. The States are also advised to adopt economic criteria for the determination of the backwardness of a particular class. But the Governments in the States which are really concerned with the implementation of these proposals have yet to change their attitudes. Most of them are still so much influenced by caste and communal considerations that it seems unrealistic to expect much from them in the near future. Rapid industrialisation and the availability of plenty of new jobs along with a simultaneous expansion of educational opportunities for the backward sections of the community as well as a change in the outlook and attitude of those classes and groups which held a traditional monopoly in public services will gradually facilitate the realisation of the ultimate goal of equal opportunity in public services.

The Abolition of Untouchability
(Art. 17)

Article 17 abolishes "Untouchability", and its practice in any

---

[1] The Public Employment (Requirement as to Residence) Act, 1957.

[2] In the name of providing employment to "sons of the soil" State authorities in India are still pandering to the worst form of parochialism. For example, according to an order of the Maharashtra Government of 1974 preference should be given to local persons and a "local person" is defined as one who has stayed in the State for over fifteen years.

form is made an offence punishable under the law. No article in
the Constitution was adopted with such unanimity and so great
an acclamation and enthusiasm as this article. It was the only
one which had the special distinction of having been adopted
with cries of "Mahatma Gandhi Ki Jai". Some critics of the Constitution ask the question: "What is the right that is created by
this article?" It is true that it does not create any special privileges for any one. Yet, it is a great fundamental right, a charter
of deliverance to one-sixth of the Indian population from perpetual subjugation and despair, from perpetual humiliation and dis-
grace. We have already seen, while discussing the nature of fundamental rights, that a right is a remedy against a disability. The
abolition of untouchability becomes a right in that sense. The
custom of untouchability had not only thrown millions of the
Indian population into abysmal gloom and despair, shame and dis-
grace, but it had also eaten into the very vitals of the nation.
There could be no better sign of the determination to eradicate
the evil than incorporating this Article into the chapter on Fundamental Rights in the Constitution.

It may not be inappropriate in this context to recall what Gandhi feelingly said on one occasion on the subject. He said: "I do
not want to be re-born, but if I am re-born, I wish that I would
be re-born as a Harijan, as an untouchable, so that I may lead a
continuous struggle against the oppression and indignities that
have been heaped upon these classes of people." Again, it may
not be inappropriate to recall here that it was an irony of fate
that a man who was driven from one school to another, who was
forced to take his lessons outside the class-room and who was
thrown out of hotels in the dead of night, all because he was an
untouchable, was entrusted with the task of framing the Constitution which embodies this Article and which dealt the death-blow
to this pernicious social custom.

With the epic fast of Mahatma Gandhi in 1932 in protest
against the "communal award" by which the Scheduled Castes
were to be given a separate electorate, a vigorous movement
against untouchability was launched on a national basis. Solemn
pledges were taken by many members of the Indian National Congress and others, that untouchability would no longer find any
asylum in the country. The movement brought forth some good

results. Many temples were thrown open, and the rigours of untouchability had become a thing of the past at least in the urban centres of the country. But the evil of untouchability still lingered in many forms and in many parts of the country. Speaking on the Untouchability Offences Bill, which was passed into an Act in 1955, the Home Minister of India said:

'This cancer of untouchability has entered into the very vitals of our society. It is not only a blot on the Hindu religion, but it has created intolerance, sectionalism and fissiparous tendencies. Many of the evils that we find in our society today are traceable to this heinous monstrosity. It was really strange that Hindus with their sublime philosophy and their merciful kind-heartedness even towards insects should have been party to such intolerable dwarfing of manhood. Yet, untouchability has been there for centuries and we have now to atone for it. . . The idea of untouchability is entirely repugnant to the structure, spirit and provisions of the Constitution."

The Untouchability Offences Act came into force in June 1955. In one sense it may be said to be an expansion of Article 15 of the Constitution. The Act intended to make the enforcement of any disability against the Scheduled Castes illegal. It provided that when the victim is a member of a Scheduled Caste, the commission of the forbidden act should be presumed to have been done on the ground of untouchability. It has laid down that whatever is open to the general public or to Hindus generally should be equally open to members of the Scheduled Castes also. Thus, for example, no shop may refuse to sell and no person may refuse to render any service to any person on the ground of untouchability. Every person is entitled to such services on the terms on which they may be obtained in the ordinary course of business by any other person. Any refusal on that ground entails cancellation of any licence required in respect of such profession. Any act which interferes in any manner with the exercise of such right by any person was made an offence punishable with imprisonment for six months or a fine upto Rs. 500 or both. A subsequent offence is punishable with both imprisonment and fine. All offences under the Act are cognisable and may be compounded with leave of the Court.

The Untouchability Offences Act was amended in 1976 making its penal clauses more stringent. The Act has been also renamed as the Protection of Civil Rights Act. One significant new provision of the Act is that a person convicted of an untouchability offence will be disqualified for contesting the elections. It was for the first time that such a provision become law in the history of elections in India.

In spite of the constitutional provisions, the operation of the Untouchability Offences Act and judicial pronouncements, India cannot yet claim to have rooted out the evil of untouchability completely. In the fight against social evils, legislation is only one of many weapons. To adopt an article in the Constitution against untouchability and make it a fundamental right, or pass an Act of Parliament making its practice an offence, and then expect overnight to have a society devoid of this centuries-old evil, would be too optimistic. There is no room for complacency in spite of the existence of these enactments. Legislation is a poor remedy for prejudices. The battle against every form of untouchability and social discrimination has to be carried to the hearts and minds of prejudiced people through mass contact, the mustering of public opinion and social action. Simultaneously, there must be a vigilant watch over offenders with a view to punishing every aggressive manifestation of caste discrimination.

The Abolition of Titles
(Art. 18)

In the creation of a society which seeks to establish political, social and economic equality and thereby aspires to become truly democratic, there is no room for some individuals to hold titles thus creating artificial distinctions among members of the same society. Recognition of titles and the consequent creation of a hierarchy of aristocracy had been denounced as an anti-democratic practice as early as the eighteenth century by both the American and the French revolutions. A democracy should not create titles and titular glories. In India, the practice of the British Government conferring a number of titles every year mostly on their political supporters and government officers, had already created a peculiar class of nobility among the people. It was difficult, on principle, for Independent India to recognise and accept these titles apart from considerations of the merit of those who held them. Article 18, therefore, abolishes all titles and the State is prohibited from conferring titles on any person. The only exception made to the strict rule of non-recognition of titles is that provided in favour of academic or military distinctions.

Ambedkar explained in the Constituent Assembly that Article 18 did not create a justiciable right:

"The non-acceptance of titles is a condition of continued citizenship, it is not a right, it is a duty imposed upon the individual that if he continues to be the citizen of this country, then he must abide by certain conditions. One of the conditions is that he must not accept a title, if he did, it would be open for Parliament to decide by law what should be done to persons who violate the provisions of this article. One of the penalties may be that he may lose the right of citizenship."

Thus, under Article 18, not only is the State in India prevented from conferring titles on any person, but Indian citizens are forbidden to accept any title from a foreign State without the consent of the President of India. The prohibition applies not only to the acceptance of titles but also to that of any present, emolument or office of any kind from any foreign State by any person holding an office of profit or trust under the State.

The battle against the titles conferred by the British monarch started with the passing of the United States Constitution in 1787 which prohibited all titles of nobility in the United States. Another British dependency, Ireland, on establishing its independence, followed suit and its constitution too prohibits the conferring of titles by the State. India and Burma were the next to follow the example, the former despite the fact that she decided to continue to be a member of the Commonwealth of Nations whose head was the British monarch.

CHAPTER 9

THE RIGHT TO FREEDOM
(*Art.* 19)

PERSONAL LIBERTY is the most fundamental of fundamental rights. Articles 19 to 22 deal with the different aspects of this basic right. Taken together, these four articles form a charter of personal liberties, which provides the backbone of the chapter on Fundamental Rights. Of these, Article 19 is the most important and it may rightly be called the key-article embodying the "Seven Freedoms" under the Constitution, guaranteed to all citizens. These are the rights.

(1) to freedom of speech and expression;
(2) to assemble peaceably and without arms;
(3) to form associations or unions;
(4) to move freely throughout the territory of India;
(5) to reside and settle in any part of the territory of India;
(6) to acquire, hold and dispose of property; and
(7) to practise any profession, or to carry on any occupation, trade or business.

It is impossible to exaggerate the importance of these freedoms in any democratic society. Indeed, the very test of a democratic society is the extent to which these freedoms are enjoyed by the citizens in general. These freedoms, as a whole, constitute the liberty of the individual, and liberty is one of the most essential ingredients of human happiness and progress. The most important among the inalienable rights of man, according to the Declaration of American Independence, are "Life, Liberty and the pursuit of Happiness." The Preamble of almost every constitution declares the same in one form or another as its objectives. The Preamble of the Constitution of the United States, for instance, declares that one of its objects is "to secure the blessings of liberty to ourselves and to our posterity". The Preamble of the Indian Constitution too proclaims that one of its objectives is to secure Liberty—"Liberty of thought, expression, belief, faith and worship."

The Articles dealing with the Right to Freedom embodied in the Constitution are the product of a compromise of two extremes. Having achieved political freedom only recently, the urge to exercise unfettered right to freedom was very much there. At the same time, there was also the realisation that the State that had been brought into existence was an infant State and if the newly-won freedom was to be guaranteed by a stable political order, it depended on the continued existence of that infant State which had yet to pass through many troubles. Therefore, the State should be preserved even if that entailed the abridgement to some extent of the rights guaranteed. The Drafting Committee, therefore, chose the golden mean of providing a proper enumeration of those rights that are considered essential for the individual and at the same time, putting such checks on them as will ensure the security of the State. They thought that the working of these rights depended on the genius of the Indian people, on how they developed their ideas of liberty which at the time of the drafting of the Constitution were in a rather undeveloped state.

As it stands now, there are seven restrictions on the freedom of speech and expression. These are: the security of the State, friendly relations with foreign States, public order, decency or morality, contempt of court, defamation, and incitement to violence. As it was passed originally by the Constituent Assembly, the restrictions were fewer and confined only to "libel, slander, defamation, contempt of court, any matter which offends against decency or morality, or which undermines the security of, or tends to overthrow the State." These were modified into their present form as a result of the First Amendment of the Constitution, 1951, necessitated by the decision of the Supreme Court in Romesh Thapar vs. The State of Madras. The Court held in this case that, unless a law restricting freedom of speech and expression were directed solely against the undermining of the security of the State or its overthrow, the law could not be held a reasonable restriction though it sought to impose a restraint for the maintenance of public order.

On the basis of this interpretation of the Supreme Court, some of the High Courts gave decisions to the effect that even incitement to individual murder or promoting disaffection among classes could not be restricted under the permissive limits set in Article

19(2). This was indeed a drawback which required rectification. The First Amendment of the Constitution made the necessary provision to obviate this difficulty by including "public order" along with other grounds for restricting the freedom of speech and expression. Thus, the scope of restriction under the present provision is broader than what it was under the original provision. Yet, in every case the judiciary gets a chance to test the validity of the executive action or legislative enactment against its reasonableness. In fact, the word "reasonable" is the life and soul of the entire Article. Interpreting the meaning of this word the Supreme Court said:

"The phrase 'reasonable restriction' connotes that the limitation imposed upon a person in enjoyment of a right should not be arbitrary or of an excessive nature beyond what is required in the interest of the public. Legislation which arbitrarily or excessively invades the right cannot be said to contain the quality of reasonableness, and unless it strikes a proper balance between the freedom guaranteed and the social control permitted under Article 19 it must be held to be wanting in reasonableness."

Freedom of the Press

There had been much criticism, both within the Constituent Assembly and outside, of the omission of a specific reference to Freedom of the Press and the failure to guarantee it along with the freedom of speech. The omission was considered a serious lapse on the part of the Drafting Committee by the protagonists of a "Free Press" as a separate right. Nevertheless, the Drafting Committee did not think it necessary to incorporate a separate right of this nature in the chapter on Fundamental Rights.

Speaking on behalf of the Committee, Ambedkar said that the Press was merely another way of denoting an individual or a citizen. "The Press has no special rights which are not to be given or which are not to be exercised by the citizen in his individual capacity. The editor of a Press or the Manager of the Press are all citizens and, therefore, when they choose to write in newspapers, they are merely exercising their right of expression and in my judgement, therefore, no special mention is necessary of the freedom of the Press at all."

The word "expression" that is used in Article 19(1) (a) in addition to "speech" is comprehensive enough to cover the Press. In fact, the lack of a specific mention of the Press in the Constitution created no difficulty when the Supreme Court was called upon to protect the freedom of the Press in Romesh Thapar's case. Further, modern science and technology have invented and are still inventing and bringing into use many forms of expression through which communication of ideas is facilitated. The radio, the cinema, the telephone and television are a few important examples of these new forms. Some of these may become in the course of time even more powerful and important media of expression than the Press itself. So, there seems to be no justification to single out any of them or mentioning all of the existing dominant forms in the Constitution, as such detailed mention would not serve any purpose which is not served by the word "expression". Hence, the criticism of the Constitution for not including the "Freedom of the Press" as a separate right can hardly be justified.

The Right of Assembly
[*Art.* 19(1)(b) *and* 19(3)]

One of the basic protections of free speech is the right of free assembly. In fact, freedom of assembly and freedom of speech go hand in hand. The framers of the Constitution knew that the right to peaceably assemble for public debate and discussion, for political activities and such other purposes, was essential to make the freedom of speech and expression real. Hence the constitutional guarantee to assemble peaceably and without arms.

The right to assembly can be restricted only in the interest of public order and the restrictions ought to be reasonable. Interpreting the scope of this provision, the Patna High Court, in the case of Indradeo Singh *vs.* the State, in which the Bihar Maintenance of Public Order Ordinance of 1949 was challenged as invalid, held that what the Court had to decide was whether or not the restrictions were reasonable:

"The question is whether the relevant section of the Ordinance relating to the banning of public processions, etc. was an unreasonable restriction in the exercise of the right conferred by the above clause [Art. 19(3)] of the Constitution. In my opinion, it is sufficient to state that the restriction imposel by the Act so far as it related to public processions, etc. was not unreasonable; and, therefore, it cannot be held that the sentence passed against the petitioners fell along with the relevant section of the Order. The restriction actually imposed cannot be said to be unreasonable judged by any standard."

The Right to Form Associations or Unions
[Art. 19(1)(c) and 19(4)]

The right guaranteed to form associations or unions is more or less a charter for all working people in this country. Trade union activity was not only discouraged by most of the Western countries until comparatively recently, but in many countries it was even looked upon as an anti-social and anti-State activity. Workers had to undergo great suffering before they could obtain even the elementary rights that vitally affected their existence as a separate group or class in society. It was only in the twentieth century, particularly after the end of the First World War, that any significant measures were undertaken to ensure the legitimate rights of workers through labour and industrial legislation. To make these rights fundamental and embody them as such in the constitution was indeed a much bolder step forward. Fully recognising the trend of the times, the Constitution of India has made the workers' right to form Unions a fundamental one.

The right to form associations or unions can be restricted only in the interests of public order or morality. There can be no association or union for an illegal or conspiratorial purpose. Nor can there be an association to further immorality. Interpreting the scope of the right the Supreme Court held in the case of the State of Madras *vs.* V. G. Rao:

"The right to form associations or unions has such wide and varied scope for its exercise and its curtailment is fraught with such potential reactions in the religious, political and economic fields, that the vesting of authority in the executive government to impose restrictions on such right, without allowing the grounds of such imposition, both in their factual and legal aspects, to be duly tested in a judicial enquiry, is a strong element which, in our opinion, must be taken into account in judging the reasonableness of the restrictions imposed on the exercise of the fundamental right under Article 19(1)(c)."

The right to form associations or unions, however, is not available to every citizen in the same measure. A member of the public services, although he is a citizen, cannot claim the right to the extent that a private citizen can. Being a government servant, he is bound by his service rules and he cannot challenge his service rules on the ground that they stand in his way of fully enjoying the right to form associations. This has been made clear by the Supreme Court in Balakotiah vs. The Union of India.

The Right to Free Movement, to Residence and to Property
[Art. 19(1)(d), (e), (f) and 19(5)]

The right to move freely throughout the territory of India, to reside and settle in any part of it and to acquire, hold and dispose of property are guaranteed under sub-clauses (d), (e) and (f) respectively of clause (1) of Article 19. The importance of the freedom of movement cannot be exaggerated. In fact, the enjoyment of the freedoms guaranteed under the other rights depends largely on the freedom of movement unhampered and uncircumscribed. The State's power to place reasonable restrictions on these freedoms is limited to two: the interests of the general public and the protection of the interests of any Scheduled Tribe. For instance, it is in the interests of the general public to restrict the free movement of a person suffering from a contagious disease. Similarly, the Scheduled Tribes form separate communities by themselves, backward and unsophisticated, with separate cultural and property interests. Although, complete segregation of the Tribal people in the name of their separate culture and general backwardness is wrong and against the ultimate aim of complete national integration, certain safeguards as are envisaged here seem to be justified. Otherwise, the Tribal people may become easy victims of exploitation at the hands of their more "civilised", shrewd and designing brethren. Hence there are various provisions disabling them from alienating their own properties except under special conditions. In their own interest and for their benefit, laws may be made restricting the ordinary rights of citizens to go and settle in particular areas inhabited by the Tribal people or acquire property in them. The reference to the interests of the Scheduled Tribes makes it clear that the free movement spoken of in the clause relates not to general rights of locomotion but to the particular right of shifting or moving from one part of the Indian territory to another, without any sort of discriminatory barriers.

The Freedom of Profession, Occupation, Trade or Business
[Art. 19(1)(g) and 19(6)]

Article 19(1)(g) guarantees the freedom to practise any profession, or to carry on any occupation, trade or business. A doubt was expressed in the Constituent Assembly whether these were fundamental rights at all. Perhaps the only other Constitutions which have given them the status of fundamental rights are those of Ireland and Switzerland. It seems that the framers of the Indian Constitution had been influenced by the complex social system that prevailed in India, in seeking to guarantee rights such as these. It has been a bane of India's social life that professions were inherited rather than acquired. A society dominated by caste, and professions based upon caste or religion, have little to offer for the building up of a community enlivened by social mobility and dynamism. Such a society is often intolerant to persons who change the traditional profession of their ancestors and is eager to maintain a petrified social order. A constitutional guarantee of the right to take up the profession, calling, trade or business of one's choice is indeed a significant aid to the building up of a dynamic and democratic society. The framers of the Constitution have done well to incorporate these rights in the chapter on Fundamental Rights and have thereby helped the evolution of a truly democratic society. The State's power to restrict the enjoyment of these freedoms is limited to the making of any law imposing reasonable restrictions in the interests of the general public in so far as it relates to: (a) the prescribing of professional or technical qualifications necessary for practising any profession or carrying on any occupation, trade or business or (b) the carrying on by the State or by a corporation owned or controlled by the State, of any trade, business, industry or service.

In Rashid Ahmed *vs.* The Municipal Board, Kairana, the Supreme Court had occasion to discuss in detail the scope of the rights guaranteed under the clause regarding the freedom of profession. Rashid Ahmed was carrying on wholesale business in fruits and vegetables in one of the bazars of Kairana, a town in Uttar Pradesh. In April 1949, a set of new by-laws framed by the Kairana municipality came into force. Anticipating the coming into force of the by-laws, the Board had auctioned the contract for wholesale trade in vegetables on the basis of a monopoly right. The contract was given to one Habib Ahmed. Subsequently the Board notified a specified place as the market for wholesale business in vegetables. Thereupon the petitioner applied for a licence to carry on his business at his shop. The Board rejected the application and the decision was communicated to the petitioner. It said: "According to resolution number 188 dated 22 December 1949, the application of Mr. Rashid Ahmed is rejected and he be informed accordingly". The resolution contained no reason for the rejection of the application. Soon after, notice was served on the petitioner by the Board asking him to stop selling vegetables at the appointed market or at his own shop where he had been doing business at least for two years prior to the coming into effect of the by-laws. His business had been wholly stopped and he was being prosecuted for alleged breach of the by-laws. By-law 2 ran thus: 'No person shall establish any new market or place for wholesale transaction without obtaining the previous permission of the Board and no person shall sell or expose for sale any vegetable, fruit, etc. at any place other than fixed by the Board for the purpose."

Speaking on behalf of a unanimous Court, Justice S. R. Das observed:

"The Constitution by Article 19(1)(g) guarantees to the Indian citizen the right to carry on trade or business subject to such reasonable restrictions as are mentioned in clause 6 of that Article. The position, however, under by-law 2 is that while it provided that no person shall establish a market for wholesale transactions in vegetables except with the permission of the Board, there is no by-law authorising the respondent to issue the licence. The net result is that the prohibition of this by-law, in the absence of any provision for issuing licences, becomes absolute. Further, the Board has granted a monopoly to Habib Ahmed and has put it out of its power to grant a licence to the petitioner to carry on wholesale business in vegetables either at the fixed market or at any other place within the municipal limits of Kairana. This certainty is much more than reasonable restrictions on the petitioner as are contemplated by clause (6) of Article 19 of the Constitution. . . . We are satisfied that in this case the petitioner's fundamental rights have been infringed and he is entitled to have his grievance redressed. The proper order in such circumstances would be to direct the respondent Board not to prohibit the petitioner from carrying on the trade of wholesale dealer and commission agent of vegetables and fruits within the limits of the Municipal Board of Kairana, except in accordance with the by-laws as and when framed in future according to law and further to direct the respondent Municipal Board to withdraw the pending prosecution of the petitioner and we order accordingly."

In Chintaman Rao *vs.* The State of Madhya Pradesh the Supreme Court held invalid the Central Provinces and Berar Regulation of Manufacture of Bidis (Agricultural Purposes) Act, 1948, because it totally prohibited the manufacture of bidis during the agricultural season in certain parts of the State. The Court said that such a prohibition, on the face of it, was of an arbitrary nature and, therefore, could not be said to be a reasonable restriction on the exercise of the right to carry on a profession, trade or business. But in another decision the Court held that the requirement of a permit as required by the law cannot be regarded as an unreasonable restriction on the citizen's right under the freedom of profession clause. In Kapur *vs.* The State of Punjab the Court upheld the nationalisation of text-books by the Government of the Punjab. "The action of the Government may be good or bad. It may be criticised and condemned in the Houses of Legislature or outside but this does not amount to an infraction of the fundamental right guaranteed by Article 19(1)(g)."

As a whole, the tendency of the judiciary with regard to the freedom of profession has been not to block in any way the increasing state activity that is bound to take place in a Welfare State but, at the same time, to give the individual maximum protection from high-handed executive actions or discriminatory legislative enactments. Whenever the action of the State was in the interest of the general public, even if it involved the restriction of the individual's freedom of action in the economic sphere, the Courts did not seem hesitant to support it.[1] This was the main reason that impelled them to uphold many legislative enactments of nationalisation of public utilities such as road transport, electricity, etc. even before the First Amendment had made a special provision in support of such State actions and the consequent expansion of the economic and commercial activities of the State.

Protection in Respect of Conviction for Offences *(Art. 20)*

Article 20 affords protection against arbitrary and excessive punishment to any person who commits an offence. There are four such guaranteed protections: (1) A person can be convicted of an offence only if he has violated a law in force at the time when he is alleged to have committed the offence; (2) No person can be subjected to a greater penalty than what might have been g'ven to him under the law that was prevalent when he committed the offence; (3) No person can be prosecuted and punished for the same offence more than once; (4) No person accused of an offence can be compelled to be a witness against himself. The Draft Constitution did not contain the term "prosecuted" in the clause prohibiting double pun'shment. It was pointed out in the Constituent Assembly that such a word was necessary because

---

[1] R. M. D. Chamarbaughwalla *vs.* Union of India 1957, S. C. J. 593; Li'avati Bai *vs.* The State of Bombay 1957, S. C. J. 557; Bhatnagar *vs.* The Union of India 1957, S. C. J 546 and Diwan Sugar and General Mills *vs.* The Union of India 1959, S. C. J. 663. Also see H. C. Narayanappa *vs*. The State of Mysore (1961) I S. C. J. 7; G. Nageswara Rao *vs*. Andhra Pradesh State Road Transport Corporation 1959, S. C. J. 967; Fedco (P.) Ltd. *vs*. S. N. B'grami, 1960, S.C.J. 235; R. D. J. Parkash *vs*. Union of India (1962) II 445 and A. H. Quraish *vs*. The State of Bihar (1962) II S. C. J. 523.

punishment here meant only that which was given by a court of law. Departmental punishment would not be taken as "punishment" in the sense in which the word is used in the Constitution. Nor would any punishment given in a court of law preclude departmental action leading to punishment for the same offence committed by the same official. This means that disciplinary action may be taken by the Government against an official despite the sentence of a court of law and such action will not infringe the right guaranteed under this Article.

Taken together, these provisions guard against retrospective application of a punitive law and double punishment for the same offence. These are, indeed, guarantees of great importance which establish "the primacy of law over the passions of man."

Protection of Life and Personal Liberty
(Art. 21)

Article 21 is one of the shortest in the Constitution over which there took place one of the longest and most thorough-going discussions in the Constituent Assembly. It enacts that "no person shall be deprived of his life or personal liberty except according to procedure established by law." The Article as it stands now is a revised version of what it originally was in the Draft Constitution, according to which "no person was to be deprived of his life or liberty *without due process of law*." The Drafting Committee gave two reasons for this change. First, the word "liberty" should be qualified by the word "personal" in order to avoid the possibility of too wide an interpretation which might include even the freedom already dealt with under Article 19. Secondly, the expression "procedure established by law" is more definite and such a provision finds place in the same context in the Japanese Constitution of 1946.

The key word in Article 21 is "law". What does it mean, law enacted by a competent legislative body, or fundamental or natural law? This was the question that confronted the Supreme Court soon after the inauguration of the Constitution. The question was discussed at length in A. K. Gopalan *vs.* The State of Madras.

Chief Justice Kania said that there was no ambiguity in the meaning of the Article:

8

"Normally read, and without thinking of other Constitutions, the expression 'procedure established by law' must mean procedure prescribed by the law of the State. . . . To read the word 'law' as meaning rules of natural justice will lead one in difficulties because the rules of natural justice as regards procedure, are nowhere defined and in my opinion, the Constitution cannot be read as laying down a vague standard. This is particularly so when in omitting to adopt 'due process of law' it was considered that the expression 'procedure established by law' made the standard specific."

This opinion of the Chief Justice was supported by four other judges of the Court.

The importance of the right embodied in Article 21, even if it does not place limitations on legislative power, is indicated by Justice Mukherjea in the same case in the following words:

"The fundamental rights not merely impose limitations upon the Legislature, but they serve as checks on exercise of executive powers as well, and in the matter of depriving a man of his personal liberty, checks on the high-handedness of the executive in the shape of preventing them from taking any step, which is not in accordance with law, could certainly rank as fundamental rights. In the Constitution of various other countries, the provisions relating to protection of personal liberty are couched very much in the same language as in Article 21. It is all a question of policy as to whether the Legislature or the judiciary would have the final say in such matters and the Constitution makers of India deliberately decided to place these powers in the hands of the Legislature. Article 31 of the Japanese Constitution, upon which Article 21 of our Constitution is modelled, also proceeds upon the same principle."

To sum up: Article 21 gives protection to life and personal liberty to the extent therein mentioned. It does not recognise the right to life and personal liberty as an absolute right but limits the scope of the right itself. The absolute right is, by the definition in that article. qualified by the risk of its being taken away in accordance with the procedure established by law. It is this circumscribed right which is substantively protected by Article 21, as against the executive as well as the legislature, for the Constitution has conditioned its deprivation by the necessity for a procedure established by law made by the legislature. While sub-clauses 2 to 6 of Article 19 have put a limit on the fundamental right of a citizen, Article 21 along with Article 22 puts a limit on the power of the State given under Article 246, read with the legislative lists. Under the Constitution, the life and personal liberty are balanced by restrictions on the rights of the citizens as laid down in Article 19, and by the checks put upon the State by Articles 21 and 22.

Protection against Arrest and Detention
(Art. 22)

Article 22 guarantees three rights. First, it guarantees the right of every person who is arrested to be informed of the cause of his arrest; secondly, his right to consult, and to be defended by a lawyer of his choice. Thirdly, every person arrested and detained in custody shall be produced before the nearest Magistrate within a period of twenty-four hours and shall be kept in continued custody only with his authority. All these rights are without any qualifications and are, therefore, in absolute terms.

There are, however, two exceptions to the universal application of the rights guaranteed under the first two clauses of Article 22. These relate to:

(1) any person who is for the time being an enemy alien; or
(2) any person who is arrested or detained under any law providing for preventive detention.

The first exception was accepted by the Constituent Assembly without any opposition as it embodied a sound principle. For instance, if India were at war with another country, considerations of national security may demand the arrest and detention of a person who is the citizen of the enemy country. He may not be given the rights guaranteed under Article 22(1) and (2). But no such easy justification is available for the second exception which provides for preventive detention even during normal times.

Discussion on this clause in the Constituent Assembly was stormy and acrimonious.

The reason for the introduction of such a clause were explained by Ambedkar thus:

> "It has to be recognised that in the present circumstances of the country, it may be necessary for the Executive to detain a person who is tampering either with public order or with the Defence Services of the country. In such case, I do not think that the exigency of the liberty of the individual shall be placed above the interests of the State."

Ambedkar's explanation, however, failed to satisfy a considerable section of the Assembly who criticised the provision in strong terms.

Replying to the debate, Ambedkar laid emphasis on the special safeguards embodied in the Constitution even when a person is arrested and detained under a preventive detention law. He said:

> "If all of us follow purely constitutional methods to achieve our objective, I think the situation would have been different and probably the necessity of having preventive detention might not be there at all. But I think in making a law we ought to take into consideration the worst and not the best.... There may be many parties and persons who may not be patient enough to follow constitutional methods but are impatient in reaching their objective and if for that purpose [they] resort to unconstitutional methods, then there may be a large number of people who may have to be detained by the Executive. In such a situation, would it be possible for the Executive to prepare the cases and do all that is necessary to satisfy the elaborate legal procedure prescribed? Is it practicable?"

Ambedkar, however, pointed out the safeguards provided in the Constitution to mitigate the rigours of an apparently absolute power of preventive detention permitted under Article 22(3). First, every case of preventive detention must be authorised by law. It cannot be at the will of the Executive. Secondly, no law of preventive detention shall normally authorise the detention of a person for a longer period than three months. Thirdly, every case of preventive detention for a period longer than three months must be placed before an Advisory Board composed of persons qualified for appointment as judges of a High Court. Such cases must be placed before the Board within the three months period. The continued detention after three months should be only on the basis of a favourable opinion by the Board. The only exception to this provision is when Parliament prescribes by law the circumstances under which a person may be kept in detention beyond three months even without the opinion of the Advisory Board. Fourthly, no person who is detained under any preventive detention law can be detained indefinitely. There shall always be a maximum period of detention which Parliament is required to prescribe by law. Fifthly, in cases which are required to be placed before the Advisory Board, the procedure to be followed by the Board shall be laid down by Parliament. Sixthly, when a person is detained under a law of preventive detention, the detaining authority shall communicate to him the grounds on which the order has been made. It should also afford him the earliest opportunity of making a representation against the order.

The greatest safeguard, according to Ambedkar, is that preventive detention takes place only under the law. It cannot be at the will of the Executive. It is also necessary to make a distinction between different categories of cases. There may be cases of detention where the circumstances are so serious and the consequences so dangerous that it would not even be desirable to permit the members of the Board to know the facts regarding the detention of any particular individual. The disclosure of such facts may be too dangerous to the security of the State or its very existence. But even here there are two mitigating circumstances. First, such cases will be defined by Parliament. They are not to be arbitrarily decided by the Executive. Secondly, in every case there shall be a maximum period of detention prescribed by law.

The First Preventive Detention Act was passed by Parliament in 1950. The validity of the Act was soon challenged before the Supreme Court in Gopalan vs. The State of Madras. The case was heard by six judges of the Court and each of the judges wrote a separate opinion. Each has examined in general the scope of fundamental rights under the Constitution besides analysing in detail the content of personal liberty. By a 4:2 majority, the Court upheld the Act except section 14 of the Act which was unanimously declared invalid. The invalidity of this section, however, did not affect the rest of the Act as it could be severed from the remaining provisions.

For a period of two decades — from 1950 to 1970 — a Parliamentary enactment on preventive detention had continued to exist in the country. The Preventive Detention Act of 1950 was amended seven times, each time for a period of three years, thus extending it upto 31 December 1969. It was not further extended, hence since then there has been no preventive detention law for the country as a whole. Some of the States, however, passed laws on preventive detention in 1970. In 1971 Parliament passed a modified version of the old Preventive Detention Act under the title Maintenance of Internal Security Act (MISA) which continued to exist until 1978 when it was abolished.

Every time in the past when the Government moved to extend the Preventive Detention Act, it provoked a heated debate in Parliament. This was particularly so in 1957 and 1960. Opposing the extension of the life of the Act, some members of the Opposition made the serious allegation that the Act had been used primarily to suppress political opposition. This allegation was refuted by the Government spokesmen by pointing out that out of a total of 106 detained on 30 September 1960, there were only 8 who could be categorised as members of opposition parties. But they denied that the detention was for political reasons. The Government spokesman went further and asserted that for a large country like India where many fissiparous tendencies against national integrity still existed and subversive elements operated, the number of persons detained under the Act (about 500 between 1959 and 1960) in the interest of the security of the nation was not too much of a price. According to the Home Minister, as against nearly 11,000 persons who were in detention in 1950, there were only about a 100 at the time of extending the Act in 1960. In September 1957 the total was 205, December 1959, 96; January 1960, 98; and September 1960, 106. He added that there was a time when the number of detenus under the Act for the whole of India fell to as low a figure as a dozen.

The Opposition, however, was not impressed by these figures. Nor were they convinced of the need of extending the Act. They were almost unanimous in condemning it as a black Act and characterising it as repugnant to all that was decent and precious in the political life of the country. One Member said that the right of individuals is not measured in quantitative terms. To say that only 500 were detained showed a 'blunting of sensitivity'. Even one person's liberty is precious and in guarding and protecting it the conscience of the whole nation had to be aroused. It was also pointed out that the circumstances which prevailed in 1950 when the Act was first passed had completely changed and that there was no justification for such a measure in 1960. Of course, the cry of the State in danger has been used in all ages in all countries by those who wanted to perpetuate themselves in power; but often, this cry has little relation to reality. Those who make laws should remember that a law misused is worse than no law at all. Some of the leaders of the Opposition made a joint appeal to the Prime Minister to refer the matter to the Law Commission so that the Commission could examine the provisions of the Act, "particularly the procedures which give authority to the executive to act in an arbitrary manner so as to undermine civil liberties of the citizens. We continue to be not convinced of the need of such wide powers which are repugnant to the spirit of the Constitution and the rule of law we cherish. If the Act has to be extended, it should be extended only till the new parliament is elected (1962) and the new House should be given an opportunity at the earliest to review the law *de novo*."

The Government did not, however, agree to refer the Act to the Law Commission as it was a matter for the Executive to decide and no points of a constitutional nature were involved which required a verdict of the Commission. The spokesmen of the Government emphasised that the retention of the Act in the Statute Book had by itself a restraining influence on anti-social and subversive elements. They also pointed out that the powers under the Act were used only sparingly as was shown by the figures of detention during the first decade since the Act was first passed. No one could seriously contest the fact that there existed in the country forces of separatism, parochialism, linguism and anti-nationalism. Some of these forces were in conspiracy with foreign powers who had evil designs on the country's integrity. Where large groups of citizens indulge in hostile activities or are suspected of espionage, where members actively participate in the process of law-making within the Legislatures but undermine the very same laws through coercive methods, such as, civil disobedience and fasting, where democratic freedoms are abused by organised sections to destroy the very same freedoms of others, the State should have effective powers, it was forcefully argued on behalf of the Government, for the protection of the civil liberties of the millions and the security of the State.[2]

Looking back on the progress so far of Republican India, one may feel reasonably satisfied with the extent of personal liberty the Indian people at large have been enjoying. A short period of about two years, however, 1975-77, was a rare exception from this point of view. During this period the country was under double emergency — the external emergency declared in the wake of Pakistan's attack on India in December 1971 and the internal emergency declared in June 1975 owing to threatened internal disturbances, and its adverse impact on personal liberty was indeed unprecedented. A continuation of the provisions of the emergency and those of the Maintenance of Internal Security Act made personal liberty a precarious fundamental right. No reliable figures are yet available of the number of people who were taken into custody and kept in detention without the due process of law. But certainly the number was very large indeed.

India won freedom from foreign rule as a result of great sacrifices by thousands of patriots. Many of them died in British jails in the course of the struggle for Independence. Many others spent

---

[2] In April 1973, by a unanimous decision in Sambhu Nath Sarkar *vs.* State of West Bengal, the Supreme Court struck down Sec. 17(A) of the Maintenance of Internal Security Act as being inconsistent with Clause 7(A) of Article 22 of the Constitution. Section 17(A) had provided that during the period of operation of the emergency issued on December 3, 1971 "any person including a foreigner in respect of whom an order of detention has been made under this Act, may be detained without obtaining the opinion of the Advisory Board for a period longer than three months, but not exceeding two years, from the date of his detention." In this case Sarkar was kept in detention for 21 months without consulting an Advisory Board under orders of the District Magistrate of Hooghly.

During the period of internal emergency from June 1975 to March 1977, MISA was misused in an unprecedented manner making it the most dreaded legislative enactment in the history of independent India.

years of their lives in prison. Naturally freedom and liberty are gifts too precious to all of them who lived to see India free. And they wanted to safeguard these rights and facilitate their enjoyment as best as possible. Against this background it is easy to understand and appreciate the deep-seated feeling against what happened to personal freedom during the emergency.

At the same time it must be remembered that democratic freedom in India is still too young and tender a plant to be capable of defending itself easily against overt or covert onslaughts that may be directed against it by elements which have no regard either for democratic liberties or orderly progress. Vigilance is still required to protect the country's hard-won freedom and national unity from forces of subversion and violent revolution. Until and unless every party or group accepts constitutional means to achieve its objectives and practises them, special provisions such as the preventive detention law may still be needed in India. But, whatever be the justification, so long as any provision similar to preventive detention or Maintenance of Internal Security Act remains on the statute book, there will also remain an unseemly blot on the face of democracy in India.[2]

[2] In 1978 the Union Government repealed the Maintenance of Internal Security Act. Most of the States had also done so already or during the same year. However, five of the States still retained their individual detention laws. The States concerned are Andhra Pradesh, Rajasthan, Uttar Pradesh, Madhya Pradesh and Jammu and Kashmir.

CHAPTER 10

THE RIGHT AGAINST EXPLOITATION

(*Arts.* 23 *and* 24)

ARTICLES 23 and 24 deal with the right against exploitation. Article 23 which prohibits traffic in human beings and *begar* and similar forms of forced labour is comparable to the Thirteenth Amendment of the American Constitution abolishing slavery or involuntary servitude. At the time of the adoption of the Constitution there was hardly anything like slavery or the widespread practice of forced labour in any part of India. The national freedom movement, since the twenties of this century, had been a rallying force against such practices. However, there were many areas of the country where the "untouchables" were being exploited in several ways by the higher castes and richer classes. For example, in parts of Rajasthan in Western India, which was in pre-independence days a cluster of Princely States, there existed a practice under which labourers who worked for a particular landlord could not leave him to seek employment elsewhere without his permission. Very often this restriction was so severe and the labourer's dependence on the "master" was so absolute that he was just a slave in reality. The local laws had supported such practices.

Evils like the *Devadasi system* under which women were dedicated in the name of religion, to Hindu deities, idols, objects of worship, temples and other religious institutions, and under which, instead of living a life of dedication, self-renunciation and piety, they were the life-long victims of lust and immorality, had been prevalent in certain parts of southern and western India. Vestiges of such evil customs and practices were still there, in many parts of the country. The Constitution-makers were eager to proclaim a war against them through the Constitution as these practices could have no place in the new political and social concept that was emerging with the advent of independence. The ideal of "one man, one vote, one value", equality before law and equal protection of laws, freedom of profession and the right to move freely throughout the country—all these would have no meaning if "one man" was subjugated by "another man" and one's life was at the mercy of another.

Although any form of forced labour is an offence punishable under law just as untouchability is an offence, this Constitutional guarantee is only against private individuals and organisations. An important exception is made in favour of the State which may impose compulsory service for public purposes. Compulsory military service or compulsory work for nation-building programmes may provide examples of such service. The State may, for instance, pass a law by which it may compel every University graduate to spend six months in villages immediately after leaving the University, on literacy work or other social service among the village people. Such a law, however, should not make any discrimination on grounds of religion, caste or class, or any of them.

Prohibition of Child Labour

According to Article 24, no child below the age of fourteen years shall be employed to work in any factory or mine or engaged in any other hazardous employment. This Article is intimately related to a directive principle of state policy which calls upon the State to enforce universal compulsory and free primary education to all children in the country upto the age of fourteen years. This comes of the realisation that children should prepare during this period for the task of the future as useful and responsible citizens. Employment of children is an uncivilised and even inhuman practice. It is exploitation. It stunts their growth, corrupts their morals and often drives them to delinquency. Naturally, it must be prohibited and incentives to divert them from employment should be provided.

In spite of the existence of several laws which seek to provide protection of the right against exploitation, there still remain in many parts of the country many forms of exploitation that come within the scope of this right. The efforts so far made by the State in this direction are marked by timidity rather than determination. There is an under-current of indifference even in the law-enforcing officials with respect to these rights. Many of them

think, for ins ance, that attempts to close down brothels altogether
are fore-doomed to failure. Society must awaken to the full
realisation that *begar* and immoral traffic are the products of
poverty and neglect. A Committee appointed some years ago by
the Central Social Welfare Board to go into all aspects of immoral
traffic reported that the question of exploitation of women and
girls generally, is so closely linked up with prostitution that it is
not possible to suggest measures to wipe out the one without taking
into consideration the other. The question cannot be considered
except in the context of national progress, full employment,
economic advancement, social justice and the general raising of
the standard of living of all sections of the people. Nevertheless,
the adoption of preventive measures would reduce the incidence
of these evil practices. For this, it is necessary for the State to
pursue a more vigorous policy.

CHAPTER 11

THE RIGHT TO FREEDOM OF RELIGION

(*Arts.* 25 *to* 28)

IT IS a paradox that while almost every religion stands for and preaches the universal brotherhood of man, religion has been a constant source of conflict in human history. India has been most unfortunate in this respect, particularly during the last thousand years of her history. The British did not desist from exploiting this situation for their own advantage and to continue their rule in India as long as they could. We saw in the earlier part of this discussion how religion shattered the unity of the nation and how the country was partitioned on a religious basis. Yet the problem of religious minorities in independent India was not solved and remained as difficult as ever. Despite the creation of Pakistan, there were more than forty million Muslims in India scattered all over the country. There were, in addition, some ten million Christians, five million Sikhs and considerable numbers of Parsees, Jains, Buddhists and Jews. Those who professed the Hindu religion formed an overwhelming majority, some 85 per cent of the total population. If they chose to act together as a religious group in representative institutions, they could pass any law they liked and have absolute control over the governmental machinery in all its activities. The slightest tendency towards such an attitude would have undermined the confidence of the religious minorities, and democracy in India might have become a label without meaning, a form without substance.

The idea of guaranteed fundamental rights itself was a device directed towards the avoidance of such a contingency. The right to freedom of speech and expression, and the right to form associations and unions are also rights which guarantee religious speech and expression and the right to form religious associations and unions. But the Constituent Assembly was not satisfied with such provisions alone in its bid to infuse complete confidence in the religious minorities. It went a step further and adopted a separate group of articles dealing solely with the right to freedom of religion. The freedoms provided in Articles 25, 26, 27 and 28 are conceived in most generous terms to the complete satisfaction of religious minorities. They were in fact the result of an agreement with the minorities, almost unanimously arrived at in the Minorties Committee constituted by the Constituent Assembly. Such unanimity created an atmosphere of harmony and confidence in the majority community. Further, these provisions embodied in detail one of the objectives of the Constitution declared in the Preamble: "to secure to all its citizens...liberty of faith, belief and worship."

Religious Freedom and the Secular State

It was argued on the floor of the Assembly that the religious freedom guaranteed under the Constitution was opposed to the concept of a secular State which the Constitution aimed to establish. This proposition was successfully challenged by several prominent members including those of the Drafting Committee. Some of the observations made in this context deserve reproduction in original. According to Lakshmi Kant Maitra the above mentioned conception of a secular State was wholly wrong. He said:

"By secular State, as I understand it, is meant that the State is not going to make any dicrimination whatsoever on the ground of religion or community against any person professing any particular form of religious faith. This means in essence that no particular religion in the State will receive any State patronage whatsoever. The State is not going to establish, patronise or endow any particular religion to the exclusion of or in perference to others and that no citizen in the State will have any preferential treatment or will be discriminated against simply on the ground that he professed a particular form of religion. In other words, in the affairs of the State, the processing of any particular religion will not be taken into consideration at all. This I consider is the essence of a secular State."

H. V. Kamath said:

"When I say that a State should not indentify itself with any particular religion, I do not mean to say that a State should be anti-religious or irreligious. We have certainly declared India to be a secular State. But to my mind, a secular State is neither a God-less State nor an irreligious nor an anti-religious State."

Participating in the debate on the Hindu Code Bill in Parliament, Ambedkar explained the concept of secularism as follows:

"It (secular State) does not mean that we shall not take into consideration the religious sentiments of the people. All that a secular State means is that this Parliament shall not be competent to impose any particular religion upon the rest of the people. That is the only limitation that the Constitution recognises."

The significance of secularism as it relates to the State in India has been dealt with at length by India's President, Dr. S. Radhakrishnan, in the following words:

"When India is said to be a secular State, it does not mean that we reject the reality of an unseen spirit or the relevance of religion to life or that we exalt irreligion. It does not mean that secularism itself becomes a positive religion or that the State assumes divine prerogatives. Though faith in the Supreme is the basic principle of the Indian tradition, the Indian State will not identify itself with or be controlled by any particular religion. We hold that no one religion should be given preferential status, or unique distinction, that no one religion should be accorded special privileges in national life or international relations for that would be a violation of the basic principles of democracy and contrary to the best interests of religion and government. This view of religious impartiality of comprehension and forbearance has a prophetic role to play within the national and international life. No group of citizens shall arrogate to itself rights and privileges which it denies to others. No person should suffer any form of disability or discrimination because of his religion but all alike should be free to share to the fullest degree in the common life. This is the basic principle involved in the separation of Church and State. The religious impartiality of the Indian State is not to be confused with secularism or atheism. Secularism as here defined is in accordance with the ancient religious tradition of India. It tries to build up a fellowship of believers, not by subordinating individual qualities to the group-mind but by bringing them into harmony with each other."

Thus the distinguishing features of a secular democracy as contemplated by the Constitution of India are: (1) that the State will not identify itself with or be controlled by any religion; (2) that while the State guarantees to every one the right to profess whatever religion one chooses to follow (which includes also the right to be an agnostic or an atheist), it will not accord any preferential treatment to any of them; (3) that no discrimination will be shown by the State against any person on account of his religion or faith, and (4) that the right of every citizen, subject to any general condition, to enter any office under the State will be equal to that of his fellow-citizens. Political equality which entitles any Indian citizen to seek the highest office under the State is the heart and soul of secularism as envisaged by the Constitution. It secures the conditions of creating a fraternity of the Indian people which assures both the dignity of the individual and the unity of the nation.

Freedom of Conscience, etc.

Article 25(1) enacts that all persons are equally entitled to freedom of conscience and the right freely to profess, practice and propagate religion. The wording of the article has been largely based upon the judicial interpretation of freedom of religion in the United States. Interpreting the scope of religious freedom as guaranteed under the First Amendment, the American Supreme Court held: "Freedom of religious belief and to act in the exercise of such belief cannot override the interests of peace, order or morals of the society and to that extent the freedom of religion is subject to the control of the State." This is in conformity with the modern idea that anything may not, in the name of religion, have the unrestricted right to practise or propagate itself.

The problem of interpreting the right to freely practise and propagate religion, however, has never been an easy task for the Courts. This is evident from the contradictory decisions of the United States Supreme Court on such an apparently simple matter as to whether an Ordinance enjoining every citizen to salute the National Flag interferes with religious freedom. As Justice Felix Frankfurter pointed out in one of these decisions:

"Of course patriotism cannot be enforced by the flag salute. But neither can the liberal spirit be enforced by judicial invalidation of illiberal legislation.... Reliance for the most precious interests of civilisation, therefore, must be found outside of their vindication in courts of law. Only a persistent positive translation of the faith of a free society into the convictions and habits and actions of a community is the ultimate reliance against unabated temptations to fetter the human spirit."

Yet in its zeal to uphold the right of religious enthusiasts, the Court has on occasions gone to the fantastic limit of approving actions such as ringing door bells and disturbing householders, accosting passers-by and insulting them in their religious beliefs, soliciting funds even in an intimidating manner and "peddling doctrinal wares in the streets." These decisions of the Court show how essential it is for the text of the Constitution to give a positive lead to the Courts by specifically laying down as clearly as possible the permissive limits to which legislation regulating the practice and propagation of religion can go. The idea of laying down such restrictions finds today wide acceptance.

The framers of the Indian Constitution accepted this idea and made it a part of Article 25(1) by placing three restrictions to the freedom of religion, namely, public order, morality and health. The full implications of these qualifications have not yet been discovered. Naturally, they will have to grow with the growing social and moral conscience of the people as well as authoritative judicial pronouncements. The State is also permitted to regulate economic, financial, political or other secular activities which may be associated with religious practice. Further, it may also

9

provide for social welfare and reform or the throwing open of Hindu religious institutions of a public character to all classes and sections of Hindus.

The word "propagate" does not find a place in any other constitution where it deals with religious freedom. A few members of the Constituent Assembly were vehemently opposed to the inclusion of this term as they thought that it might be perilous to guarantee it and might freely be used for the purpose of wholesale conversion. But the overwhelming majority of members did not agree with this view. As one member pointed out:

"After all propagation is merely freedom of expression. I would like to point out that the word 'convert' is not there. ...Those who drafted this Constitution have taken care to see that no unlimited right of conversion has been given. People have freedom of conscience, and if any man is converted voluntarily owing to freedom of conscience, then well and good. No restrictions can be placed against it."[1]

Speaking on behalf of the Drafting Committee, K. M. Munshi said:

"....Moreover, I was a party from the beginning to the compromise with the minorities... and I know that it was on this word the Indian Christian Community laid the greatest emphasis, not because they wanted to convert people aggressively, but because the word 'propagate' was a fundamental part of their tenet. Even if the word were not there, I am sure, under the freedom of speech which the Constitution guarantees, it will be open to any religious community to persuade other people to join their faith. So long as religion is religion, conversion by free exercise of the conscience has to be recognised."[2]

Advocating the inclusion of the word "propagate", another member observed:

[1] K. Santhanam, C.A.D. VII, p. 835.
[2] Ibid, p. 837.

"It is generally understood that the word propagate is intended only for the Christian Community. But I think it is absolutely necessary, in the present context of circumstances, that we must educate our people on religious tenets and doctrines. So far as my experience goes, the Christian community has not transgressed their limits of legitimate propagation of religious views, and on the whole, they have done well indeed. It is for other communities to emulate them and propagate other religions as well. . . . The different communities may well. . .propagate their religion and what it stands for. It is not to be understood that when one propagates his religion he should cry down other religions. It is not the spirit of any religion to cry down another religion. Therefore, this is absolutely necessary and essential."[3]

According to Alladi Krishnaswami Aiyar,

"it was probably unnecessary to have included the expression 'propagate' in view of the fact that freedom of expression is already guaranteed under Article 19, but the expression was inserted by way of abundant caution to satisfy certain missionary interests who were zealous about it."[4]

The Supreme Court had occasion to interpret the right to religious freedom under Article 25 in the case of Commissioner of Hindu Religious Endowment vs. L. T. Swamiar. The Court held that

"Article 25 guarantees to every person, subject to public order, health and morality a freedom not only to entertain such religious belief as may be approved of by his judgment and conscience, but also to exhibit his belief in such outward acts as he thinks proper and to propagate or disseminate his ideas for the edification of others. . . . The expression 'practice of religion' denotes that the Constitution not only protects the freedom of religious opinion but also acts done in pursuance of a religion."

[3] L. Krishnaswami Bharati, C.A.D., VII, p. 833.
[4] The Constitution and Fundamental Rights, p. 45.

Article 26 is, in fact, a corollary to Article 25 and guarantees the freedom to manage religious affairs. According to this, every religious denomination is given the right (*a*) to establish and maintain institutions for religious and charitable purposes; (*b*) to manage its own affairs in matters of religion; (*c*) to own and acquire movable and immovable property, and (*d*) to administer such property in accordance with law. Article 27 provides an additional protection to religious activity by exempting funds appropriated towards the promotion or maintenance of any particular religion from the payment of taxes.

However, the right of a religious denomination to manage its own affairs in matters of religion is subject to any law protected by Article 25(2)(b) throwing open a Hindu Public temple to all classes and sections of Hindus. The object of this provision is to remove a potent cause of disunion and inequality among the various castes of the Hindus. It is indeed a corollary to the abolition of untouchability.

A provision that is similar to the above is that which deals with social reform. A secular state which gives protection to all religions equally is by no means bound to protect every kind of human activity under the guise of religion. There are religions which bring under their own cloak every human activity and it would be absurd to suggest that a secular state should protect them all. Here again, Indian conditions, especially the degradation of certain social institutions such as caste have had their particular impact in the minds of the fathers of the constitution. As Ambedkar explained in the Constituent Assembly, the conception of religion in India is so vast that it covers every aspect of life from birth to death. If the State were to accept this conception of religion, the country would come to a standstill in regard to reforms. At the same time, no sensible State, in the name of social reform, would interfere with the essence of any religion.

Religious Instruction in Schools

Article 28 prohibits religious instruction in any educational institution wholly maintained out of State funds whether such instruction is given by the State or by any other body. But this prohibition will not apply to any educational institution which is established under any endowment or trust which requires that religious instruction should be imparted in such institution, even if it happens to be administered by the State. After having thus settled the question of religious instruction in State Schools, the Constitution deals with the same in State-aided or State-recognised schools. No person attending such institutions can be compelled to take part in any religious instruction without the consent of the person concerned or, if the person is a minor, without the consent of his guardian. This again is a provision which seeks to accommodate the interests of religious minorities. Although educational institutions run by them may receive State aid, this does not prohibit their imparting religious instruction to those who are willing to attend. Thus, while the secular character of the State is demonstrated by all State educational institutions, private or denominational institutions, even when they receive State aid, are given freedom to maintain their religious character.

Chapter 12

CULTURAL AND EDUCATIONAL RIGHTS

(*Arts.* 29 *and* 30)

UNDER ARTICLES 29 and 30, certain cultural and educational rights are guaranteed. Section (1) of Article 29 guarantees the right of any section of the citizens residing in any part of the country having a distinct language, script or culture of its own, to conserve the same. Section (2) prohibits any discrimination based only on religion, race, caste, language or any of them in the matter of admission to State or State-aided educational institutions. Section (1) of Article 30 provides that "all minorities, whether based on religion or language, shall have the right to establish and administer educational institutions of their choice." According to section (2) the State shall not, in granting aid to educational institutions, discriminate against any educational institution on the ground that it is under the management of a minority, whether based on religion or language.

These provisions are unique in their thoroughness. There is nothing comparable to these in the Bill of Rights of the American Constitution. When provisions under Articles 29 and 30 are considered along with other provisions in the chapter on Fundamental Rights and elsewhere in the Constitution safeguarding the rights of religious, linguistic and racial minorities it will become clear that the sole purpose of these provisions is to reassure the minorities that certain special interests of theirs which they cherish as fundamental to their life are safe under the Constitution. These are in conformity with the right to religious freedom and an extension to certain specific aspects of that right, like the freedom to maintain separate educational institutions, etc. already referred to. One special feature of these provisions, however, is that the term 'minority' has been given a wide connotation. Here a minority is recognised as such not only on the basis of religion but also on language, script or culture. The importance of the provision will be evident in view of the existence of not less than a dozen well-developed languages within the territory of India.

Interpreting the scope of Article 29, the Bombay High Court held that it embodied two important principles:

"One is the right of the citizen to select any educational institution maintained by the State and receiving aid out of State funds. The State cannot tell a citizen, 'you shall go to this school which I maintain and not to the other'. Here we find reproduced the right of the parent to control the education of the child."

The scope of Article 29 (2) came up for detailed interpretation before the Supreme Court in two cases, both of which were appeals from decisions of the Madras High Court, relating to Admission to educational institutions maintained by the State. After analysing the facts in detail the Court said:

"It will be noticed that while clause (1) protects the language, script or culture of a section of the citizens, clause (2) guarantees the fundamental right of an individual citizen. The right to get admission into any educational institution of the kind mentioned in clause (2) is a right which an individual citizen has as a citizen and not as a member of any community or class of citizens. This right is not to be denied to the citizen on grounds only of religion, race, caste, language or any of them. If a citizen who seeks admission into any such educational institution has not the requisite academic qualifications and is denied admission on that ground, certainly he cannot be heard to complain of an infraction of his fundamental right under this Article. But, on the other hand, if he has the academic qualifications but is refused admission only on grounds of religion, race, caste, language or any of them, then there is a clear breach of his fundamental right."

On behalf of the State it was contended that Article 46 charged the State with promoting, with special care, the educational and special interests of the weaker sections of the people and, in particular, of the Scheduled Castes and Scheduled Tribes and with protecting them from social injustice and all forms of exploitation. But the Court rejected this argument on the ground that this was a Directive Principle — a non-justiciable right — and it could not override a Fundamental Right which was justiciable. It was the duty of the Court to enforce a Fudamental Right.

With the passing of the forty-second Amendment of the Constitution this argument of the Court has lost much of its force. According to the Amendment where there is a conflict between a Fundamental Right and a Directive Principle, Parliament may by law give precedence to the Directive Principle.

Article 30 is a charter of educational rights. It guarantees in absolute terms the right of linguistic and religious minorities to establish and administer educational institutions of their choice and, at the same time, claim grants-in-aid without any discrimination based upon religion or language. The fact that the Constitution does not impose any express restriction in the scope of the enjoyment of this right, unlike most of the rights included in the chapter on Fundamental Rights, shows that the framers intended to make its scope unfettered. This does not, however, mean that the State cannot impose reasonable restrictions of a regulatory character for maintaining standards of education. This point has been made abundantly clear in judicial pronouncements.

The scope of Article 30 was interpreted at length by the Supreme Court in a reference made to it by the President. The subject of the reference was the constitutional validity of certain provisions of the Kerala Education Bill, 1957, which was submitted to the President for his assent. The Bill has been the cause of agitation in the State of Kerala ever since its introduction in the State Assembly in 1957, and those who opposed it contended that it violated the fundamental rights guaranteed under the Constitution, especially those under Article 30. In a six to one decision, the Court held that clause 3 (5) of the Bill was invalid. The clause read as follows:

"After the commencement of this Act, the establishment of a new school or the opening of a new class in any private school shall be subject to the provisions of this Act and the rules made thereunder and any school or higher class established or opened otherwise than in accordance with such provisions shall not be entitled to be recognised by the government."

Speaking for the majority on the content of Article 30 (1), Chief Justice Das said that:

"What the Article said was that the religious and linguistic minorities should have the right to establish educational institutions of their choice.

"It did not say that minorities based on religion should establish educational institutions for teaching religion only, or that linguistic minorities should have the right to establish educational institutions for teaching their language only. What the Article said and meant was that the religious and linguistic minorities should have the right to establish educational institutions of their choice. As such, minorities would ordinarily desire that their children should be brought up properly and efficiently and be eligible for higher university education, educational institutions of their choice would necessarily include institutions imparting general secular education also."

The Chief Justice said that the Article gave all minorities whether based on religion or language, two rights namely, the right to establish and the right to administer educational institutions of their choice. The key to the understanding of the true meaning and implication of the Article under consideration was the words, "of their own choice."

The educational institutions established or administered by the minorities in exercise of the rights conferred by Article 30(1), the Chief Justice said, might be classified into three categories: (1) those which did not seek either aid or recognition from the State, (2) those which wanted aid, and (3) those which wanted only recognition but not aid. In regard to educational institutions in the first category, he held that by Clause 38 of the Bill, they were *prima facie* outside the purview of the Bill. As regards the second category, the Chief Justice said that they had to subdivide it into two classes, namely, (1) those which were by the Constitution itself expressly made eligible for receiving grants, and (2) those which were not entitled to such grant, but nevertheless seek to get aid.

The Chief Justice observed that the Anglo-Indian educational institutions established prior to 1948 used to receive grants from

the Governments of those days.   Article 337 of the Constitution
preserved this bounty for a period of ten years.   The Anglo-Indian
educational Institutions in Kerala had, before the passing of the
Bill, been receiving grants from the Madras State and also the
Travancore-Cochin State.   After the formation of Kerala too the
bounty continued.   In the circumstances, the amount received by
the Anglo-Indian institutions as grant under Article 337 should
be construed as aid within the meaning of the Bill and educational
institutions in receipt of such grants payable under Article 337
should accordingly be regarded as aided schools.

Referring to the argument that no conditions could be imposed
in regard to the administration of institutions run by minorities,
the Chief Justice said the right to administer could not obviously
include the right to maladminister.   It stood to reason that the
constitutional right to administer an educational institution of
their choice did not necessarily militate against the claim of the
State to insist that in order to grant aid the State might prescribe
reasonable regulations to ensure the excellence of the institutions
to be aided.

In regard to educational institutions of minorities which sought
only recognition, but not aid from the State, the Chief Justice
said that without recognition the educational institutions established
or to be established by minority communities could not fulfil the
real object of their choice.   The right to establish educational
institutions of their choice should, therefore, mean the right to
establish real institutions which would effectively serve the needs
of their community and the scholars who attended such institutions.   To deny recognition to educational institutions except on
terms tantamount to the surrender of their constitutional right to
administer educational institutions of their choice was in truth
and effect to deprive them of their right under Article 30(1).

"We the people of India," the Chief Justice said, "had given
unto ourselves the Constitution which is not for any particular
community or section but for all.   Its provisions are intended to
protect all, minority as well as majority communities.   There
can be no manner of doubt that our Constitution has guaranteed
certain cherished rights of the minorities concerned—their
language, culture and religion.   These concessions must have

been made to them for good and valid reasons.

"So long as the Constitution stands as it is and is not altered, it is, we conceive, the duty of this Court to uphold the fundamental rights and thereby honour the sacred obligations to the minority communities who are of our own. Throughout the ages endless inundations of men of diverse creeds, cultures and races—Aryans and non-Aryans, Dravidians and Chinese, Sythians, Huns, Pathans and Mughals—have come to this ancient land from distant regions and climes. India has welcomed them all. They have met and gathered, given and taken and got mingled, merged and lost in one body. India's traditions have thus been epitomised in the noble lines: 'None shall be turned away from the shores of this vast sea of humanity that is India' (Tagore). Indeed India has sent out to the world her message of goodwill enshrined and proclaimed in our national anthem. It is thus that the genius of India has been able to find universality in diversity by assimilating the best of all creeds and cultures."

There were several other decisions of the Supreme Court since 1959 interpreting the scope of Articles 29 and 30. These decisions lead us to the following conclusions:

1. Articles 29 and 30 create two separate rights although it is possible that they may meet, in a given case.

2. Whether a particular community is a minority or not is to be judged on the basis of the entire population of the area to which the particular legislation applies.

3. A minority can effectively conserve its script, language and culture by and through the establishment and maintenance of educational institutions of its choice.

4. The language of Article 29(2) is wide and unqualified and covers all citizens whether they belong to the majority or minority groups.

5. The right of getting admission to an educational institution is a right which an individual citizen has as a citizen and not as a member of a community or class of citizens. Hence this right cannot be denied to citizens on grounds only of religion, race, caste, language or any of them.

6. In the case of a minority based on religion or language, the right to impart instruction in their own institutions to the children of their community in their own language must be protected. In such a case, the power of the State to determine the medium of instruction must yield to the fundamental right of the minority to the extent it is necessary to give effect to that right.

7. The words establish and administer in Article 30(1) must be read conjunctively and if done so the minority is entitled to the right to administer an educational institution provided the said institution has been established by the minority and not otherwise.

8. The protection implied in Articles 29 and 30 applies not only to educational institutions established after the commencement of the Constitution but also to those established before it.

The rights of the minorities, however cannot be absolute. They must be subject to restrictions in the interest of education as well as in pursuance of socio-economic objectives embodied in the Constitution. The purpose of these rights was not to create vested interests in separateness of minorities but to maintain their individuality as well as distinct identity of their language and culture. But the preservation of such distinctiveness should not result in the minorities remaining isolated from the mainstream of national life. As the nation makes progress, the barriers that divide citizens into majority and minority compartments should gradually disappear and the tradition-bound, rigid society in India should become transformed into a composite, dynamic and progressive society cherishing common national ideals and aspirations. Educational and cultural institutions should become the agents of such change rather than perpetuating narrow barriers between citizen and citizen.

Taking the rights guaranteed under religious, educational and cultural fields as a whole, it will be noted that these are couched in the most comprehensive language and the maximum possible freedom is guaranteed to the minorities, religious and linguistic. The special significance of these provisions is that while the impact of other rights in Part III of the Constitution is on the people of India as a whole, irrespective of religion, caste, race or language, that of these rights is only on the minorities. The democratic basis of the Constitution would be lost if the minorities were not given adequate protection to preserve their religious beliefs, and institutions of education and culture. The Constitution may then be branded as an instrument for the furtherance of the majority community and the language of the majority. Naturally, resentment against such a position would manifest all over the country, as religious minorities live in all States of India and linguistic minorities total not less than 200 millions. Moreover, such a position would have discredited the foundation of the national movement against foreign rule, in which every religious and linguistic minority in India was represented and solemn promises had been made by representatives of the majority community to safeguard the legitimate interests of the minorities against all forms of tyranny in a free India.

CHAPTER 13

THE RIGHT TO PROPERTY

(*Arts.* 31, 31A, 31B, 31C and 31D)

ONE OF the Articles that experienced the greatest difficulty in getting into shape in the Constituent Assembly was that which dealt with the right to property under Article 31. We have already seen the scope of the right to acquire, hold and dispose of property under Article 19. We have seen also under the same Article the right to practise any profession or to carry on any occupation, trade or business. The Assembly thought fit to have in addition an altogether separate section to deal with property rights, because it realised that in the absence of such a section it would be impossible to solve the conflicts involved in the right of the individual to own property and the duty of the State to enter the economic field with a view to bringing about badly needed reforms. In fact, Articles 31 and 31A, attempt to reconcile the competing claims of the right of the individual to property and the duty of the State to acquire private property for public purpose or general welfare.

Article 31 as originally passed reads as follows:

"31 (1) No person shall be deprived of his property save by authority of law.

"(2) No property, movable or immovable, including any interest in, or in any company owning, any commercial or industrial undertaking, shall be taken possession of or acquired for public purposes under any law authorising the taking of such possession or such acquisition, unless the law provides for compensation for the property taken possession of or acquired and either fixes the amount of the compensation, or specifies the principles on which, and the manner in which, the compensation is to be determined and given.

"(3) No such law as is referred to in clause (2) made by the Legislature of a State shall have effect unless such law, having been reserved for the consideration of the President, has received his assent.

"(4) If any Bill pending at the commencement of this Constitution in the Legislature of a State has, after it has been passed by such Legislature, been reserved for the consideration of the President and has received his assent, then, notwithstanding anything in this Constitution, the law so assented to shall not be called in question in any court on the ground that it contravenes the provisions of clause (2).

"(5) Nothing in clause (2) shall affect—

(a) the provision of any existing law other than a law to which the provisions of clause (6) apply, or

(b) the provisions of any law which the State may hereafter make—

(i) for the purpose of imposing or levying any tax or penalty, or

(ii) for the promotion of public health or the prevention of danger to life or property, or

(iii) in pursuance of any agreement entered into between the Government of the Dominion of India or the Government of India and the Government of any other country, or otherwise, with respect to property declared by law to be evacuee property.

"(6) Any law of the State enacted not more than eighteen months before the commencement of this Constitution may within three months from such commencement be submitted to the President for his certification; and thereupon, if the President by public notification so certifies, it shall not be called in question in any court on the ground that it contravenes the provisions of clause (2) of this Article or has contravened the provisions of sub-section (2) of section 299 of the Government of India Act, 1935."

While the Constitution thus affords protection to private property in general, it declared under clauses (4) and (6) that the validity of certain specific laws affecting property rights shall not be challenged in any Court on the ground that they violated the safeguards detailed above. These were laws which abolished the Zamindari system or absentee landlordism in different States. The object of this special provision was to remove any uncertainty and make safe the main agrarian reform which sought to do away with this evil system and thwart the attempts of the landlords to fight these laws through the Courts of law. The Constitution also provided under clause (5) that the compensation clause would not apply in the following cases: (1) Laws providing for the imposition or levying of any tax or penalty; (2) laws made for the promotion of public health or the prevention of danger to life or property; and (3) laws relating to evacuee property.

The special protection given to the various Zamindari abolition laws, however, did not prove to be of much avail. Soon after the inauguration of the Constitution the Zamindars tested the validity of these laws against some of the fundamental rights. The first round of the battle was fought in the High Courts of Patna, Allahabad and Nagpur. In the Patna High Court they succeeded in getting the Bihar Land Reforms Act, 1950, declared invalid. The decision of the High Court was unanimous. It was based on the equality provision (Art. 14) of the Constitution and not under the property right clause (Art. 31). The Allahabad High Court, however, found the Uttar Pradesh Zamindari Abolition and Land Reforms Act, 1950, valid in all respects. The decision of the Nagpur High Court also went in favour of the State law. But the Zamindars were not disheartened. They carried the battle to the Supreme Court in appeal.

The First Amendment

When it was found that the legal battle was going to consume an unduly long time with consequent frustration for the general mass of people and the loss of confidence in the Governments, new ways and measures were sought to combat the deteriorating situation. Accordingly, it was decided to amend the Constitution whereby judicial road-blocks could be removed and immediate implementation of the land reform legislation could be made possible. The First Amendment of the Constitution was accordingly passed in 1951 adding two new Articles, 31A and 31B, with a view to fully safeguarding the various land reform laws against possible attack arising from any fundamental right in the Constitution. Further, a new Schedule containing all such State laws —the Ninth Schedule—was added to the Constitution to make the scope of the new amendment abundantly clear. The Amendment read as follows:

"31A, (1) Notwithstanding anything in the foregoing provisions of this Part, no law providing for the acquisition by the State of any estate or of any rights therein or for the extinguishment or modification of any such rights shall be deemed to be void on the ground that it is inconsistent with, or takes away or abridges any of the rights conferred by, any provisions of this Part.

"Provided that where such law is a law made by the legislature of a State, the provisions of this Article shall not apply thereto unless such law, having been reserved for the consideration of the President, has received his assent.

"(2)   In this Article—

    (a) the expression 'estate' shall, in relation to any local area, have the same meaning as that expression or its local equivalent has in the existing law relating to land tenures in force in that area, and shall also include any Jagir, Inam or muafi or other similar grant:

    (b) the expression 'rights' in relation to an estate, shall include any rights vesting in proprietor, sub-proprietor, under-proprietor, tenure-holder or other intermediary and any rights or privileges in respect of land revenue.

"31B.   Without prejudice to the generality of the provisions contained in article 31A, none of the Acts and Regulations specified in the Ninth Schedule nor any of the provisions thereof shall be deemed to be void, or ever to have become void, on the ground that such Act, Regulation or provision is inconsistent with, or takes away or abridges any of the rights conferred by any provision of this Part, and notwithstanding any judgement,

10

decree or order of any court or tribunal to the contrary, each of the said Acts and Regulations shall, subject to the power of any competent Legislature to repeal or amend it, continue in force."

The appeals to the Supreme Court were still pending when the First Amendment was passed. Anticipating the strong position of the State under the new Amendment, the Zamindars carried their battle even against the Constitutional amendment on the plea that Parliament as it was then constituted was not competent to pass the amendment. Since the decision of the Court on this question was to affect the fate of the appeal cases, the Court instead of proceeding with the appeals, first considered the validity of the Amendment itself. The main attack on the amendment was that it was passed by a Parliament which had only one House whereas the amendment procedure prescribed in the Constitution spoke of two Houses of Parliament. The intention of the framers of the Constitution, therefore, was to undertake any amendment of the Constitution only after the new Parliament consisting of both the Houses had been constituted as the result of a general election. The Court rejected this plea and gave a unanimous verdict in favour of the competence of the Provisional Parliament to amend the Constitution.

By 1952, the Court also finally disposed of the appeals which at last put the stamp of final authority on these hotly contested legislative measures. There were, however, interpretations of the Court which did not quite accord with some of the observations of the Prime Minister which he had made while moving the property right clause in the Constituent Assembly. These related mainly to the terms "public purpose" and "compensation". According to the Court

"the existence of a 'public purpose' is undoubtedly an implied condition of the exercise of compulsory powers of acquisition by the State, but the language of Article 31(2) does not expressly make it a condition precedent to acquisition. It assumes that compulsory acquisition can be for a public purpose only which is thus inherent in such acquisition. Hence, Article 31 (4) does not bar the jurisdiction of the Court from enquiring

whether the law relating to compulsory acquisition of property
is valid, ... to see whether the acquisition has been made for
a public purpose. It is unnecessary to state in express terms
in the statute itself the precise purpose for which property
is being taken, provided from the whole tenor and intendment
of the Act it could be gathered that the property was being
acquired either for purposes of the State or for the purposes
of the public and that the intention was to benefit the community
at large. The Legislature is the best judge of what is good for
the community, by whose suffrage it comes into existence and
it is not possible to say that there was no public purpose behind
the acquisition.... The phrase 'public purpose' has to be
construed according to the spirit of the times in which the
particular legislation is enacted...."

The result of this pronouncement seemed to be that while the
Court had the ultimate power of determining what a public
purpose was, generally it would uphold the will of the legislature as
expressed in the statute. Here the Court appeared to be quite
close to the intention of the Constitution-makers.

But the position was quite different in the case of the term
"compensation". Although the Constitution does not say "just"
or "full" or "adequate" compensation, the Court said that
compensation here meant *just compensation* determined on the
basis of the market value of the property acquired. They went one
step further and said that in addition to 100 per cent market value
to be paid in every case of acquisition, a solatium of 15 per cent
more was to be given to compensate the compulsory nature of
the acquisition which was already in vogue in India under the Land
Acquisition Act of 1894. According to the Allahabad High Court,

"Compensation in Article 31 (2) means the equivalent in
value of property taken or acquired, subject only to this qualification that such equivalent need not be paid in money. Any
provision for giving by way of compensation less than the
equivalent will not amount to compensation in law and will
constitute a contravention of that clause". The Calcutta High
Court also expressed the same view: "Article 31, clause 2
requires a just amount to be given for any property acquired

and if the amount law gives be not just or reasonable, then it cannot be regarded as compensation within that clause."

Other High Courts also gave interpretations to the same effect. The Supreme Court affirmed this interpretation of the High Courts in its decision on the Zamindari abolition cases. In Mrs. Bella Banerjee *vs.* State of West Bengal the Court went a step further and said.

"While it is true that the legislature is given the discretionary power of laying down the principles which should govern the determination of the amount to be given to the owner for the property appropriated, such principles must ensure that what is determined as payable must be compensation, that is, a just equivalent of what the owner has been deprived of."

In Dwarkadas Shrinivas *vs.* Sholapur Spinning and Weaving Company the Court examined the correlation of Articles 31 (1) and 31 (2) and said:

"From the language employed in the different sub-clauses of Article 31, it is difficult to escape the conclusion that the words 'acquisition' and 'taking possession' used in Article 31 (2) have the same meaning as the word 'deprivation' in Article 31(1)."

It further said that the protection in Article 31 is against loss of property to the owner and there is no protection given to the State by the Article. The decision of the Court in this case made invalid a Central enactment by which the above-mentioned Company was taken over by the Government. According to the Court, the Statute had overstepped the limits of legitimate social control legislation and had infringed the fundamental right of the Company guaranteed to it under Article 31 (2) and was, therefore, unconstitutional.

These judicial pronouncements had far-reaching consequences. They showed that legislation on social and economic welfare, which necessitated the acquisition of various forms of private property, was virtually impossible because of the prohibitive cost involved in the payment of compensation. Zamindari abolition

was only the first stage in a planned programme of legislation for
social and economic welfare. Other equally important legislative
measures were planned to follow suit. Some of the most important
of these were: (1) the fixing of limits to the extent of agricultural
land that may be owned or occupied by any person, the disposal
of any land held in excess of the prescribed minimum and the
further modification of the rights of land-owners and tenants in
agricultural holdings; (2) the proper planning of urban and rural
areas, the beneficial utilisation of vacant and waste lands and
clearance of slum areas; (3) the taking over of the control of
the mineral and oil resources of the country in the interests of
national economy; (4) the taking over of the management by the
State, for temporary periods, of commercial and industrial undertakings in the public interest or to secure better management;
(5) reforms in company law administration including the elimination of the managing agency system; (6) nationalisation of public
utility undertakings. But so long as the compensation clause of
the Constitution remained in the manner in which it was interpreted
by the Supreme Court, it was pointed out by spokesmen of the
Government, that no progress could be made along these lines.
Thus, according to them, the compensation clause and the power
of the Courts to enforce it stood in the way of planning and the
implementation of a programme of planned development. The
Government wanted to remove this hindrance and have a free
hand in the evolution of a new society. The only way to
accomplish this was by further amending the Constitution. The
result was the Fourth Amendment of 1955.

The Fourth Amendment

The chief provision of the Amendment is that compensation under
Article 31 is no more a justiciable matter under the Constitution.
The Amendment does not say that no compensation will be paid
in future for property compulsorily acquired, nor is its intention to
abolish compensation altogether. All that it does say is that
although compensation should be paid in all cases of acquisition,
it is the sole business of the legislature to determine the amount
of compensation or the principles or the manner in which it will
be paid and no Court of Law will sit over it in judgement. Thus,

the question of compensation is withdrawn from the field of judicial determination and placed exclusively at the will of the legislature. The following is the text of the Amendment:

"31 (2)   No property shall be compulsorily acquired or requisitioned save for a public purpose and save by authority of a law which provides for compensation for the property so acquired or requisitioned and either fixes the amount of the compensation or specifies the principles on which, and the manner in which, the compensation is to be determined and given; and no such law shall be called in question in any court on the ground that the compensation provided by that law is not adequate.

"(2A)   Where a law does not provide for the transfer of the ownership or right to possession of any property to the State or to a corporation owned or controlled by the State, it shall not be deemed to provide for the compulsory acquisition or requisitioning of property, notwithstanding that it deprives any person of his property.

"31A.   (1) Notwithstanding anything contained in Article 13, no law providing for—

(a) the acquisition by the State of any estate or of any rights therein or the extinguishment or modification of any such rights, or

(b) the taking over of the management of any property by the State for a limited period either in the public interest or in order to secure the proper management of the property, or

(c) the amalgamation of two or more corporations either in the public interest or in order to secure the proper management of any of the corporations, or

(d) the extinguishment or modification of any rights of managing agents, secretaries and treasurers, managing directors, directors or managers of corporations, or of any voting rights of shareholders thereof, or

(e) the extinguishment or modification of any rights accruing by virtue of any agreement, lease or licence for the purpose of searching for, or mining, any mineral oil, or the premature termination or cancellation of any such agreement, lease or licence,

shall be deemed to be void on the ground that it is inconsistent with, or takes away or abridges any of the rights conferred by Article 14, Article 19 or Article 31:

"Provided that where such law is a law made by the Legislature of a State, the provisions of this Article shall not apply thereto unless such law, having been reserved for the consideration of the President, has received his assent."

With the passing of the Fourth Amendment it was hoped that the bitter legal controversy about the meaning of the compensation clause of the Constitution would come to an end and it would facilitate the passing of legislation embodying economic reforms. It was also hoped that such legislation would be immune from challenge in courts on the ground of its alleged inconsistency with Articles 14, 19 and 31. But this was not to be. The Supreme Court still continued to interpret Article 31-A rather narrowly. This was evident in its decision in Kochunni *vs.* State of Madras.

The Court held: "Under Article 31(1) a person cannot be deprived of his property save by authority of law. The law must be a valid law. Under Article 13(2) a law depriving a person of his property cannot take away or abridge the rights conferred by Part III of the Constitution. Hence a law depriving a person of his property will be invalid if it infringes Article 19(1)(f) unless it imposes reasonable restrictions on the citizen's fundamental right."

In the light of this decision it was fairly clear that the Court might not uphold every piece of legislation for economic reform. The Seventeenth Amendment of the Constitution (1964) was the result.

The Amendment introduced the following new provisions:

(*i*) in clause (1), after the existing proviso, the following proviso shall be inserted, namely:

Provided further that where any law makes any provision for the acquisition by the State of any estate and where any land comprised therein is held by a person under his personal cultivation, it shall not be lawful for the State to acquire any portion of such land as is within the ceiling limit applicable to him

under any law for the time being in force or any building or
structure standing thereon or appertinant thereto, unless the
law relating to the acquisition of such land, building or
structure, provides for payment of compensation at a rate which
shall not be less than the market value thereof.

(*ii*) In Clause (2), for sub-clause (a), the following sub-
clause shall be substituted and shall be deemed always to have
been substituted, namely:

(*a*) the expression "estate" shall, in relation to any local area,
have the same meaning as the expression or its local equivalent
has in the existing law relating to land tenures in force in that
area and shall also include—

(*i*) any *jagir, inam* or *muafi* or other similar grant and in the
States of Madras and Kerala, any *Janmam* right;

(*ii*) any land held under ryotwari settlement;

(*iii*) any land held or let for purposes of agriculture or for
purposes hereto, including waste land, forest land, land for
pasture or sites of buildings and other structures occupied by
cultivators of land, agricultural labourers and village artisans.

The Ninth Schedule of the Constitution has been amended to
add 44 new land reform enactments to the original list of 20.
Thus the Ninth Schedule then consisted of a total of 64 such
enactments. By making them part of the Constitution they have
been taken out of the reach of judicial review so far as their
validity with respect to any provision embodied in Part III of the
Constitution is concerned.

The validity of the Seventeenth Amendment was soon challenged
in Sajjan Singh *vs.* The State of Punjab. The Supreme Court
upheld its validity but two years later, in 1967, the Court made a
somersault and the spirit of its earlier decision was nullified by its
decision in the Golak Nath Case. The Court also held that Parliament had no power to amend the Fundamental Rights and it would
not tolerate any amendments in the future. In several subsequent
decisions the attitude of the Court regarding questions of
compensation became rigid. In fact the Court appeared to be
assuming the role of a champion for full compensation every time
private property was acquired or requisitioned by the State for a
public purpose. The net result of the many decisions of the

Court on this subject has been utter confusion and uncertainty regarding the meaning of the Constitution. Further, it defeated the clearly expressed intention of the Constitution that a law of acquisition would not be challenged in Courts on the ground that the compensation it provided was inadequate. The decision of the Court in the Bank Nationalisation case (1970) is a classic example in this context.

The only way to remedy this unsatisfactory situation was further amending the Constitution. But since the Golak Nath decision still held the ground and prohibited Parliament from amending the Fundamental Rights, the first step required was to restore to Parliament its power to modify any part of the Constitution including the chapter on Fundamental Rights. The Twenty-fourth Amendment (1971) restored Parliament's amending power. Soon after, the Twenty-fifth Amendment was passed suitably amending the provisions dealing with property rights to remove all uncertainties created by conflicting judicial pronouncements.

The Twenty-fifth Amendment has tremendous political, economic and constitutional significance. Parliament has, through this Amendment, reasserted its position as the most important agency for bringing about radical socio-economic changes. The Courts can no more sit in judgement on the adequacy of the *amount* (no more compensation) payable by the State when it takes over private property for a public purpose. The Amendment for the first time, in clear terms, established the principle that in a matter of public importance, the Fundamental Rights of the individual will give place to the Directive Principles of State Policy. (Clause B and C of Article 39). The Forty-second Amendment (1976) went a major step further and made it possible to widen the scope of the Article further through Parliamentary action so as to cover all the Directive Principles enumerated in Part IV of the Constitution.

A new Article also has been added — 31D — providing for the making of a Parliamentary law to prevent or prohibit anti-national activities and to prevent or prohibit the formation of anti-national associations. The law made by virtue of this amendment shall not be deemed to be void on the ground that it takes away or abridges any of the Fundamental Rights conferred by Articles 14, 19 and 31.

Of all the rights included in the chapter on Fundamental Rights and indeed of all provisions in the Constitution, the right to property has been the one whch was subjected to the largest number of amendments so far. It shows on the one hand the complex nature of the right itself and on the other the difficulty of the State to find a satisfactory balance between the individual's right to property and its social control under laws made by the State.

Right to Property has again figured prominently when the Forty-fifth Amendment to the Constitution was taken up by Parliament in 1978. There was, however, a striking contrast this time to the approaches of the past. According to the Forty-fifth Amendment the right to property will no longer be a fundamental right. However, the right of persons holding land for personal cultivation and within the ceiling limit to receive compensation at the market value will not be affected. Looking back at the several constitutional amendments and the bitter and costly legal battles on the right to property as a Fundamental right, the latest amendment appears like an anti-climax the effect of which the future alone can unfold.

CHAPTER 14

THE RIGHT TO CONSTITUTIONAL REMEDIES

(*Arts.* 32 *and* 32A)

A DECLARATION of fundamental rights is meaningless unless there is an effective machinery for the enforcement of the rights. Hence the framers of the Constitution were in favour of adopting special provisions guaranteeing the right to constitutional remedies. This, again, is in tune with the nature in general of the various provisions embodied in the chapter on fundamental rights.

Article 32 has four sections. The first section is general in scope and says that "the right to move the Supreme Court by appropriate proceedings for the enforcement of the rights conferred by this Part is guaranteed." The second section deals, in more specific terms, with the power of the Supreme Court to issue writs including writs in the nature of *habeas corpus, mandamus,* prohibition, *quo warranto* and *certiorari* for the enforcement of any of the rights. The third section empowers Parliament to confer the power of issuing writs or orders on any other Court without prejudice to the power of the Supreme Court in this respect. So far, Parliament has not passed any law conferring the power of issuing writs on any Courts. The last section deals with the conditions under which this right can be suspended.

The first three sections of the Article, taken together, make fundamental rights under the Constitution real and, as such, they form the crowning part of the entire chapter. Adverting to the special importance of this Article, Ambedkar declared in the Assembly:

"If I was asked to name the particular article in this Constitution as the most important without which this Constitution would be a nullity, I could not refer to any other article except this one. It is the very soul of the Constitution and the very heart of it and I am glad that the House has realised its importance. Hereafter, it would not be possible for any legislature to take away the writs which are mentioned in this article.

It is not that the Supreme Court is left to be invested with the power to issue these writs by a law to be made by the legislature at its sweet will. The Constitution has invested the Supreme Court with these writs and these writs could not be taken away unless and until the Constitution itself is amended by means left open to the legislatures. This in my judgement is one of the greatest safeguards that can be provided for the safety and security of the individual."

This opinion of the Chairman of the Drafting Committee has been reaffirmed by the Court itself on several occasions. In Romesh Thappar *vs.* The State of Madras the Court held:

"Article 32 provides a guaranteed remedy for the enforcement of the rights conferred by Part III (of the Constitution) and this remedial right is itself made a fundamental right by being included in Part III. The Court is thus constituted the protector and guarantor of fundamental rights and it cannot, consistently with the responsibility so laid upon it, refuse to entertain applications seeking protection against infringements of such rights."

However, the Court will not entertain any application under Article 32 unless the matter falls within the scope of any of the fundamental rights guaranteed in Part III of the Constitution.

As the guardian of Fundamental Rights the Supreme Court has two types of jurisdiction, original and appellate. Under its original jurisdiction, any person who complains that his fundamental rights have been violated within the territory of India, may move the Supreme Court seeking an appropriate remedy. The fact that he may have a remedy in any of the High Courts does not preclude him from going directly to the Supreme Court.

We have already seen under Article 32 (4) that the Right to Constitutional Remedies may be suspended under certain circumstances. These circumstances are dealt with in detail in the chapter on Emergency Provisions of the Constitution. Chiefly, these emergencies are three: external aggression, internal disturbance and breakdown of constitutional machinery in the States. Under such conditions the President of India is empowered to proclaim an emergency. During the period of emergency he *may* by order declare that the right to move any Court for the enforcement of any Fundamental Right shall remain suspended up to a maximum period of the existence of the emergency (Art. 359). Every such order should be placed before each House of Parliament as soon as possible.

Until 1976 the Supreme Court had power to consider the constitutional validity of any State law in any proceedings initiated under Article 32. But this power was taken away by the Forty-second Amendment (1976). As a result the Supreme Court could consider the constitutional validity of any State law only if the constitutional validity of any Central law was also an issue in such proceedings. The Forty-third Amendment (1978) however has restored the original position.

A NOTE ON WRITS

HABEAS CORPUS

"Habeas corpus" is a Latin term which literally means 'you may have the body'. Under the law of England, as a result of long usage, the term came to signify a prerogative writ, a remedy with which a person unlawfully detained sought to be set at liberty. It is mentioned as early as the fourteenth century in England and was formalised in the Habeas Corpus Act of 1679. The privilege of the use of this writ was regarded as a foundation of human freedom and the British citizen insisted upon this privilege wherever he went whether for business or colonisation. This is how it found a place in the Constitution of the United States when the British colonies in America won their independence and established a new State under that Constitution.

In India, under the Constitution, the power to issue a writ of habeas corpus is vested only in the Supreme Court and the High Courts. The writ is a direction of the Court to a person who is detaining another, commanding him to bring the body of the person in his custody at a specified time to a specified place for a specified purpose.

A writ of habeas corpus has only one purpose: To set at liberty a person who is confined without legal justification: to secure release from confinement of a person unlawfully detained. The writ does not punish the wrongdoer. If the detention is proved unlawful, the person who secures liberty through the writ may proceed against the wrongdoer in any appropriate manner. The writ is issued not only against authorities of the State but also to private individuals or organisations if necessary.

MANDAMUS

The Latin word "mandamus" means "we order". The writ of mandamus is an order of the High Court or the Supreme Court commanding a person or a body to do that which it is his, or its, duty to do. Usually, it is an order directing the performance of ministerial acts. A ministerial act is one which a person or body is obliged by law to perform under given circumstances. For instance, a licensing officer is obliged to issue a licence to an applicant if the latter fulfils all the conditions laid down for the issue of such licence. Similarly, an appointing authority should issue a letter of appointment to a candidate if all the formalities of selection are over and if the candidate is declared fit for the appointment. But despite the fulfilment of such conditions, if the officer or the authority concerned refuses or fails to issue the licence or the appointment letter, the aggrieved person has a right to seek the remedy through a writ of mandamus.

There are three essential conditions for the issue of a writ of mandamus. First, the applicant must show that he has a real and special interest in the subject matter and a specific legal right to enforce. Secondly, he must show that there resides in him a legal right to the performance sought, and finally, that there is no other equally effective, convenient and beneficial remedy.

PROHIBITION

A writ of prohibition is issued primarily to prevent an inferior court from exceeding its jurisdiction, or acting contrary to the rules of natural justice, for example, to restrain a judge from hearing a case in which he is personally interested. The term "inferior courts" comprehends special tribunals, commissions, magistrates and officers who exercise judicial powers, affecting the property or rights of the citizen and act in a summary way or in a new course different from the common law. It is well established that the writ lies only against a body exercising public functions of a judicial or quasi-judicial character and cannot in the nature of things be utilised to restrain legislative powers.

The writ of prohibition is the counterpart of the writ to certiorari which too is issued against the action of an inferior court. The difference between the two was explained by Justice Venkatarama Ayyar of the Supreme Court in the following terms:

"When an inferior court takes up for hearing a matter over which it has no jurisdiction, the person against whom the proceedings are taken can move the superior court for a writ of prohibition and on that an order will issue forbidding the inferior court from continuing the proceedings. On the other hand, if the court hears the cause or matter and gives a decision, the party aggrieved would have to move the superior court for a writ of certiorari and on that an order will be made quashing the decision on the ground of want of jurisdiction."

CERTIORARI

Certiorari is an ancient prerogative writ which orders the removal of a suit from an inferior court to a superior court. It may be used before a trial to prevent an excess or abuse of jurisdiction and to remove the case for trial to a higher Court. It is invoked also after trial to quash an order which has been made without jurisdiction or in defiance of the rules of natural justice.

Speaking on the scope of the writ, the Supreme Court, in the State of Bombay vs. Advani, held:

"(i) Whenever any body of persons having legal authority to determine questions affecting the rights of subjects and having the duty to act judicially, act in excess of their legal authority, a writ to certiorari lies. It does not lie to remove an order merely ministerial or to remove or cancel executive or administrative acts. (ii) For this purpose, the term judicial does not necessarily mean acts of a judge or legal tribunal sitting for the determination of matters of law, but for the purpose of this question a judicial act seems to be an act done by competent authority, upon consideration of facts and circumstances, and imposing liability or affecting the rights of others."

Often a writ of certiorari is sought along with prohibition, so that not merely may an invalid act be reviewed by a superior court (certiorari), but its operation may also be restrained (prohibition). While prohibition and certiorari are so intimately related to each other, prohibition is the converse of mandamus. The former is invoked to prevent a Court or other authority from doing something which it has not the power to do, while the latter is called in aid to require it to do something which it is bound to do.

QUO WARRANTO

The writ of quo warranto is a common law process of great antiquity. According to this, the High Courts or the Supreme Court may grant an injunction to restrain a person from acting in an office to which he is not entitled and may also declare the office to be vacant. What the Court has to consider in an application for a writ of quo warranto is whether there has been usurpation of an office of a public nature and an office substantive in character, i e. an office independent in title. It is a remedy given by law at the discretion of the Court and is not issued as a matter of course.

An application for the issue of a writ of quo warranto is maintainable only in respect of offices of a public nature which are the creation of statute and not against private institutions. In the case of domestic tribunals, the order of the tribunal will not be disturbed unless it is attacked on the ground of bona fides or vires. Thus, it has been held that a member of a Legislative Assembly has every right to know by what authority the Speaker of the body functions as such, if he bona fide thinks that the Speaker holds his office without authority and the application for a writ of quo warranto is maintainable.

CHAPTER 15

AN ASSESSMENT

THE CHAPTER on Fundamental Rights in the Constitution has been the subject of criticism both in India and outside, ever since its adoption. Broadly classified, the critics are of three types. First, there are those who think that the Constitution does not embody fundamental rights in reality but only an apology for them. According to them, many fundamental rights such as the right to work, education, etc. which ought to have found a place in the chapter have been ignored. Secondly, there are those who think that the spirit of the whole chapter and much of its substance are taken away by the extraordinary provisions such as preventive detention, suspension of the right to constitutional remedies, etc. These critics allege that what has been given by one hand has been taken away by the other. Thirdly, there are those who argue that even those rights that are attempted to be safeguarded are hedged in with so many exceptions, explanations and qualifications that it is difficult to understand what exactly is available to the individual by way of fundamental rights. One of these critics sarcastically suggested that the chapter on Fundamental Rights should be renamed as "Limitations on Fundamental Rights, or Fundamental Rights and Limitations Thereon."

It is true that the right to work, the right to rest and leisure, material security, etc. are not included in the chapter on Fundamental Rights. Even the right to education does not find a place there. The reason why they have not been included is not far to seek. Every one of the rights in this chapter is a justiciable right. For every violation of these rights, there is a judicial remedy, which makes the right a practical proposition. On the other hand, take, for example, the right to education: "Every child under the age of fourteen shall have the right to free education." It is a positive right. To translate it into reality, the State must provide immediately thousands of schools all over the country. Was it possible under the conditions prevailing in India at the time of the adoption of the Constitution to have this right realised in practice? Needless to say, it was impossible. It is a right which can be made available to every one only in the course of decades. This is why the right to education has been included in the chapter on Directive Principles of State Policy and a time limit of ten years was fixed.

The difference between Fundamental Rights and Directive Principles is that the former are justiciable rights—rights that can be enforced by a court of law—while the latter are non-justiciable rights. The fact that certain rights have been made non-justiciable does not make them useless or meaningless as has been alleged by some critics. The distinction can be understood only in the light of the evolution of theory and practice relating to Fundamental Rights in the nineteenth and twentieth centuries. Consequent upon the industrial revolution in Europe, the labouring classes became politically conscious and realised that the conditions which they required for the development of their personality, whose fulfilment they demanded, were different from those which the middle classes of the seventeenth and eighteenth centuries required and demanded. What the working classes wanted was better conditions of work in the factories: better housing, better sanitation, medical relief and social security. They wanted education for their children. They stood for more equitable distribution of wealth and higher and heavier taxation of the wealthy. The right to freedom of expression and religion, etc. demanded by the middle classes called for negative action by the State. These rights could become real when governments abstained from doing certain things such as imposing restrictions on the press or dictating religion to its subjects. But the conditions of good life demanded by the labourers called for positive action by the State, such as factory legislation, compulsory and free education, old age pensions, unemployment relief and so on. This is the difference between the rights demanded during the seventeenth and eighteenth centuries and those demanded during the nineteenth and the twentieth centuries. Those who question the utility of non-justiciable rights do not appreciate this distinction. The right to employment or education are not rights which can be safeguarded by courts of law. When they start safeguarding such rights they will cease to be courts. These are rights which ought to come within the scope of legislative policy. They are not appropriate

11

for judicial action. The remedy for them lies in the legislature which is elected on the basis of adult franchise. In a democracy based upon adult suffrage, legislatures are bound to take action and see that such rights remain not mere platitudes on paper but as effective as justiciable rights.

The provisions dealing with preventive detention and the suspension of constitutional remedies are not easy to defend. Nevertheless, there are considerations which can be urged in their favour. It has already been pointed out that restrictions on individual freedom are necessary in the interests of society. The framers of the Constitution were not unaware of the dangers to the existence and safety of the Republic they were establishing. They were giving it shape at a time when the country was passing through extraordinary stress and strain. There were groups and parties in India who made no secret of their opposition to the new democratic order that was emerging in the country. The assassination of Gandhiji was itself the most eloquent indication of this. Where organised groups swear by force and violence to achieve their objectives which strike at the very roots of democratic institutions no constitution can be accused of whittling down fundamental rights if a freely elected Parliament is given power to enact a law of preventive detention. In the opinion of a British writer on Fundamental Rights in India, preventive detention

"is an administrative necessity in India, and likely to cause less human misery than might result from likely alternative measures to deal with persons who cannot be successfully prosecuted for their activities, though they are a menace to public security and order. The danger and the consequences of public disturbances in India are too grave to justify any Indian Government in giving the tub-thumping demagogue, and the conspiratorial member of a political cell the freedom he enjoys in Britain."

It goes to the credit of democratic India that, in spite of the extremely trying circumstances under which she had been functioning during the first two decades, the number of persons taken into custody under the preventive detention laws had been comparatively small in relation to the gigantic proportions of the country, both in area and population and in the magnitude of the problems confronting it.

During the third decade, however, and especially as a result of the declaration of internal emergency in 1975, unlike in the past, a large number of persons were taken into custody. While this was assailed by the opposition as politically motivated, the spokesmen of the Government justified it to protect the country from chaos and anarchy which were to result from the unconstitutional and violent activities of a number of political parties and groups. Fortunately the situation did not last long. With the announcement of Parliamentary elections in January 1977 the Central Government issued instructions to all the States to release political prisoners held under the Maintenance of Internal Security Act and allow all forms of political activity normally undertaken, especially during election time. The election results went against the ruling Congress Party and as a result, the emergency was fully withdrawn and the Fundamental Rights were restored. In 1978 the Maintenance of Internal Security Act was abolished.

As to the question of suspension of constitutional remedies, so far there has been no occasion for it in spite of the declaration of national emergency on four occasions, in 1962, 1965, 1971 and 1975.

The operation of several other Fundamental Rights, however, was seriously affected by the Proclamation of Emergency by the President in 1962 and later in 1965, 1971 and 1975. The Proclamation was followed by the Defence of India Act, investing the Government with vast powers over the liberty of the citizen. In fact, Article 358 of the Constitution provides for the automatic suspension of the seven freedoms such as the right to freedom of speech, assembly, association, movement, etc. embodied in Article 19 of the Constitution as a result of the proclamation. Article 359 enables the President by order to suspend the right to constitutional remedies provided under Article 32. Since there is no provision for the automatic suspension of any other fundamental right, orders were issued soon after the Proclamation suspending the enforcement of Article 14 (equality before the law), Article 21 (right to life and personal liberty), and Article 22 (protection against unlawful arrest and detention) in so far only as they might affect the constitutionality of the Defence of India Act, the Rules made under it and also any order made in pursuance of them.

In addition to the already existent powers under the Preventive Detention Act,[1] the Defence of India Act provides for the detention of any person "whom the authority suspects on grounds appearing to that authority to be reasonable, of being of hostile origin, of having acted, acting, being about to act or being likely to act in a manner prejudicial to the defence of India and civil defence, the security of the State, the public safety or interest, the maintenance of public order, India's relations with foreign States, the maintenance of peaceful conditions in any part of India or the efficient conduct of military operations." The Government may also impose restrictions, short of detention, regulating the conduct in any such particular as may be specified in the order. Restrictions may also be imposed in respect of employment, association or communication with other persons or against propagation of opinion.

Suffice it to say that these are by any standard extraordinary powers to be exercised by the Executive under a democratic system of Government. This is particularly so when there is no provision for an independent review of orders made under the Act. Under the cloak of emergency these powers could be abused by an unscrupulous and power-seeking party in office to destroy for ever the cherished ideals of the Constitution. If the emergency is unnecessarily prolonged or the powers under it are misused for political purposes, then it will sound the death-knell of the democratic character of the Constitution. It is true, as Lord Justice Scrutton once observed, that a war could not be conducted on the principles of the Magna Carta or those of the Sermon on the Mount. Fundamental Rights are bound to be curtailed during a period of grave national emergency in the interests of the security of the State. But the term 'security' of the State has to be properly interpreted and it should not be equated with the 'security of the Government' of the day. The extent of regulation of individual liberty even during a war emergency should conform to the spirit of Lord Atkin's celebrated dictum: "Amid the clash of arms, the laws are not silent. They may be changed but they speak the same language in war as in peace."

[1] Later the Maintenance of Internal Security Act (MISA).

The third line of criticism that the Fundamental Rights are couched in difficult language, that they are beyond the comprehension of an ordinary reader of the Constitution, that the rights are hedged in with numerous exceptions and qualifications, is justified. It is a feature that runs through the entire Constitution which made a critic remark that it is not a Constitution but a constitutional treatise. Compared with the Indian Fundamental Rights, a similar document like the American Bill of Rights is a marvel of clarity and conciseness. The fathers of the American Constitution reduced their ideas of fundamental liberties to a few simple propositions and made them part of their Constitution. The rest of the job was left trustfully to the judges. The Constituent Assembly, on the contrary, instead of leaving it to the courts to read into the law the necessary exceptions and limitations, sought to express them in a compendious form in the Constitution itself. It is also well to remember in this connection that the difficulty of understanding the different constitutional provisions is not actually a problem of language alone. It also arises out of the unfamiliarity of a new constitutional system that requires close study and deep understanding which alone can make it a part of the common, national heritage.

A close study of the provisions of the chapter on Fundamental Rights will show that it is not the product of a consistent philosophy. Such a philosophy was perhaps possible a century ago and in countries characterised by a homogeneity of language, religion and culture. But India presented something totally different, complex, heterogeneous and diversified. Naturally, the Constitution was bound to reflect it; and the chapter on Fundamental Rights is its most powerful mirror. There is some justification in the following words of a critic of this chapter:

"A thread of nineteenth century liberalism runs through it; there are consequences of the political problems of Britain in it; there are relics of the bitter experience in opposition to British rule; and there is evidence of a desire to reform some of the social institutions which time and circumstances have developed in India. The result is a series of complex formulae, in twenty-four articles, some of them lengthy, which must become the basis of a vast and complicated case law."

It is generally true that, in the ultimate analysis, Fundamental Rights are not protected by courts of law but by public opinion. But the effectiveness of public opinion as the guardian of fundamental rights depends upon how well organised and effective is public opinion in a country. India is vast in size and has a huge population. It is also a poor and backward country. Education and civic consciousness are yet to reach a commendable level in India. How difficult it is to organise effective public opinion in a country like India needs no special emphasis. In the absence of really effective public opinion, it would have been suicidal to leave the protection of fundamental liberties to the discretion of executive authorities or the caprices of legislative majorities. Even in England it took centuries for public opinion to assert itself as a champion of human rights. It is this that adds to the importance of incorporating the right to constitutional remedies as an integral part of the chapter on Fundamental Rights. Nevertheless, there is the utmost need for the building up of vigorous, effective public opinion in India as an important additional safeguard to fundamental rights. Eternal vigilance is the price of liberty.

By no means was it an easy problem for the Constituent Assembly to draw up a simple list of fundamental rights. What has been finally adopted is the product of a difficult compromise. It is still too early to pronounce a final verdict on the wisdom of the Assembly. One thing, however, is already clear. The Supreme Court of India has been deciding more cases dealing with Fundamental Rights than those connected with the rest of the Constitution. The Court's decisions as the guardian of these rights have had, indeed, a salutary influence both on the executive and the legislature against whom those rights have been primarily guaranteed. The Court has been prompt and forthright in curbing legislative exuberance by declaring those enactments of Parliament and the State Legislatures invalid whenever it found them transgressing the defined limits within which they are permitted to impose reasonable limitations on the freedom of the individual. Similarly, it has successfully prevented on many occasions the excess and abuse of administrative power and the illegal and high-handed actions of the executive. Further, every time a Fundamental Right of the individual has been upheld against the executive or the legislature, it has had wholesome and far-reaching repercussions. Despite the fact that some of the Rights have been substantially modified in scope as a result of constitutional amendments, the chapter on Fundamental Rights, taken as a whole, remains a formidable bulwark of individual liberty, a code of public conduct and a strong and sustaining basis of Indian democracy.

Nevertheless, a word of caution seems to be appropriate here. The fact that a remedy is available from the High Court or the Supreme Court for the violation of every fundamental right does not mean in fact that it is available to all. This is because of the heavy cost involved in the process of moving the Court. Effective enforcement of those rights from the point of view of the ordinary Indian citizen is possible only when justice becomes cheap, speedy and simple.

CHAPTER 16

THE DIRECTIVE PRINCIPLES

PART IV of the Constitution dealing with the "Directive Principles
of State Policy" provides one of the most novel and striking
features of modern constitutional government. The framers of the
Constitution were in this respect influenced most by the Constitution of the Irish Republic which embodies a chapter on "Directive
Principles of Social Policy." The Irish themselves had, however,
taken the idea from the Constitution of Republican Spain which
was the first ever to incorporate such principles as part of a
Constitution. But the idea of such principles can be traced to
the Declaration of the Rights of Man and Citizen proclaimed by
Revolutionary France and the Declaration of Independence by
the American Colonies. The influence of these declarations was
so profound on millions of people in Europe and America that
they inspired organised efforts, on the one hand, to overthrow all
forms of political tyranny, and, on the other, to compel the State
to take positive measures for the removal of many anti-social
practices which had been considered as normal in those days.

In more recent times, thinkers on political and social reforms,
who did not agree with the Marxian approach for the removal of
the ills and evils of modern society, advocated such principles
to be made the guiding force of State activity. The ideas of
Jeremy Bentham, the political and social stand of the Liberal and
Radical Parties of Western Europe, the major principles of Fabian
Socialism and, to some extent, those of Guild Socialism, are all
akin to much of what is embodied in this Part of the Constitution.
Sir Ivor Jennings claims that the ghosts of Sidney and Beatrice
Webb stalk through the pages of the entire text and this part of the
Constitution expresses Fabian Socialism without the word
"socialism", "for only the nationalisation of the means of
production, distribution and exchange is missing". But this would
be to give an exaggerated importance to the Fabian influence, for
one finds other documents and proclamations, of more recent date,
that have influenced the framers even more. Mention has already

168

been made of the Irish Constitution. The Constitution Act of India (1935) itself provided for 'Instruments of Instructions' which were a fruitful idea. Ambedkar provides a clue to this in the following passage:

"The Directive Principles are like the Instruments of Instructions which were issued to the Governor-General and the Governors of Colonies, and to those of India by the British Government under the 1935 Government of India Act. What is called 'Directive Principles' is merely another name for the Instrument of Instructions. The only difference is that they are instructions to the legislature and the executive. Whoever captures power will not be free to do what he likes with it. In the exercise of it he will have to respect these instruments of instructions which are called Directive Principles. He cannot ignore them."

But there were other influences too. The Charter of the United Nations as well as the Universal Human Rights Charter influenced the Constitution-makers. The discussions on the Charter of Human Rights were in progress during the same period as the Constituent Assembly was deliberating upon the Constitution.

It would however be wrong to suppose that the various principles embodied in this chapter are mere foreign borrowings or adaptations of principles of recent Western Political or Social Philosophy. In fact, a number of these principles are entirely Indian, particularly those which formed an integral part of the very foundations of the national movement. Provisions dealing with village panchayats, cottage industries, prohibition, protection against cow-slaughter, Scheduled Castes, Scheduled Tribes and other socially and educationally backward classes, are all formally and essentially Indian and some of these were the cherished ideas for the recognition of which Gandhiji had striven throughout his life.

As the title itself indicates, the principles embodied in this chapter are directives to the various governments and government agencies (including even village panchayats) to be followed as fundamental in the governance of the country. It shall be the duty of the State to apply these principles in making laws. Thus, they place an ideal before the legislators of India while they frame new legislation for the country's administration. They lay down a code of conduct for the administrators of India while they discharge their responsibilities as agents of the sovereign power of the nation. In short, the Directive Principles enshrine the fundamentals for the realisation of which the State in India stands. They guide the path which will lead the people of India to achieve the noble ideals which the Preamble of the Constitution proclaims: Justice, social, economic and political; Liberty, Equality and Fraternity. It is this realisation that impelled a member in the Constituent Assembly to demand the placing of this chapter immediately after the Preamble in order to give it "greater sanctity" than others. There was also a suggestion to change the title of the chapter to "Fundamental Principles of State".

There are sixteen articles of the Constitution, from 36 to 51, that deal with the Directive Principles. These cover a wide range of State activity embracing economic, social, legal, educational and international problems. The most important of these are the following:

(1) To secure and protect a social order which stands for the welfare of the people (Art. 38).

(2) In particular, the State shall direct its policy towards securing:

(a) adequate means of livelihood to all citizens; (b) a proper distribution of the material resources of the community for the common good; (c) the prevention of concentration of wealth to the common detriment; (d) equal pay for equal work for both men and women; (e) the protection of the strength and health of workers and avoiding circumstances which force citizens to enter avocations unsuited to their age or strength; and (f) that children are given opportunities and facilities to develop in a healthy manner and in conditions of freedom and dignity and the protection of childhood and youth against exploitation or moral and material abandonment (Art. 39).

The State shall secure that the operation of the legal system promotes justice, on a basis of equal opportunity, and shall in particular provide free legal aid, by suitable legislation or schemes or in any other way, to ensure that opportunities for securing justice are not denied to any citizen by reason of economic or other disabilities (Article 39A).

(3) To organise village panchayats as units of self-government (Art. 40).

(4) To secure the right to work, education (Art. 40) and public assistance in cases of undeserved want, such as unemployment, old age, sickness, etc. (Art. 41).

(5) To secure just and humane conditions of work and maternity relief (Art. 42).

(6) To secure work, a living wage, a decent standard of life, leisure and social and cultural opportunities for people, and in particular to promote cottage industries (Art. 43).

(7) The State shall take steps, by suitable legislation or in any other way, to secure the participation of workers in the management of undertakings, establishments or other organisations engaged in any industry (Art. 43A).

(8) To secure a uniform civil code applicable to the entire country (Art. 44).

(9) To provide, within ten years from the commencement of the Constitution, free and compulsory education to all children upto the age of fourteen years (Art. 45).

(10) To promote with special care the educational and economic interests of the weaker sections of the people, especially the Scheduled Castes and Tribes (Art. 46).

(11) To secure the improvement of public health and the prohibition of intoxicating drinks and drugs (Art. 47).

(12) To organise agriculture and animal husbandry on scientific lines and preserve and improve the breeds and prohibit the slaughter of cows, calves and other milch and draught cattle (Art 48).

(13) The State shall endeavour to protect and improve the environment and to safeguard the forests and wild life of the country (Art. 48A).

(14) To protect all monuments of historic interest and national importance (Art. 49).

(15) To bring about the separation of the judiciary from the executive (Art. 50).

(16) To endeavour to secure: (a) the promotion of inter-

national peace and security; (*b*) the maintenance of just and honourable relations between nations; and (*c*) the settlement of international disputes by arbitration (Art. 51).

Taken together, these principles lay down the foundations on which a new democratic India will be built up. They represent the minimum of the ambitions and aspirations cherished by the people of India, set as a goal to be realised in a reasonable period of time. Indeed, when the State in India translates these principles into reality, she can justly claim to be a "Welfare State".

How far the State has moved, so far, towards the realisation of these principles is a question that deserves an answer in this context. It may be stated in general that the achievements of the last three decades have not yet made the country a welfare State. Nevertheless, no impartial observer can miss the direction towards which it is moving, if not fast, at least at a reasonable pace.

The efforts of the State to translate the Directive Principles into reality are concentrated primarily in the national Five Year Plans, the first of which was initiated soon after the inauguration of the Constitution. The central objective of public policy and national endeavour as evinced through these plans has been the promotion of rapid and balanced economic development which will raise living standards and open out to the people new opportunities for a richer and more varied life. Such development is intended to expand the community's productive power and to provide the environment in which there is scope for the expression and application of diverse faculties and urges. It follows, therefore, that the pattern of development must be related to the basic objectives which the Constitution has kept in view. These objectives are defined and explained from time to time in order that they may guide the State in planning as well as ensure their conformity with the Directive Principles. The basic objectives may be summed up in the phrase 'socialist pattern of society'. What it stands for is explained by the Second Five Year Plan in the following terms:

"Essentially this means that the basic criterion for determining the lines of advance must not be private profit but social gain, and that the pattern of development and the structure of socio-economic relations should be so planned that they result not only in *appreciable increases in national income and employment, but also in greater equality in incomes and wealth.* Major decisions regarding production, consumption and investment—in fact all significant socio-economic relationship—must be made by agencies informed by social purpose. The benefits of economic development must accrue more and more to the relatively less privileged classes of society, and there should be a progressive reduction of the concentration of incomes, wealth and economic power. The problem is to create a milieu in which the small man who has so far had little opportunity of perceiving and participating in the immense possibilities of growth through organised effort is enabled to put in his best in the increase of a higher standard of life for himself and increased prosperity for the country. In the process, he rises in economic and social status.... For creating the appropriate conditions, the State has to take on heavy responsibilities as the principal agency speaking for and acting on behalf of the community as a whole...."

The Third Five Year Plan spells out even more explicitly the meaning and implications of the Indian concept of socialist pattern. In the first chapter of this document[1] entitled the Objectives of Planned Development, it is stated:

"Progress towards socialism lies along a number of directions, each enhancing the value of others. Above all, a socialist economy must be efficient, progressive in its approach to science and technology, and capable of growing steadily to a level at which the well-being of the mass of the population can be secured.... In the second place a socialist economy should ensure equality of opportunity to every citizen.... In the third place, through the public policies it pursues, a socialist economy must not only reduce economic and social disparities which already exist, but must also ensure that rapid expansion of the economy is achieved without concentration of economic power

[1] This chapter is reported to have been written by Prime Minister Nehru himself.

and growth of monopoly. Finally, a society developing on the basis of democracy and socialism is bound to place the greatest stress on social values and incentives and developing a sense of common interest and obligations among all sections of the community."[2]

This statement of objectives makes it clear that the Directive Principles are not allowed to remain in the Constitution as platitudes, but are systematically put into application with a view to transforming Indian society and bringing about a social order in conformity with these principles. It is difficult to bring within the scope of this discussion a detailed survey of the concrete measures the State has taken so far and the results achieved therefrom. Yet, one may broadly indicate the trends which would help the better appreciation of the situation. For example, there has been a substantial increase in the vesting of both ownership and control of material resources of the community in the State during the last three decades. The great multi-purpose river valley projects such as Bhakra-Nangal, Damodar Valley and Hirakud, iron and steel producing concerns such as Bhilai, Rourkela and Durgapur, ship-building centres like Vizag and other concerns such as the Sindri-Fertilizers, Hindustan Machine Tools, Chittaranjan Locomotives, Hindustan Aircrafts, which contribute substantially to the basic economic development of the country, are owned and managed by the State. The choice in fact, is being forced on the State almost continuously and as a result new economic functions are being undertaken by the State machinery. According to one estimate, by 1977 the total investment in the public sector had risen to nearly 100,000 million rupees from a negligible figure in 1950.

It is true that the State has not yet moved very far on the road of achieving objectives such as full employment, public assistance during old age, sickness, etc. Nevertheless, most of them have found a place in the development plans. Great emphasis is now being laid on the creation of employment opportunities. Steps are being taken to bring into being a scheme of unemployment insurance. A limited scheme of workmen's insurance against sickness, accident and disease is already in operation. Minimum

[2] Third Five Year Plan (1961), pp. 9-10.

wages are fixed in a number of spheres of employment. Equal wages for equal work are being paid to both men and women in almost every area of activity. The community development programme which has been in operation in many parts of the country seeks the transformation of the rural economy, particularly the reorganisation of agriculture and animal husbandry on scientific lines. Besides, most of the States have passed laws designed to prohibit the slaughter of cows, calves and other milch and draught cattle. Mention has already been made of a number of laws which have been passed with a view to protecting children and youth against exploitation. The Central Council of Health established in 1952 deals with matters connected with health, hygiene, nutrition, etc. on a national basis. Most of the villages in India have now their own panchayats which form the primary units of administration.

The passing of a uniform civil code is not an easy measure in India where adherents of every religion have their own personal laws. The Hindu Code that is being passed in instalments (e.g. The Hindu Marriage Act, 1955, and the Hindu Succession Act, 1956) is a right move towards the ultimate realisation of a uniform civil code for the entire country. In the field of free and compulsory primary education for children, great strides have already been made. But it is now widely realised that the ten year limit that was set in the Constitution to make such education available to every child in the country was too ambitious. It seems that India will require another decade to make this principle a practical proposition. A number of measures have already been taken to promote the educational and economic interests of the weaker sections of the people, especially the Scheduled Castes and Tribes. With a view to specially benefiting the backward classes of citizens economically, efforts are being made for the setting up of more and more cottage and small scale industries and also to give liberal financial aid for such activities undertaken by them. A vigorous policy of prohibition was inaugurated with the adoption of the Constitution, and at least a few of the States have achieved the goal of complete prohibition of intoxicating liquors throughout their territory. The remaining States have made considerable progress in this direction. The principle of the complete separation of the judiciary from the executive is yet to be fully realised. But every State has adopted a definite programme in this respect and according to this every year a certain number of districts are being brought under the scheme. Finally, it is perhaps unnecessary to detail the efforts made by India towards the promotion of international understanding, peace and security. Suffice it to say that her contribution in this field is widely and generously acknowledged by almost all nations of the world.

According to Article 37, Directive Principles, though they are fundamental in the governance of the country and it shall be the duty of the State to apply these principles in making laws, are expressly made non-justiciable. It means that the Courts in India including the Supreme Court have no power to enforce them. This is in contrast with the position of Fundamental Rights which are justiciable and, therefore, enforceable by the Courts of law. Thus, while there is a judicial remedy for every violation of a Fundamental Right, there is none for the enforcement of Directive Principles. Would this mean that these are a set of platitudes designed by clever politicians to hoodwink the credulous Indian masses? Is there no remedy at all if the government that is in power ignores and even flagrantly violates these principles which are of a fundamental character in the governance of the country? The answer is "no" to the first and "yes" to the second. No doubt, there is no direct judicial remedy, except when parliament has made special provision under Article 31C of the Constitution. There are however other remedies and they are reasonably effective.

It must be remembered in this connection that the Constitution establishes a democratic form of Government, a representative government. It is also a responsible government, one that is continuously and always responsible for all its actions to the representatives of the people and through them to the people in general. Those who are in power are there because the people of India, who have been guaranteed universal adult suffrage, have given them that power. They are not the masters of the people but their 'servants'. They are voted into power to translate into practice the provisions of the Constitution which the people have given unto themselves. If they fail in this solemn duty, then they have no right to continue in office and they can be and should be removed from office when the stock-taking of their work is done at the end of every five years at the time of the General Election in the country. Since the Constitution ensures free choice by the people from amongst competing candidates with differing policies and programmes, the electorate can choose those who, in their opinion, are likely to transform these principles into reality. These directives, thus seen, constitute a kind of basic standard of national conscience and those who violate its dictates do so at the risk of being ousted from the positions of responsibility to which they have been chosen. The agents of the State at a given time may not be answerable to a court of law for their breach of these principles, but they cannot escape facing a higher and more powerful court which will at regular intervals do the reckoning. When a member in the Constituent Assembly moved an amendment which sought to make the Directive Principles justiciable, another pointed out:

"There is no use being carried away by sentiments. We must be practical. We cannot go on introducing various provisions here which any government, if it is indifferent to public opinion, can ignore. It is not a Court that can enforce these provisions or rights. It is the public opinion and the strength of public opinion that is behind a demand that can enforce these provisions. Once in four (or five) years election will take place and then it is open to the electorate not to send the very same persons who are indifferent to public opinion. That is the real sanction and not the sanction of any court of law."

There are, however, two important questions that are intimately related to the non-justiciable character of these principles and have created some confusion in the minds of those interested in India's Constitutional law. Of these, the first deals with the attitude of the President or the Governor towards a Bill containing provisions that contravene any of these principles. One view is that since the President, or the Governor, as the case may be, has taken oath to defend and uphold the Constitution, he should refuse to give his assent to a Bill which violated a Directive Principle. Ambedkar is opposed to this view and characterised it as a "dangerous doctrine" and contended that "the Constitution does not warrant it". The apprehension that these principles might lead to a conflict between the President and the Prime Minister or between the Governors and the Provincial Ministers was expressed in the Constituent Assembly itself. "What happens if the Prime Minister of India ignores these Instructions?" There have so far been no such occasion for such a conflict. Yet the problem has to be faced if and when it arises. The main factor that should be remembered in this context is the system of Government which the Constitution establishes—a parliamentary system under which the executive is responsible to the legislature. So long as the executive has the confidence of the legislature, a Constitutional head of the State will find it difficult to go against the will of the legislature.

It is also relevant to remember in this context that the President is not directly elected by the people and hence can claim no direct mandate. If at any time Parliament or a State legislature decides to pass a law which contravenes a Directive Principle, there must be weighty reasons for it. And if it is the considered opinion of the legislature to pass such a law and if the voting on it reflects a substantial majority in its favour, the President will have little justification to withhold his assent to the Bill. Perhaps the President could send the Bill back to Parliament for reconsideration in the light of his objections to it. And if Parliament passes it a second time, the President will have no justification to withhold his assent. After all, Parliament alone is competent to change even the Directive Principles by a Constitutional amendment. Moreover, however fundamental these principles might be today, they can have no claim to permanent sanctity. They cannot be considered as embodying eternal verities. As society changes in character, its needs also undergo corresponding changes. What is considered as fundamental today may become inessential and unimportant a few decades hence or earlier. Under a democratic system, all these questions are first to be determined by the representatives of the people and finally by the people themselves. Hence, it would seem wise for the President not to use his veto power over a Bill that is passed by the legislature merely on the ground that it violates a directive principle.

The second question is this: Where there is a conflict between a Fundamental Right and a Directive Principle, which should prevail? This question was answered by the Supreme Court, for the first time in Champakam Dorairajan's case (1952). Speaking for a unanimous Court, Justice S. R. Das said:

"The Directive Principles of State Policy which by Article 37 are expressly made unenforceable by a court cannot override the provisions found in Part III which, notwithstanding other provisions, are expressly made enforceable by writs, orders or directions under Article 32. The chapter on Fundamental Rights is sacrosanct and not liable to be abridged by any legislative or executive act or order except to the extent provided in the particular Article in Part III. The Directive Principles of State Policy have to conform to and run subsidiary to the chapter on Fundamental Rights. In our opinion, that is the correct way in which the provisions found in Part III and Part IV have to be understood."

It was mainly this decision of the Court that led to a constitutional amendment to Article 15 in 1951, under which the State was permitted to make special provisions to protect the interests of socially and educationally backward classes. A year later, when the Court dealt with the Zamindari Abolition cases, its attitude was considerably modified. In the State of Bihar *vs.* Kameswar Singh, the Court used the Directive Principles for its guidance in determining a crucial question on which the validity of the Bihar Act hinged. The question was whether there was any "public purpose" to justify the legislation which acquired compulsorily vast lands of private owners. Answering the question, Justice Mahajan said, after quoting Article 37:

"Now it is obvious that the concentration of big blocks of land in the hands of a few individuals is contrary to the principles on which the Constitution of India is based. The purpose of the acquisition contemplated by the Act, therefore, is to do away with the concentration of big blocks of land and means of production in the hands of a few individuals and to distribute the ownership and control of the material resources which come in the hands of the State, so as to subserve the common good as best as possible."

Here the judge was guided absolutely by the Directive Principles. Justice S. R. Das substantially reproduced the same language in the same case. After quoting Articles 38 and 39 of the chapter on Directive Principles, he said:

"In the light of this new outlook, what I ask is the purpose of the State in adopting measures for the acquisition of Zamindaris and the interests of intermediaries. Surely, it is to subserve the common good by bringing the land which feeds and sustains the community and also produces wealth by its forest, mineral and other resources, under State ownership or control. This State ownership or control over land is a necessary preliminary step towards the implementation of Directive Principles of State Policy and it cannot but be a public purpose."

This question came up again in the course of arguments in the President's Reference to the Supreme Court of the Kerala Education Bill (1958). The Court had no hesitation to uphold its earlier stand in the Zamindari abolition cases, namely, that the Directive Principles cannot be altogether ignored by it in spite of their non-justiciable character.

Speaking on the motion by which he introduced the Fourth Amendment to the Constitution in Parliament, Prime Minister Nehru observed that where there was conflict between a Fundamental Right and a Directive Principle, the latter should prevail. This opinion may appear to be in direct conflict with the view of the Supreme Court. But on closer examination it will be seen that the conflict is apparent rather than real. For, as far as the Supreme Court is concerned, where there is a clear conflict between the two, it should uphold the Fundamental Right being justiciable, against the Directive Principle which is a non-justiciable right. But this solution is only a judicial solution of the matter. The courts cannot go further than that, but Parliament can. The final solution is arrived at only when the social conflict arising out of the competing claims of a justiciable and a non-justiciable right are resolved. The guiding principle here is the superiority of the social interest over that of the individual. To facilitate the putting into effect of this principle, the Constitution may have to be amended and the Directive Principle allowed to prevail. The

Constitution was amended several times with this object in view. It should, however, be added that whenever the Court is called upon to resolve a conflict between a Fundamental Right and a Directive Principle, it is the duty of the Court to resolve the conflict with an eye on the spirit of the Constitution and with a view to harmonising differences to the extent that is possible and feasible.

The significance of Directive Principles in relation to that of Fundamental Rights can be determined only by making a reference to the object of the Constitution-makers in making these principles an integral part of the Constitution. As has already been pointed out, they represent the basic principles which aim at the creation of a welfare state. Taken together, these principles form a charter of economic and social democracy in India. On the one hand, they are assurances to the people as to what they may expect, while on the other, they are directives to the governments, Central and State, as to what policies they ought to pursue. It is unfair to the people as well as inconsistent with the spirit of the Constitution to allow these principles to remain pious wishes. Every effort should be made by the representatives of the people and the agents of the government to translate them into reality. Nothing should be allowed to stand in their way, even the fundamental rights guaranteed to the individual. After all, the progress and welfare of society as a whole should not be hampered by the rights of the individual. This is why every fundamental right is subject to reasonable restrictions in the interests of the general public, whether such restrictions are on account of public order, morality, decency, health or anything else. It is in this sense that the Fundamental Rights are to subserve the Directive Principles. Indeed, there can be no real conflict between the two. They are intimately related to and inseparably bound up with each other.

A constitution framed in the middle of the twentieth century could hardly do without a chapter on directive principles of the type the Indian Constitution has. The establishment of political democracy is a fundamental aim of a Constitution. But that in itself is not enough. The sustaining forces of that political democracy have to be carefully built up. The most effective force which will sustain a political democracy is the simultaneous existence of an economic democracy. Where there is no economic democracy, political democracy is bound to degenerate soon into a dictatorship.   If the fundamental rights guarantee a political democracy in India, the directive principles ensure the eventual emergence of an economic democracy to sustain the former. Thus, the Directive Principles of State Policy become the greatest guarantee for a genuine democracy in India.   In the light of these considerations, it would betray a lack of discernment to consider these directives as a mere political manifesto without any legal sanction, or to characterise them as vague and indefinite serving no useful purpose or to dismiss them as a mere moral homily. The last three decades demonstrate that such criticism has neither substance nor relevance today.   If K. T. Shah were alive now, he should certainly have revised the opinion that he expressed in the Constituent Assembly that these principles "are like a cheque on a bank payable when able—only when the resources of the bank permit."

Another apparently weighty criticism of the Directive Principles is implied in the question whether it is worth while to insert in a constitution of today a collection of political principles taken from the experience of nineteenth century Engand or western Europe, and to deem them to be suitable for India in the middle of the twentieth century.   The question whether they would be suitable for the twenty-first century when the Constitution is hoped to be still in operation is difficult to answer.   It is probable that they may become outmoded by then.   Who can predict the precise nature of the potentialities of an atomic or a hydrogen age?   It may revolutionise the whole economic system of the present day and convert India into a land of plenty where all human wants in the material field are fully satisfied.   In such a state of affairs, the Directive Principles will indeed look not only outmoded but even reactionary.   But as far as the twentieth century is concerned, India has yet to reach in many spheres of economic activity a standard comparable to that which existed in the nineteenth century in western Europe.   Thus, even assuming that the Directive Principles reflect the nineteenth century political ideas of the West, their value in twentieth century India is not lost.   Besides, it is not quite correct to characterise these principles as borrowings from abroad.   As has been pointed out elsewhere, there are many provisions in this chapter which prove the originality of the Constitution-makers and reflect the genius of the Indian people.

If and when the Directive Principles become outmoded, they can be suitably amended or altogether abolished. The process of amending these provisions is simple. But by the time such amendments take place, India will have benefited immensely by the Directive Principles, and an economic democracy will have sent its roots deep into the Indian soil and the present form in which these principles are embodied will have realised its goal. Moreover, these principles would have become part and parcel of the Indian heritage. Thus, one can see the immense educative value of these principles. They will instil in the minds and thoughts of the coming generations of Indian youth the fundamental values of a stable political order and a dynamic economic system. A constitution is primarily concerned with the present. The future will take care of itself if the present is built on solid foundations. It is quite unnecessary, therefore, to think of the distant future with reference to certain provisions of a constitutional document.

The real importance of the Directive Principles is that they contain the positive obligations of the State towards its citizens. No one can say that these obligations are of an insignificant type, or that even if they are fulfilled, the pattern of society in India will still remain more or less the same. In fact they are revolutionary in character and yet to be achieved in a constitutional manner. Herein lies the real value of embodying these principles as an integral part of the Constitution. Through the Directive Principles of State Policy, the Constitution of India will steer clear of the two extremes, a proletarian dictatorship which destroys the liberty of the individual and a capitalist oligarchy which hampers the economic security of the masses.

Fundamental Duties

The Forty-second Amendment of the Constitution added a new part to the Constitution Part IV A — incorporating ten Fundamental Duties of the citizen under Article 51-A. "What is the use of mere enumeration of such duties in the Constitution in the absence of suitable provisions to enforce them?" it may be asked and it is not easy to give a very satisfactory answer. However, the intention is quite clear and that is to place before the country a code of conduct which the citizens are expected to follow in their actions and conduct.

It shall be the duty of every citizen of India:

(*a*) to abide by the Constitution and respect its ideals and institutions, the National Flag and the National Anthem;

(*b*) to cherish and follow the noble ideals which inspired our national struggle for freedom;

(*c*) to uphold and protect the sovereignty, unity and integrity of India;

(*d*) to defend the country and render national service when called upon to do so;

(*e*) to promote harmony and the spirit of common brotherhood amongst all the people of India transcending religious, linguistic and regional or sectional diversities; to renounce practices derogatory to the dignity of women;

(*f*) to value and preserve the rich heritage of our composite culture;

(*g*) to protect and improve the natural environment including forests, lakes, rivers and wild life, and to have compassion for living creatures;

(*h*) to develop the scientific temper, humanism and the spirit of inquiry and reform;

(*i*) to safeguard public property and to abjure violence;

(*j*) to strive towards excellence in all spheres of individual and collective activity, so that the nation constantly rises to higher levels of endeavour and achievement.

THE MACHINERY OF THE UNION GOVERNMENT

CHAPTER 17

THE UNION EXECUTIVE

THE CONSTITUTION of India has adopted the British model of the Cabinet system of responsible government. On the question of the form of government, opinion in the Constituent Assembly was at first divided. There were those who advocated the adoption of the Presidential system of government prevalent in the United States of America. But they formed only a small minority. At least one member pleaded for the Swiss form of Collegiate Executive which combined the merits of both the Presidential and Parliamentary systems by providing stability and responsibility at the same time. As against these, the overwhelming majority was decisively in favour of the Cabinet system of government.

The decision to adopt the Cabinet system was the result of a long discussion in the Assembly in one of its earlier sessions. It had in its support the favourable recommendation of the Constitution committee (for the Union Government) presided over by Nehru. The two issues which were raised during the discussion were: (1) What would make for the strongest executive consistent with a democratic constitutional structure? (2) What was the form of executive which was suited to the conditions of this country? Giving his views in answer to these questions, K. M. Munshi said:

"The strongest government and the most elastic executive have been found to be in England and that is because the executive powers vest in the Cabinet supported by a majority in the Lower House which has financial powers under the Constitution. As a result, it is the rule of the majority in the legislature; for it supports its leaders in the Cabinet, which advises the head of the State, namely, the King. The King is thus placed above party. He is made really the symbol of the impartial dignity of the Constitution. The Government in England is found strong and elastic under all circumstances. . . . "We must not forget a very important fact that, during the last hundred years, Indian public life has largely drawn upon

187

the traditions of British Constitutional law. Most of us have looked up to the British model as the best. For the last thirty or forty years, some kind of responsibility has been introduced in the governance of this country. Our constitutional traditions have become parliamentary and we have now all our Provinces functioning more or less on the British model. Today, the Dominion Government of India is functioning as a full-fledged parliamentary government. After this experience, why should we go back upon the tradition that has been built for over a hundred years and try a novel experiment. . . .?"

Office of the President

Since India is a Republic, the Constitution provides for a President of India and the executive power of the Union Government, including the supreme command of the defence forces, is vested in him. The Constitution prescribes only simple qualifications for a Presidential candidate. He should be a citizen of India who has completed the age of 35 years and is qualified to be elected as a member of the House of the People. No person who holds any office of profit under the Government of India or any State Government or local authority is eligible for election as President. But there are certain positions in the Government which are excluded from the scope of this provision. These are the offices of the President, Vice-President, Governors and Ministers of the Central and State Governments. The President cannot be a member of Parliament or a State Legislature. Any member of a legislature who is elected as President shall cease to be such a member on the date he assumes the office of President. Further, the President is prohibited from holding any other office of profit. He is entitled to have his official residence free of rent. He is also entitled for such salaries, allowances and privileges as may be determined by Parliament. At present, his salary is fixed at Rs. 10,000 per mensem. His salaries and allowances cannot be diminished during his term of office.

Election

The President is elected for a period of five years by an electoral college which is composed of (a) the elected members of Parliament and (b) the elected members of the State Legislative

Assemblies. With a view to ensuring uniformity of representation of the different States at the Presidential election and parity between the States as a whole and the Union, the Constitution has prescribed an ingenius method. Normally it should have been possible to achieve this uniformity by the simple device of assigning each member of the electoral college one vote. Such uniformity would, however, have been invidious because in different States different ratios prevailed between the population and the number of legislators. For example, in one State it may be one representative for every 50,000 of the population while in another the proportion may be one to 75,000 or more. The most populous State in the Union, Uttar Pradesh, has only 430 members in the Legislative Assembly for a population of over 90 millions while Assam has 108 members for a population of about 15 millions. That being so, the problem was to ensure that the votes will have a value in proportion to the population that the votes represented.

According to the special method devised to ensure this, each elected member of the State Assemblies has a certain number of votes on the basis of the relation between the total number of the elected members of the State Assembly and the total population of the State. The number is worked out in the following manner: Divide the total population of the State, first by the total number of elected members in the Assembly. Divide the quotient obtained by the above division by 1,000. Fractions of half or more should be counted as one and added to the quotient which will be the number of votes each member of the Assembly will have in the Presidential election.

The following illustration will help to make the process clear. We may work out the actual number of votes a member of the Uttar Pradesh Legislative Assembly had in the Presidential election in 1957.

Total population of Uttar Pradesh	63,215,742
Total number of elected members in the Legislative Assembly	430
	63,215,742
The number of votes of each member	$\dfrac{63,215,742}{430 \times 1000}$

$$= 147 \; \frac{13}{1000} = 147$$

The number of votes each elected member of Parliament is entitled to in the Presidential election is arrived at by dividing the total number of votes given to all the elected members of the State Assemblies by the total number of elected members of both Houses of Parliament. The election is held in accordance with the system of proportional representation by means of the single transferable vote. The voting at the election is by secret ballot. On the whole, this is a unique system of Presidential election and one is tempted to ask what prompted the constitution-makers to adopt such a system.

First, in view of the adoption of a Cabinet system of Government under which the President was to function as constitutional head of the State, direct election by the entire electorate as in the case of the President of the United States (in practice) was considered neither necessary nor advisable. Yet, it was thought desirable to have the President elected by as popular a body as possible. Both these purposes have been realised under the present system. The election becomes indirect and also simple when the electorate consists of only the elected members of the State Legislative Assemblies and Parliament. The elected members of the State Assemblies are themselves elected on adult suffrage. The House of the People of Parliament is also elected on the same basis. The Council of States is elected by the State Assemblies which are also elected on adult suffrage. The electoral college is thus not only broad-based but also is substantially large in size.

In the 1952 election there were 3,559 members in the electoral college and a total of 616,913 votes were cast. In the 1957 election the total number of valid votes polled was 463,196; of these, Rajendra Prasad secured 459,698, Nagendra Narayan Das, 2,000 and Chowdhry Hari Ram, 1,418.

In 1962 the electoral college had a strength of 3,920. Of these, 3,094 participated in the election. The total number of valid votes was 562,945. Of these, S. Radhakrishnan secured 553,067, Chowdhry Hari Ram 6,341 and Yamuna Prasad Trisulia, 3,537 votes.

The most hotly contested Presidential election so far was that of 1969. There were three principal candidates in that election: V. V. Giri, N. Sanjiva Reddy and C. D. Deshmukh. When the first preference votes were counted, Giri obtained 401,505 votes, Reddy 313,545 and Deshmukh 112,769. As no one got the requisite quota of 50 per cent plus one of the votes polled, second preference votes were counted. As a result, Giri secured 420,077 as against Reddy's 405,427. Hence Giri was elected President. In contrast, in 1977 the Presidential election produced no heat. It was uncontested and Sanjiva Reddy was elected unanimously.

The significance of an electoral college composed of not only the members of both Houses of Parliament but also those of the various State Assemblies needs emphasis. In an election where the Head of the Nation is chosen, if the members of Parliament alone participate, it is possible that a Party that has a clear majority in Parliament can easily see its candidate elected. But when the members of the State Assemblies also participate in the election, the picture is likely to undergo a substantial change. For, it is quite possible that the Party which has won a majority in Parliament may be a minority in many State Assemblies or even in most of them. Under such conditions, a Party supported by a majority of members in Parliament will not by itself be able to get its candidate elected.

The use of the term "proportional representation" was objected to in the Assembly because only one person was to be elected as President. Critics asked: "What significance has it in the absence of a multi-member constituency?" It is significant because, first it ensures that an absolute majority of the total number of votes are polled for a candidate to be elected, instead of a simple majority or a plurality of votes as in the elections to Parliament and the State Legislative Assemblies. Since the President is the head of the State and represents the nation which includes all parties and groups, and since he should stand above party consi-derations, it is desirable that he is elected with as large a majority as possible. But under the simple majority system there is no guarantee for this. The present system ensures his elec-tion with at least an absolute majority. Secondly, it often helps the smaller parties in Parliament or regional parties who are strong only in some State Assemblies to have some voice in the election of the President. If no Party can claim an absolute majority of the total votes of the electoral College, a candidate, to win the election, has to seek the support of two or more

Parties. This gives an opportunity to smaller parties to influence the election.

Although, on paper, the Presidential election is a complicated process, in practice it is a comparatively simple process. Moreover, this method of electing the President seems to be much more in consonance with the federal principle than that which obtains in the United States, where the President is supposed to be elected by the electors but, in reality, directly by the people. The election of the American President raises the greatest political battle in the world for the election of any Head of State. But, in India, such a contest will pass off without a ripple of popular excitement.[1] No doubt, it is a matter of all-India significance. And yet, since those who directly participate in it number just a few thousands (about 4000) it passes off in a quiet, business-like manner.

Although the President is only a constitutional Head of the State who has little effective power at his disposal, the office of the President carries with it great dignity and prestige. These are reflected in certain legal privileges which the President enjoys. Thus, he is not answerable to any Court of law for the exercise and performance of the powers and functions of his office. No criminal proceedings can be instituted against him nor can he be arrested or imprisoned during the tenure of his office. No civil proceedings even can be instituted against him without, at least, two months' written notice regarding the relief claimed.

Before entering upon his office, the President has to take and subscribe in the presence of the Chief Justice of India, an oath or affirmation to the effect that as President he will, "preserve, protect and defend the Constitution and the law and devote himself to the service and well-being of the people of India."

Normally, the President's Office becomes vacant in three ways: death, resignation or removal by impeachment. The Constitution lays down a detailed procedure for the impeachment of the President, which is almost identical to that in the United States except for one major difference. In India the charge may be preferred by either House of Parliament while in the United

---

[1] The Presidential election of 1969 was an exception to this normal feature because of the unusual political circumstances, that followed the split in the Congress Party earlier that year.

States the House of Representatives alone has the power to try the impeachment. The President can be impeached only for the violation of the Constitution, a form which is comprehensive enough to cover crimes such as treason, bribery and other crimes. Before the charge is preferred by either House of Parliament, the proposal should be embodied in a resolution moved after a notice of at least fourteen days. The notice must be signed by at least one-fourth of the total membership of the House. The charge shall be preferred only if such a resolution is passed by a two-thirds majority of the total membership of the House. Once the charge has been so preferred in one House, the other House will investigate the charge or appoint a special body for such investigation. If the result of such investigation is that the charge against the President has been sustained and to this effect a resolution is passed by the House with a two-thirds majority of its total membership, the President ceases to hold the office of the President of India from the date of passing such resolution.

When a vacancy arises in the office of the President owing to any one of the above causes, it will be filled by the Vice-President until a new President is elected. But the new President should be elected before six months elapse after the vacancy has occurred. When a new President is elected in this manner he will hold office for the full term of five years. There is no constitutional bar against the President's re-election. Every doubt and dispute arising out of the Presidential election shall be finally decided by the Supreme Court of India.

Powers of the President

Under Article 53 of the Constitution the executive power of the Union is vested in the President who is empowered to exercise it either directly or through officers subordinate to him. The list of powers which the Constitution confers upon the President is long and impressive. These may be broadly classified under three categories, Executive powers, Legislative powers and Emergency powers.

Executive Powers

The Constitution lays down the general principle that the execu-

13

tive power of the Union is co-extensive with its legislative power. Interpreting the scope of this power the Supreme Court held that it embraced not only matters upon which Parliament has already passed legislation but also those on which it is competent to pass legislation. Since the President is the Head of the Union Executive, naturally his executive power embraces the entire field of activities of the Union. It has already been pointed out that he is the Commander-in-Chief of the Defence Forces. By making the President the Commander-in-Chief, the Constitution ensures the subordination of the entire Armed Forces to the civil authority at all times. In addition, the President has vast powers of appointment. He appoints the Prime Minister and other members of the Council of Ministers and makes rules for the transaction of the business of the Government of India and for the allocation, among the Ministers, of that business. He appoints the Attorney-General, the Chief Justice and justices of the Supreme Court and those of the High Courts, the members of the Union Public Service Commission, the Election Commission, the Comptroller and Auditor-General of India, Ambassadors and other diplomatic representatives of India abroad, the Commissioner for the Scheduled Castes, Tribes, Backward Classes and Minorities, the Governors, Chief Commissioners of Union Territories, members of the Finance Commission and of the Inter-State Council. In fact, every appointment in the Union Government is made in the name of the President or under his authority. But in the above cases the appointments are made by the President "by warrant under his hand and seal".

Under Article 72 the President is given the power to grant pardons. According to this, in all Court Martial cases as well as cases involving the breach of a Union law where a punishment or sentence is inflicted on any person, the President may grant pardon or any other appropriate mercy such as reprieve, respite, remission, or suspension, or commutation of the sentence.

Legislative Powers

In the legislative field too the President has important powers. In fact, the President forms an integral part of the legislative process in that without his assent, no central Bill can become law. He summons the Houses of Parliament, prorogues the

Houses and may dissolve the House of the People. He may address either House of the Parliament or both Houses assembled together or send messages to them. He nominates 12 members to the Council of States and may nominate two members of the Anglo-Indian community to the House of the People. Every Bill passed by Parliament must be presented to the President for his assent. He may withhold his assent or return it to Parliament for reconsideration. He causes to be laid before Parliament the annual budget showing the estimated receipts and expenditure of the Union for each year. No demand for a financial grant can be made in Parliament except on his recommendation.

Perhaps, the most important legislative power of the President is his power to promulgate ordinances under Article 123. According to this, the President is empowered to promulgate Ordinances, except when both the Houses of Parliament are in session, if he is satisfied that circumstances exist compelling him to take immediate action. A Presidential Ordinance has the same force and effect as an Act of Parliament. However, every such Ordinance should be laid before both Houses of Parliament within six weeks from the re-assembly of Parliament. Failure to comply with this condition, or Parliamentary disapproval within the six weeks' period, will make the Ordinance invalid. The President may also withdraw the Ordinance at any time he likes.

Emergency Powers

The President is empowered to declare three different types of emergency. He may declare an emergency either in any part or the whole of India, if he is satisfied that there is a threat of war or external aggression or internal disturbance. Further, he is empowered to declare an emergency in case of a breakdown of the constitutional machinery in any State of the Union. He may also declare, in case of a financial breakdown, a financial emergency. (As there is a separate chapter dealing with these powers and their implications, it is not proposed to deal with the subject in detail here.)

The President, a Constitutional Head of the State

Taken as a whole, and on their face value, the Presidential powers are formidable indeed. There is hardly any other constitution which gives such a long and detailed list of powers to its Chief Executive. The question, however, is how far all or any of these powers will be really exercised by him. On the answer to this question will depend the real position of the President in the governmental system established by the Constitution, rather than what may appear from a literal reading of the Constitutional provisions. It is here that we have to turn to the nature as well as the working of the Government of India. It has already been pointed out that the form of government which the Constitution aims to establish is modelled on the British Parliamentary or Cabinet System and not the Presidential type of the United States. Under the British system, the monarch (the King or the Queen) is only a ceremonial head of the State. The tremendous powers, technically ascribed to him, he does not possess. They belong to a convenient myth or "working hypothesis" called the Crown. Almost all the powers which theoretically belong to the Crown are in reality exercised by the Cabinet. The position under the Indian Constitution too is the same, that the President of India is only the Constitutional Head of the State who is a necessary adjunct of Cabinet Government, his position and powers being more or less the same as those of the British monarch.

This question was discussed at length in the Constituent Assembly at different times and every time the point that was stressed most was the constitutional character of the Head of the State. Introducing the Draft Constitution, Ambedkar said:

"In the Draft Constitution there is placed at the head of the Indian Union a functionary who is called the President of the Union. The title of this functionary reminds one of the President of the United States. But beyond identity of names there is nothing in common between the form of Government prevalent in America and the form of government proposed under the Draft Constitution. The two are fundamentally different. Under the Presidential system of America, the President is the Chief head of the Executive. The Administration is vested in him. Under the Draft Constitution the President occupies the same position as the King under the English Constitution. He is the head of the State but not of the Executive. He represents the nation but does not rule the nation. He is the symbol of the nation. His place in the Administration is that of a ceremonial device on a seal by which the nation's decisions are made known."

Participating in the discussion towards the end of the deliberations in the Constituent Assembly, President Prasad said:

"We have had to reconcile the position of an elected President with an elected legislature, and in doing so, we have adopted, more or less, the position of the British monarch for the President. . . . His position is that of a constitutional President. Then we come to the Ministers. They are, of course, responsible to the Legislature and tender advice to the President who is bound to act according to that advice. Although there are no specific provisions, so far as I know, in the Constitution itself making it binding on the President to accept the advice of his Ministers, it is hoped that the convention under which in England the King acts always on the advice of his Ministers will be established in this country also and the President, not so much on account of the written word in the Constitution, but as a result of this very healthy convention, will become a constitutional President in all matters."

With this background in view one may examine the Constitutional provisions that deal with the relationship of the President with the Council of Ministers in order to see how far these claims are justified. Articles 74, 75 and 78 are important in this connection. They provide: (1) There shall be a Council of Ministers with the Prime Minister at the head to aid and advise the President in the exercise of his functions.[2] (2) No Court of

[2] The Forty-second Amendment of the Constitution (1976) modified this provision to the effect that in the exercise of his functions, the President "shall act in accordance with such advice." The Forty-fifth Amendment (1978) however, seeks to add the following Proviso to Article 74(1):

law has power to enquire as to whether any advice was given by the Ministers and if so, what it was. (3) The Prime Minister shall be appointed by the President and on the advice of the Prime Minister, the President will appoint other Ministers. (4) The Ministers shall hold office during the pleasure of the President. (5) The Council of Ministers shall be collectively responsible to the House of the People. (6) It shall be the duty of the Prime Minister (a) to communicate to the President all decisions of the Council of Ministers; (b) to furnish such information relating to the administration of the Union and proposals for legislation as the President calls for; and (c) to submit for the consideration of the Council if the President so desires, any matter on which a decision has been taken by a Minister but which has not been considered by the Council.

These provisions, taken as a whole, fairly establish the claim of Ambedkar and his colleagues that the authors of the Constitution wanted to adopt the British pattern of Cabinet Government. At the same time, it is also clear that they did not want to use expressions which would take away the flexibility that is the heart and soul of the British system. The difficulty of the Drafting Committee was to state precisely in a written Constitution certain well-established constitutional conventions that regulate the relationship between the King and the Cabinet in Britain. This is why, while certain provisions convey their meaning in unmistakable terms, there are others that are not equally clear. Thus, it is quite clear that, for the exercise of his functions, there must be a Council of Ministers with the Prime Minister at the head to aid and advise the President. But does this mean that the President is always bound by the advice of the Council? Ambedkar answered it in the positive. "The President of the Indian Union will be generally bound by the advice of his Ministers. He can do nothing contrary to their advice, nor can he do anything without their advice."

"Provided that the President may require the Council of Ministers to reconsider such advice either generally or otherwise, and the President shall act in accordance with the advice tendered after such reconsideration."
Discussing the significance of this proviso, the Law Minister who piloted the Amendment Bill in Parliament said: "This proviso seeks to make explicit what was implicit before the Forty-second Amendment was passed."

According to those who supported Ambedkar, "It is the Prime Minister's business, with the support of the Ministers, to rule the country and the President may be permitted now and then to aid and advise the Council of Ministers. Therefore, we should look at the substance and not at the mere phraseology which is the result of conventions."

In a Parliamentary system of Government, the Executive is responsible to the Legislature. As such, the Council of Ministers hold their offices not as a grace of the President (or literally during his pleasure) but because of the confidence of Parliament which they enjoy. They go out of office not because the President has lost confidence in them, but because they have lost the confidence of Parliament to which they are jointly and directly responsible. There can be no conflict between the will of Parliament, the representative of the electorate, and that of the President. If at all there arises such a conflict, the will of Parliament ought to prevail. That is why the Constitution vests in Parliament the power to impeach the President. Therefore, so long as the Council of Ministers have the confidence of Parliament, the President is literally bound by their advice and, in reality, it is the President who is cast in the role of an adviser.

This view about the position of the President vis-a-vis the Council of Ministers is shared also by the Supreme Court which expressed its opinion in the following language:

"In India, as in England, the executive has to act subject to the control of the Legislature; but in what way is this control exercised by the Legislature? Under Article 53 (1) of our Constitution, the executive power of the Union is vested in the President but under Article 75 there is to be a Council of Ministers with the Prime Minister at the head to aid and advise the President in the exercise of his functions. The President *has thus been made a formal or Constitutional head of the executive and the real executive powers are vested in the Ministers or the Cabinet.* . . . In the Indian Constitution, therefore, we have the same system of Parliamentary executive as in England, and the Council of Ministers consisting as it does of the members of the legislature is, like the British Cabinet, 'a hyphen which joins, a buckle which fastens the legislative part of the State to the executive part'. The Cabinet enjoying, as it does, a majority in the legislature concentrates in itself the virtual control of both legislative and executive functions; and as the Ministers constituting the Cabinet are presumably agreed on fundamentals and act on the principle of collective responsibility, the most important questions of policy are all formulated by them."

The Forty-second Amendment expressly lays down that the President is bound to act in accordance with the advice of the Council of Ministers.

The experience of the *first* twenty-six years also clearly indicates, that the President is, in reality, only the constitutional head of the State. On the eve of the 1951-52 General Elections in India, President Rajendra Prasad sent a message to Parliament explaining his views on the Hindu Code Bill which was then under its consideration. In that message he said that personally he was opposed to the passing of the Bill but if adopted by Parliament, he would give his assent to it, however reluctant that might be. During the first twenty-five years the country has had five General Elections each followed by a reconstitution of the Council of Ministers. During this period there were also major political changes and economic development programmes. The States Reorganisation Act, 1956, has brought about a complete redrawing of the political map of India. There were over forty constitutional amendments some of which were of a far-reaching character. In all these cases, the decisions were of the Ministry (the Cabinet) and there was never a question of the "President exercising executive powers and the Ministers only advising him".

Fortunately for India, there was during this period a stable government, one that always enjoyed the confidence of Parliament.

CHAPTER 18

THE COUNCIL OF MINISTERS AND THE
PRIME MINISTER

WE HAVE already seen the relationship of the President with the Council of Ministers. In that connection we saw the special status the Constitution confers on the Prime Minister as the head of the Council of Ministers. The special position of superiority given to the Prime Minister is essential in the interest of the principle of collective responsibility to the House of the People as laid down under Article 75 (3). The essence of collective responsibility is that all members of the Council of Ministers will speak in public with a united voice. This does not necessarily mean that all of them see eye to eye with one another on every problem the Ministry faces. The different points of view are expressed freely in the meetings of the Council so as to arrive at the best decision in the circumstances. Once such a decision is taken, every Minister is expected to stand by the decision without any reservation. Thus, responsibility for governmental action becomes collective on the part of the Ministry which will "sink or sail as a whole", as a united body.

Nevertheless, if a Minister violates the principle by openly criticising the decision of the Ministry, he cannot be prosecuted in a court of law for a breach of the principle of collective responsibility. Obviously, there is no legal sanction for collective responsibility. What is expected of a Minister as normal practice is that he should tender his resignation if he finds himself so sharply in conflict with his colleagues that it is no longer honestly possible for him to defend the Government's policies. But if he fails to do so, the Prime Minister can enforce collective responsibility through either of two ways. He may advise the President to dismiss the Minister, for the President has appointed the Ministers on the advice of the Prime Minister. If the Prime Minister is not inclined to adopt this course, he may tender the resignation of the entire Ministry and form a new Ministry excluding the undesirable Minister. Thus, the realisation of the principle of collective responsibility is made possible by placing the Ministers under the Prime Minister in the matter of appointment as well as dismissal.

A striking feature of the Cabinet system of Government is that Ministers who hold the top positions in the executive are, at the same time, members of Parliament also. But a rigid adherence to this rule might deprive the executive of the services of men of ability who may not, for the time being, be members of the legislature. To avoid this difficulty, the Constitution provides a maximum period of six months for a Minister to become a member of the legislature if he is already not such a member.

We have already seen the position of importance which the Constitution confers upon the Prime Minister. Though the President appoints him formally, it is only a constitutional formality, as the person appointed has the political and parliamentary support to claim such an appointment. Similarly, though the President also appoints the other Ministers, they are so appointed only on the advice of the Prime Minister and, in reality, they are the nominees of the Prime Minister. The Ministry's decisions and actions are transmitted to the President only through the Prime Minister. Again, the Ministry is jointly responsible to the House of the People whose leader is the Prime Minister. Thus, the Prime Minister is a connecting link between the Ministry and the President on the one hand, and also between the Ministry and Parliament on the other. This special position that he enjoys both in the Government and in Parliament makes his office the most important under the Constitution of India.

The long list of powers that are vested in the President are normally powers exercised in reality by the Prime Minister. As the leader of the Party that commands the majority in Parliament and thus in fact as the leader of Parliament itself, and in addition, as the head of the Council of Ministers, he really leads the Council of Ministers, Parliament and the Nation. This is what makes him the most powerful functionary under the governmental system established by the Constitution. During any period of emergency, his power will increase as the administration of the area affected by the emergency comes directly under the Union Government. Naturally the personality of the Prime Minister will have an influence either in enhancing the actual powers of the President or limiting them to his constitutional functions.

India is gradually developing a well defined party system which is an indispensable aid to the evolution of a successful parliamentary government. The national election in the United States once every four years is meant primarily to select the President who would become the head of the nation and the chief of the Executive. In India, the general election once every five years becomes a great battle which determines the Party that will rule the country. But, to some extent, it will also decide the person who will become the Prime Minister of India. For, the Party which secures a majority in Parliament is sure to have its leader appointed Prime Minister by the President. In fact, the President himself is often the nominee of the Party and the leader of the Party is sure to have a substantial influence in the selection of the Presidential candidate.

Nevertheless, the Office of the President is one of great dignity and authority. Although a constitutional head of the State, the British monarch enjoys great dignity mainly because of the hereditary nature of the office behind which there lies the history of centuries. But an indirectly elected constitutional head of the State who holds office for a limited period often becomes a mere figure-head as the French President under the Fourth Republic was. The framers of the Constitution had a very difficult task in designing the office of the President. For unlike the British monarch's, his was to be an elective office. But like that of the British monarch his was to be of great dignity. In the words of Nehru: "We want to emphasise the ministerial character of the Government, that power really resided in the Ministry and in the legislature and not in the President as such. At the same time, we did not want to make the President a mere figure-head like the French President. We did not give him any real power but we have made his position one of great authority and dignity." From the working of the Constitution so far, it is not an exaggeration to say that the framers have been vindicated in their expectations.

The Council of Ministers and the Cabinet

There is some confusion as a result of the indiscriminate use of the terms "Cabinet" and "Council of Ministers" in connection with the activities of the Government. Often they are used as interchangeable terms. But in fact, they are not. The Council of Ministers, or the Ministry as it is usually called, consists of all the different categories of Ministers of the Government of India. At present, there are three such categories, namely, Cabinet Ministers, Ministers of State and Deputy Ministers. Of these, the Cabinet Ministers by themselves form a separate body called the Cabinet which, in fact, is the nucleus of the Council of Ministers. There is not a word mentioned about the Cabinet in the Constitution which, as we have already seen, speaks only of the Council of Ministers. Yet, today, the functions of the Cabinet, for all practical purposes, are identified with those assigned to the Council under the Constitution.

The Cabinet provides the best example of conventions so far established under the Constitution. No doubt, the organisation and working of the British Cabinet have provided the example. Yet, the Indian Cabinet is not a carbon copy of the British original, for it has developed its own special features. At the time when power was tansferred to Indians in 1947, there was no such institution as a Cabinet in India. What existed then as a comparable body at the highest level in the Government was the Governor-General's Executive Council. But with the establishment of responsible government on August 15, 1947, the Executive Council was transformed into a Ministry responsible to Parliament. The two significant results of this transformation were the recognition of the principle of collective responsibility and the acceptance of the Prime Minister as the leader and head of the Ministry. The term "Cabinet" was used thereafter as an alternative to "Ministry", so much so that for some time these two terms were in use as synonymous to each other. All members of the Ministry or the Cabinet except the Prime Minister had the same status. But the situation soon underwent a change on account of the appointment of junior Ministers to the Council of Ministers.

Accordingly a three-tier ministerial hierarchy was established, with the Cabinet Ministers at the top, Ministers of State in the middle and Deputy Ministers in the lowest rung of the ladder. A clear distinction was drawn between Ministers who were members of the Cabinet and others. The Cabinet was composed of the senior-most Ministers who were not mere departmental chiefs but whose responsibilities transcended departmental boundaries into the entire field of the administration. It was, naturally, a smaller body and the most powerful body in the Government. Thus, the growth of the Cabinet as a separate body from the Council of Ministers was only a natural product of the application of the administrative theory of organisation. Soon, the Cabinet became not only a distinct entity, different from the Council of Ministers, but also an institution with its own detailed organisation. In the process, it has also taken over functions assigned by the Constitution to the Council. For instance, the constitutional responsibility of advising the President is the Council's. But this function today is exercised exclusively by the Cabinet.

The Cabinet and Parliament

The most distinguishing feature of a parliamentary system of government is the unqualified and continuous responsibility of the Cabinet to Parliament for all its actions. Besides collective responsibility, there is also the individual responsibility of Ministers to Parliament for their actions arising out of their own administrative charges. Under the Constitution, ministerial responsibility is confined to the House of the People, the Lower House of Parliament. This is in recognition of the popular character of that House which is a directly elected body, whereas the Council of States (the Upper House of Parliament) is indirectly elected.

There are two special features of the Parliamentary Government in India which deserve mention in this connection. A person who is not a member of either House of Parliament can be a Minister. Secondly, a Minister whether he is a member of Parliament or not has the right to attend both Houses and participate in the discussions. The only restriction placed upon him is that he cannot vote. Similarly, a Minister who is a member of either House has the right to appear in the other House and participate in its proceedings, except for voting. Although Mrs. Gandhi continued to be a member of the Council of States even after her appointment as Prime Minister in 1966, the established practice of the Prime Minister belonging to the House of the People has become a convention of great merit and, therefore, it is expected to be followed in future also.

There are several methods by which Parliament ensures ministerial responsibility. Questions in Parliament, budget discussions, adjournment motions, discussions on reports by departments, are some of the common and regular devices by which accountability is ensured. But the most important device at the disposal of Parliament is a no-confidence motion with which Parliament's confidence in the Ministry can be tested. A successful no-confidence motion will result in the defeat and overthrow of the Ministry. Thus, under the Parliamentary system of Government, the Cabinet is the creature of Parliament. But the working of the Parliamentary system will show that although the Cabinet is the creature of Parliament, it is a creature that leads its creator.

The strength of the Indian Cabinet today is the result of the support that it receives from the party to which it belongs and the overwhelming strength of the party in Parliament. With a stable parliamentary support, the Cabinet, in reality, becomes the leader of Parliament. The initiative for all the policies and programmes of the Government are in the hands of the Cabinet. Nevertheless it must be pointed out that the Indian Cabinet has been treating Parliament with greater consideration and respect than is usual elsewhere under conditions of overwhelming parliamentary majorities. This has been mainly due to two reasons. First, on some occasions, on questions of great importance which vitally affect the nation as a whole, the Cabinet itself has given over the initiative to Parliament. The best example of this is provided by the initiative taken by Parliament in settling the question of the re-organised State of Bombay at the time of the adoption of the State Reorganisation Act of 1956. Secondly, members of Parliament have often evinced a willingness to forget party affiliations when questions of purity in administration are brought before it. On such occasions, the Indian Parliament has shown that it is the mirror and custodian of public opinion in the country and a true representative of the electorate and is second only to the electorate itself. The manner in which Parliament dealt with the allegations brought before it against a state enterprise like the Life Insurance Corporation in 1957 is a classic example in point. Parliamentary pressure has also brought about perceptible changes in later years in the policies of the Government towards industry, labour, taxation, defence, etc.

We must also point out in this connection the willingness and even the open-mindedness displayed by the Indian Cabinet in dealing with such matters. The Government, with its steam-roller majority and ability to crack the party whip against every recalcitrant member showing any sign of defiance, could have imposed its will on Parliament and carried on in a dictatorial manner. But experience so far shows that cabinet dictatorship is still somewhat foreign to India although the conditions and circumstances have been abundantly in its favour. It must be pointed out, however, that during a short period of Internal Emergency from June 1975 to March 1977, the country had experienced a form of dictatorship, although not cabinet dictatorship. It was largely the concentration of governmental power in the hands of one individual in the Cabinet, the Prime Minister, who exercised it with the assistance of a few others who were not even members of the Cabinet. The situation, however, did not last long. The Parliamentary elections of March 1977 and the change of Government as a consequence, restored Parliament's original position of importance as the mirror of public opinion in India. Adherence to the fundamental principles of parliamentary government has been almost a passion with the Indian Cabinet especially during the Nehru era which had been eager to build up conventions of an abiding nature to make Parliament's working smooth and successful. That tradition has been maintained to a large extent in later years also. The flowering of parliamentary government may yet be a long way off in India. But its roots are growing fast in the Indian soil and there is reason to believe that, in the fulness of time, it will flourish and become a proud part of the best of parliamentary heritage.

CHAPTER 19

THE VICE-PRESIDENT AND THE
ATTORNEY-GENERAL

THE CONSTITUTION provides for a Vice-President whose role in the Government is comparatively insignificant. Going through the provisions dealing with his office, one can easily see a striking similarity between the role of the Vice-President of India and that of his counterpart in the United States. The American Vice-President is sometimes called "His Superfluous Highness" to characterise his comparative insignificance in the administration. But there is a provision in the American Constitution which makes the Vice-President potentially important. According to this, if the President dies in Office, or is removed from Office, the Vice-President takes over the President's Office and continues in that capacity for the full length of the unexpired term. But under the Indian Constitution, if the President dies or resigns or is otherwise incapacitated and, as a result, the presidential office becomes vacant, the Vice-President will act as President only for a maximum period of six months.

The main function of the Vice-President like that of his American prototype is to preside over the Council of States. He is its *ex officio* Chairman.

The Vice-President is elected by the members of both Houses of Parliament at a joint meeting. The election will be conducted in accordance with the system of proportional representation by means of the single transferable vote. The voting will be by secret ballot.

The Vice-President will take over the office of the President, normally, under four situations: death of the President; resignation of the President; removal of the President from his office through impeachment or otherwise; and finally, when the President is unable to discharge his functions owing to absence, illness or any other cause. The last of these clearly provides for any temporary period of incapacity which makes the President incapable of discharging his responsibilities.

During the period when the Vice-President is acting for the President, he will have all the powers and immunities of the President. He is also entitled for such salary and allowances and privileges as may be determined by Parliament by law for the purpose. At present, according to the Second Schedule to the Constitution, the Vice-President is entitled to the same emoluments, allowances and privileges as the President while he discharges the functions of, or is acting as the President.

Any Indian citizen who has completed the age of thirty-five years and who is qualified for election as a member of the Council of States is eligible for election as Vice-President. But no person who holds an office of profit under the Government of India or any State or local or other authority in India is eligible for the purpose. The Vice-President cannot be a member of either House of Parliament or a member of any State legislature. He can be removed from office by a resolution of the Council of States passed by a majority of all the then members of the Council and agreed to by the House of the People. But this procedure does not seem to be sufficient, if at the time such removal is sought the Vice-President is acting for the President. If he is to be removed from office while he acts in the latter capacity, the provisions ought to be exactly the same as are applicable to the impeachment of the President.

Although the Constitution does not confer upon the Vice-President, the great authority that it vests in the President as the Head of the State, the office of the Vice-President has been one of great dignity and prestige. The personality of its incumbents who have all been eminent men has been one of the major reasons. The dignity and prestige that are established today may be expected to remain with the office of the Vice-President in the years to come.

The Attorney-General

In order to advise the Union Government in legal matters as well as to perform such other duties of a legal character as may be assigned by the President, the Constitution has provided for the office of the Attorney-General for India. The Attorney-General must have the qualifications of a judge of the Supreme

Court of India. He is appointed by the President and shall hold office during the pleasure of the President. The President may determine the remuneration to be paid to the Attorney-General.

The Attorney-General is a member of the Cabinet in Britain. But in India, there is a Minister of Law in the Cabinet to deal with legal affairs at Government level. The Attorney-General, however, has the privilege of addressing both Houses of Parliament, just as a Minister has, irrespective of his membership of the House. He also enjoys the same privileges and immunities as the members of Parliament. The Constitution expressly guarantees his right of audience in all courts in India in the performance of his duties.

CHAPTER 20

THE UNION LEGISLATURE—THE PARLIAMENT
OF INDIA

UNDER THE Constitution, the Legislature of the Union is called Parliament. The Indian Parliament is constituted on the basis of the principle of bicameralism, that is, the legislature having two Houses or Chambers. As the Constitution established a federal system of government, there was almost unanimity among the framers for achieving a balance between the direct representation of people and the representation of units as such, by setting up two Houses, one representing the people as a whole and the other the federated units. The two Houses of Parliament are the House of the People (the *Lok Sabha*) and the Council of States (the *Rajya Sabha*). The names of the Houses fairly reflect the character of their composition. The House of the People is composed of directly elected representatives on the basis of adult franchise and territorial constituencies. The Council of States is composed mainly of representatives of the States elected by the State Assemblies.

As has been pointed out earlier, the President is an integral part of Parliament. Under Article 79, Parliament shall consist of the President and the two Houses. Making the President a part of Parliament is in conformity with the principles and traditions of parliamentary government. In England, Parliament is constituted of the King, the House of Lords and the House of Commons. In contrast, the President of the United States is not a part of the American Congress. Whereas the presidential system of government emphasises the separation of the executive and legislative powers, the parliamentary system lays stress on the intimate relationship and the interdependence of the executive and the legislature. Members of the Government are at the same time members of the legislature. Although the President himself is not a member of the legislature, his participation in the legislative process is ensured by making him a part of Parliament. The fact that he is the chief executive authority and that the executive power is co-extensive with the legislative power also makes it necessary that he should become an integral part of the legislature.

The House of the People (The Lok Sabha)

The House of the People is commonly known as the "Lower House" of Parliament, and its members are elected directly by the people. Unlike many other constitutions, the maximum number of members to be elected to the *Lok Sabha* is fixed by the Constitution. Originally, this number was fixed at 500. But the Seventh Amendment of the Constitution following the reorganisation of States in 1956, raised it to 520. The Forty-second Amendment of the Constitution further raised it to 545 (Art. 81). Of these a maximum of 20 seats are reserved for members from the Union territories. The remaining members are to be chosen by direct election from territorial constituencies in the States. For this purpose, to each State is allotted a certain number of seats on the basis of its population in proportion to the total population of all the States. For the purpose of election, each State is divided into territorial constituencies which are more or less of the same size in regard to population.

The present total strength of the House includes two Anglo-Indian representatives who have been nominated to the House by the President. This is in accordance with a special provision in the Constitution under which the President will nominate not more than two members of the Anglo-Indian community to the *Lok Sabha* if no member of that community is elected to that House. On the basis of the 1951 census, India had a population of 360 million. But in 1971 it was about 600 million.

With 545 elected members in the House, one member at present represents over one million of the population, a very low rate of representation indeed. The representation from the various States may be seen in the table on p. 213.

The election to the House is conducted on the basis of adult franchise, every man or woman who has completed the age of 21 years being eligible to vote. The Constitution provides for secret ballot. According to the present system, a candidate who secures the largest number of votes is declared elected. Some members had advocated the system of proportional representation for the election of members to the *Lok Sabha*. This was opposed by Ambedkar who pointed out that with the present standard of literacy India was not ready for proportional representation. Further, proportional representation might bring about a multiplicity of political parties and a chronic instability in government.

TABLE 5
HOUSE OF THE PEOPLE (LOK SABHA)

Name of the State		Number of Members
1.	Andhra Pradesh	42
2.	Assam	14
3.	Bihar	54
4.	Gujarat	26
5.	Haryana	10
6.	Himachal Pradesh	4
7.	Jammu and Kashmir	6
8.	Karnataka	28
9.	Kerala	20
10.	Madhya Pradesh	40
11.	Maharashtra	48
12.	Manipur	2
13.	Meghalaya	2
14.	Nagaland	1
15.	Orissa	21
16.	Punjab	13
17.	Rajasthan	25
18.	Sikkim	1
19.	Tamil Nadu	39
20.	Tripura	2
21.	Uttar Pradesh	85
22.	West Bengal	42
Union Territories		
1.	Andamans	1
2.	Arunachal Pradesh	1
3.	Chandigarh	1
4.	Dadra and Nagar Haveli	1
5.	Delhi	7
6.	Goa	2
7.	Lakshadweep	1
8.	Mizoram	1
9.	Pondicherry	1
Special Representation		
	Anglo Indians	2

The normal life of the House of the People is six years from the date of its first meeting,[1] but it may be dissolved earlier by the President of India. The President is also empowered to extend the life of the House for one year at a time during a national emergency. But in any case, the life of the House cannot be extended beyond six months after the emergency has ceased to operate. The House shall meet at least twice a year and the interval between two consecutive sessions shall be less than six months. The time and the place of meeting will be decided by the President who will summon the House to meet. He has also the power to prorogue the House.

There is hardly any qualification that the Constitution prescribes for a member of Parliament except that he should be an Indian citizen and has completed the age of twenty-five years if he seeks election to the House and thirty years if he seeks election to the Council. A striking feature of the electoral law is that a candidate for election to the House of the People may stand from any Parliamentary constituency from any of the States in India. Such a provision, which is almost unknown in other federal States, is an incidence of the principle of single citizenship which emphasises the unity of the nation. In the United States, for instance, a contesting candidate for a seat in the House of Representatives must be, when elected, "an inhabitant of that State in which he shall be chosen." A person who seeks election to the Council of States, however, should be an elector in any of the Parliamentary constituencies of the State from which he is standing for election. This emphasises the principle that the Council of States is a representative of the States.

The Constitution has laid down certain disqualifications for membership. These are (1) no person can be a member of both Houses of Parliament or a member both of Parliament and of a State Legislature. There is no bar to a candidate contesting at the same time as many seats as he likes or to as many legislatures as he likes. But if he is elected to more than one seat, he should vacate all except one according to his choice. If the same person is elected to both a Parliamentary seat and a seat in a State Legislature and if he does not resign his seat in the State Legis-

[1] As orginally provided the normal life of the House was five years but the Forty-second Amendment made it six years.

lature before a specified period, his seat in Parliament will become vacant; (2) a person will be disqualified, if he absents himself for a period of sixty days from the meetings of the House without the permission of the House; (3) if he holds an office of profit under any Government in India; (4) if he is of unsound mind; (5) if he is an undischarged insolvent; (6) if he voluntarily acquires the citizenship of another State or is under any acknowledgement of allegiance to a foreign State.

In pursuance of the powers granted under Article 327 to regulate matters of election, Parliament passed in 1951 the Representation of the People Act which too lays down certain conditions for disqualification. These are: (1) a member of Parliament should not have been found guilty by a Court or an Election Tribunal of certain election offences or corrupt practices in election; (2) he should not have been convicted by a Court in India of any offence and sentenced to imprisonment for a period of not less than two years; (3) he should not have failed to lodge an account of his election expenses within the time and in the manner prescribed; (4) he should not have been dismissed for corruption or disloyalty from Government service; (5) he should not be a Director or Managing Agent or hold an office of profit under any corporation in which the Government has any financial interest; and (6) he should not have any interest in government contracts, execution of government work or service. These disqualifications should not exist on the date of nomination of a candidate for election and on the date when the results are declared.

Officers of Parliament

The Speaker

The House of the People is presided over by the Speaker who is elected by the House from among its own members. The office of the Speaker has been held in great esteem throughout the history of over three hundred years of Parliamentary government in Britain. This is because of the manner in which he has discharged his responsibilities as a presiding officer, the detachment and objectivity which he brought to bear upon all his decisions. That the framers of India's Constitution were quite cons-

cious of this role of impartiality of the Speaker is evident from
the provisions in the Constitution that deal with the office of
the Speaker. For instance, Article 94 (c) provides for the
removal of the Speaker by a resolution of the House passed by
a majority of all the then members of the House. Removal of
officers from their positions in this manner, namely, by such special resolutions and by such special majorities is restricted to
only a few officers such as the President, the Vice-President,
the Presiding Officers of both Houses of Parliament, Judges
of the Supreme Court, etc. as these officers are expected
to discharge their responsibilities without political and party
considerations.

The importance of the office of the Speaker can be seen also
from the functions that he performs and the powers that he
exercises. He presides over the meetings of the House. He
adjourns the House or suspends its meeting if there is no quorum.
While questions are decided in the House, he is not entitled to
vote in the first instance (which emphasises his impartiality) but
he shall exercise a casting vote in case of a tie. Any member of
the House who resigns his office should address his letter of
resignation to the Speaker. The decision of the Speaker as to
whether or not a Bill is a Money Bill shall be final. The Speaker
will have to endorse or certify it before such a Bill is transmitted
to the Council of States or presented to the President for his assent.
He will be consulted along with the Chairman of the Council of
States by the President while making rules of procedure with
respect to joint sittings of the two Houses. In such sittings it is
the Speaker's right to preside. In conformity with the Speaker's
power to conduct the business of the House, he is empowered to
allow any member to speak in his mother tongue if he cannot
adequately express himself either in Hindi or English. With
respect to the discharge of his powers and functions, the Speaker
is not answerable to anyone except the House. No court of law
can go into the merits of a ruling given by the Speaker.

In addition to these constitutional provisions, the Rules of Procedure of the House confer upon the Speaker a variety of powers
in the detailed conduct of the business of the House. Under these,
his decision to admit notices of questions, motions, resolutions,
bills, amendments, etc. is final. There are certain guiding princi-

ples which the Rules of Procedure lay down for determining the admissibility of notices of motions, etc. The interpretation of these rules as well as their application to specific situations and circumstances is the prerogative of the Speaker. He is the sole authority for giving priority or urgency to a matter so that it may be placed before the House in the national interest. He is not expected to give reasons for his decisions which cannot be challenged by any member. His powers to maintain discipline in the House and to conduct its proceedings in accordance with the rules are formidable. Similarly his powers in connection with the constitution as well as the working of Parliamentary Committees also are enormous. The Speaker is thus the guardian and custodian of the rights and privileges of the members, both in their individual capacity and on the group or party basis. The Speaker, in short, is the representative of the House itself in its powers, proceedings and dignity.

A special feature of the Speaker's office is that even when the House is dissolved, the Speaker does not vacate his office. He will continue in office until a new Speaker is elected when the new House meets. Parliament is empowered to fix the salary and allowances of the Speaker and these are charged on the Consolidated Fund of India.

Within the short period of three decades during which the Speaker's Office has been in existence, conventions of an abiding nature have already been established and the Speaker has, indeed, become a true symbol of the dignity and independence of the House as well as the guardian of the rights and privileges of its members.

The Deputy Speaker

The Deputy Speaker who presides over the House in the absence of the Speaker is elected in the same manner in which the Speaker is elected by the House. He can be removed from office also in the same manner. When he sits in the seat of the Speaker, he has all the powers of the Speaker and can perform all his functions. One of his special privileges is that when he is appointed as a member of a Parliamentary Committee, he automatically becomes its Chairman. By virtue of the office that he holds, he has a right to be present at any meeting of any

Committee if he so chooses and can preside over its deliberations. His rulings are generally final, in any case, so far as they are related to the matters under discussion, but the Speaker may give guidance in the interest of uniformity in practice. Whenever the Deputy Speaker is in doubt, he reserves the matter for the ruling of the Speaker.

The Deputy Speaker, however, is otherwise like any ordinary member when the Speaker presides over the House. He may speak like any other member, maintain his party affiliation and vote on propositions before the House as any ordinary member. The Deputy Speaker is entitled to a regular salary.

Panel of Chairmen

To facilitate the work of the House in the absence of the Speaker and the Deputy Speaker, there is provision for one of the members of the House out of a panel of six Chairmen, whom the Speaker nominates from time to time, to preside over its deliberations. When the Chairman sits in the Speaker's chair, he has all the powers of the Speaker just as the Deputy Speaker has when he acts for the Speaker. The Chairman, however, is just an ordinary member as soon as he vacates the Speaker's Chair. A healthy convention has been built up by which the Speaker nominates members on the Panel of Chairmen irrespective of their party affiliations. As a result, some of the members of the Panel come from the ranks of the opposition parties.

Secretary

The Constitution authorises each House of Parliament to have its own secretarial staff and also gives them the power to regulate by law the conditions of service of those appointed to the secretarial staff. The *Lok Sabha* Secretariat is headed by a Secretary who is a permanent officer. He discharges on behalf of the Speaker the various administrative and executive functions connected with the work of the House. In many ways, he is like an Adviser to the House, its Committees, the Speaker, the Deputy Speaker, and individual members. His role in the work of the House is that of a permanent civil service officer in the Secretariat of the Government of India. In discharging his functions, he is not concerned with the party affiliations of the members or the political cross currents within the House.

Chairman and Deputy Chairman of the Council of States

While the presiding officers of the House of the People are called the Speaker and the Deputy Speaker, their opposite numbers in the Council of States are called the Chairman and the Deputy Chairman respectively. It has already been mentioned that the Vice-President of India is the *ex-officio* Chairman of the Council of States. We have also seen in that connection the method of his election, the manner in which he may be removed from office and his functions and powers. As the presiding officer of the *Rajya Sabha* his functions and powers are the same as those of the Speaker. He is however not a member of the House. We have seen how the Vice-President will act for the President under certain contingencies. During such periods, he will not perform the duties of the office of the Chairman of the Council nor will he draw the salary or allowances payable to the Chairman.

In the absence of the Chairman, the Council is presided over by the Deputy Chairman. He is a member of the House and is elected by the members of the House. When he ceases to be a member of the Council, he automatically vacates the office of the Deputy Chairman. He can resign his office by writing to the Chairman. He may be removed from his office by a resolution passed by a majority of all the then members of the Council. The Deputy Chairman is empowered to discharge all the functions and to perform all the duties of the office of the Chairman, whenever the Chairman's Office is vacant or when the Vice-President is acting for the President. As a presiding officer of the Council he is also given a regular salary and other allowances such as Parliament by law has fixed. The Council of States also has a panel of members called "Vice Chairmen" nominated by the Chairman for the purpose of presiding over the House in the absence of both the Chairman and the Deputy Chairman. The Secretariat of the *Rajya Sabha* is headed by a Secretary who discharges the same functions as the Secretary of the *Lok Sabha*.

The Council of States

The Council of States is the "Upper House" of Parliament and is sometimes called the "House of Elders". In spite of the academic and theoretical denunciations of second chambers, the Constituent Assembly was practically unanimous about the usefulness and necessity of the Council of States as an integral part of the general scheme of the Union Government. There was however divergence of opinion with respect to its composition, maximum membership and functions. One member wanted the numerical strength of the House to be fixed at 150. Several suggestions were made in connection with the composition of the House. Some wanted equality of status among the States in the matter of representation while others denounced it as undemocratic and outmoded. Some were bitterly opposed to nomination of members while others wanted functional representation. While indirect election was opposed by some, election by the method of proportional representation was welcomed by others. One member suggested that an advisory body of professional and special interests should be set up to advise Parliament. Despite the large number of amendments based upon these and other ideas, the provisions embodied in the Draft Constitution were passed without any substantial modification except in regard to the method of the election of members.

The maximum membership of the Council of States is limited to 250, just about half of the maximum membership originally fixed for the House of the People. Its composition has unique features. Here is an attempt to combine different principles of representation in the composition of the same legislative body. The American principle of equality of States in representation which has been followed by several federal constitutions was rejected as undemocratic. At the same time, the election of the majority of its members by the State assemblies is intended to give recognition to the federal principle. The provision for nomination seeks to bring into the Council persons of special talents and accomplishments who may not otherwise ever become members.

The present strength of the Council is 244. Of these, 232 are elected by the various State Legislative Assemblies, thus making the Council predominantly an indirectly elected body. For the purpose of this election, to each State is allotted a certain number of seats in the Council. The main basis of such allotment is the strength of the population in each State. But this is not the sole consideration. The smaller States have been accorded some weightage in representation. Thus, for example, Uttar Pradesh, with a population of over 73 million, has been given only 34 seats while 7 seats have been allotted to Assam with a population of a little over 11 million. While Kerala with a population of 16.8 million has 9 seats, only 22 seats have been allotted to Bihar with a population of over 46 million. To take a more glaring example, Delhi with a population of less than three million has 3 seats while West Bengal has only 16 seats despite her population being over 34 million. (These figures of population are of the 1961 census).

Members of each State Legislative Assembly form the electorate for the purpose of electing the requisite number of members allotted to each State, thus ensuring the principle of State representation in the "Upper Chamber" of Parliament. The election of members to the Council from the State Assemblies is conducted in accordance with the system of proportional representation by means of the single transferable vote and voting is by secret ballot.

Another principle that is given recognition in the composition of the Council of States is representation of talent, experience and service. Here the example of the "Seanad Eireann" of the Irish Republic seems to have influenced the Constitution-makers of India. However, the number of members nominated by the President of India to the Council is very small in comparison with the number of elected members. The number of nominated members is constitutionally limited to twelve. Such members should be persons having special knowledge or practical experience in respect of matters like literature, science, art or social service. The table on p. 222 will show the State-wise representation in the Council of States.

The Council of States is a permanent body like the American Senate. Like the American Senators the members of the *Rajya Sabha* are elected for six years. At the end of every second year, one-third of the members are re-elected. This provision enables the Council to retain its political complexion in a more stable manner than the House of the People which after every election is a completely new House.

The Relationship between the Two Houses

Although the participation and collaboration of both the Houses are essential for all legislative activities and without such collaboration practically nothing can be done in the legislative field, the Constitution has recognised the superiority of the House of the People over the Council in certain respects. The first and perhaps the most important of these is the relationship between

TABLE 6

COUNCIL OF STATES

Name of the State	Number of Members
1. Andhra Pradesh	18
2. Assam	7
3. Bihar	22
4. Gujarat	11
5. Haryana	5
6. Himachal Pradesh	3
7. Jammu and Kashmir	4
8. Karnataka	12
9. Kerala	9
10. Madhya Pradesh	16
11. Maharashtra	19
12. Manipur	1
13. Meghalaya	1
14. Nagaland	1
15. Orissa	10
16. Punjab	7
17. Rajasthan	10
18. Sikkim	1
19. Tamil Nadu	18
20. Tripura	1
21. Uttar Pradesh	34
22. West Bengal	16

Union Territories

1. Arunachal Pradesh	1
2. Delhi	3
3. Mizoram	1
4. Pondicherry	1
Nominated	12
Total	244

Parliament and the Council of Ministers. The Upper House has hardly any control over the Ministers who are jointly and individually responsible for their actions to the House of the People. Not that the Ministers, if they so choose, can ignore the Council of States. The Council has every right to be fully informed of all matters connected with the Government's activities which are raised on its floor. But it has no right to pass a censure motion against the Government of the day. The confidence of Parliament means the confidence of the House of the People, and the responsibility of the executive means responsibility to the House of the People. This principle can be justified only on the basis of the popular character of the House. In a Parliamentary democracy, the government of the day must be accountable to the people. Within the mechanism of the government such accountability is made possible through the people's representatives, and the House of the People alone is composed of the directly elected representatives of the people. It was England which first established this principle by ensuring Cabinet responsibility to the House of Commons and, today, it has become an accepted principle in every parliamentary democracy including India.

Secondly, the power of the Council with regard to Money Bills is almost negligible. Every Money Bill should be introduced in the House of the People. It is the fundamental principle of every taxation measure that it should be taken only with the consent of the people. In a democracy, the people's consent is essential both for the raising of public revenues and their spending. Here again, the people's consent can be expressed only by a House which is elected *directly* by the people. Under the procedure established by the Constitution, however, the Council is not altogether prevented from scrutinizing Money Bills. But its power is only of an advisory character. Every Money Bill passed by the House will go to the Council for its consideration and within fourteen days after the receipt of the Bill, the Council must take whatever action it deems fit. It may pass it in which case the Bill goes to the President for his assent. If the Bill is amended or rejected by the Council it goes back to the House where it is reconsidered and voted by a simple majority and sent to the President. Thus, in financial matters, the Council has only an advisory role and the House has the final say.

In all other matters of legislation, including constitutional amendments, the extent of the Council's power is the same as that of the House. A Bill can be initiated either in the House or in the Council. The Council may amend or reject a Bill that is passed by the House. If the House does not agree with the action of the Council, the contested measure is placed before a joint sitting of both the Houses and passed by a simple majority. As the total membership of the Council is less than even half the total strength of the House of the People, the House is naturally bound to win in a conflict of this nature between the two.[2] A Bill passed in a joint sitting is sent straight to the President for his assent. Thus, unlike its counterpart in the U.S.A., namely, the Senate, the Council of States has comparatively less power. The American Senate with its special powers in connection with appointments and treaty making, in addition to its normal powers of legislation, is immensely more powerful than the House of Representatives of the American Congress, and is easily the most powerful Second Chamber in the World. In contrast, the Canadian Senate, which was modelled on the House of Lords, stands at the other extreme.

The relative status of the two Houses of Parliament was the subject of discussion at least once so far in the life of Parliament. It was raised in the *Rajya Sabha* by one of its Members who referred to the exception taken by a Member of the *Lok Sabha* to the discussion of the Railway and General Budgets by the *Rajya Sabha* first. The Vice-President who was in the Chair at the time said that "under the Constitution there was no question of any superiority of one House over the other. It was incontrovertible".

Of all the Second Chambers in the Commonwealth of Nations every one of which has a parliamentary system of government, the Australian Senate seems to be the most powerful. It shares power with the House of Representatives on the basis of equality. Even in the case of Money Bills, it has the power of rejection. By the exercise of this power it may even force a dissolution of

---

[2] So far there has been only one occasion (1961) when the two Houses sat in joint session. It was to resolve their differences with respect to certain provisions of the Dowry Prohibition Bill of 1960. The joint sitting lasted for two days during which the differences between the two Houses were resolved and the Bill was passed.

both chambers. Nevertheless, in practice, the Australian Senate has not established any position as a rival, not to speak of a position of superiority, to the Australian House of Representatives.

In India, the Council of States in relation to the House of the People is nowhere near as powerful as the American Senate, nor is it on a par with its Australian counterpart; but it is much more powerful than the Canadian Senate. It is true that the Constitution clearly recognises the supremacy of the House of the People over the Council in certain matters, but not in all. The co-equal power of the Council on constitutional amendment is of great significance. It means that the Constitution cannot be amended unless the Council of States as the representatives of the States also agrees to such change. This provision alone will show the significantly important role the framers of the Constitution have assigned to the Council. In addition, in all matters of legislation except finance it shares equal powers with the House.

Besides, there are two other provisions which confer upon the Council, as the sole representative of the States, powers in its own right and to the exclusion of the House. These are of considerable importance from a constitutional point of view. Under Article 249, the Council with the support of two-thirds of its members sitting and voting, is empowered to declare that, in the national interest, Parliament should make laws with respect to a matter that is included in the State legislature list. On the passing of such a resolution, it becomes lawful for Parliament to make laws with respect to that matter for the whole or any part of India for a period of one year.

The second exclusive power of the Council is connected with the setting up of All India Services. The special characteristic of an All India Service is that it is common to the Union and the States. As such, the setting up of such a service affects the powers of the States. Therefore, here again, the Council is given the power to decide by a resolution supported by a two-thirds majority the question of setting up of an All India Service. Hence, any laws connected with such a service can be initiated only if the Council passes such a resolution. Thus, in both these cases, the House of the People comes into the picture only after the Council has acted and the House does not share the power of the Council in deciding as to what action is necessary under both

15

the contingencies.

These provisions make the Council an important part of the governmental machinery and not an ornamental super-structure or an inessential adjunct. It was not designed to play the humble role of an unimportant adviser, nor of an occasional check on hasty legislation. Its comparatively small and therefore compact size, its permanent character which ensures a certain degree of stability and continuity in thought and action, and its having a large number of "elder statesmen" among its members, and its broad-based representative character, all these, in course of time, should help to establish it not only as a respectable but also beneficial and influential body though not equal in power in all respects with the House of the People.

Conduct of Business

Each House has a Roll of Members which is to be signed by every member before taking his seat. Every member should also make and subscribe to an oath or affirmation in order to formally assume his seat. With the Speaker or any other presiding officer in the Chair and in the presence of at least one-tenth of its total membership which is the quorum, the House can begin its business. If at any time during a meeting of the House there is no quorum, the presiding officer will either adjourn or suspend the work of the House. Normally, all questions are decided by a majority of the votes of members present and voting. The presiding officer may vote only when the House is equally divided.

The first hour of each sitting is devoted to Parliamentary questions and interpellations. Normally, this is the time when the House is most lively. The main purpose of questions is to seek information and draw attention to grievances of public importance. There are elaborate Rules of Procedure to determine the admissibility of questions. The Speaker's decision in this respect is final. Usually every question is sent days in advance of the session so that all relevant information is collected in the department concerned and transmitted to the House. There is, however, a provision for asking short notice questions under certain conditions.

After the question hour the House takes up, item by item, the business that is allotted for the day. The business takes different forms and, for each of these, a separate procedure is prescribed. The more important of these which deserve special mention are adjournment motions, resolutions, no-confidence motions, other motions for discussion, legislative business and financial business. There are also other types of business such as statements on policy made by Ministers from time to time and laying of papers and documents on the Table of the House. In the latter case, the Minister concerned will rise in his seat and make a formal statement drawing the attention of the House to the document that is placed on the Table.

Adjournment motions are an unusual feature. A motion for adjournment is meant to draw the attention of the House to a matter of public importance which has arisen suddenly and which deserves immediate attention. It should deal with a specific matter of recent occurrence and of urgent public importance. Such a motion is intended to focus the attention of the House to a particular action or inaction of the Government. It also compels the Government to act in a manner that is appropriate to the situation on penalty of otherwise losing the confidence of the House.

A Resolution is a device by which the House is made to declare an opinion on a particular matter. A Resolution should deal with only one issue and should be worded clearly and precisely. It should not contain arguments, imputations or defamatory statements nor refer to the conduct and character of persons except in their official or public capacity.

No-confidence or Censure Motions are a rare feature.[3] A censure motion is an expression of want of confidence in the Ministry. Permission to move such a motion will be given only if at least fifty members in the House rise in support of it. If leave is granted to move the motion, a date is fixed for discussion and the Speaker may allot one or more days for the purpose. Resort to a no-confidence motion is not usually made unless the Opposition has a reasonable chance of defeating the Ministry. But sometimes it is also made use of as a political weapon to discredit a Ministry or highlight its various failures in the public

[3] Until 1963 there was never moved a no-confidence motion in the *Lok Sabha*. But during the next four years a motion was moved each year.

eye with a view to bringing down its prestige. In the annals of
the Indian Parliament so far there has been no censure motion
against the government.

Under the Rules of Procedure, a member can, with the consent
of the Speaker move a motion for the discussion of a matter of
general public interest. If admitted,[4] the Speaker will allot a day
or more for its discussion. The possibility of such discussion
depends upon the availability of time during a particular session.
Sometimes, the Government itself may bring forward such motions
in view of the importance of the matter involved. This provision
is, in a way, one that enables members as well as the Government
to bring to the floor of the House any matter of public importance which is not covered by legislative proposals and other
parliamentary business.

There is also provision to cut short the discussion on any
matter by moving what is known as a "closure motion". Any
member can move such a motion and if the House adopts it,
discussion is stopped forthwith and the matter before the House
is voted upon. Sometimes when the time set for a particular
measure is already over despite the fact that the discussion on
all its parts has not been completed, a vote is taken on the
motion before the House. Then the rest of the measure is put
to vote without discussion. This procedure is described as the
"guillotine".

There are at present 389 Rules which regulate the procedure
in the House covering every aspect of its activities. These are
supplemented by "Directions by the Speaker". There are 123 such
Directions by the Speaker which are codified for the use of
members and others concerned. Taken together, these form the
foundations of Parliamentary procedure in India, which facilitate
the orderly transaction of business in Parliament. But the picture is not complete with these alone. One must add to it the
numerous rulings of the presiding officers, precedents and conventions, all of which, in a substantial measure, serve the successful working of the Houses of Parliament.

---

[4] At least 10 per cent of the total membership of the House should
support the motion for its admission.

CHAPTER 21

LEGISLATIVE PROCEDURE

THE PRIMARY function of Parliament is law-making. Histori-
cally, it was the function of making laws that made the legislature a distinctly separate department of government. In spite of
all the additional functions that a parliament takes up as a result
of the complexities of modern government, law-making still
remains its most important activity. A parliament without legislative work ceases to be a parliament in the real sense, whatever
else it might be.

A law-giver has to look to the future, while being rooted in the
experience of the past. He has to take into consideration the
conditions and circumstances of the society to which the laws
would be applicable. Modern society is so complex that laws
which govern it have necessarily to be complex. Naturally, law-
making too has become a complex process. This will be illus-
trated by the process prescribed under the Constitution of India.

The first stage of legislation is the introduction of a Bill
embodying the provisions of the proposed law, accompanied by
the "Statement of Objects and Reasons". If a private member
desires to introduce a Bill, he must give notice of his intention
to the Speaker. Every Bill that is introduced in the House has
to be published in the Gazette. There is provision, however, for
the publication of any Bill with the consent of the Speaker even
before its formal introduction. Usually, at the time of the introduction of a Bill there is no debate. The person who is given
leave to introduce the Bill, if he so chooses, may make a short
statement indicating broadly its aims and objects. But if the
introduction of the Bill is opposed, then the Speaker may allow
one of the opposing members to give his reasons too, after which
he will put the question to vote. If the House is in favour of the
introduction of the Bill, then it goes to the next stage. The introduction of the Bill is also called the first reading of the Bill.

There are four alternative courses of action open at the second
stage: The Bill may be taken into consideration; it may be refer-

red to a select committee of the House; it may be referred to a joint committee of both the Houses; or it may be circulated for the purpose of eliciting public opinion on it. In the case of every proposed legislative measure which is likely to arouse public controversy and agitate public opinion, resort to the last alternative is invariably made. But there are many Bills which are of minor importance or pertain to routine matters, and others of an emergent nature, which may not therefore permit any long delay. In their cases one or the other of the first three alternatives is adopted.

The Select Committee or Joint Committee is expected to give its report within a specified date. The members of the Select Committee are selected generally on the basis of their ability or expert knowledge on the subject. The usual practice is that the mover of the Bill will himself propose the names of members of the Committee and the House adopts them. Members of the Opposition are well represented on the Committee. In the case of a Joint Committee, the concurrence of the other House is taken. Of the total number of members on the Joint Committee, two-thirds belong to the *Lok Sabha* and one-third to the *Rajya Sabha*. The Committee may give a unanimous report or a majority report. In the latter case, members in a minority have the right to give "minutes of dissent". Submission of the report of the Committee may be taken as the beginning of the third stage. It is during this stage that members can send in their amendments to the different provisions of the Bill.

After the Committee's report has been considered and the motion that the Bill as reported by the Committee be taken into consideration is adopted, the fourth stage begins when a detailed clause to clause discussion of the Bill begins. Each clause is taken up by the House and amendments are moved, discussed and disposed of. The amendments that are moved in the House are those which have already been checked by the Secretariat with a view to seeing that they are within the scope of the Bill and relevant to the subject matter and satisfy all the conditions laid down in regard to their admissibility. This is the stage when the Bill undergoes substantial changes, should they be found necessary. It is also the most time-consuming stage. Once the clause by clause consideration is over and every clause is voted, the second reading of the Bill is over.

The next stage is the third reading stage when the member in charge who has piloted it moves that "the Bill be passed". Such a motion may be moved either immediately after the second reading or on a subsequent date. Unless there is any great urgency, the third reading takes place after sufficient time is given to members to study the Bill in the amended form in which it was passed at the second reading. At the third reading, normally only verbal or purely formal amendments are moved and discussion is limited and progress is quick. When once all the amendments are disposed of, the Bill is finally passed as a whole. And, when the work in one House is over, the Bill is sent to the other House for its action.

A sixth stage starts with the consideration of the Bill by the other House where it goes through the same procedure and the different stages. The House has three alternatives before it. It might finally pass the Bill as sent by the originating House. It might amend or altogether reject the Bill. In both these latter cases, the Bill may be returned to the originating House. Or it may not return it at all within six months after the receipt of the Bill, which will mean the same as rejection.

At the seventh stage, the returned Bill is considered by the House in the light of the amendments made by the other House. If the amendments are accepted, it sends a message to the other House to that effect. If they are not accepted then the Bill is returned to the other House with a message to that effect. If in this process of sending the Bill up and down, the Houses do not come to an agreement, the only solution is a joint sitting of the two Houses called for the purpose by the President. The disputed provision is finally adopted or rejected by a simple majority vote of those who are present at voting.

A Bill that is finally passed by both the Houses, goes with the signature of the Speaker, to the President for his assent. This is normally the last stage. If the President gives his assent, the Bill becomes an Act and is placed on the Statute Book. But even at this last stage, the Bill can be stopped from becoming an Act. The President, as we have already seen, is empowered, if he so chooses, to refuse assent to a Bill that is placed before him. He may send the Bill back to Parliament for reconsideration.

This will reopen almost the whole process and if the Bill is passed by both the Houses again with or without amendments, it will be sent to the President for a second time. At this stage, the President shall not withhold his assent. Thus, it can be seen how long, detailed and time-consuming is the process of modern legislation and how difficult it is if a Bill has to be passed within a short time. The magnitude of the work will be fully understood only if one takes into consideration the number of bills which Parliament is called upon to pass every year. This also highlights the importance of drafting, a highly skilled technical job, which would facilitate the smooth passage of the Bill without unnecessary discussions on matters of minor importance such as language, sequence of sentences, arrangement of matter, numbering of clauses, punctuation, etc. If a Bill is properly drafted, when it is introduced, its passage to a great extent, becomes easy and smooth. Successful and expeditious law-making involves also the skilful handling of the provisions of a Bill on the floor of the House by those who are in charge of piloting it and the maximum measure of support they can enlist from members in general and particularly from those in opposition.

Financial Procedure

It is the unquestioned right of Parliament under any responsible system of Government not only to ensure that public funds are raised only with its consent but also to exercise complete control over the way in which the nation's revenues are spent by the Government. The framers of the Constitution had kept in view these basic considerations while laying down the principles which would guide the operation of public finance and the procedure that would regulate the financial transactions of the Government. The basic principles underlying the financial provisions of the Constitution are as follows: (1) There shall be no taxation without a law authorising it. If any levy is to be made upon the people, the sanction must be that of law. (2) There shall be no expenditure without the authority of Parliament. Such authority should be embodied in an Act of Parliament and not merely expressed by a Resolution. (3) As an essential safeguard for the sound administration of the nation's finances, Parliament should have unrestricted power to superintend, scrutinise, regulate and determine financial administration. (4) The executive should alone have the initiative in making proposals for taxation and expenditure and no such proposals can be initiated by a private member. (5) The House of the People should have supremacy over the Council of States in all financial matters. (6) All revenues received by the Union Government should form the "Consolidated Fund of India" from which alone the government shall withdraw money for its expenditure and repayment of debts. (7) To meet unforeseen requirements exceeding the authorised expenditure, a reserve fund called the "Contingency Fund of India", should be placed at the disposal of the Government facilitating advances subject to subsequent regularisation. (8) The President shall not withhold his assent from a Money Bill passed by Parliament. In the matter of finance, Parliament is supreme.

On the basis of these principles, the Constitution proceeds to lay down a detailed financial procedure. In laying down such a detailed procedure the framers were influenced by a set of established principles. These are:

(1) Procedures should not obscure fundamental issues.

(2) Procedures should ensure that no bad or irresponsible decisions are taken by the executive.

(3) Procedures should make it possible to consider the budget as a whole and as an integral part of national accounting rather than as a series of unrelated parts.

(4) Procedures should ensure a complete and coordinated circuit between expenditure and resources.

(5) Procedures should leave ample room for long-term economic planning and development, treating annual allocations and sanctions as effective and strong links of such planning and development.

With these principles in view one may examine the mechanics of the financial procedure. Under Article 112, every year "the President shall cause to be laid before both the Houses of Parliament" the annual financial statement, popularly known as the Budget. The person through whom the President acts in this respect is the Finance Minister who is the custodian of the nation's finances. The budget will show the estimated receipts and expenditure for that financial year. According to custom, it is presented on the last day of February in order that Parliament will have sufficient time to discuss the proposals in general and authorise appropriation before the beginning of the new financial year on the first day of April. There will be no discussion of the budget on the day on which it is presented to Parliament; this is to give members time to study the proposals before the discussion of the budget begins.

The expenditure embodied in the budget is divided into two separate parts: the expenditure charged upon the "Consolidated Fund of India" which are "non-votable", and the sums required to meet other expenditure from the Consolidated Fund which are "votable". The following items belong to the charged expenditure:

(a)   the salary and allowances of the President;
(b)   the salaries and allowances of the Presiding Officers of the Houses of Parliament;
(c)   debt charges of the Government of India;
(d)   the salaries and allowances of the judges of the Supreme Court and High Courts, the Comptroller and Auditor-General and pension payable to retired judges of the Federal Court;
(e)   sums required to satisfy any Court decree or award and any other expenditure declared by the Constitution or by Parliament to be so charged.

Although Parliament does not vote on these items as these payments are guaranteed under the Constitution, there is no bar to a discussion on any of them by either of the two Houses. With respect to the second part of expenditure, estimates are to be submitted in the form of demands for grants to the House of the People. The House has the power to assent to, reduce or reject these demands. Every demand for a grant should be made only with the recommendation of the President.

Under the rules of procedure, ordinarily, a separate demand has to be made in respect of the grant proposed for each Ministry and each demand should contain not only a statement of the total grant proposed, but also a detailed estimate under each grant divided into items. The discussion on the budget can be divided into two parts: a general discussion, and a detailed discussion which takes place when every time a separate demand is placed before the House. During the general discussion, the accent is on general problems connected with the nation's finances and the principles involved in the budget proposals. At the end of the discussion the Finance Minister has a right to reply.

It is during the second stage that members get the opportunity to move cut motions to reduce the amount of a demand. Every cut motion to a demand for grants represents disapproval of some aspect or other of the governmental policy or administration involved in the demand. The procedure recognises three different types of cut motions. If the cut motion aims to reduce the demand by one rupee only, the motion will be known as "Disapproval of Policy Cut". The motion in this case represents disapproval of the policy underlying the demand. If the reduction demanded is either in the form of a lump sum of omission or reduction of an item in the demand, the motion which embodies such cut is known as "Economy Cut". Here the object of the motion is economy in Government spending. If the motion seeks to reduce the demand by a cut of Rs. 100, it aims to ventilate a specific grievance which is within the sphere of the responsibility of the Government and such a motion is known as a "Token Cut." The admissibility of these cut motions is regulated by rules laying down conditions. The cut motions provide the maximum opportunity for members to examine every part of the budget and subject it to detailed criticism and offer sugtions for improvement.

Voting on demands by itself does not complete the formalities connected with the provision of funds to the Government. There should be legal sanction for the appropriation of sums from the Consolidated Fund. To facilitate this the procedure provides for two different pieces of financial legislation. One is the Appropriation Act and the other is the Finance Act. The former fixes the amount which can be drawn out of the Consolidated Fund for meeting the expenditure against each grant. The Constitution does not permit any withdrawal in excess of the amount provided in the Act. The latter deals with the legislation which authorises the raising of funds through taxation as embodied in the financial proposals of the year.

Mention has been made earlier of the constitutional prohibition against funds being withdrawn from the Consolidated Fund except under appropriations made by law. But it has been found, from time to time, that the expenditure voted by Parliament for a Department is not enough because of unforeseen or unexpected reasons. If the expenditure is incurred without Parliamentary authorisation, it would be illegal. But if the executive awaits Parliamentary sanction before incurring the expenditure, the Department concerned will be put to great inconvenience. Besides, the expenditure may be urgently required and the inability of the Government to make provision for it may be detrimental to the public interest. To provide for such contingencies, Parliament is authorised under Article 267, to establish a "Contingency Fund of India into which shall be paid, from time to time, such sums as may be determined by law". This Fund is placed at the disposal of the President to enable advances to be made by him for the purpose of meeting unforeseen expenditure pending its authorisation in accordance with the established financial procedure. The idea of the Contingency Fund, as most of the other ideas in the financial field, is taken from England. The Contingency Fund stands at Rs. 150 million now.

Once advances have been made available from the Contingency Fund for meeting the unforeseen and urgent financial needs of a Department in excess of the authorised amount, such advances have to be regularised. As we have seen, the executive cannot spend funds without the specific authority of Parliament. The situation is met through the device of a "supplementary budget". A supplementary budget is one which includes all those sums which the Department has drawn in excess of the annual grant. It is presented during the course of the financial year. The procedure for getting supplementary grants is similar to that prescribed for the annual budget. When the supplementary demands are passed, advances taken from the Contingency Fund are returned to it in order to restore the Fund to its original amount.

A discussion of the financial procedure is not complete without going into the respective roles of two Committees of Parliament whose activities have an important bearing on the financial affairs of the Government. These are the Estimates Committee and the Public Accounts Committee. Mention must also be made of the role of the Comptroller and Auditor-General of India in this connection. These are dealt with separately. Taking into consideration the impact of all these controlling agencies on the financial policies, programmes and activities of the Government, one major conclusion emerges, namely, that the fundamental principles which have been embodied in the financial provisions of the Constitution are substantially realised in practice. The fact that the Government of the day enjoys the support of a Party with an overwhelming majority in Parliament has not made the Parliamentary control of public finances any the less real.

CHAPTER 22

PRIVILEGES AND COMMITTEES

THE PROVISIONS of the Constitution dealing with Parliamentary privileges and immunities bear a special mark of indebtedness to the centuries-old conventions established and maintained in this regard by the mother of Parliaments, the British Parliament. In fact, this is the only section where a direct reference to the House of Commons was originally made in the Constitution.[1] Article 105 deals with the powers, privileges and immunities of the Houses of Parliament, their members and Committees. It guarantees to every member freedom of speech in Parliament and grants immunity from proceedings in any Court of law in respect of anything said or any vote given by him in Parliament or in any of its Committees. A similar immunity is granted in respect of any publication under the authority of either House of Parliament of reports, papers, votes or proceedings.

So far Parliament has not been able to do much with regard to the codification of the powers, privileges and immunities of its members, Committees and the Houses. What has been done is included in the Rules of Procedure. This deals mainly with two questions: Questions of Privilege, and arrest or detention of members. A question of privilege can be raised by any member provided it satisfies the conditions laid down for its admissibility. The matter is then referred to the Committee of Privileges if the House agrees to that and appropriate action is taken by the House on the basis of the recommendations of the Committee.

The *Lok Sabha* made history on August 29, 1961 by reprimanding a journalist at the Bar of the House for publishing words calculated to bring a Member of the House into odium, contempt and ridicule. Administering the reprimand the Speaker said: "This offence of yours was further aggravated by the type of explanation you chose to submit to the Committee of Privileges. In the name of the House, I accordingly reprimand you for committing a gross breach of privilege and contempt of the

[1] That reference was taken away by Section 21 of the Forty-second Amendment of the Constitution (1976).

238

House." The Journalist concerned, the Editor of *Blitz*, a Bombay Weekly, had earlier moved the Supreme Court in a desperate bid to challenge the warrant issued against him summoning him before the Bar of the House on the ground that it was in violation of a fundamental right guaranteed to him by the Constitution. The Supreme Court, however, rejected the petition and reaffirmed its decision in an earlier case[2] of a similar nature when it held that the right to freedom of speech was subject to the right or privilege of the Legislature to prohibit the publication of even a true and faithful report of the proceedings that took place in the House. According to the Court, the real remedy lies only with the Legislature itself by passing a comprehensive law defining and codifying its privileges. Then the citizen will know how far these parliamentary privileges restrict his fundamental right to freedom of speech and expression.

It is true that, under a system of parliamentary government, the privileges of the legislature, its members and committees are an essential guarantee of its efficient working. The concept of parliamentary privileges, however, rests mainly on parliamentary privileges in England. There, these have been evolved for the purpose of maintaining the independence and dignity of the House and its members. In the words of Erskine May, "the distinctive mark of a privilege is its ancillary character. They are enjoyed by individual members because the House cannot perform its functions without unimpeded use of the service of its members, and by each House for the protection of its members and the vindication of its own authority and dignity." By the very origin and nature of these privileges, they do not accrue by reason of any exalted position of the House or its members, but because they are absolutely necessary for the proper and effective discharge of the functions of a legislative body. But the manner in which issues on privilege are raised again and again on the floor of the Houses of Parliament and the State Legislatures gives one the impression that the parliamentarians in India are too sensitive to criticism from outside. This is not a trend meriting encouragement from any quarter. After all, parliaments and their

---

[2] M. S. M. Sharma *vs.* Sri Krishna Sinha, 1959 S.C.J. 925.

members and committees are neither infallible nor embodiments of all wisdom. Being the representatives of the people they must always be prepared to face public criticism and should never consider themselves to be above such criticism.

The Indian Parliament, it should be pointed out, is very different in at least one important respect from the British Parliament. While the latter has sovereign powers at least in theory, the Indian Parliament has only limited powers. Parliamentary supremacy is inconsistent with the written constitution of India which has imposed prohibitions on Parliament to pass certain kinds of legislation.[3] Such a Parliament cannot pretend, under the cover of Article 105(3), to have unlimited powers and privileges.

When a member is arrested or detained on a criminal charge or sentenced to imprisonment by a Court, the authority concerned should immediately inform the Speaker or the Chairman, as the case may be, indicating the reasons for the arrest, detention or imprisonment. Similarly, when a member is released from detention, such fact also should be communicated to the Speaker. The Speaker will inform the House of the contents of such communications as early as possible. No member can be arrested within the premises of Parliament without the permission of the Speaker. Similarly, no legal process, civil or criminal, can be served on members within the precincts of the Houses without obtaining the Speaker's or the Chairman's permission.

Under Article 106, members are entitled to receive such salaries and allowances as may from time to time be determined by law made by Parliament. At present, members draw a salary of Rs. 500 per month and per diem allowance for a sitt ng of the House. On an average, it works out to over Rs. 1,200 per month. In comparison with the emoluments of members of Parliament in other countries, particularly in Europe and America, this amount is low. Nevertheless, in the context of the general standard of living in this country, it is not inconsiderable. One must add to this the privilege of free first class railway travel throughout India all the year round, that is extended to every member by the Indian Railways.

---

[8] These prohib tions are the result of the existence of constitutionally guaranteed Fundamental Rights as well as the division of powers between the Union of India and the constituent States.

Parliamentary Committees

Under a parliamentary system of government, Committees of Parliament are a necessary adjunct of the work of Parliament. They make parliamentary work smooth, efficient and expeditious. They provide a certain expertise to the deliberations of Parliament. They enable Parliament to feel the pulse of the public on proposals of legislation that are introduced for its consideration. They also help to realise better and more constructive co-operation from the opposition for various measures initiated by the Government.

According to the *Rules of Procedure and Conduct of Business in the Lok Sabha,* there are twelve Committees of Parliament. The following is a brief survey of the work of these Committees which should give one a general perspective of the work of Parliament itself.

(1) *The Business Advisory Committee*

This Committee is constituted at the commencement of the House with a view mainly to regulating the time-table of the work of the House and has fifteen members. The Speaker himself is its Chairman.

(2) *The Committee on Private Members' Bills and Resolutions*

This again is a Committee of fifteen whose main function is to examine all private members' Bills from different points of view before recommending them to be placed before the House for its consideration.

(3) *Select Committees on Bills*

The occasion for the appointment of a Select Committee on any Bill arises as and when a motion that the Bill be referred to a Select Committee is made. Members of a Select Committee are appointed by the House. A Select Committee may hear expert evidence and representatives of special interests affected by the measure before them, and submit its report to the House.

(4) *The Committee on Petitions*

The Committee is nominated by the Speaker at the commencement of the House and it has a strength of fifteen members.

16

(5) *The Estimates Committee*

The financial business of Parliament, as we have already seen, is so complex that, constituted as it is, Parliament is unable to devote to it the time and energy required for discharging satisfactorily its responsibilities for financial control. Hence two Committees have been set up to enable Parliament to discharge its functions in this connection more efficiently, viz. the Estimates Committee and the Public Accounts Committee.

The Estimates Committee is charged with the detailed examination of the budget estimates and, therefore, is in a powerful position to influence the activities of the Government not only in the financial field but also in other fields. There are four specific functions allotted to the Committee:

(1) to report what economies, improvements in organisation, efficiency or administrative reform, consistent with the policy underlying the estimates, may be effected;

(2) to suggest alternative policies in order to bring about efficiency and economy in administration;

(3) to examine whether the money is well laid out within the limits of the policy implied in the estimates; and

(4) to suggest the form in which the estimates shall be presented to Parliament.

The Committee has thirty members who are elected in accordance with the system of proportional representation from among the members of the *Lok Sabha* for a period of one year. One special feature of the work of the Committee is that its work is not over with the final passage of the budget even though it is mainly concerned with estimates. It goes on working all the year round, selecting according to its own choice, any department or agency of the Government for the purpose of its scrutiny.

(6) *The Public Accounts Committee*

The Public Accounts Committee is the twin-brother of the Estimates Committee. If the latter is concerned with the examination of estimates, the former is concerned with the manner and results of spending public funds. The Public Accounts Committee is not new to India. As early as 1923, a Public Accounts Committee was set up by the Central Legislative Assembly. Consequently, the Committee today has behind it a set of well-established traditions.

The Committee consists of twenty-two members of whom seven are from the *Rajya Sabha*. The members are elected by the system of proportional representation. No Minister can be a member of the Committee. The term of office of the members is not to exceed one year.

The function of the Committee is the examination of accounts of the Government in all its financial transactions. In this respect it is its duty to scrutinise the appropriation accounts and the report of the Comptroller and Auditor-General of India. The Committee should satisfy itself:

(*a*) that the moneys shown in the accounts as having been disbursed were legally available for, and applicable, to the service or purpose to which they have been applied or charged;

(*b*) that the expenditure conforms to the authority which governs it; and

(*c*) that every reappropriation has been made in accordance with the provisions made in this behalf under rules framed by competent authority. It is also the duty of the Committee to examine the statements of accounts showing the income and expenditure of state corporations, and manufacturing concerns, autonomous and semi-autonomous bodies, together with their balance sheets and profit and loss accounts. If any money has been spent on any service during a financial year in excess of the amount granted by the House for that purpose, the Committee shall examine with reference to the facts of each case the circumstances leading to such an excess and make such recommendation as it deems fit.

Unlike the Estimates Committee, the **Public Accounts Committee** has at its disposal the expert advice of the Comptroller and Auditor-General based upon a thorough study and detailed examination of the Government's accounts.

(7) *The Committee on Privileges*

The Speaker nominates this Committee at the commencement of

the House and it consists of fifteen members. It is concerned with the examination of questions of privilege and the determination of any breach of privilege in the cases which are referred to it.

(8) *The Committee on Subordinate Legislation*

The main function of this Committee is to scrutinise and report to the House whether the powers to make regulations, rules, sub-rules, bye-laws, etc. conferred by the Constitution or delegated by Parliament are being properly exercised within the limits of such delegation. It will have a maximum membership of fifteen who will hold office for a year. The members are nominated by the Speaker. Membership of this Committee is not open to Ministers.

(9) *The Committee on Government Assurances*

It is the function of this Committee to scrutinise the various assurances, promises, undertakings, etc. given by Ministers, from time to time, on the floor of the House and to report on the extent to which such assurances have been implemented.

(10) *The Committee on Absence of Members from the Sittings of the House*

This also is a fifteen-member Committee whose members are nominated by the Speaker for a year. The Committee considers all applications from members for leave of absence from the sittings of the House and will examine every case where a member has been absent for a period of sixty days or more, without permission, from the sittings of the House and will report whether the absence should be condoned or the seat of the member be declared vacant.

(11) *The Rules Committee*

The main function of the Rules Committee is to consider matters of procedure and conduct of business in the House and to recommend any amendments or additions to these rules that may be deemed necessary. The Committee is nominated by the Speaker, has fifteen members, and the Speaker himself is its *ex officio* Chairman.

(12) *The Committee on Public Undertakings*

The *Lok Sabha,* in November 1963, adopted a motion to set up a Committee on Public Undertakings consisting of ten members of the *Lok Sabha* and five of the *Rajya Sabha.* The Committee will examine (*a*) the reports and the accounts of the Public Undertakings, (*b*) the reports, if any, of the Comptroller and Auditor-General on the Public Undertakings, and (*c*) in the context of the autonomy and efficiency of the Public Undertakings whether their affairs are being managed in accordance with sound business principles and prudent commercial practices. It will also examine such functions at present vested in the Public Accounts Committee and the Estimates Committee in relation to Public Undertakings as may be allotted to that Committee by the Speaker from time to time. Matters of major Government policy as distinct from business or commercial functions, matters of day to day administration, and matters for the consideration of which machinery is established by any special statute, will not be examined by the new Committee.

One-fifth of the Committee shall retire every year by rotation and members to retire by rotation every year shall be those who have been longest in office since their last election. The Public Undertakings over which the Committee will have jurisdiction are: the Damodar Valley Corporation, Industrial Finance Corporation, Indian Airlines Corporation, Air-India International, Oil and Natural Gas Commission and all Government Companies.

Although the decision to constitute the Committee was taken in 1963, it came into being only in 1964.

Parliament and the Party System

The essence of Parliamentary democracy is party government. And a party government cannot succeed without an organised party system. To maintain the democratic character of a party government, there should be continuous and responsible criticism both within the legislature and elsewhere. In the absence of such criticism, the government would soon become an autocracy and later, a tyranny. But criticism cannot be effective if it is only sporadic, and it becomes even useless when it is only casual. To make it sustained and effective, it should be organised. Hence the necessity for deliberately organised political parties whose

TABLE 7

RELATIVE STRENGTH OF ALL INDIA PARTIES IN THE HOUSE OF THE PEOPLE

Parties	1952 No. of seats won	1952 Percentage of valid votes polled	1957 No. of seats won	1957 Percentage of valid votes polled	1962 No. of seats won	1962 Percentage of valid votes polled	1967 No. of seats won	1967 Percentage of valid votes polled	1971 No. of seats won	1971 Percentage of valid votes polled	1977 No. of seats won	1977 Percentage of valid votes polled
1. Congress Party	364	45.0	371	47.78	361	44.72	283	40.73	—	—	153	34.54
2. Congress (R)	—	—	—	—	—	—	—	—	350	43.64	—	—
3. Congress (O)	—	—	—	—	—	—	—	—	16	10.56	—	—
4. Janata/CFD	—	—	—	—	—	—	—	—	—	—	299	43.17
5. Jana Sangh	3	3.1	4	5.93	14	6.44	35	9.41	22	7.48	—	—
6. Swatantra	—	—	—	—	18	7.89	44	8.68	3	3.08	—	—
7. Communist Party of India	16	3.3	27	8.92	29	9.96	23	5.19	23	4.89	7	2.82
8. Communist Party of India (Marxist)	—	—	—	—	—	—	19	4.21	25	4.97	22	4.30
9. Socialist (divided into various parties)	21	16.14	19	10.41	18	9.33	36	7.98	5	3.41	—	—
10. Dravida Munnetra Kazhagam	—	—	—	—	7	2.02	25	3.90	23	3.80	1	—
11. Other Parties	44	16.4	34	7.57	30	7.37	20	6.15	30	9.84	51	9.15
12. Independents	41	15.8	39	19.39	20	12.27	35	13.75	13	8.33	7	6.02
Total	489	100.0	494	100.0	497	100.0	520	100.0	515	100.0	540	100.00

business it is to oppose the government, to expose its defects and depose it when the time is ripe.

It is true that the Constitution does not give expression to them except in an oblique manner. The only provision which has anything directly to do with this is Article 75(3) which ensures the collective responsibility of the Council of Ministers to the House of the People. But the spirit that underlies the fundamentals of the Constitution envisages a party system which implies all the above principles. To a great extent, even legal sanction has been given to them, by the Election Commission of India officially recognising political parties in India on an all-India or regional basis for the purposes of conducting elections. The Commission had given recognition of an all-India status to five parties, the Indian National Congress, the Praja Socialist Party, the Communist Party, the Swatantra Party and the All India Jan Sangh. In 1977 by the time the Sixth General Elections took place, the number of recognised all-India parties came down to four because of the emergence of the Janata Party consisting of the Socialist Party, the Jan Sangh, the B.L.D. and the Old Congress. The four all-India parties so recognised were: Indian National Congress, Janata Party, Communist Party of India and Communist Party (Marxist).

CHAPTER 23

THE UNION JUDICIARY—THE SUPREME COURT

Why a Supreme Court

THE ESSENCE of a federal constitution is the division of governmental power between a Central government and State governments and this division is expressed in written words. Since language is apt to be ambiguous, and its meaning may not be taken as the same by all at all times, it is certain that in any federation there will be disputes between the centre and the units about the terms of the division of powers and the respective areas of their authority. All such disputes are to be settled with reference to the Constitution which is the supreme law and which embodies the manner in which powers are divided between the centre and the units. Justice demands, at the same time, that such conflicts should be settled by an independent and impartial authority. A supreme court under a federal constitution is one such and is, therefore, an essential part of a federal system. It is at once the highest interpreter of the Constitution and a tribunal for the final determination of disputes between the Union and its constituent units. This is one of the most important functions of the Supreme Court of India under the federal system established by the Constitution.

The Supreme Court of India, however, is more than a federal supreme court. For, as we have already seen, under Article 32, the Court is made the protector of all the Fundamental Rights embodied in the Constitution and it has to guard these rights jealously against every infringement at the hands of either the Union Government or the State Governments. By declaring the significance and operation of these rights, from time to time, it protects the citizens from unconstitutional laws passed by the legislatures and arbitrary acts done by the administrative authorities.

The Supreme Court is also an all-India supreme appellate court having both criminal and civil jurisdictions. The Constitution invests the Court with extensive powers of reviewing the decisions of the courts below it in criminal as well as civil cases. In the process, it gets an opportunity to interpret not only the Constitution and the laws enacted by Parliament but also the laws passed by the various State Legislatures.

Further, the Supreme Court of India plays a unique role by giving its advice, from time to time, to the President of India on questions of law or fact which are of such a nature and of such public importance that the President refers them to the Court for its consideration and opinion. It is doubtful whether there is any other court of law to which has been assigned so much power under any constitution.

A Single Judicial System

Unlike many countries with federal constitutions, India has a single judicial system. This, however, is not an altogether novel feature that has come in with the present Constitution. It was there, in a limited sense, under the Constitution Act of 1935 with the Federal Court as the highest Court within India in all constitutional matters. But the Federal Court was not the ultimate judicial authority, as appeals could go to the Judicial Committee of the Privy Council in London even from the Federal Court. There are no such limiting factors in the Supreme Court filling the role. The Court stands at the apex of India's judicial hierarchy, with effective power to supervise and control the working of the entire system and to ensure the realisation of the high judicial standards that it might set as an integral part of the democratic system of government sought to be established by the Constitution.

This single hierarchical system of judiciary has brought about not only jurisdictional unity, but also the establishment of a single judicial cadre, as it were, for the whole country. Although there is nothing that prevents a direct appointment to the Supreme Court from the Bar, there has been none so far, and all the appointments to the Supreme Court were made from the High Courts. Similarly, a good many appointments to High Courts are made from among the judges of the lower courts, particularly the District and Sessions judges. Further, there is also a provision for the transfer of judges from one High Court to another in any part of the country. The Indian judiciary, thus, with the Supreme Court at its apex, is a fully integrated system in every sense of the term. The writ of the Supreme Court runs not only all over the country, Central,

State and Local areas, but also within all fields of law, constitutional, civil and criminal.

An Independent Court (Art. 124)

The Supreme Court consisted of the Chief Justice and fifteen other judges in 1978. In 1950, when the Court was inaugurated with the new constitution, it had only eight judges. But a parliamentary enactment in 1960 increased the strength to eleven and a subsequent enactment in 1968, raised it to fourteen. That was the position until 1978 when an amendment further raised the authorised strength of the judges from 14 to 18.

The Constitution envisages an independent Court. The independence of the judges is ensured by the following provisions:

(1) Appointment

Every judge of the Supreme Court is appointed by the President of India after consultation with such of the judges of the Supreme Court and the High Courts of the States as the President may deem necessary for the purpose. But in the appointment of a judge, other than the Chief Justice, consultation of the Chief Justice of India by the President is obligatory.

(2) Qualifications

The elimination of politics in the appointment of judges is further achieved by prescribing high minimum qualifications in the Constitution itself. This is also intended to enhance the competence of those appointed as the judges of the highest court in the land. The qualifications are: the person concerned must be a citizen of India and (a) has been a judge of a High Court at least for five years; or (b) has been for at least ten years an advocate of a High Court; or (c) is in the opinion of the President a distinguished jurist. The inclusion of the last provision which would enable the President to appoint a distinguished jurist on the Supreme Court, even if he did not qualify by a specified number of years of practice at the Bar, was intended to open a wider field of choice. Under this provision, for instance, a distinguished jurist who holds a chair in a University will be qualified for appointment to the Supreme Court.

(3) *Tenure*

Although the Constitution does not provide for life tenure, the existing provision in effect amounts to nearly the same, as judges once appointed, hold office until they complete the age of sixty-five years. A retiring age of sixty-five is by Indian standards, very high, considering the average expectation of life in India and the average fitness of persons for work in old age.

(4) *Prohibition of Practice after Retirement*

A retired judge of the Supreme Court is prohibited from practising law before any Court or authority within the territory of India. But there is no constitutional prohibition against a retired judge being appointed for a specialised form of work by the Government.

(5) *Removal*

A judge of the Supreme Court can be removed from his position only on the ground of proved misbehaviour or incapacity. Parliament is empowered to regulate the procedure for the investigation and proof of such misbehaviour or incapacity. But whatever be the procedure, each House, in order to remove the judge, will have to pass a resolution supported by two-thirds of the members present and voting and a majority of the total membership of the House. Such a resolution will be addressed to the President who will then pass the order of removal of the judge.

(6) *Remuneration*

A very important element that determines the independence of any functionary is the remuneration that he receives as well as its dependence or otherwise on the will of somebody else. With respect of the judges of the Supreme Court, the Constitution has taken good care of this. Unlike many other constitutions which leave the fixation of salary to the legislature, it has prescribed that a salary of Rs. 4,000 per month should be paid to every judge except the Chief Justice who should receive a salary of Rs. 5,000 per month. In addition, each judge is also entitled to a free house and certain other allowances and privileges. Neither the salary, allowances and privileges, nor his rights in respect of leave of absence or pension (to which he is entitled after retirement) can be varied to his disadvantage after his appointment. There is, however, one exception to this almost absolute rule. The salaries of the judges may be reduced by a law of Parliament during a grave financial emergency proclaimed by the President.

(7) *Establishment*

The framers were not content with this alone. They went a step further and authorised the Supreme Court to have its own establishment and to have complete control over it. In the absence of such a provision they thought that the Court's independence may become illusory. If the establishment looks for preferment or for promotion to other quarters, it is likely to sap the independence of the judiciary. Hence all appointments of officers and servants of the Supreme Court are to be made by the Chief Justice or any other judge or officer whom he may direct for the purpose. The conditions of service of such officers and servants also are determined by the Court. Further, all administrative expenses, salaries, etc. connected with these officials and servants as well as the other maintenance charges of the Court's establishment as a whole, are charged on the Consolidated Fund of India.

(8) *Immunities*

Finally, the independence of the Court is further safeguarded by making all the actions and decisions of the judges in their official capacity immune from criticism. This does not mean that no one may subject a decision of the Court or an opinion of a judge to a critical academic analysis. All that is prohibited is the imputation of motives on the part of the judges in arriving at decisions and taking action. Even Parliament may not discuss the conduct of a judge except when a resolution for his removal is before it. In order to maintain the dignity of the Court and to protect it from malicious and tendencious criticism, it has the power of initiating contempt proceedings against any alleged offender and take appropriate action.

As Ambedkar said in the Assembly, it was the intention of the framers to create a judiciary and to give it ample independence so that it could act without fear or favour of the Executive or anybody else. There was no intention, however, to create an *imperium in imperio* which would have created unwanted rivalries between the judiciary and the executive resulting in unexpected conflicts. The last three decades of the work of the Court have vindicated the expectations of the framers of the Constitution.

The Court's Jurisdiction

A survey of constitutions would show that the Supreme Court of India has wider jurisdiction than any other superior court in any part of the world. The jurisdiction of the Court can be divided into three categories, original, appellate and advisory.

Original Jurisdiction (Art. 131)

The Supreme Court has original exclusive jurisdiction in any dispute (*a*) between the Government of India and one or more States; or (*b*) between the Government of India and any State or States on one side and one or more other States on the other; or (*c*) between two or more States. It is also provided that the dispute should involve a question, whether of law or fact, on which depends the existence or the extent of a legal right which the Court is called upon to determine.

Appellate Jurisdiction (Arts. 132 to 136)

The appellate jurisdiction of the Court can be divided into four main parts, constitutional, civil, criminal and special.

Article 132 (1) provides that "an appeal shall lie to the Supreme Court from any judgement, decree or final order of a High Court in the territory of India, whether in a civil, criminal or other proceeding, if the High Court certifies that the case involves a substantial question of law as to the interpretation of the Constitution". Even if the High Court refuses to give such a certificate, the Supreme Court can grant special leave to appeal if the Court is satisfied that the case involves a substantial question of law as to the interpretation of the Constitution. When once such a certificate is given or such leave is granted, any party to the case may raise before the Supreme Court any matter which in its opinion has been wrongly decided by the High Court in that particular case. Thus, in every matter which involves an interpretation of the Constitution, whether it arises under civil, criminal or any other proceeding, the Supreme Court has been made the final authority to expound the meaning and intent of the Constitution. This is what makes the Court the ultimate interpreter and guardian of the Constitution.

The Supreme Court's appellate jurisdiction in civil cases is of a restricted character. According to this, a party to a civil suit is permitted to appeal to the Supreme Court if the High Court certifies that the value of the subject matter of the dispute is not less than Rs. 20,000 or that the case is fit for appeal to the Supreme Court. Further, when once the Court is seized of the appeal, it is open to any party to challenge a decision of the High Court in that case as invalid so far as it dealt with the interpretation of the Constitution. The appellate jurisdiction of the Court in civil cases can be enlarged if Parliament passes a law to that effect.

There are three circumstances under which criminal appeals to the Supreme Court will be permitted: that is, if a High Court

(1) has on appeal reversed an order of acquittal of an accused person and sentenced him to death; or

(2) has withdrawn for trial before itself any case from any court subordinate to its authority and has in such trial convicted the accused person and sentenced him to death; or

(3) certifies that the case is a fit one for appeal to the Supreme Court. Parliament is empowered, in this connection also, to enlarge the Court's jurisdiction. These provisions, according to Ambedkar, "ought to be made, having regard to the enlightened conscience of the modern world and of the Indian people."

One might wonder why the Constitution makes separate sets of provisions dealing with questions of constitutional law and those which do not raise such questions. The reason why this separation is made between the two sets of appeals is to be made clear. Under Article 132, whenever an appeal comes before the Supreme Court and if it involves questions of constitutional law, the minimum number of judges who would sit to hear such a case shall be five, while in other cases of appeal, the matter is left to the Supreme Court to determine the number of judges. According to the practice established by the Court, in constitutional matters, often more than five judges sit to hear the case. But in civil and criminal appeals the Bench will consist of three judges only. As it is, with seventeen judges on the Court, there could be one Constitutional Bench and four Benches for civil or criminal appeal cases at the same time.

Special Appeal

From a jurisdictional point of view Article 136 is of utmost importance. It enacts: "Notwithstanding anything in this Chapter, the Supreme Court may, in its discretion, grant special leave to appeal from any judgement, decree, determination, sentence or order in any cause or matter passed or made by any Court or tribunal in the territory of India". The only exception to this all-embracing power of judicial superintendence is the decisions of any Courts constituted under any law relating to the Armed Forces. Explaining the comprehensive nature of the Article and the plentitude of jurisdiction that it confers on the Supreme Court, Alladi Krishnaswami Aiyar said: "The jurisdiction of the Supreme Court extends over every order in every cause or matter passed by any Court, or tribunal in the territory of India. Secondly, the Supreme Court is free to develop its own rules and conventions in the exercise of its jurisdiction. For example, there is nothing to prevent the Court from interfering even in a criminal case where there is miscarriage of justice, where a Court has misdirected itself or where there is a serious error of law. . . . The Supreme Court is able to develop its own jurisprudence according to its own light, suited to the conditions of the country in such a way that it could do complete justice in every kind of case or matter."

Although the Court's intervention under this jurisdiction is often sought, it has been reluctant to make frequent use of it. "On a careful examination of Article 136 along with the preceding Article," the Court held in one case, "it seems clear that the wide discretionary power with which the Supreme Court is invested under it is to be exercised sparingly and in exceptional cases only, and as far as possible a more or less uniform standard should be adopted in granting special leave in the wide range of matters which can come up before it under this Article." In another case the Court held: "It is not possible to define with any precision the limitations on the exercise of discretionary jurisdiction vested in the Supreme Court by the Constitutional provision made under Article 136. The limitations, whatever they be, are implicit in the nature and character of the power itself. It being an exceptional and overriding power, naturally it has to be exercised sparingly and with caution and only in special and extraordinary situations. Beyond that, it is not possible to fetter the exercise of this power by any set formula or rule. All that can be said is that the Constitution having trusted the wisdom and good sense of the judges of the Supreme Court in this matter, that itself is a sufficient safeguard and guarantee that the power will only be used to advance the principles which govern the exercise of overriding constitutional powers."

The special appellate power has become a handy weapon in the hands of the Court to review the decision of Election, Labour and Industrial Tribunals. In the Calcutta Tramways Company's case the Court said that "wide and undefinable with exactitude as the powers of the Supreme Court are, it is now well settled that generally the necessary prerequisites for the Court's interference to set right decisions arrived at by Tribunals on questions of fact are final. These can be classified under the following categories, namely, (i) where the Tribunal acts in excess of the jurisdiction conferred upon it under the statute or regulation; (ii) where there is an apparent error on the face of the decision, and (iii) where the Tribunal has erroneously applied well accepted principles of jurisdiction. It is only where errors of this nature exist that interference is called for."

The Court, however, held that "it is not the practice of the Supreme Court in special leave cases and in exercise of its over-riding powers to interfere with a matter which vests in the discretion of the High Court except in very exceptional cases." Similarly, the Court held on another occasion that it would normally be slow to interfere, in appeal, with an order passed by virtue of such wide powers as are vested in the Custodian-General under the Administration of the Evacuee Property Act of 1950. Nevertheless, the reach of Article 136 is indeed formidable. It has become a convenient instrument at the disposal of the Court to check arbitrary acts and unjust decisions of the ever-increasing number of administrative tribunals which the Union and the States are setting up almost daily in the process of realising the objectives of a socialist pattern of society.

Review

As a measure of abundant caution the framers have invested the Court with the power of reviewing its own decisions and orders. It has been said that while a lower Court is concerned with facts and a High Court with error (of judgement of the Lower Court), a Supreme Court is concerned with wisdom. But even a Supreme Court may go wrong and there must be a provision by which such wrongs can be rectified. This has been ensured under Article 137 which empowers the Court to review its own judgements or orders. So far, there have been very few occasions for the Court to exercise its powers under this provision.

Enlargement of Jurisdiction

Parliament is empowered to enlarge the jurisdiction of the Supreme Court with respect to any matter included in the Union List of legislative powers. The Government of India and the Government of any State may enter into an agreement under which any matter may be placed under the jurisdiction of the Supreme Court provided Parliament passes a law for the purpose. Further, Parliament may by law confer on the Supreme Court power to issue directions, orders or writs for purposes even other than the enforcement of Fundamental Rights already provided for under Article 32 of the Constitution. Parliament may also confer upon the Supreme Court such supplemental powers not inconsistent with any of the provisions of the Constitution as to enable the Court to exercise its jurisdiction more effectively.

The Court as an Adviser (Art. 143)

The role of the judiciary as adviser to the executive or legislative department of the government was unknown to India until the inauguration of the Government of India Act of 1935. The enunciation of this principle as embodied in section 213 of the Act evinces an attempt to follow the old English practice of the Executive consulting the Judiciary. With the establishment of the Federal Court of India in 1937 and the number of important

17

advisory opinions rendered by the Court since then, judicial circles in India were by and large convinced of the usefulness of conferring a jurisdiction of this nature on the highest Court of the land. There was, therefore, hardly any criticism in the Constituent Assembly on Article 143 of the Constitution which provides for the advisory role of the Supreme Court.

Article 143 (1) enacts: "If at any time it appears to the President that a question of law or fact has arisen or is likely to arise, which is of such a nature and of such public importance that it is expedient to obtain the opinion of the Supreme Court upon it, he may refer the question to that Court for consultation, and the Court may, after such hearing as it thinks fit, report to the President its opinion thereon." The President can, thus, refer to the Court either a question of law or a question of fact provided that it is of public importance. There is, however, no constitutional compulsion for the Court to give its advice. Further, it is up to the Court to decide as to what type of hearing it will adopt for the purpose. In this respect, the Court has adopted the same procedure as in the case of a regular dispute that comes before it. The hearing is in the open Court; interested parties are heard in the usual manner, and the opinion of the Court is announced in the open Court. Judges are allowed to divide themselves and give their opinions jointly or severally, concurring or dissenting.

Under section (2) of Article 143, the President is empowered to refer to the Supreme Court for its opinion disputes arising out of any treaty, agreement, etc. which had been entered into or executed before the commencement of the Constitution. In such cases, it is obligatory for the Court, under the Constitution, to give its opinion to the President. The treaties, agreements, etc. referred to here, are those which the Government of India have entered into with the former Princely States and their Rulers between 1947 and 1950 during which period the territorial integration of the Indian Union was accomplished.

There have been only seven occasions during the last three decades when the President referred questions to the Supreme Court for its opinion. The first of these was in 1951, and dealt with the scope of delegation of legislative power in India. The Court was asked to determine the validity or otherwise of certain provisions of three enactments, the Delhi Laws Act, 1912, the

Ajmer-Merwara (Extension of Laws) Act, 1947 and the Part C States (Laws) Act, 1950. The Court was unable to give a unanimous opinion in answer to the specific questions referred to it. Yet the different opinions expressed by the judges who heard the case are hailed as "momentous" on the subject of delegation of legislative power.

The second reference, by the peculiar nature of its subject matter, is almost unprecedented in the annals of advisory jurisdiction. It dealt with a Bill passed by the Legislature of the State of Kerala, in 1957, which sought to reorganise the educational system, at the primary and secondary stages in that State. As the Bill contained certain provisions which authorised the State Government to take over schools managed by private agencies and, as such, came within the scope of the property right provisions of the Constitution, Presidential assent became necessary for its validity. Since there were serious and acrimonious controversies within the State about the validity of several provisions of the Bill in the light of some of the Fundamental Rights under the Constitution, and representations were made to the President not to give his assent to such an "unconstitutional piece of legislation," the President decided to send the Bill for the opinion of the Court. Here again, the opinion of the Court has become one of the most important ever given by the Court, interpreting the scope of the constitutional guarantees ensuring the cultural and educational rights of minorities.

The third reference relates to the question of ceding certain territories of the Indian Union to a foreign State, namely, Pakistan. The question arose out of an agreement between the Prime Ministers of India and Pakistan in 1958, by which certain territories were to be exchanged between the two countries. Such an agreement involving transfer of Indian territory was attacked as unconstitutional both in Parliament and outside. The matter was hence referred to the Supreme Court for its opinion and the Court declared that for a valid transfer of Indian territory to a foreign State a constitutional amendment was absolutely necessary.

The three opinions[1] of the Court are enough to prove the

[1] In 1964 the President referred to the Supreme Court the conflict of jurisdiction that arose between the Legislative Assembly and the High Court of the State of Uttar Pradesh regarding legislative privileges. In

beneficent results of its advisory jurisdiction.

A Court of Record (Art. 129)

Article 129 makes the Supreme Court a Court of Record. The significance of a court of record is twofold: First, the records of such a Court are admitted to be of evidentiary value and are not questioned when they are produced before any Court. Secondly, once a Court is made a Court of Record by statute, its power to punish for contempt necessarily follows from that position. In spite of this, the Constitution has specifically provided for the power of the Supreme Court to punish for contempt of itself.

Court Rules (Art. 145)

The Supreme Court is authorised, with the approval of the President and subject to any law made by Parliament, to make rules for regulating the practice and procedure of the Court.

The Court's Judicial Supremacy

We have already seen how the Supreme Court is the ultimate interpreter of the Constitution and, as such, its guardian. The authority of the Court is further enhanced by the provision that "the law declared by the Supreme Court shall be binding on all Courts within the territory of India" (Art. 141). Further, in the exercise of its jurisdiction, the Court is authorised to pass appropriate decrees or orders in the interests of complete justice in any case before it. Such decrees and orders are enforceable throughout the territory of India in such manner as may be prescribed by the law of Parliament. The Supreme Court has also the power to secure the attendance before it of any person within the territory of India or to order the discovery and production of any documents, or the investigation or punishment of any contempt of itself (Art. 142).

An enumeration of the various powers of the Supreme Court will show how impressive and formidable they are. To recount the most important of them: The Court is the ultimate interpre-

---

1978 the President sought the Court's advice on the Constitutional validity of setting up special courts to try emergency offences.

ter of the Constitution. As the final interpretational authority of the Constitution, its power embraces not only the interpretation of the Constitution but also that of the laws of the Union, the States and local authorities. Under its original jurisdiction, it finally settles all disputes between the States and the Union or those between the States themselves. Its appellate jurisdiction embraces not only constitutional but also civil and criminal matters. And through the exercise of its power to grant special leave to appeal, it is competent to review any decision by any Court or Tribunal in the country. It is also empowered under certain conditions to give advice to the President. The law declared by the Supreme Court is binding on every Court in India. Further, it has the power of superintendence and control over every High Court in India. Its orders are enforceable throughout the country and it can order any one to appear before it or call for any document. Its decisions can invalidate the laws made by even the highest legislative authority in the land—the Parliament of India. Above all, the Court is the protector of the Fundamental Rights guaranteed under the Constitution. In the exercise of this power it can declare Union or State laws invalid or issue writs or orders to any administrative authority in any part of India with a view to preventing the infringement of any Fundamental Right guaranteed under the Constitution. The combination of such wide and varied powers in the Supreme Court makes it not only the supreme authority in the judicial field but also the guardian of the Constitution and the laws of the land.

GOVERNMENT MACHINERY IN THE STATES

PART V

GOVERNMENT MACHINERY IN THE
STATES

CHAPTER 24

THE STATE EXECUTIVE: THE GOVERNOR

THE MACHINERY of government in the States is organised on the same pattern as that of the Union Government. Hence, in the light of our discussion on the machinery of the Union Government, the task of analysing the organisation and working of the State Government becomes comparatively easy. As in the Union, the government in the States also is organised on the parliamentary model. The Head of the State is called the Governor who is the constitutional head of the State as the President is for the whole of India. The Chief of the State Government is called the Chief Minister who is the counterpart in the State, of the Prime Minister of India. There is a Council of Ministers for each of the States as in the Union. The organisation of the State Legislature is also more or less on the model of the Indian Parliament. In the judicial field, the High Courts, for all practical purposes, occupies the same position within the States as the Supreme Court does for the whole of India. Thus, the State Government is a true copy of the Union Government within the jurisdiction of each State; this helps the States to draw examples and inspiration from the working of the Union Government in almost every field of activity.

The executive power of the State is vested in a Governor who is appointed by the President and who holds office during the pleasure of the President. The vesting of the entire executive power of the State in the Governor shows that he occupies the same constitutional position within the State as the President does with respect to the Government of India. Normally, the Governor holds office for a period of five years from the date on which he enters upon his office.

The qualifications for appointment as a Governor are simple and few. He should be a citizen of India and must have completed the age of thirty-five years. The Governor cannot be a member of either House of Parliament or of a State Legislature. Nor can he hold any other office of profit. He is entitled to a free official residence, a regular monthly salary and other allowances. At present, his salary is fixed at Rs. 5,500 per month. His salary and allowances cannot be reduced during his term of office. These are charged on the Consolidated Fund of the State and, as such, are non-votable. Before entering upon his office, the Governor has to make and subscribe, in the presence of the Chief Justice of the High Court of the State, an oath or affirmation to preserve, protect and defend the Constitution.

Why the Governor is Appointed and not Elected

In the beginning, the framers of the Constitution had decided upon an elected Governor for each of the States. This decision was in conformity with their idea of giving each State the maximum autonomy as units of a federation. The position of the State Governor in the United States must have been the greatest influence upon them in this connection. However, within two years, they decided to abandon this idea in favour of an appointed Governor. What made them to do so deserves some consideration.

(1) In a Parliamentary system of Government a popularly elected Governor does not fit well. If the Governor is elected directly by the people, he becomes a direct representative of the people and may very well exercise his powers not as the constitutional head of the State, but as its real head. Such a position is very likely to create a rivalry between the Governor and the Council of Ministers whose members also are directly elected by the people. Since the American States have a Presidential system of Government just as in the case of the Federal Government in the United States, they do not face a problem of rivalry between the Governor and his Cabinet.

(2) Instead of the Governor being elected directly by the people, if he is elected by the State Legislature, there seems to be not much chance of a rivalry between him and the Ministry. This is because the Ministry is responsible to the same legislature which has elected the Governor. But a serious defect of such an arrangement seems to be the danger of the Governor becoming a pawn in the hands of a political party or parties that secure his election. Since he is not elected to the office on a permanent basis, the temptation for him to play into the hands of a legisla-

tive majority for the sake of re-election is, indeed, irresistible.

(3)   Either a directly elected or an indirectly elected Governor is unlikely to fit into a highly centralised federal system of government.   For, the Governor in either case is a representative of the State who receives his authority from the people of the State. In case of a conflict between the State and the Union, such a Governor may not very likely prove an obedient servant or a convenient instrument of the Union Government.   On the other hand, the Governor may create difficulties in the path of the Union's authority extending in any form to the State's sphere. This is not something in harmony with the idea of emergency powers under which the Union becomes all-powerful and the federal system ceases to function.

The original idea of the framers to have a *weak* Union and *strong* States had yielded place to one of a *strong* Union and *weak* States.   A number of causes contributed for this major change in the basic structure of the Constitution.   Among these were the partition of the country, the various problems created by the partition, the food crisis, the urge for economic and social planning for the country as a whole, the upsurge of provincialism and the fear of possible instability of State Ministries.   It was thought that both for the preservation of the newly won independence and the planned development of the country, central direction was essential.   For this purpose, an elected Governor was not desirable.   The Governor should be one who could be commanded by the President in times of emergency for translating the will of the Union into action within the State.

(4)   It was thought that in the wake of a newly established self-government, the emergence of rival groups and factions was inevitable within the State Legislature and the State as a whole. Under such conditions, a Governor who was a resident of the State might become an interested party rather than an impartial and independent mediator or conciliator of the rival factions. When the Governor is the President's nominee there is very little possibility for such a danger.

(5)   Even if the Governor is appointed by the President, so long as the State politics is of a stable character, so long as the Ministry has a solid backing within the legislature, he is bound to function as a constitutional head of the State just as the

President himself. The change in his role is envisaged only under exceptional circumstances. Hence, this is a provision that arose out of abundant caution and the Constitution-makers have been fully justified by events in some of the States during the last few years.

The Canadian Constitution which has a strong Centre seems to have particularly influenced the Constituent Assembly in this connection. There, the Governor-General appoints all the Governors who hold office during his pleasure. But this provision as such has not affected the smooth working of the Canadian federation. On the contrary, it has on several occasions proved beneficial.

As Alladi Krishnaswami Aiyar said in the Constituent Assembly: "On the whole, in the interests of harmony, in the interests of a good working, in the interests of sounder relations between the Provincial Cabinet and the Governor, it will be much better if we accept the Canadian model."

Thus, the Constitution vests complete power in the President for the selection and appointment of the Governor. This means in effect that he is a nominee of the Central Government. But a healthy convention has grown up during the past years which makes the Governor not merely a nominee of the Central Government but also one who is agreeable to the State concerned. Such a result is obtained by the Central Government consulting the State Cabinet prior to the appointment of a new Governor. This enables the selection of an agreed candidate who is capable of discharging his responsibilities as the head of the State and "a sagacious counsellor and adviser to the Ministry, one who can throw oil on the troubled waters" of the State politics. Thus, the present method of selection has removed the evils which would have otherwise resulted from any of the alternative methods of selection originally contemplated by the Constituent Assembly.

Another convention has also been fairly well established and this too has contributed to making the position of the Governor one above party and group politics within the State. According to this, the person selected as the Governor of a State is normally an outsider, a resident of another State, one who has had no political entanglements within the State. This has, on the whole, proved to be of great advantage. Not only does this keep the

Governor out of the local politics, but it also enables him to look at the problems of the State and the problems of Union-State relationship with detachment and objectivity.

Powers and Functions of the Governor

The executive power of the State is vested in the Governor who is empowered to exercise it either directly or through officers subordinate to him. And the executive power of the State extends to all matters on which the State Legislature has the power to make laws. In the discharge of his responsibilities as the Head of the State, the Governor exercises functions similar to those of the President as the Head of the Union. He appoints the Chief Minister and other members of the Council of Ministers who hold office during his pleasure. He allocates the business of the Government among the Ministers and makes rules for the more convenient transaction of such business. All executive actions of the Government are taken in his name. He appoints the Advocate-General and other officers of the State. In the States of Bihar, Madhya Pradesh and Orissa, it is the special responsibility of the Governor to see that a Minister is placed in charge of tribal welfare. In Assam, the Governor is given certain special powers with respect to the administration of the tribal areas as povided in the Sixth Schedule of the Constitution.

Like the President's power of pardon, the Governor too is empowered to grant pardons. This applies to all persons convicted of any offence against any law relating to a matter to which the executive power of the State extends.

In the legislative field, the Governor has considerable powers. He is an integral part of the State Legislature. He convenes the State Legislature, addresses it in person or sends messages to it, and can prorogue or dissolve it. During every financial year, he causes the budget to be laid before the House. Demands for grants in the Legislature can be made only on his recommendation. Every Bill that is passed by the State Legislature has to be presented to the Governor for his assent. The Governor has three alternatives before him with respect to such a Bill. He may give his assent to it, in which case it becomes law. Or, he may return it to the Legislature with a message suggesting alterations or modifications. The

Governor has, however, no power to return a Money Bill. Or again, he may reserve the Bill for the assent of the President if, in his opinion, it contains provisions which might endanger the position envisaged for the High Court under the Constitution.

The Governor has also the special legislative power of promulgating Ordinances during the recess of the State Legislature, if he is satisfied that there exist circumstances which make it necessary for him to take immediate action. But with respect to three matters, the Governor is prohibited from promulgating Ordinances without prior instructions from the President. These are: (1) if the Ordinance contains provisions which, if embodied in a Bill, would require the previous sanction of the President for introduction in the State Legislature; or (2) if the Governor would have deemed it necessary to reserve a Bill containing the same provisions for the consideration of the President; or (3) if an Act of the State Legislature containing the same provisions would be invalid without the assent of the President.

Every Ordinance promulgated by the Governor has the same force and effect as an Act of the State Legislature. But every such Ordinance should be laid before the State Legislature when it reassembles and if the Ordinance is not upheld by the Legislature, then it becomes invalid. The Governor is empowered to withdraw the Ordinance any time he likes. The Ordinance will be invalid if it has provisions which would not be valid if enacted in an Act of the State Legislature to which the Governor gives his assent.

During a period of emergency, the Governor comes into his own as the real head of the executive in the State. With the proclamation of an emergency by the President, the entire State administration comes directly under the control of the Union. Being the "man on the spot" and the "agent" of the President in the State, the Governor during the period of emergency, takes over the reins of administration directly into his own hands and runs the State with the aid of the civil service.

CHAPTER 25

THE GOVERNOR AND THE COUNCIL OF MINISTERS

IN THE exercise of all his functions, except when he is expressly required to act in his discretion, the Governor is aided and advised by a Council of Ministers headed by a Chief Minister. But if there is a conflict of opinion between the Governor and the Ministry as to whether or not a particular matter falls within the scope of the Governor's discretionary power, the decision of the Governor in his discretion shall be final. Further, the validity of anything done by the Governor cannot be called in question on the ground that he ought or ought not to have acted in his discretion. Although the Governor has to act on the advice of the Ministers, the question whether any, and if so what, advice was tendered by the Ministers to the Governor cannot be enquired into in any Court.

The Governor appoints the Chief Minister and on the advice of the Chief Minister he appoints the other Ministers. The Ministers hold office during the pleasure of the Governor. The Ministers are collectively responsible to the Legislative Assembly of the State just as the Central Ministers are responsible to the *Lok Sabha.* The Governor administers the oath of office to each Minister before he enters upon his office. The Governor can appoint as Minister a person who is not a member of the State Legislature at the time of the appointment. But such a Minister should become a member of the Legislature within six months after entering upon his office.

We have already noticed that all executive action of the State Government is taken in the name of the Governor. In this connection the Governor is authorised to make rules for the more convenient transaction of the business of the State Government. He is also empowered to allocate among the Ministers the business of the Government except where he is expected to act in his discretion. It is the duty of the Chief Minister as the head of the Council of Ministers to communicate to the Governor all decisions of the Council relating to the administration of the affairs of the State and proposals for legislation. He has also to furnish any information which the Governor calls for and which is connected with any administrative or legislative matter of the State. Again, it is the duty of the Chief Minister to place before the Council, if the Governor so requires, any matter on which a decision has been taken by a Minister but which has not been considered by the Council.

These provisions of the Constitution vest in the Governor a fairly long list of powers which, if taken on their face value, will add up to formidable proportions. Yet, as we have already seen from statements made in the Constituent Assembly, the Governor normally is only the constitutional head of the State. This means that although he is the "Chief Executive", in the exercise of his functions, the real power is in the hands of the Council of Ministers. This was pointed out again and again by authoritative spokesmen in the Constituent Assembly.

Interpreting the scope of the provision that "the Ministers shall hold office during the pleasure of the Governor", Ambedkar said: "I have no doubt that it is the intention of this Constitution that the Ministry shall hold office during such time as it holds the confidence of the majority. It is on this principle that the Constitution will work. The reason why we have not so expressly stated it is because it has not been stated in that fashion or in those terms in any of the Constitutions which lay down a parliamentary system of Government. 'During pleasure' is always understood to mean that the 'pleasure' shall not continue notwithstanding the fact that the Ministry has lost the confidence of the majority it is presumed that the Governor will exercise his 'pleasure' in dismissing the Ministry and, therefore, it is unnecessary to differ from what I may say the stereotyped phraseology which is used in all responsible governments."

It is difficult to think of a Governor under a fully responsible system of government established on the broadest possible popular basis, to behave in an authoritarian manner. When a Cabinet composed of popular Ministers, collectively responsible to the Legislature, is to aid and advise the Governor in the discharge of his functions, occasions are almost non-existent for him to overrule them or act in a manner contrary to their advice. But does this mean that he is a mere figure-head, "a rubber-stamp of his Cabinet or a post-office between his Cabinet and the President or between his Cabinet and the official gazette?" A careful reading of the constitutional provisions and an appreciation of them in the perspective of the totality of the constitutional scheme, will show that the Governor is neither a figure-head nor a rubber-stamp but a functionary designed to play a vital role in the administration of the affairs of the State.

The occasions which will give such an opportunity to the Governor to act in his discretion seem to be the following: (1) the selection of a Chief Minister prior to the formation of a Council of Ministers; (2) dismissal of a Ministry; (3) dissolution of the Legislative Assembly; (4) asking information from the Chief Minister relating to legislative and administrative matters; (5) asking the Chief Minister to submit for the consideration of the Council of Ministers any matter on which a decision has been taken by a Minister but which has not been considered by the Council; (6) refusing to give assent to a Bill passed by the Legislature and sending it back for reconsideration; (7) reserving a Bill passed by the State Legislature for the assent of the President; (8) seeking instructions from the President before promulgating an ordinance dealing with certain matters; (9) advising the President for the proclamation of an emergency; and (10) in the case of the Governor of Assam, certain administrative matters connected with the tribal areas and settling disputes between the Government of Assam and the District Council (of an autonomous District) with respect to mining royalties.

It should be pointed out however that the Governor's discretionary powers cannot in reality be absolute. For, absolute discretion is an element of autocracy. The Governor can under no circumstances be an autocrat, so long as he functions within the framework of a democratic Constitution. What, then is the check on his discretionary power? Neither the Ministry nor the State Legislature can control the Governor in this respect; but the President can. This means that the Governor is not a free agent in the exercise of his discretion. If he misuses it either as a result of personal ambitions or as a partisan in the currents and cross-currents of State politics, the President can always check him and if necessary he may even dismiss him. Thus, in the final analysis, the Governor is not a free agent, either during normal times or abnormal times. For, in the discharge of his functions,

18

normally he is aided and advised by the Council of Ministers. So long as the Council has the confidence of the State Legislature, the Governor will not be able to substitute his discretion for the advice of the Council. If he attempts to do that, it will lead to political complication which will ultimately lead to his dismissal. On the contrary, under abnormal conditions such as an emergency caused by war, internal rebellion or breakdown of the constitutional machinery in the State, he will be acting as an agent of the President and not as the absolute master of the situation himself. No doubt, during such times his powers are more real than during normal times when his powers are practically nominal.

All things taken together, the emphasis on the Governor's office seems to be on his role as an adviser. On the one hand, he is a non-partisan adviser to the Ministry. By virtue of his position as the Head of the State he has a right to be consulted, the right to encourage and the right to warn. He is a detached spectator, from a position of vantage and authority, of what is going on in the State. Placed in that position, he maintains the dignity, the stability and the collective responsibility of the State Government. On the other, he is the agent of the President, his adviser on the affairs of the State and the "representative" of the Union in the State. He is the link that fastens the federal-state chain, the channel which regulates the Union-State relationship. Thus, he is an essential part of the constitutional machinery, fulfilling an essential purpose and rendering an essential service. In the words of one who was privileged to know the position from inside: "A Governor can do a great deal of good if he is a good Governor and he can do a great deal of mischief, if he is a bad Governor, in spite of the very little power given to him under the Constitution we are framing."

The Advocate-General for the State

Like the Attorney-General who is the legal adviser to the Union Government, the Constitution provides for a legal adviser to the State Government known as the Advocate-General for the State. He is appointed by the Governor and holds office during his pleasure. To be appointed as Advocate-General, a person should have the same qualifications as would make him eligible for appointment as a judge of the High Court. The Advocate-General will receive such remuneration as the Governor may determine.

It is the duty of the Advocate-General to give advice to the State Government on legal matters referred to him as well as to perform certain other duties of a legal character which are assigned to him from time to time. In the discharge of these duties he is entitled to appear before any court of law within the State or address the State Legislature as and when required.

CHAPTER 26

THE STATE LEGISLATURE

THE CONSTITUTION provides for a Legislature for every State in
the Union. But it does not adhere to the principle of bicameralism in the case of every State Legislature. There are ten States,
namely, Andhra Pradesh, Bihar, Jammu and Kashmir, Maharashtra, Madhya Pradesh, Tamil Nadu, Karnataka, Punjab, Uttar
Pradesh and West Bengal, each of which has two Houses in the
Legislature, while the remaining States have unicameral legislatures. Where there are two Houses of the Legislature, one is
known as the Legislative Assembly and the other the Legislative
Council. Where there is only one House, it is known as the
Legislative Assembly. The Governor of the State is an integral
part of the Legislature.

The State Legislative Assembly is modelled on the House of
the People while the Legislative Council has a resemblance to the
Council of States. Although the Constitution provides for bica-
meral Legislatures for certain States and unicameral ones for
others, the question of the organisation of State Legislatures in a
single House or two Houses is still left an open one. For, Article 169 provides a special procedure for the creation and abolition
of Legislative Councils in the future. According to this, Parliament is empowered to create a Legislative Council in a State having no such Council or abolish the Council where it exists, provided the Legislative Assembly of the State passes a Resolution
to that effect supported by not less than a majority of the total
membership of the House and a majority of not less than two-
thirds of those who sit and vote. Any law passed by Parliament in
this regard should contain the necessary amendment to the provisions of the Constitution which are affected by such law. But these
amendments will not be considered as regular amendments to the
Constitution for which a special procedure is prescribed.

The Legislative Assembly

Composition

The Assembly is composed of members chosen by direct election. The only exception to this rule is the representation of the Anglo-Indian community. If no member of that community secures election to the Assembly, the Governor is empowered to nominate one or more members on behalf of it as members of the Assembly. The Constitution has fixed a maximum number of 500 members for any State Assembly and a minimum of 60 members. For purposes of election, the State is divided into as many territorial constituencies as there are seats in the Assembly. As far as possible, the ratio between the population of each constituency and the number of seats allotted to it will be the same throughout the State. At the end of each decennial census, the constituencies will be recast to make the necessary adjustments to meet the variations in population. At present, the number of voters in each constituency is about 75,000. The number of members in each State Legislative Assembly may be seen from table 8 on p. 278 which contains the figures both before and after the reorganisation of States in 1956.

The Legislative Council

Composition

Several members in the Constituent Assembly were opposed to the idea of constituting an Upper House for the States. They thought that an additional House to the Legislative Assembly in the States was superfluous. Some of them even doubted the financial ability of several States to maintain this "costly ornamental luxury". These criticisms were mainly responsible for the Assembly allowing the members from different States to decide the question themselves, and leaving the future of the Councils in a fluid state in the Constitution itself. The basis of the composition of the Council is as follows:

(1) The total number of members in the Legislative Council should not exceed one-third of the total number of members in the Legislative Assembly. But in any case, it should not be less than forty.

(2) There are five different categories of representation to the Council. These are:

(a) One-third of the total membership to be elected by electo-

TABLE 8

LEGISLATIVE ASSEMBLY

Name of the State	Total Members		On the basis of 1971 census	Nominated
	Before Re-organisation	After re-organisation (1957)		
1. Anchra Pradesh	196	302	294	1
2. Assam	105	105	126	—
3. Bihar	330	318	324	1
4. Gujarat	—	133	182	—
5. Haryana	—	81	90	—
6. Himachal Pradesh	—	60	68	—
7. Jammu & Kashmir	75	75	76	—
8. Karnataka	105	209	224	1
9. Kerala	109	133	140	1
10. Machya Pradesh	232	289	320	1
11. Maharashtra	—	264	288	1
12. Maripur	—	60	60	—
13. Meghalaya	—	60	60	—
14. Nagaland	—	60	60	—
15. Orissa	140	140	147	—
16. Punjab	126	154	117	—
17. Rajasthan	160	176	200	—
18. Sikkim	—	—	30	—
19. Tamil Nadu	234	205	234	—
20. Tripura	—	60	60	—
21. Uttar Pradesh	431	431	425	1
22. West Bengal	238	258	294	4

rates consisting of members of self-governing local bodies like Municipalities, District Boards, etc. in the States.

(b) One-third to be elected by the members of the Legislative Assembly of the State.

(c) One-twelfth to be elected by electorates consisting of University graduates (of at least three years' standing) or others recognised as possessing equivalent qualification and who are residing in the State.

(d) One-twelfth to be elected by electorates consisting of secondary school teachers or those in higher educational institutions with at least three years' experience in teaching.

(e) The remainder to be nominated by the Governor on the

basis of their special knowledge or practical experience in literature, science, art, the co-operative movement or social service.

(3) The election of the first four categories is to be held in accordance with the system of proportional representation by means of the single transferable vote.

(4) Voting shall be by secret ballot.

(5) Parliament is empowered to make any change with regard to the nature of representation detailed above.

These provisions, it must be said, are not the result of sufficient thinking on the question. As it stands at present, there is a combination of direct election, indirect election and nomination which make the Council a hotchpotch of representation. The right of franchise given to teachers and members of local government bodies indicates that the emphasis is primarily on functional representation. But, from that point of view, the representation is too narrow. There are many professions and interests in addition to these whose representation in the Council is desirable and likely to prove of great benefit. Too much weight has been given to the members of the Assembly by providing for one-third of the Council membership to be elected by them. The percentage of seats reserved for nomination, on the other hand, seems to be too small. Men of merit from the fields of art, science, literature and social service should have formed a larger number among the members of the Council in order to make it a body of meritorious elders who can effectively help in the work of legislation, supervise or watch over the administration with the wisdom born of their maturity and experience.

Table 9 on p. 281 shows the membership of the Legislative Councils in different States with a detailed statement of the constituencies from which they are elected.

The normal life of the Assembly is six years;[1] but it may be dissolved earlier by the Governor. In case of an emergency, its life may be extended by a law of Parliament, one year at a time, but in any case not beyond six months after the Proclamation of Emergency has ceased to operate. The Council, on the other hand,

---

[1] Originally it was five years. But the Forty-second Amendment has made it six years.

is a permanent body which renews one-third of its membership after every two years. In this respect, it follows the pattern of the Council of States.

There is hardly any special qualification fixed for election to the State Legislature except one of age. As in the case of a member of the House of the People, a member of the Assembly should have completed the minimum age of twenty-five years at the time of election. In the case of a member of the Council the minimum age prescribed is thirty years.

The Assembly has two elected officers, the Speaker and the Deputy Speaker, to conduct its business. The position of these two officers in the conduct of the business of the House, and their powers and functions in the Assembly, are respectively the same as those of the Speaker and the Deputy Speaker of the House of the People. They may be removed from office by a resolution of the House supported by at least a majority of all the existing members of the House. The Council has a Chairman and a Vice-Chairman both elected by the Council, and they have the same powers and functions as their counterparts in the Assembly. They can also be removed from office by a resolution of the Council supported by a majority of the existing members in the Council at the time of passing such resolution. The Constitution provides for each House of the State Legislature a separate secretarial staff whose members are independent of the Executive in matters of recruitment and conditions of service.

Conduct of Business

There is hardly anything special to be pointed out in this context which is different from that of the two Houses of Parliament. Most of the articles in this part of the Constitution are a reproduction, almost verbatim, of those which deal with corresponding provisions regarding the two Houses of Parliament. Ambedkar acknowledged this in the Constituent Assembly and pointed out that that was one of the reasons why there were very few amendments to the various articles in that part of the Constitution. In view of the detailed discussion on Parliamentary procedure given in an earlier chapter, it is not considered necessary to go into any details regarding the procedure in the State Legislatures. A brief resume of the same is given below.

TABLE 9

LEGISLATIVE COUNCIL

Name of the State	Total number of members	Elected by the Legislative Assembly	Elected by Local Authorities	Elected by Graduates	Elected by Teachers	Nominated
1. Andhra Pradesh	90	31	31	8	8	12
2. Bihar	72	25	23	6	6	12
3. Jammu & Kashmir	36	21	7	Nil	2	6
4. Karnataka	63	21	21	6	6	9
5. Madhya Pradesh	90	31	31	8	8	12
6. Maharashtra	78	31	21	7	7	12
7. Punjab	42	18	10	3	3	8
8. Tamil Nadu	50	16	16	6	4	8
9. Uttar Pradesh	72	24	24	6	6	12
10. West Bengal	51	17	17	4	4	9

The State Legislature must meet at least twice a year and the interval between any two sessions should not be more than six months. Usually, a new session begins with an opening address by the Governor which outlines the policy of the State Government. The address is then subjected to a debate and finally voted upon in the form of a resolution expressing thanks to the Governor. It is during this debate that Opposition Parties get the best opportunity to criticise in general the policies and programme of the Government.

Every bill, except Money Bills, may be introduced in either House of the Legislature. The Bill is finally passed with its third reading. Then it goes to the Governor for his assent. But the Governor may send it back for reconsideration. When it is passed again by the Legislature, the Governor cannot withhold his assent. But he may reserve it for the consideration of the President, who may ask the Governor to place it before the Legislature for reconsideration. When it is passed again, with or without amendment, it goes to the President for his consideration. The President is not bound to give his assent even though the Bill has been reconsidered and passed for a second time by the State Legislature.

Assembly vs. Council

A significant point of difference between the relationship of the two Houses of Parliament and that of the two Houses of the State Legislature (wherever the two Houses exist) is the comparatively less important role which the Legislative Council plays in contrast to that of the Council of States. As we have already seen, the Council of States has, excepting in the field of Money Bills, co-equal powers with the House in all legislative matters. When there is an irreconcilable conflict between the two, the deadlock is resolved in a joint sitting of the two Houses. In the State Legislature, on the contrary, the Council is designed to play a definitely inferior role. Its functions are of an advisory nature only. Ambedkar pointed out in the Constituent Assembly that the provisions adopted by the Constitution to resolve conflicts between the two Houses of the State Legislature were based on the provisions of the (British) Parliament Act of 1911.

According to this, a Bill can have only two journeys from the

Assembly to the Council. When a Bill goes to the Council for the first time from the Assembly the Council has four alternative courses of action: (1) it may reject the Bill; (2) it may amend the Bill; (3) it may take no action on it; (but when three months have elapsed since its receipt by the Council and the Council does not inform the Assembly as to what action it has taken on the Bill, it is deemed to have been rejected by the Council); and (4) it may pass the Bill as sent by the Assembly. In the first three cases the Assembly takes up the consideration of the Bill for a second time. It may or may not accept the amendments made by the Council and pass the Bill. It now goes for the second time to the Council which can adopt any of the above alternative courses of action except that it can delay the Bill only for a month instead of the three months in the first instance. The Assembly acts again according to the same procedure as before, if the Council does not again agree with it. Thus, only twice will the Bills travel from the Assembly to the Council and the latter has only the power of a suspensory veto, the first time for a period of three months and the second time for a month. These provisions clearly establish the absolute superiority of the Assembly over the Council. In respect of Money Bills, the powers of the State Assembly are the same as those of the House of the People, which we have already dealt with. There is also a special procedure prescribed for financial matters on the same pattern as what obtains in Parliament.

Privileges

The powers, privileges and immunities of the State Legislature, its committees and their members are the same as those of Parliament, its committees and its members. Members are entitled to receive such salaries and allowances as are determined by the Legislature. At present, there is no uniformity with regard to these among the various States. Nevertheless all of them give regular monthly salaries and certain allowances to their legislators.

The question of the privileges and immunities of the legislature and its members figured prominently in three cases where an attempt was made to persuade the High Courts and the Supreme Court to interfere with the working of the State Legislative Assemblies. Of these Misra *vs.* Nand Kishore was a case which came up before the Orissa High Court in which the petitioner challenged the action of the Speaker who disallowed certain questions which he asked on the floor of the Orissa Assembly.

The High Court declined to interfere as this was a matter which fell within the exclusive rights of the Legislature to regulate. In the second case, Singh *vs.* Govind, the Allahabad High Court was asked to determine the legality or otherwise of certain disciplinary action taken against the petitioner as a member of the Uttar Pradesh Assembly. Here again, the Court refused to interfere. Speaking on behalf of the Court, Justice Sapru said: "Obviously, this Court is not, in any sense whatever, a Court of appeal or revision against the Legislature or against the rulings of the Speaker, who as the holder of an office of the highest distinction, has the sole responsibility cast upon him of maintaining the prestige and dignity of the House." He added that under Article 194, the legislature has the right (1) to be the exclusive judge of the legality of its own proceedings, (2) to punish its members for their conduct in the House, and (3) to settle its own proceedings.

The matter came before the Supreme Court for the first time in the case of *The Searchlight* and the Court gave its verdict in favour of the legislature. The case arose out of the publication by *The Searchlight,* an English language daily newspaper, of certain references in the Legislative Assembly of the State of Bihar relating to the conduct of the Chief Minister of the State and an ex-Minister. The newspaper reported that a member of the Assembly made a bitter attack on the Chief Minister and his ex-colleague with respect to their activities regarding the selection of Ministers and the glaring instances of encouragement of corruption by the Government. Soon after, the Secretary, Bihar Legislature, issued a notice to the Editor of *The Searchlight* for the breach of privilege of the House inasmuch as he was alleged to have published a perverted and unfaithful report of the proceedings. The notice asked the Editor to appear before the Privileges Committee which had found a *prima facie* case against him, and show cause why action should not be taken against him. The Editor challenged the validity of the notice by a petition filed in the Supreme Court under Article 32 of the Constitution.

The Court said that it was called upon to answer two questions: (*i*) whether the House of the Legislature could prohibit the publication of publicly seen and heard proceedings; (*ii*) whether the privileges of the House under Article 194 (3) prevailed over the Fundamental Rights of the citizen under Article 19 (1) (a). A four to one majority of the Court answered both the questions in the affirmative. Speaking on behalf of the majority, Chief Justice S. R. Das held that in the absence of a law made by the Legislature, the Legislature shall have all the privileges, powers and immunities enjoyed by the House of Commons in England at the commencement of the Constitution of India and the citizen could not insist on the faithful publication of the proceedings of the Legislature if the Legislature chose not to permit him to do so. The Fundamental Right of freedom of speech guaranteed to a citizen under Article 19(1)(a) could not override the privileges of the Legislature. It must not be overlooked that they (the privileges) were conferred by constitutional laws and not ordinary laws made by Parliament and, therefore, they are as supreme as the Chapter on Fundamental Rights.

In his dissent, Justice Subba Rao said that the reasoning adopted in the majority judgment would unduly restrict and circumscribe the wide scope and content of one of the cherished Fundamental Rights, namely, the freedom of speech in its application to the press. The learned judge asked: "Why should Article 194 be preferred to Article 19 (1)(a) and not *vice versa*?" According to him, if there is a conflict between a legislative privilege and a Fundamental Right, the former should yield to the latter to the extent that it is necessary to uphold the Fundamental Right. The legislature has only the privilege of preventing *mala fide* publication of the proceedings. Article 19 (2) gives ample scope for such reasonable restrictions to be imposed by a duly enacted law. The privilege of the legislature can be adequately protected by applying the test of reasonable restrictions envisaged under Article 19(2). Hence it is unnecessary to accord a preferred position to the privilege of the legislature over the Fundamental Right of the citizen expressly guaranteed by the Constitution.

In spite of the Supreme Court's verdict in *The Searchlight* case upholding the supremacy of legislative privilege over the right to freedom of expression, it must be emphasised that the interests of a parliamentary democracy demand the need to ensure the freedom of the press in an adequate measure. The press should not get the impression that the House was trying to "terrorise" it into refraining from fair comment. As there is no possibility for appeal against any decision taken by the House, fairness demands of members to act with great responsibility and utmost impartiality in deciding what they should object to and what action they should take. Unfortunately, however, there exists a tendency among legislators in India to invoke privilege too frequently. This seems to be the product either of insufficient appreciation of the rights of others to criticise what they do on the floor of the House or an exaggerated feeling of importance of their parliamentary role.

The best example of this was provided by the unprecedented jurisdictional fight between the Uttar Pradesh Assembly and the Allahabad High Court. The circumstances which led to this unusual incident were as follows: The U.P. Legislative Assembly passed a resolution on March 14, 1964 recommending that a socialist worker, Keshava Singh, be sentenced to simple imprisonment for seven days for committing contempt of the House by defying its order. Subsequently, the High Court, acting on a writ petition, released Keshava Singh on bail pending the final disposal of the petition. The Assembly discussed the action of the Court and decided by an overwhelming majority that it amounted to a contempt of the House. Hence it adopted a motion that the two judges who heard the writ petition as well as Keshava Singh and his counsel should be produced before the bar of the House for the breach of privilege. The High Court reacted to this move of the Assembly swiftly and firmly. A full bench of the Court consisting of twenty-eight judges, on the following day, passed an interim order staying the implementation of the Assembly's controversial resolution which had already provoked an unprecedented constitutional crisis. Further, the Court reserved orders on three petitions intended to institute contempt of court proceedings against the Assembly, the Speaker, the Marshal (who was asked to serve the warrant on the judges) and the mover and the supporter of the resolution in the Assembly.

By now, the U.P. happenings were attracting nation-wide attention and attempts were made to discuss the matter in the Lok Sabha of Parliament. A few days later, having failed to find a satisfactory solution to the constitutional impasse, the ruling Congress Party steam-rolled a resolution requesting Presidential intervention under Article 143 of the Constitution in order to settle its conflict with the High Court. Thus the matter reached the President who, under Article 143, referred it to the Supreme Court for its advice. The Court held that the High Court was competent to entertain the petition filed by Keshava Singh challenging the legality of the sentence of imprisonment imposed on him by the Assembly. It also held that the Assembly was not competent to direct the production of the two judges of the High Court who ordered the release of Keshava Singh.

The extent to which claims to parliamentary privileges can go was further shown in a decision of the Supreme Court in January 1961. In this—a defamation case—a member of the West Bengal State Assembly contended that there was an absolute privilege in favour of a member and that he, therefore, could not be prosecuted for having published subsequently questions which had been disallowed by the Speaker. In January 1954, he had given notice of his intention to ask certain questions in the Assembly. The questions were disallowed. He then published them in a local journal. The person whose conduct had formed the subject matter of the questions filed a complaint against the Assembly member, and also the editor and publisher of the journal, alleging that the published matter contained scandalous imputations against him and was intended to tarnish his reputation. In an unanimous verdict the Supreme Court held that there was no absolute privilege attaching to the publication of extracts from proceedings and that, if the extracts contained defamatory matter, the member concerned should face the consequences as in any ordinary case of defamation.

CHAPTER 27

JUDICIARY IN THE STATES

The High Court

EVERY STATE has a High Court operating within its territorial jurisdiction and every High Court is a Court of Record which has all the powers of such a Court including the power to punish for contempt of itself. Neither the Supreme Court nor the Legislature can deprive a High Court of its power of punishing a contempt of itself.

We have already seen the position of the Supreme Court with the inauguration of the new Constitution in 1950, and how it affected the position of the High Courts by bringing them directly under the Supreme Court as parts of a single, integrated, hierarchical, all-India judicial system. The Constitution does not, however, vest in the Supreme Court any direct administrative control over the High Courts which would substantially affect their functioning as independent judicial institutions.

The position of the High Courts under a federal constitution like that of India is substantially different from that of the State Courts under most other federations, notably that of the United States of America. There, the State Courts are constituted under the State Constitutions and, as such, do not in any way link themselves up with the federal judicial system. The method of appointment and conditions of service of the judges of the State Courts as well as their respective jurisdictions vary from State to State. In India, on the contrary, there is uniformity in all these matters and the Constitution lays down detailed provisions dealing with them. Neither the State Executive nor the State Legislature has any power to control the High Court, or to alter the constitution or organisation of the High Court. Whatever that is permissible, short of a constitutional amendment, is vested in Parliament. These provisions have great importance in determining the independence of the High Courts.

Unlike the Supreme Court, there is no fixed minimum number of judges for the High Court. The President, from time to time, will fix the number of judges in each High Court and it varies from Court to Court. For example, the Jammu and Kashmir High Court, has at present only five judges whereas the Calcutta High Court has as many as thirty-seven judges.

Every judge of the High Court is appointed by the President of India after consultation with the Chief Justice of India, the Governor of the State and, in the case of the appointment of a judge other than the Chief Justice, the Chief Justice of the High Court concerned. If he is appointed on a permanent basis, he will hold office until he completes the age of sixty-two years. The minimum qualifications prescribed for appointment are Indian citizenship and at least ten years' experience either as an advocate of a High Court in India or a judicial officer in the territory of India.[1] In computing the ten-year period for the purpose of appointment, experience as an advocate can be combined with that of a judicial officer. A judge of the High Court can be removed from office only for proved misbehaviour or incapacity and only in the same manner in which a judge of the Supreme Court is removed.

The Chief Justice and the other judges, of the High Court are paid monthly salaries of Rs. 4,000 and 3,500 respectively. In addition, they are also entitled to certain allowances and a pension on retirement. The salary and allowances of a judge of the High Court cannot be varied to his disadvantage after his appointment. Further, these sums are charged on the Consolidated Fund of the State and, as such, are excluded from voting in the State Legislature. The Constitution imposes on retired judges of High Courts certain restrictions with respect to legal practice after retirement. According to this, they cannot practise before any Court except the Supreme Court and High Courts other than those in which they were judges. These provisions which are almost identical with those dealing with the judges of the Supreme Court are intended to safeguard the independence of the High Courts.

There are, however, certain special provisions which make the organisation and functioning of the High Court different from those of the Supreme Court. Of these, the power of the President to transfer a judge from one High Court to another seems to be the most important one. Every such transfer is to be made only after

[1] A person who is, in the opinion of the President of India, a distinguished jurist is also eligible to be appointed a judge of the High Court.

consultation with the Chief Justice of India. The provision may not seem to be quite in harmony with the concept of judicial independence. Yet, it has some justification. The services of a competent judge may be required in any part of the country as a matter of national interest, and this provision enables the President to choose such a judge from any of the High Courts in the country. This will also facilitate the better selection of judges and to keep the question above State or regional barriers. Secondly, unlike the provisions in regard to the Supreme Court, there is a provision for the appointment of additional and acting judges to the High Court. Additional judges are appointed for a period not exceeding two years, in order to meet any temporary increase in the work of the Court or to dispose of arrears of accumulated work. An acting judge is appointed in the place of a permanent judge of the Court when the latter is away on leave or on some other duty.

Jurisdiction

The Constitution does not attempt detailed definitions and classification of the different types of jurisdiction of the High Courts as it has done in the case of the Supreme Court. This is mainly because most of the High Courts at the time of the framing of the Constitution, had been functioning with well-defined jurisdictions whereas the Supreme Court was a newly-created institution necessitating a clear definition of its powers and functions. Moreover, the High Courts were expected to maintain the same position that they originally had as the highest courts in the States even after the inauguration of the Constitution. It was provided, therefore, that the High Courts would retain their existing jurisdiction subject to the provisions of the Constitution and any future law that was to be made by the appropriate legislature. Further, in future, there would be no restriction as in the past to the exercise of original jurisdiction by the High Courts in matters concerning "revenue or its collection". The High Courts have also been given full powers to make rules to regulate the business before them and such other incidental power as is required in relation to the administration of justice which falls within their jurisdiction.

Apart from the normal original and appellate jurisdiction, the Constitution also vests four additional powers in the High Courts.

These are: (1) the power to issue writs or orders for the enforcement of the Fundamental Rights or for any other specified purpose; (2) the power of superintendence over all Courts in the State; (3) the power to transfer cases to itself from subordinate Courts concerning the interpretation of the Constitution; and (4) the power to appoint officers and servants of the High Court.

Under Article 226, the High Courts have been made the protectors of the Fundamental Rights guaranteed under the Constitution within their respective territorial jurisdiction. We have already seen that under Article 32, the Supreme Court is the ultimate protector of these fundamental rights. But if the protection of Fundamental Rights was entirely entrusted to the Supreme Court alone, many an aggrieved citizen would have found it impossible to approach the Court for the enforcement of a right which has been violated. By giving this power to the High Courts also, these rights have been made more real for the ordinary citizen. In the exercise of this power, the Court may issue the same type of writs, orders or directions which the Supreme Court is empowered to issue under Article 32.

Speaking on the scope of this power of the High Courts, the Supreme Court said: "The jurisdiction under Article 226 is exercised by the High Court in order to protect and safeguard the rights of the citizens and whenever the High Court finds that any person within its territories is guilty of doing an act which is not authorised by law or is violative of the Fundamental Rights of the citizens, it exercises that jurisdiction in order to vindicate his rights and redress his grievances and the only conditions of its exercise of that jurisdiction are: (1) the power is to be exercised throughout the territories in relation to which it exercises jurisdiction, that is to say, the writs issued by the Court do not run beyond the territories subject to its jurisdiction; (2) the person or authority to whom the High Court is empowered to issue such writs must be within those territories which clearly implies that they must be amenable to its jurisdiction either by residence or location within territories."

Under Article 227, every High Court has the power of superintendence over all Courts and tribunals except those dealing with the Armed Forces functioning within its territorial jurisdiction. In the exercise of this power the High Court is authorised (1) to call for returns from such courts, (2) to make and issue general rules and prescribe forms for regulating the practice and proceedings of such Courts, and (3) to prescribe forms in which books, entries and accounts shall be kept by the officers of any such Courts. Interpreting the scope of this power, the Supreme Court said that all types of tribunals including the Election Tribunals operating within a State are subject to the superintendence of the High Courts and further, that the "superintendence is both judicial and administrative." While under Article 226 the High Court can only annul the decision of the Tribunals, it can under Article 227 do that, and also issue further directions in the matter.

Article 228 vests in the High Courts the power to transfer constitutional cases from Lower Courts. According to this, if the Court is satisfied that a case pending in one of its subordinate Courts involves a substantial question of law as to the interpretation of the Constitution, the determination of which is necessary for the disposal of the case, it shall then withdraw the case and may either dispose of the case itself or determine the constitutional question and then send the case back to the Court wherefrom it was withdrawn. By vesting this power in the High Court, the framers of the Constitution have safeguarded against the possible multiplicity of constitutional interpretations at the level of subordinate Courts. As it is, in addition to the Supreme Court every High Court is authorised to interpret the Constitution which means that there are at least sixteen Courts undertaking this interpretation work. Conflicts in interpretation are not unusual or unnatural under such conditions. The Supreme Court does not get an opportunity in every case to resolve such conflicts as there is no provision for automatic revision by the Court in every such case of conflict. If every subordinate Court also were invested with the power of interpreting the Constitution, it would have created an extremely confusing situation. That possibility has been completely eliminated by the provisions under Article 228.

If the High Courts are to function independently they should also have at their disposal adequate staff and the power of controlling the members of that staff. These are ensured under Article 229. According to this, the Chief Justice of the High Court is empowered to appoint officers and servants of the Court. The Governor may in this respect require the Court to consult the

Public Service Commission of the State. The Chief Justice is also authorised to regulate the conditions of service of the staff subject to any law made by the State Legislature in this respect. The rules relating to the salaries, allowances, leave or pension require the approval of the Governor. The power of the Chief Justice to appoint any member of the staff of the High Court also includes his power to dismiss any such member from the service of the Court. The Constitution also provides for charging all the administrative expenses of the High Court on the Consolidated Fund of the State.

We have already noted that, subject to the provisions of the Constitution, the State Legislature is empowered to modify the jurisdiction of the High Court. Thus, for instance, the Legislature may enlarge or restrict the scope of the Court's jurisdiction in civil matters by prescribing a pecuniary limit, as Ambedkar pointed out in the Constituent Asembly. But Parliament alone is empowered to enlarge or restrict the territorial jurisdiction of a particular High Court by extending or excluding such jurisdiction from any Union Territory. The Legislature of a Union Territory, if it has one, has no power to deal with the jurisdiction of the Court in any manner. Parliament is also empowered to establish common High Courts for two or more States or for two or more States and a Union Territory. Although no such common High Court has so far been established, the provision is pregnant with possibilities for better organisation of the judicial system at the level of the High Courts as and when appropriate conditions present themselves in future.

Table 10 on p. 294 shows the various High Courts in India, the places where they are located and the number of judges in each High Court.

Subordinate Courts

A Constitution, being the basic law, does not usually go into such details as the provisions dealing with the organisation and working of subordinate courts. Such subjects are left to be dealt with by the Legislature. The Constitution of India departs from this practice by incorporating detailed provisions concerning even the subordinate judiciary. This is mainly due to certain peculiar conditions which existed in India at the time of the making of the Constitution.

TABLE 10

HIGH COURTS

Name of State	Seat of the Court	Number of Judges
Andhra Pradesh	Hyderabad	18
Assam	Shillong	6
Bihar	Patna	23
Gujarat	Ahmedabad	16
Jammu & Kashmir	Srinagar	5
Karnataka	Bangalore	13
Kerala	Ernakulam	15
Madhya Pradesh	Bhopal	20
Maharashtra	Bombay	30
Orissa	Bhubaneshwar	7
Punjab	Chandigarh	17
Rajasthan	Jaipur	10
Tamil Nadu	Madras	20
Uttar Pradesh	Allahabad	34
West Bengal	Calcutta	37

During the British rule, in order to suit the convenience of a foreign government, executive and judicial functions were combined in the same officer at the lower levels of the administration. Under the British, each province was divided into a number of districts which became the pivotal units of administration. Each of these districts was headed by an officer called the Collector Magistrate who combined in his office both the executive and judicial functions. As an instrument of the alien, imperial government, this officer behaved, more often than not, as a local dictator. What really made him a dictator was the combination of both the executive and judicial powers in his office. The evils of this system were so far-reaching that it became an instrument of terror during the national movement for political liberation. There was almost universal condemnation of the system and the demand for the complete separation of the judiciary from the executive was persistent and vociferous. This accounts for the Constitution-makers dealing with this problem in detail. As we have seen earlier, one of the Directive Principles is the separation of the judiciary from the executive. They were not satisfied with this alone. They wanted also to see that the judiciary at the lower levels was made completely independent of the executive; they sought to establish a judicial system under which from the highest court in the land to the lowest, every layer and each unit in every layer functioned in a spirit of judicial independence. The special significance of the powers of superintendence which the High Court exercises over the subordinate judiciary is to be assessed in this context.

The constitutional provisions dealing with the Subordinate Courts, therefore, are intended to secure a two-fold objective. First, to provide for the appointment of District and Subordinate Judges and their qualifications. Secondly, to place the whole of the civil judiciary under the control of the High Court. The importance of these provisions can hardly be exaggerated in the context of the Indian situation. It is the subordinate judiciary that comes into most intimate contact with the ordinary people in the judicial field. Therefore, it is particularly necessary that its independence is placed beyond question in order to infuse public confidence in it. This is the justification for incorporating these provisions in the Constitution.

The Constitution draws a distinction between two categories of Subordinate Courts, namely the District Courts and others. Judges of the District Courts are appointed by the Governor in consultation with the High Court. Further, a person to be eligible for appointment as a District Judge should be either an advocate or a pleader of seven years' standing, or an officer in the service of the Union or of the State. In the case of every advocate or pleader, the appointment should be on a recommendation by the High Court.

Appointment of persons other than district judges to the judicial service of a State is made by the Governor in accordance with rules made by him in that behalf after consultation with the High Court and the State Public Service Commission. The practice that exists in most States at present is that the Public Service Commission conducts competitive examinations for the selection of candidates for appointment in the state judicial service. The Commission lays down certain minimum educational and professional qualifications for candidates who intend to compete in these examinations. At least three years' experience as an advocate or a pleader is one of the principal qualifications. The selected candidates are given special training for a certain period before regular appointment to the service, and thereafter they come under the superintendence of the High Court in the discharge of their responsibilities.

Article 235 specifies the nature and extent of the High Court's control over the subordinate judiciary. According to that Article, the High Court exercises control over the District Courts and the Courts subordinate to them, in matters such as posting, promotions and the granting of leave to all persons belonging to the State Judicial Service. The Governor is empowered to extend the scope of these provisions in order to include also different classes of magistrates in the State who do not belong to the regular judicial service.

Except for minor local variations, the structure and functions of the subordinate courts are uniform throughout the country. Each State, for the purpose of judicial administration is divided into a number of districts, each under the jurisdiction of a District Judge. Under him is a hierarchy of judicial officers exercising varying types of jurisdiction. As a result of the progressive implementation of the principle of the separation of the judiciary from the executive, the subordinate judiciary in most parts of the country is already functioning separately. The Constitutional safeguards are bound to provide for its firm establishment as a truly independent institution as the framers intended it to be.

CHAPTER 28

UNION TERRITORIES

WHILE DISCUSSING the reorganisation of States which took place in 1956, we had occasion to deal with the Part C States and the Territories under Part D, established under the original Constitution. There were in all ten Part C States. The Territories under Part D were Andaman and Nicobar islands. What should be the status of these states and territories under the reorganised set-up was a question which the States Reorganisation Commission was called upon to deal with. There were three alternative courses of action possible. First, to recommend the continuance of the Part C States and make them equal in status to the Part A States; secondly, to allow the *status quo* to continue; thirdly, to abolish them as separate entities and merge them with the neighbouring States. The Commission gave adequate consideration to the pros and cons of each of these alternatives. They said:

"Separated from each other by long distances they have greater economic, linguistic and cultural affinities with the neighbouring States than with each other. Politically, economically and educationally, they are in varying phases of development. Even in the constitutional field, they do not follow a uniform pattern in that some of them have legislatures and ministries and others only advisory councils. Two are adminstered through Lieutenant Governors and the remaining through Chief Commissioners."

Summing up their discussion on these States, the Commission said: "The position is that there is a general consensus of opinion that the existing set-up of the Part C States is unsatisfactory. The solution suggested by the official representatives of the Part C States, namely, a constitutional status which is identical with that of Part A States will only remove the constitutional anomalies. These small units will still continue to be economically unbalanced, financially weak, and administratively and politically unstable."

"The democratic experiment in these States, wherever it has been tried, has proved to be more costly than was expected or intended and this extra cost has not been justified by increased administrative efficiency or rapid economic and social progress. Quite obviously, these states cannot subsist as separate administrative units without excessive dependence on the Centre, which will lead to all the undesirable consequences of divorcing the responsibility for expenditure from that for finding the resources."

"Taking all these factors into consideration, we have come to the conclusion that there is no adequate recompense for all the financial, administrative and constitutional difficulties which the present structure of these States presents and that, with the exception of two, to be centrally administered, the merger of the existing Part C States with the adjoining States is the only solution of their problems."

The reorganisation plan of the Commission envisaged only two categories of units in the Indian Union: (1) 'States' forming primary constituent units of the Indian Union having a Constitutional relationship with the Centre on a federal basis. These units were to cover virtually the entire country. (2) 'Territories' which for vital strategic or other considerations, cannot be joined to any of the States and are, therefore, centrally administered. This plan was accepted and given effect to in the Seventh Amendment of the Constitution and the States Reorganization Act, 1956. This is the story of the origin of the present Union Territories.

There are in all nine Union Territories. These are:

(1) Delhi

(2) Andaman and Nicobar Islands

(3) The Laccadive, Minicoy and Amindivi Islands

(4) Goa, Daman and Diu

(5) Dadra and Nagarhaveli

(6) Pondicherry

(7) Chandigarh

(8) Mizoram

(9) Arunachal Pradesh

Of these, Delhi is the federal capital. As such, it could not be made part of a full-fledged constituent unit of the Indian Union. Even under a unitary system of Government, the normal practice is to place national capitals under a special dispensation. London and Paris are perhaps the best examples of this where there is a greater degree of central control over the city administration than over other municipalities. Under a federal system there is an additional consideration. Any constitutional division of powers, if it is applicable to a unit functioning in the seat of the national government, is bound to give rise to embarrassing situations. This is why most federal capitals are under the Central Government. Washington, the capital of the United States, and Canberra, the federal capital of the Australian Commonwealth, are two good examples.

The next two Union Territories in the list are islands in the Bay of Bengal and the Arabian Sea respectively. They are not contiguous with any of the States and are comparatively backward and undeveloped. The former French and Portuguese colonies have distinct cultures of their own and as such deserved a special status. In 1966 when Punjab was reorganised to form two separate States, Punjab and Haryana, Chandigarh, the Capital of undivided Punjab was made a Union Territory. Mizoram was made a Union Territory in 1972 and Arunachal Pradesh in 1971.

The Constitutional provisions dealing with these Union Territories attempt to set out the basic pattern of administration for them. Its main features are as follows:

(1) The Union Territories will be administered by the President through an administrator to be appointed by him with a suitable designation. Parliament, however, is empowered to make any other provision by law for the administration of any of these Territories.

(2) The President may, if he so chooses, appoint the Governor of a State as the administrator of an adjoining Union Territory. In the exercise of his functions as administrator of a Union Territory, the Governor will act independently of his Council of Ministers.

(3) The President may make regulations for the peace, progress and good government of the Union Territories of the Andaman and Nicobar islands, and the Laccadive, Minicoy and Amindivi islands. Any such regulation made by the President may repeal or amend any existing Act dealing with the administration of these islands and will have the same effect as a Parliamentary enactment.

(4) Parliament is empowered to constitute a High Court for any Union Territory or to declare any existing court there to be a High Court. Such a High Court will have the same functions and powers as any other High Court in India except for such

modifications or exceptions as Parliament may provide by law. Until such a High Court is established, those High Courts under whose jurisdiction these territories had remained, will continue to exercise such jurisdiction in relation to these territories. Parliament has the power to make any change with respect to this jurisdiction.

PART VI

THE FEDERAL SYSTEM

CHAPTER 29

THE SCHEME OF DIVISION OF POWERS

MOVING CONSIDERATION of the Draft Constitution in the Constituent Assembly, Ambedkar said that the form of the Constitution was federal. "It establishes a dual polity with the Union at the Centre and the States at the periphery, each endowed with sovereign powers to be exercised in the field assigned to them respectively by the Constitution." The Union is not a League of States, united in a loose relationship, nor are the States the agencies of the Union, deriving powers from it. Both the Union and the States are created by the Constitution, both derive their respective authority from the Constitution. The one is not subordinate to the other in its own field; the authority of one is coordinate with that of the other.

Dealing with the criticism of over-centralisation in the Constitution, Ambedkar said:

"A serious complaint is made on the ground that there is too much centralisation and that the States have been reduced to municipalities. It is clear that this view is not only an exaggeration but is also founded on a misunderstanding of what exactly the Constitution contrives to do.

"As to the relations between the Centre and States it is necessary to bear in mind the fundamental principle on which it rests. The basic principle of federalism is that the Legislative and Executive authority is partitioned between the Centre and the States not by any law to be made by the Centre but by the Constitution itself. This is what the Constitution does. The States are in no way dependent upon the Centre for their legislative or executive authority. The States and the Centre are co-equal in this matter.

"It is difficult to see how such a Constitution can be called centralism. It may be that the Constitution assigns to the Centre a larger field for the operation of its legislative and executive authority than is to be found in any other federal constitution. It may be that residuary powers are given to the Centre and not to the States. But these features do not form the essence of federalism.

303

"The chief mark of federalism lies in the partition of the legislative and executive authority between the Centre and Units by the Constitution. This is the principle embodied in our Constitution. There can be no mistake about it. It is therefore wrong to say that the States have been placed under the Centre. The Centre cannot by its own will alter the boundary of this partition. Nor can the judiciary. For as has been well said: 'Courts may modify, they cannot replace. They can revise earlier interpretations as new arguments, new points of view are presented, they can shift the dividing line in marginal cases, but there are barriers they cannot pass, definite assignments of power they cannot re-allocate. They can give a broadening construction of existing powers, but they cannot assign to one authority the powers explicitly granted to another'."

Ambedkar was supported in these views by his colleagues on the Drafting Committee and by others whose opinions carried weight and authority in the deliberations of the Assembly. Yet, the controversy continued. A large number of members still thought that the Centre was invested with excessive power and, in the process, the federal principle which was to form the very foundation of the States system under the Constitution was almost destroyed.

The controversy did not end even with the adoption of the Constitution. From the floor of the Assembly it migrated to a wider arena, among political scientists and constitutional lawyers both within and outside the country. According to some, the Constitution is 'quasi-federal'; it establishes a unitary State with subsidiary federal features rather than a federal State with subsidiary unitary features. Others are of opinion that the unitary features are so strong that the federal framework of the Constitution is nothing but a facade without the substance of federalism in it. But there are others who think that the Constitution embodies the federal principle in such a substantial measure that it is truly a federal Constitution.

These conflicting opinions arise from the conflicting ideas on federation that prevail among constitutional theorists. Hence, the question whether the Constitution is federal or not cannot be satisfactorily answered without going into the meaning of federalism and the essential elements that constitute a federal State.

Federalism in the modern age is a principle of reconciliation between two divergent tendencies, the widening range of common interests and the need for local autonomy. This is why Lord Acton said: "Of all checks on democracy, federalism has been the most efficacious and the most congenial.... The federal system limits and restrains the sovereign power by dividing it, and by assigning to the government only certain defined rights." The reconciliation that is established in a State between the individual self-sufficiency of the citizen and his allegiance to the State is, in a measure, federal in essence. Modern forms of federations arose either out of the imperfections or limitations of the large, unitary democracy or the defence and economic necessities of the small individual state. What is needed is neither complete independence nor total dependence but an inter-dependence that creates harmony, orderly progress and prosperity. It looks almost contradictory in appearance, but it is the essence of federalism; and only federalism can provide such an effect. Unity while allowing diversity, oneness while providing for division, is the outstanding characteristic of modern federalism. It finds an institutional means whereby the solution of conflicts between social interests could be provided for, and the means remain the same in different parts of the world, however much they vary in detail to suit environment and circumstances. When federalism is viewed in this broad sense, there is hardly any possibility for a controversy on the federal character of the Constitution. For, (1) there is a clear division of governmental power between the Central and State governments; (2) each government is independent of the other in its own field; and (3) the Constitution establishes an independent judiciary to settle the disputes between the Union and the States with respect to the division of powers. This will become clear as we progress with the analysis of the federal provisions of the Constitution.

Legislative Relations between the Union and the States

A common feature of many federal constitutions which follow the American federal model is to enumerate a list of legislative powers and assign them to the Union and leave the residue to the States. The Canadian Constitution, on the other hand, follows a different

20

system according to which there are two lists of legislative powers, one for the Centre and the other for the Provinces and the residue is vested in the Centre. The Constitution of India follows a system similar to the Canadian, but with more elaborate lists which include an additional one called the Concurrent List. In drawing up an elaborate Concurrent List, the framers followed the Australian pattern of federal division of powers. Under the Australian Constitution concurrent subjects are 39. Under the Draft Constitution, they were 37. (In the final form of the Constitution the number increased to 47). The scheme is almost the same as in the Government of India Act of 1935. The three lists are embodied in the Seventh Schedule of the Constitution.

The Union List which consists of ninety-nine items is the longest of the three. It includes items such as defence, armed forces, arms and ammunition, atomic energy, foreign affairs, diplomatic representation, United Nations, treaties, war and peace, citizenship, extradition, railways, shipping and navigation, airways, posts and telegraphs, telephones, wireless and broadcasting, currency, coinage and legal tender, foreign loans, the Reserve Bank of India, foreign trade, inter-state trade and commerce, incorporation and its regulation, banking, bills of exchange, insurance, stock exchange, patents, establishment of standards in weights and measures, control of industries, regulation and development of mines, minerals and oil-resources, maintenance of national museums, libraries and such other institutions, historical monuments, the Survey of India, Census, Union Public Services, elections, Parliamentary privileges, audit of Government accounts, constitution and organisation of the Supreme Court, High Courts and the Union Public Service Commission, income-tax, customs duties and export duties, duties of excise, corporation tax, taxes on capital value of assets, estate duty, terminal taxes, taxes on the sale or purchase of newspapers, etc. which are of common interest to the Union and with respect to which uniformity of legislation throughout the Union is essential. As such, Parliament has exclusive powers of legislation with regard to the items mentioned in this List.

The State List consists of sixty-two items. The selection of these items is made on the basis of local interest and it envisages the possibility of diversity of treatment with respect to different items in the different States of the Union. The scope of the application of the federal principle in India is to be determined by the scope of State Legislation arising out of items included in this List. Some of the more important of these items are as follows: public order, police, administration of justice, prisons and reformatories, local government, public health and sanitation, intoxicating liquors, burials and burial grounds, libraries and museums controlled by the State, intra-State communications, agriculture, animal husbandry, water supplies and irrigation, land rights, fisheries, trade and commerce within the State, gas and gas-works, markets and fairs, money lending, theatres, betting and gambling, local elections, legislative privileges, salaries and allowances of all State officers, State public services and the State Public Service Commission, treasure trove, land revenue, taxes on agricultural income, taxes on lands and buildings, estate duty, and succession duty on agricultural land, duties of excise on alcoholic liquors, opium, etc. produced within the State, taxes on the entry of goods into a local area, taxes on electricity (its sale and consumption), taxes on the sale and purchase of goods other than newspapers, taxes on goods and passengers carried by road or inland waterways, taxes on vehicles, taxes on animals and boats, tolls, taxes on professions, trades and callings, capitation taxes, taxes on luxuries, etc. The State Legislature has the exclusive power of legislation with regard to every one of the items included in the State List.

The Concurrent List consists of fifty-two items. These are items with respect to which *uniformity of legislation throughout the Union* is *desirable* but not essential. As such, they are placed under the jurisdiction of both the Union and the States. The List includes items such as: detention for reasons connected with the security of the State, marriage and divorce, transfer of property other than agricultural land, contracts, bankruptcy and insolvency, trust and trustees, civil procedure, contempt of Court, vagrancy, lunacy and mental deficiency, adulteration of food-stuffs, drugs and poisons, economic and social planning, commercial and industrial monopolies, trade unions, social security, labour welfare, education, forests, legal, medical and other professions, vital statistics, trade and commerce in a number of items, price control, factories, electricity, newspapers, books and printing presses, stamp duties, etc. The Parliament of India and the State Legislatures have concurrent power of legislation over the items included in this List.

So long as Parliament does not pass a law on any of these items, the States may pass any law they like on the same. But once Parliament does enact a law on such items, Parliamentary law shall prevail over any State law in this regard. There is, however, one exception to this general rule. According to this, a later law of the State Legislature on any item in the Concurrent List shall prevail over an earlier law of Parliament on the same subject, if the State law was reserved for the consideration of the President and received his assent. This is a novel and original feature which enables a State to pass a more advanced piece of legislation than an existing Parliamentary law, or to provide through a new law with the consent of the Union, for any special conditions and circumstances which prevail in the State.

As in Canada, the residuary powers of legislation are vested in the Union. This power includes the power of making laws imposing any taxes not mentioned in either of the State or Concurrent Lists. Parliament is also empowered to establish additional Courts for the better administration of laws made by it on any matter included in the Union List. Besides, Parliament has the exclusive power of legislation to give effect to any treaty, agreement or convention with any other country or international body.

Although the States have the exclusive power of legislation over every item in the State List, there are two exceptions to this general rule.

(1) Under Article 249: If the Council of States declares by a resolution supported by two-thirds of the members present and voting, that it is necessary or expedient in the national interest that Parliament should make laws with respect to any matter enumerated in the State List, then Parliament is competent to make laws on that matter for the whole or any part of India. Such a resolution remains valid for a year. If, however, the situation under which the resolution was passed continues to exist even at the end of the one-year period, another resolution to the same effect may be passed. In the absence of such a resolution, the Parliamentary law passed in this connection will automatically cease to be in force within six months after the end of the year.

(2) Under Article 250: Parliament is empowered to make laws on any item included in the State List for the whole or any part of India while a Proclamation of Emergency is in operation. The

maximum period for which such a law can be in force is the period for which Emergency lasts and six months beyond that period.

In addition to these two occasions when the Union, on its own initiative, extends its legislative power to embrace that of the States, there could be a third occasion when action on the part of two or more States will enable Parliament to make laws on any item included in the State List. Article 252 deals with this contingency. According to this, if the Legislatures of two or more States pass resolutions to the effect that it is desirable to have a Parliamentary law regulating any of the matters included in the State List, then, it is lawful for Parliament to make laws regulating that matter. Such laws can be extended to any other State as and when the Legislature of that State passes a resolution to that effect. If any such law is to be amended or repealed, it can be done only by Parliament alone but the initiative for it rests with the States. The merit of this provision is that Parliamentary action is the result of the initiative taken by the States in a matter in which they have a common interest but are unable to act individually because the suggested legislation goes beyond their respective territorial jurisdictions. Further, the States will retain the same initiative to amend or repeal such Parliamentary law when it no longer serves the purpose for which it was originally passed or its need has ceased to exist.

A comparison with other federal constitutions will show, first of all, that none of them has attempted such a detailed division of legislative powers between the Union and the States. In the Indian Constitution, the subjects have been precisely formulated so as to lead to a minimum of controversy and litigation. If the framers, for the sake of brevity, had dealt with this subject in such general terms as in the United States Constitution, it would have led to an immense amount of litigation. The litigation that centres on the "commerce clause" of the American Constitution is sufficient to indicate the vast scope of judicial interpretation and the dependence on such interpretation whenever the Centre or the States wish to take any particular action that they consider as falling within their own respective fields.

The provision for a Concurrent List consisting of a fairly large number of items has a special merit in this context. The Concurrent List is like a twilight zone as it were, for both the Union and the States are competent to legislate in this field without coming into conflict. The possibility of mutual encroachment between the Union and the States is reduced to a minimum by including in the Concurrent List all those matters over which conflicts of jurisdiction are most likely to arise. While the State List is based upon local interests and the Union List on national interests, the Concurrent List includes matters which have varying degrees of local and national interests. If these matters had figured in either the State List or the Union List, conflicts would have arisen. As it is, the Concurrent List is like a shock-absorber which enables both the Union and the States to go beyond their own exclusive legislative spheres, as necessity arises, so as to meet exigencies without transgressing the boundaries of each other. This has already been demonstrated during the last three decades of the working of the Constitution.

A clear understanding of the federal provisions will show that the makers of the Indian Constitution were eager to avoid the long, winding way along which federal power had advanced slowly and painfully in the older federations. If India, struggling for political unity and economic stability, were to depend on judicial intervention for the enhancement of national powers, no one could say how successful she would have been in realising these objectives. In all probability, she might have failed in both. The Constitution had to provide for any contingency that might arise in future. In short, the special virtue of the division of powers under the federal system established by the Constitution is its unique combination of rigidity and flexibility, which provides for adaptability to suit the needs of the political and economic situation in the country.

The entire scheme of the distribution of legislative powers undoubtedly displays a strong tendency towards a high degree of centralisation. This has been praised by some as the product of realism and a genuine understanding of the general tendency towards centralisation in all federations whatever be the nature of the division of powers in them as shown by the original, written provisions. At the same time, others have denounced it as deviation from a strictly federal pattern and an attempt to embody unitarism in a federal form. Here we may recall our earlier discussion on the meaning of federalism and point out that there is no strictly rigid federal system set as a pattern for all to copy, nor any sanctity attached to any particular form of federation. Federal government is not always and everywhere good government. It is not an end in itself, but a means for ensuring good government. Nevertheless, there are critics who point out that in a vast country like India, the danger of excessive centralisation which may lead to "apoplexy at the Centre and anaemia at the circumference" cannot altogether be ruled out in practice.

The Union Government, by virtue of its position, is called upon to co-ordinate the activities of the various State Governments in the interests of uniformity without which there is the risk of fissiparous tendencies growing unchecked. Moreover, the trend towards centralisation is not peculiar to India. War, economic depression, the growth of social services, the mechanical revolution in transport and industry, planning, the receipt by the States of financial assistance from the Union and judicial interpretation, all these have promoted the increase of federal power in the United States, Canada, Australia and Switzerland. As pointed out by an Indian critic of the Constitution, "What, notwithstanding the fiercely avowed intentions and policies of the founders of the American Constitution, has taken place in the United States, and what local and provincial antagonisms have been unable to prevent in Canada and Australia, has now been statutorily formulated in India."

Nevertheless, a careful reading of the sixty-two items over which the States have exclusive jurisdiction along with the power they enjoy in the Concurrent field, should make it clear that the States are not reduced to a position of insignificance in the scheme of division of powers. On the contrary, they have at their disposal substantial powers covering a large area which enable them to function as effective agencies of the sovereign power which they share with the Union. Take, for instance, items like public health, agriculture and fisheries which are placed within the jurisdiction of the States. Considering the importance of these items from a national point of view, one could even doubt the wisdom of leaving them in the State List. As a keen observer of the working of the administrative system has pointed out:

"Epidemics respect no State boundaries, and for other reasons too national health is increasingly a national problem. Neither agriculture nor fisheries has greater local significance than national if as much. In a nation dedicated to the Welfare State ideal, the food supply and the welfare of farm families are inescapably national responsibilities. Almost all economic activities are carried on in localities but this fact does not make their significance local. The Constitutional effort to specify scopes of national and state powers so precisely would appear to raise the most serious barriers before national needs to develop and execute national programmes in the interest of national economy and the national public."

Yet, these powers are there with the States, making them function as units of a federal system that attempts a balanced division of powers in the context of the complex problems of the present day.

CHAPTER 30

ADMINISTRATIVE RELATIONS BETWEEN THE UNION AND THE STATES

ONE OF the most difficult problems under a federal system is the adjustment of administrative relations between the Union and the States. In the absence of clear provisions in the Constitution, considerable difficulty is often experienced by the Union and the States in the discharge of these responsibilities. The framers of the Indian Constitution therefore decided to include detailed provisions so as to avoid clashes between the Union and the States in the administrative field. Here again the pattern that is adopted is based mainly on that which was established under the Government of India Act of 1935.

According to Article 256, the executive power of every State is to be exercised in such a way as to ensure compliance with the laws made by Parliament. Further, the Union Executive is empowered to give such directions to a State as may appear to the Government of India to be necessary for the purpose. The idea of the Union giving directions to the States is foreign to most federations. It is looked upon with suspicion and distrust in the United States. In Australia too, the position is more or less the same. Yet it is difficult to see how this can altogether be avoided in practice.

Explaining the object of Article 256, Ambedkar said that it envisaged two propositions:

"The first proposition is that generally the authority to execute laws which relate to what is called the Concurrent field, whether the law is passed by the Central Legislature or is passed by the State Legislature shall ordinarily apply to the State. The second proposition it lays down is that if in any particular case Parliament thinks that in passing a law which relates to the Concurrent field, the execution ought to be retained by the Central Government, Parliament shall have the power to do so."

Ambedkar also said that if the Centre did not have such power,

it would become impossible to secure the proper execution of
the laws which Parliament was obliged to enact. Take, for
instance, laws such as the untouchability abolition law, factory
legislation, child marriage abolition law.

"Is it desirable that these legislations of the Central Government be mere paper legislations with no effect given to them?
Is it logical, is it fair, that the Centre on which responsibility
has been cast by the Constitution in the matter of untouchability should merely pass a law and sit with folded hands waiting
and watching as to what the State Governments are doing in
the mater of executing all these particular laws?"

Not satisfied with the general power of the Union to give directions to the States, the Constitution goes a step further and calls
upon every State (under Article 257) not to impede or prejudice
the executive power of the Union in the State. If any Union
agency finds it difficult to function within a State, the Union
Executive is empowered to issue appropriate directions to the
State Government to remove all obstacles. The Union's power
of giving directions in this regard includes certain specific matters
such as
(1) the construction and maintenance of means of communication which are of national or military importance, and
(2) the protection of railways within the States. This power
of giving directions does not in any way affect the power of
Parliament to declare highways or waterways or the power of
the Union to construct and maintain means of communication as
part of its functions with respect to naval, military or air force
works.

It is possible that by reason of the special directions given by
the Centre some extra cost above normal may be incurred by
the States in the performance of the service. The Constitution
provides for compensating the States for the extra expenditure
they incur on account of undertaking such tasks. Under this
provision, the Union is obliged to come to an agreement with
the States as to the amount that is to be paid. If, however, the
parties fail to reach an agreement, the matter will be referred
to an arbitrator appointed by the Chief Justice of India. Such

an arbitrator will decide the extra costs incurred which the Union should make good to the State concerned.

The Constitution also empowers the Union Executive, with the consent of the Government of a State, to entrust to that Government or its officers functions which fall within the scope of the Union's executive functions. Parliament is also empowered, in a similar manner, to confer powers or impose duties on State Officers through any of its laws which has application in a State. The Union Government will pay to the State the cost involved in the discharge of such functions by the State or its officers. Here again, if any dispute arises, it will be settled by an arbitrator appointed by the Chief Justice of India.

Under Article 260 the Government of India may undertake any executive, legislative or judicial functions in a foreign territory on the basis of an agreement with the Government of that territory. The provisions of such agreement are governed by laws relating to the exercise of foreign jurisdiction and, as such, they will not come within the scope of the provisions dealing with the normal administrative relationship between the Union and the States. The necessity of this provision is obvious in the context of territories belonging to foreign powers within the geographical boundaries of the Indian Union. It is possible, as in the case of Pondicherry, that the *de facto* control over any of these territories may be vested in the Government of India pending the *de jure* transfer of sovereignty. During such periods, these territories will be governed in accordance with the provisions of this article.

Another provision that facilitates the smooth transaction of administrative business is embodied in Article 261. According to this, full faith and credit shall be given to public acts, records and judicial proceedings of the Union and the States in all parts of Indian territory. The manner in which these acts and records will be proved and their effect determined will be provided by Parliamentary enactments. Provision is also made for the execution of final judgments or orders delivered or passed by civil courts in any part of India.

The Constitution has an important provision embodied in Article 262 dealing with the waters of inter-State rivers and river valleys. Aware of the unending inter-State disputes over this subject in other federations, particularly the United States, the Constitution-makers decided that the power to deal with this subject should be vested exclusively in Parliament. Thus, Parliament may by law provide for the adjudication of any dispute or complaint with respect to the use, distribution or control of the waters of any inter-State river or river valley. Parliament may also provide that neither the Supreme Court nor any other Court shall exercise any jurisdiction in respect of any such dispute or complaint. The importance of this provision is evident in the context of the many inter-State multi-purpose river valley projects like the Damodar Valley Corporation, which are being undertaken in different parts of the country.

Finally, to facilitate the smooth working of the administrative machinery of the country as a whole as well as to ensure the better co-ordination of policy and action between the Union and the States or between the States themselves, the Constitution empowers the President to appoint an Inter-State Council whenever the necessity is felt. The Council is charged with the following three specific duties:

(1) to enquire into and advise upon disputes which may have arisen between States;

(2) to investigate and discuss subjects in which the States or the Union and the States have a common interest;

(3) to make recommendations upon these subjects and, in particular, recommendations for the better co-ordination of policy and action with respect to these subjects.

The President is empowered not only to establish such a Council but also to determine its organisation and procedure and to define the nature of its duties. So far, no such Council has been established.

An analysis of the legislative and administrative relations between the Union and the States shows that the federal system established under the Constitution, like other similar systems, aims to achieve the fundamental objective of unity in diversity. A federation being a dual polity based on the division of authority in all the principal departments of the governments, is bound to produce diversities in laws, administration and judicial protection. Up to a certain point, the diversity is to be welcomed as an attempt to accommodate the powers of government to local needs and circumstances. But when it goes beyond a point, it is capable of creating chaos and has indeed produced chaos in many federal States. The framers of the Indian Constitution were aware of the inherent dangers of a federal system which as Professor Dicey pointed out provides for the predominance of legalism and produces a weak government. Conditions in India at the time of the transfer of power and immediately afterwards were such that those in authority feared that a federal set-up without adequate special safeguards to preserve unity would dissipate the century-old effort at national unity.

At the same time, it would have been politically unwise and impossible in practice to abandon altogether the idea of establishing a federal system. Moreover, when vast areas are brought under a single national government, perhaps no constitutional form except federalism can weld them together as willing partners of an integrated system. The urge for conserving power to rule over oneself and to be independent is as old as humanity. Dependence on others in any form is to be compensated by considerations of relative advantage. As independence without security would be short-lived, the predominant consideration in devising a Federal Union was the urge for the preservation of independence. But for this paramount consideration and the existence of a vague, underlying cultural unity, India presents a picture of perplexing diversity. It has an area almost as large as Europe minus Russia and a larger population than that of the whole of Europe. The number of well-developed languages in India is more than in the whole of Western and Central Europe and the racial and cultural differences more pronounced than in continental Europe. In these circumstances it was not easy to frame a federal constitution that could satisfy at once the urge for independence and the paramount need for security. The framers of the Constitution, in their attempt to satisfy both these objectives, designed a federal system embodying several special features not generally found in other federations.

We have dealt with most of these special features in different places. It may be appropriate here to collect them together so as to obtain a clear perspective of these distinctive features which place the Indian federation almost in a class by itself.

(1) The division of powers between the Union and the States

is the most elaborate ever attempted by a federal constitution. Although the idea of a Concurrent List of powers is not new, no other constitution has enumerated the items in such detail and included in it a variety of subjects with a view to eliminating as far as possible, litigation between the Union and the States, and also the diversity of law courts and procedures. The residuary powers are vested in the Union.

(2) Usually, under a federal system, the States have their own constitutions separate from that of the Union. This is the case in the United States. The Indian Constitution, on the contrary, embodies not only the Constitution of the Union but also those of the States. Further, the States of the Indian Union have a uniform constitution. The amending process, both for the Constitution of the Union and the States, is the same.

(3) Under the Indian federation, the territorial jurisdiction of each of the States can be changed, States themselves abolished and new States created, without resorting to the procedure prescribed for amending the Constitution (Art. 3). That is, the territorial pattern of the federal system as it exists today can be reorganised with suitable adjustments without resorting to the comparatively difficult process of a constitutional amendment.

(4) Dual citizenship is a usual feature that goes with the dual form of government established under a federation. As a result, each member-State has the right to grant its citizens or residents certain rights which it may deny, or grant on more difficult terms, to non-residents. This was a striking feature of the American federation in its early days. As time passed by, the rigours of 'dual citizenship' have become less. Still the idea continues to be associated with the federal system of government. In India, however, it has no place. The Constitution has established a single citizenship. Indians, no matter where they reside, are all equal in the eyes of the law.

(5) Dual polity involves in certain federations a double system of judiciary. For example, in the United States, the States have their own judicial systems unrelated to and unco-ordinated with, the federal judiciary. Australia too follows more or less the same pattern. But in India the Supreme Court and the High Courts form a single integrated judicial system. They have jurisdiction over cases arising under the same laws, constitutional, civil and

criminal. The civil and the criminal laws are codified and are applicable to the entire country. To ensure their uniformity, they are placed in the Concurrent List.

(6) A unique feature of the Indian federal system is its ability to adapt itself to changing circumstances. This is in contrast with the general characteristic of rigidity associated with federal constitutions. Normally, the Indian Constitution is meant to be federal. But under an emergency it can assume a unitary character. The process of change-over does not involve any complicated constitutional process.

(7) The Constitution vests certain extraordinary powers in the Union Government even during normal times. Thus, a resolution supported by a two-third majority of the Council of States can temporarily transfer any item from the State List to the Union List, enabling Parliament to pass laws on such items in the national interest. It also provides for Parliament to pass laws on items in the State List if two or more States ask for it.

(8) The Heads of the States—the Governors—are appointed by the President. They hold office during his pleasure.

(9) The Constitution has certain special provisions to ensure the uniformity of the administrative system and to maintain minimum common administrative standards without impairing the federal principle. These include the creation of All-India Services such as the Indian Administrative and Police Services and placing the members of these Services in key administrative positions in the States.

(10) Appointments to the High Courts are made by the President, and the judges of the High Courts can be transferred by the President from one High Court to another.

(11) The Comptroller and Auditor-General of India has an organisation managed by the officers of the Indian Audit and Accounts Service—a Central Service, who are concerned not only with the accounts and auditing of the Union Government but also those of the States.

(12) The Election Commission, a body appointed by the President, is in charge of conducting elections not only to Parliament and to other elective offices of the Union, but also those to the State Legislatures.

(13) Although every Bill passed by the State Legislatures

normally becomes law with the assent of the Governor, certain Bills have to be reserved for the assent of the President. Only with the assent of the President can such Bills become law.

(14) The provision for giving grants-in-aid and loans from the Union to the States and the consequent capacity which the Union has to influence the States is again a special feature of the Constitution.

(15) The Constitution vests powers in the Union and its agencies to resolve conflicts that arise between the Union and the States. The Finance Commission, the Inter-State Council, etc. are examples of such agencies.

(16) Finally, Constitutional amendment too is a comparatively simple process in India. This, again, emphasises the flexibility of the federal constitution. Ultimately, the test of a constitution is in its working. If it is found to be defective in any respect in its actual working, it should be amended. For this, the amending process should be reasonably simple and easy.

The list is indeed formidable. Almost every one of these emphasises the supremacy of the Union and its compulsive power to discipline the States. Where the Union has such predominant powers, can the system be called federal? Once again, it may seem that there is some validity in the viewpoints of some of the critics of the Constitution referred to earlier. But if we take into account the manner in which the States in India have been functioning during the last decade and the substantial autonomy they have been enjoying in ordering their affairs within the sphere of power allocated to them, the conclusion will be different. Even when the Centre took over, under the emergency provisions, the administration of some of the States for short periods, it was done only for re-establishing responsible government in those States where owing to political instability, such government had become impossible. The only occasion when the Union availed itself of Article 249 and passed a law on a subject included in the State List was in 1951 when there was acute food scarcity and such a law became essential in the economic interests of the nation. But the operation of the law lasted only for a short period and the States got back their powers in this regard when the scarcity conditions disappeared.

An objective study of the Constitution at work cannot miss a basic fact of constitutional government in India, namely, the existence and functioning of full-fledged Parliamentary and Cabinet government in the States of the Indian Union. As Professor Alexandrowicz points out: "A local executive fully responsible to a local Legislature ensures a good deal of local internal sovereignty and sovereignty means statehood, limited as it may be by the distribution of powers. Local States pursue local policies, sometimes in accordance with the policy of the Centre, sometimes not. This distinguishes them precisely from the position which prevails in administrative federations in which local units must toe the line and always follow the policy of the Centre. India is undoubtedly a federation in which the attributes of statehood are shared between the Centre and local States. Instead of defining her by the vague term of 'quasi-federation', it seems more accurate to exclude her from the category of administrative federations and to consider her a federation with vertically divided sovereignty. Moreover, the position of local States is also strengthened by two significant developments, one connected with the opposition to formation of coalition governments in a number of local States, the other with the reorganization of the Union on linguistic lines".

About the operation of the federal system from an administrative point of view and the trend it indicates for the future, here are a few significant observations which Paul Appleby made after his study of India's administrative system.

"It is not too unfair, I think, to say that except for the character of its leadership, the new national government of India is given less basic resource in power than any other large and important nation, while at the same time having rather more sense of need and determination to establish programmes dealing with matters important to the national interest. The administrative trend is evidently to go still further, to give over to the States same financial resource now in the province of the Centre, to minimize in practice some of the marginal or interpretative zones of power, and to retreat before an opposition State minister's charge of interference with the States.

"No other large and important national government, I believe, is so dependent as India on theoretically subordinate but actually rather distinct units responsible to a different political control, for so much of the administration of what are recognised as national programmes of great importance to the nation.

"The power that is exercised organically in New Delhi is the uncertain and discontinuous power of prestige. It is influence rather than power. Its method is making plans, issuing pronouncements, holding conferences. In reference to two different programme fields I have been authoritatively informed at both the Centre and in the States that the Centre's administrative function is performed by annual or semi-annual conferences. Any real power in most of the development field is the personal power of particular leaders and the informal, extra-constitutional, extra-administrative power of a dominant party coherent and strongly led by the same leaders. Dependence for achievement, therefore, is in some crucial ways apart from the formal organs of goverance, in forces which in the future may take quite different forms."

Appleby's criticisms focussing attention on the weakness of the Central power may be countered by pointing out the different instruments of control with which the Centre may bring the States to its way of thinking. The role of the Planning Commission, an extra-constitutional body created by the Centre and the manner in which it acts as a Super-Cabinet for the whole of India directing and regulating the entire socio-economic activity on a national basis, may be cited as an illustration. Yet, the basic fact remains that India is not ruled by one government but simultaneously by twenty-three governments, one national government and twenty-two State Governments sharing between them the totality of governmental power under the Constitution. Such sharing of sovereign powers by different governments under the same constitution is possible only under a federal system and that is what makes India a federal union and its constitution a federal constitution.

CHAPTER 31

FINANCIAL RELATIONS

NO OTHER federal constitution makes such elaborate provisions as the Constitution of India with respect to the relationship between the Union and the States in the financial field. In fact, by providing for the establishment of a Finance Commission for the purpose of allocating and adjusting the receipts from certain sources, the Constitution has made an original contribution in this extremely complicated aspect of federal relationship. The significance of this provision becomes evident when one takes into account the unending conflicts between the federation and the units in the financial field that characterise the working of the older federations. Often the federation and the units have tried to raise revenue by taxing the same sources such as income-tax. In theory it may look all right. But in practice it created great inconveniences. The federation thought that the States stood in its way of enhanced taxation while the States looked upon the federation as a hindrance to their financial soundness. At the same time, the people thought that they were subjected to double or excessive taxation. There was a constant challenge by the States to the authority of the federation to impose a particular tax. At the same time, the federation too resorted to the same process against the States. Individual citizens too challenged the authority of either the federation or the States so as to suit their interests. The result was an enormous amount of litigation. The Courts tried to solve the problem by propounding new doctrines of interpretation. The doctrine of Immunity of Instrumentalities as propounded by the Supreme Court of the United States is an example in point.

The Government of India Act, 1935, had attempted a solution of the problem by a better device. To avoid all confusion, it tried to allocate every possible source of taxation either to the Centre or the Provinces. In some cases, the Centre was allowed to levy and collect the tax but distribute the proceeds to the Provinces. But the real drawback of the Act of 1935 was the extremely limited revenue resources of the Provinces. The makers of the

---

under the 1935 Act, wanted to avoid the repetition of its defect.
As a result, the Constitution lays down a broad scheme for the
distribution of revenue resources between the Union and the
States. But it left the task of detailed allocation to the Finance
Commission to be set up by the President within two years after
the inauguration of the Constitution.

The basic principles that guide the allocation of resources
between the federation and the units are efficiency, adequacy and
suitability. It is indeed difficult to achieve all the three ends at the
same time. Constitutional, natural and economic considerations
often stand in the way. Even if a certain system might suggest
itself as the most acceptable, it would not satisfy the claims and
counter-claims of the various States. Hence, the Constitution has
attempted a compromise. According to this, the subject is divided
into two parts, namely, (1) the allocation of revenues between
the Union and the States, and (2) the distribution of grants-
in-aid. The following list will show the respective sources of
revenue for the Union and the States:

(I) UNION SOURCES

1. Corporation tax.
2. Currency, coinage and legal tender; foreign exchange.
3. Duties of customs including export duties.
4. Duties of excise on tobacco and certain goods manufactured or produced in India.
5. Estate duty in respect of property other than agricultural
   land.
6. Fees in respect of any of the matters in the Union List,
   but not including any fees taken in any Court.
7. Foreign Loans.
8. Lotteries organised by the Government of India or the
   Government of a State.
9. Post Office Savings Bank.
10. Posts and Telegraphs; Telephones, Wireless Broadcasting
    and other like forms of communication.
11. Property of the Union.
12. Public Debt of the Union.

13. Railways.
14. Rates of stamp duty in respect of Bills of Exchange, Cheques, Promissory Notes, etc.
15. Reserve Bank of India.
16. Taxes on income other than agricultural income.
17. Taxes on the capital value of the assets, exclusive of agricultural land, of individuals and companies.
18. Taxes other than stamp duties on transactions in stock exchanges and future markets.
19. Taxes on the sale or purchase of newspapers and on advertisements published therein.
20. Terminal taxes on goods or passengers, carried by railways, sea or air.

(II) STATE SOURCES

1. Capitation taxes.
2. Duties in respect of succession to agricultural land.
3. Duties of excise on certain goods produced or manufactured in the States, such as, alcoholic liquids, opium, etc.
4. Estate duty in respect of agricultural land.
5. Fees in respect of any of the matters in the State List, but not including fees taken in any Court.
6. Land Revenue.
7. Rates of stamp duty in respect of documents other than those specified in the Union List.
8. Taxes on agricultural income.
9. Taxes on land and buildings.
10. Taxes on mineral rights, subject to limitations imposed by Parliament relating to mineral development.
11. Taxes on the consumption or sale of electricity.
12. Taxes on the entry of goods into a local area for consumption, use or sale therein.
13. Taxes on the sale and purchase of goods other than newspapers.
14. Taxes on advertisements other than those published in newspapers.
15. Taxes on goods and passengers carried by road or on inland waterways.

16. Taxes on vehicles.
17. Taxes on animals and boats.
18. Taxes on professions, trades, callings and employments.
19. Taxes on luxuries, including taxes on entertainments, amusements, betting and gambling.
20. Tolls.

(III) TAXES LEVIED AND COLLECTED BY THE UNION BUT ASSIGNED TO THE STATES (*Art.* 269)

1. Duties in respect of succession to property other than agricultural land.
2. Estate duty in respect of property other than agricultural land.
3. Taxes on railway fares and freights.
4. Taxes other than stamp duties on transactions in stock exchanges and future markets.
5. Taxes on the sale or purchase of newspapers and on advertisements published therein.
6. Terminal taxes on goods or passengers carried by railway, sea or air.
7. Taxes on the sale or purchase of goods other than newspapers where such sale or purchase takes place in the course of inter-State trade or commerce.

(IV) DUTIES LEVIED BY THE UNION BUT COLLECTED AND APPROPRIATED BY THE STATES (*Art.* 268)

Stamp duties and duties of excise on medicinal and toilet preparations (those mentioned in the Union List) shall be levied by the Government of India but shall be collected:

(*i*) in the case where such duties are leviable within any Union territory, by the Government of India, and

(*ii*) in other cases, by the States within which such duties are respectively leviable.

(V) Taxes which are Levied and Collected by the Union but Which May be Distributed Between the Union and the States (*Arts.* 270 *and* 272)

1. Taxes on income other than agricultural income.
2. Union duties of excise other than such duties of excise on medicinal and toilet preparations as are mentioned in the Union List and collected by the Government of India.

"Taxes on income" does not include corporation tax. The distribution of income-tax proceeds between the Union and the States is made on the basis of the recommendations of the Finance Commission. According to the recommendation of the Third Finance Commission, 1962, the percentage of the States is fixed at sixty.

In spite of articles 269 and 270 which provide for the collection of taxes by the Union either to be assigned to the States or to be shared between the Union and the States, Parliament is, under article 271, authorised to impose a surcharge for the purposes of the Union on all the items of tax included in articles 269 and 270. The entire proceeds of such a surcharge will form part of the Consolidated Fund of India.

Taxes on Professions, Trades, etc. (Art. 275)

Although the imposition and collection of income-tax are within the jurisdiction of the Union, the States are permitted to impose a tax on professions, trades, callings or employments. Such a tax will not be invalid on the ground that it relates to a tax on income. Taxes on professions, etc. are generally made use of for the benefit of local self-governing institutions such as municipalities, local boards, etc. If such a tax were not allowed, an important source of income of these bodies would have come to an end, adversely affecting their already depleted sources of income. There is, however, an upper limit of Rs. 250 per annum prescribed for this tax.

Grants-in-Aid (Art. 275)

Federalism is not only a unifying but also a levelling-up force. Among the constituent States of the Union are some which are developed and advanced while others are undeveloped or underdeveloped and backward. One of the results expected of a federal union is the opportunity that it should provide for the socially and economically backward units to better their lot. A common method adopted for this purpose is the system of the Union giving grants to the needy States. Article 275 provides for this by empowering Parliament to pay, out of the Consolidated Fund of India, certain sums every year as grants-in-aid of the revenues of such States, to the extent that such assistance is adjudged as necessary. The grants so fixed are based upon the recommendations of the Finance Commission. It is not necessary that every State should get grants-in-aid every year. If, in the opinion of the Finance Commission, a particular State does not need such assistance, Parliament may leave it out while allocating such grants. The Constitution, however, makes it obligatory for the Union Government to pay such grants-in-aid to cover the schemes of development undertaken by a State with the approval of the Union for the purpose of promoting the welfare of the Scheduled Tribes in that State or raising the level of administration of the Scheduled Areas.

Bills Affecting Taxation in which the States are Interested (Art. 274)

In the case of all Bills relating to taxation in which the States are interested, the Constitution requires the prior recommendation of the President. Thus, when a Bill which affects the meaning and scope of the term 'agricultural income' as applied to Indian income-tax is to be introduced in the House of the People, the President's recommendation is necessary. The purpose of such recommendation by the President is to safeguard the interests of the States by making it obligatory for the Union Government to consult them through the President.

The Finance Commission (Arts. 280 and 281)

As has been pointed out earlier, the constitutional requirement of setting up a Finance Commission is an original idea. According to this, the President should, within two years from the inauguration of the Constitution and thereafter on the expiry of every fifth year or at such earlier intervals as he thinks necessary, constitute a Finance Commission. The Commission will consist of a Chairman and four other members who are all to be appointed by the President. As the Commission has to be constituted at regular intervals, a certain measure of continuity in the work of these Commissions is ensured. And each Commission profits by the work of its predecessors.

According to Article 280, the Finance Commission has to make recommendations to the President on two specific matters and on "any other matter referred to the Commission by the President in the interests of sound finance."

The two specific matters are:

(*i*) the distribution between the Union and the States of the net proceeds of taxes which are to be, or may be, divided between them and the allocation between the States of the respective shares of such proceeds; and

(*ii*) the principles which should govern the grants-in-aid of the revenues of the States out of the Consolidated Fund of India.

The Constitution makes it mandatory under Article 270 to divide taxes on income other than agricultural income between the Union and the States. For this purpose, taxes on income exclude corporation tax and any surcharge which may be levied for Union purposes. To the extent that the proceeds of taxes on income represent proceeds attributable to Union Territories or to taxes payable in respect of Union emoluments, they are retained by the Union. The Constitution also contains in Article 272 an enabling provision under which, if Parliament so prescribes by law, Union duties of excise other than duties of excise on medicinal and toilet preparations may be divided.

The President, after considering the recommendations of the Finance Commission with regard to income-tax, prescribes by order the percentages and the manner of distribution. Parliament is not directly concerned with the assignment and distribution of income-tax.

Article 275 deals with the grants-in-aid of the revenues of the State. These grants-in-aid are to be provided by law of Parliament; but clause (2) of this Article states that until provision is made by law, the President may exercise this power by order. His power is, however, conditioned by the proviso "that after a Finance Commission has been constituted no order shall be made under this clause by the President except after considering the recommendations of the Finance Commission." No reference to the Commission is necessary, if the grants-in-aid are provided by law of Parliament or if the President considers that no State is in need of assistance. The President did, however, refer the matter to all the Finance Commissions for their recommendations.

Under Article 280 (3)(b) the Finance Commission has the duty of making recommendations as "to the principles which should govern the grants-in-aid of the revenues of the States out of the Consolidated Fund of India."

Under Article 280 (3)(c) the President may refer to the Commission any matter which he considers to be in the interests of sound finance. Under this provision, they were asked to make recommendations as to the principles which should govern the distribution, among the States, of the net proceeds in any financial year of

(a) the estate duty in respect of property other than agricultural land;

(b) the tax on railway fares; and

(c) the additional duties of excise on mill-made textiles, sugar and tobacco (including manufactured tobacco), to be levied in replacement of the sales taxes on those articles.

In the case of the last item, the Commission had been asked to recommend the amounts which should be assured to each State as the income now derived by it from the levy of the sales taxes on these commodities.

The importance of the Finance Commission as a constitutional instrument capable of settling many complicated financial problems that affect the relationship of the Union and the States may be seen from the recommendations of the last six Commissions. The present system of allocation of finance between the Union and the States is almost entirely the result of these recommendations.

The chief merit of the work of the Commission lies in its impartial and objective outlook as a steadying force in the finances of the federal system and its ability to take the question of distribution of finances out of the vortex of federal-state political pressures and controversies. In fact, the Commission acts as a buffer between the Union and the States, checking the clamorous, finance-hungry States bent upon applying their political pressure on the Union, and, at the same time, making the latter give as much as possible to the needy States. It will be almost impossible for the Union to go against the recommendations of the Commission.

The Constitution also embodies a number of special provisions which seek to establish a certain amount of immunity from taxation by the State Governments on the income and property of the Union and *vice versa*. Further it contains several detailed provisions dealing with miscellaneous financial matters.

To examine the financial relations between the Union and the States is indeed to traverse difficult terrain. The provisions are detailed, often expressed in difficult and clumsy legal terminology. Moreover, almost every general proposition is qualified or modified by exceptions or limitations. Nevertheless, these detailed provisions have one solid merit, that of eliminating the possibility of much litigation which has been the bane of the older federations. Critics of the bulkiness of the Constitution should take special note of this. It is a striking feature in the working of the Constitution that the volume of litigation in this field has been negligible.

Thus, the financial provisions of the Constitution have on the whole avoided the pitfalls of other federal constitutions. This has been achieved by sharply demarcating the tax jurisdictions of each authority—Union and State—in order that conflicts in the concurrent zone of tax jurisdiction may not arise. The Constitution has not followed the simple dichotomy of direct and indirect tax commonly followed in some federations. Both direct and indirect taxes have been allocated to the Union and the States. The rationale of the division is the fundamental principles of federal finance, namely, efficiency and suitability. The principle of adequacy has been met by the provision dealing with federal grants-in-aid. The framework of the entire financial fabric is based upon the assumption of Union-State co-ordination, so that the fiscal relations between the Union and the States may be harmonious.

Viewing the Union-State relationship in the financial field as a whole, one finds that it is in harmony with the general nature of the Indian federalism, namely, the tendency for centralisation. The Union Government is financially stabler and stronger than the State Governments. This was necessary to facilitate the planned development of the country as a whole and to check parochial and even separatist tendencies in the economic activities within individual States. As it is, the States are, in view of their limited resources, bound to look up to the Union for financial aid for most if not all developmental projects. Naturally, they will have to follow the lead of the Union and often even submit to its dictation.

This is not a happy situation from the point of view of the States. Perhaps in the initial stages of development of India as a new politically independent country (after 1947) this was necessary both to ensure the unity of the nation and the balanced development of the different regions. But during the last thirty years the pattern of Indian economy has undergone considerable change. The States today feel that if they have to pursue their developmental objectives satisfactorily, they should have greater financial resources. And this is possible only if either the Centre gives them a larger share of the Central revenues or allowing them to have more taxation powers, if necessary, through constitutional amendment. It is not likely that the Centre would agree with either of these demands readily. But there is indication to believe that these demands are bound to gather momentum and strength in the days to come.

Financial relations between the Union and the States, especially in a developing economy, cannot remain static for long. Adjustments will have to be made in the light of the changing pattern of the economy. Legislative enactments on taxation cannot be made for all time to come. After all, the relationship between the Central Government and the States in a federal system is a dynamic one; and the problems arising out of this relationship cannot be solved once for all any more than the problems of life itself.

CHAPTER 32

INTER-STATE TRADE AND COMMERCE

FROM THE very beginning of its deliberations the Constituent Assembly was keen to ensure the freedom of inter-State trade and commerce throughout the Union. In fact, one of the primary purposes of a federal Union itself is the establishment of freedom of commerce. According to some writers, it is the Commerce Clause of the American Constitution which made the United States one united nation. For, under the Commerce Clause, the national government of the United States assumed enormous powers of regulating a wide variety of activities of the citizens and of the constituent States. But the process has involved an unending legal conflict which is still raging between the Union and the States even after nearly two centuries of the working of the Constitution. In Australia too, the situation is not happy owing to the omnibus character of the right to inter-State trade and commerce that is embodied in the Constitution.

The framers of the Indian Constitution had the benefit of these experiences at the time of drafting the provisions dealing with Inter-State Trade and Commerce as embodied in the Constitution. This is why Articles 301 to 307 form a well-thought-out scheme and, in the opinion of one of the members of the Drafting Committee, "are about as nearly perfect as human ingenuity could possibly make them." The objective behind the principle of freedom of inter-State commerce is that within the country, trade and commerce should develop to the largest possible extent and it should not be hindered by artificial barriers and restrictions imposed by the various States of the federation.

Accordingly, the Constitution has taken into account the larger interests of India as a whole as well as the interests of particular States and the wide geography of this country in which the interests of one region differ from those of another. Speaking on the general nature of the provisions, Ambedkar said: "I should also like to say that according to the provisions contained in this part, it is not the intention to make trade and commerce absolutely free, that is to say, deprive both Parliament and States

333

of any power to depart from the fundamental provision that trade and commerce shall be free. The freedom of trade and commerce is subject to certain limitation which may be imposed by Parliament or by the Legislatures of the various States, subject to the fact that the limitations contained in the power of Parliament is confined to cases arising from scarcity of goods in one part of the territory of India, and in the case of the States it must be justified on the ground of public interest."

Article 301 is general in scope and enacts that "subject to the other provisions of this Part, trade, commerce and intercourse throughout the territory of India shall be free." After having stated the general nature of the freedom of trade and commerce, the Constitution details the limitations to this freedom. There are five such limitations.

(1) Parliament may impose restrictions in any part of the territory of India in the public interest (Art. 302). The purpose of this provision is to allow the Government of India to restrict the movement of goods so as to safeguard a well-balanced economy and the proper organisation and ordering of supplies of goods and services. Famine may be raging in one part of the country while there is plenty in another part, as has been the experience of the country in regard to food during the last several decades. If Parliament has no effective powers to check such abnormal situations, freedom of trade and commerce, instead of a blessing, will become a menace to the freedom of life itself.

(2) Although Parliament is empowered to restrict the free movement of articles of trade and commerce, normally the laws passed by Parliament in this context ought to be non-discriminatory in character. In other words, it should not prefer one State to another. But when any part of the country is suffering from scarcity of goods, Parliament may, to meet such a situation, pass even a discriminatory law (Art. 303).

(3) A State Legislature may impose on goods imported from other States any tax if similar goods produced in that State also are taxed in a like manner. A State Legislature is also authorised to impose reasonable restrictions on the freedom of trade and commerce with or within that State as may be required in the public interest (Art. 304). Here is a certain amount of discretion given to the States to regulate inter-State trade and commerce

under exceptional conditions. But this is subject to Central control. According to this, any Bill which seeks to introduce such restrictions can be introduced in the State Legislature only with the previous sanction of the President. The purpose of the provision is obvious. If on account of parochial patriotism or provincialism and in disregard of the larger interests of India as a whole, a new Bill or an amending Bill to modify an existing law is introduced in a State Legislature, it will, be open to the President to withhold the sanction. The President will have the opportunity to see that the legislation is in the public interest and the restriction imposed is reasonable.

(4) Under Article 305, tax laws existing at the time of the inauguration of the Constitution were safeguarded even if they violated the freedom of inter-State trade and commerce and the power of Parliament to regulate it. At the same time, the President was empowered to make any changes to those laws as he thought fit. This Article in its present form was added by the Fourth Amendment of the Constitution, 1955, and it saves also all laws providing for State monopolies which were passed before the coming into effect of the Fourth Amendment. The fact that every restriction should be reasonable in relation to its objective leaves the Supreme Court with adequate power to examine and adjudicate upon the reasonableness of such restrictions and declare those that are unreasonable in its view invalid.

(5) Finally, under Article 307, Parliament is empowered to appoint such authority as it considers appropriate for carrying out the purposes of Articles 301 to 304 and to confer on that authority such powers and duties as it thinks necessary. Speaking on this provision, Ambedkar said: "(It) is merely an article which would enable parliament to establish an authority such as the Inter-State Commission as it exists in the U.S.A. Without specifically mentioning any such authority it is thought desirable to leave the matter in a fluid state so as to leave Parliament freedom to establish any kind of authority that it may think fit." Australia too has such an Inter-State Commission which renders valuable service in the field of inter-State trade and commerce.

Taxes on Inter-State Sales and Purchases (Art. 286)

The Constitutional provisions dealing with taxes on purchase and sale of goods were not in the original draft of the Constitution. They were introduced by Ambedkar in the form of amendments almost towards the end of the deliberations of the Constituent Assembly. Speaking on the necessity of those provisions, he said that although

> "the financial system which has been laid down in the scheme of the Draft Constitution is better than any other financial system that I know of, I think it must be said that it suffers from one defect. That defect is that the Provinces (States) are very largely dependent for their resources upon the grants made to them by the Centre. . . . I think, therefore, that while a large number of resources on which the Provinces depend have been concentrated in the Centre, from the point of view of constitutional government, it is desirable at least to leave one important source of revenue with the Provinces."

While it was felt that an important source of income should be left to the States by allowing them to tax the purchase or sale of goods, it was also keenly felt that the use of such tax power by the States should not be allowed to affect prejudicially the freedom of inter-State trade and commerce. Hence Article 286 (1) provided that no State could impose a tax on the sale or purchase of goods if such sale or purchase took place (*a*) outside the State; or (*b*) in the course of the import of the goods into, or export of the goods out of, the territory of India. There was, however, an explanation to sub-clause (*a*) above which provided that "a sale or purchase shall be deemed to have taken place in the State in which the goods have actually been delivered as a direct result of such sale or purchase for the purpose of consumption in that State, notwithstanding the fact that under the general law relating to sale of goods the property in the goods has by reason of such sale or purchase passed in another State." Section (2) of Article 286 provided that except as permitted by Parliament, "no State shall impose a tax on the sale or purchase of any goods where such sale or purchase takes place in the course of inter-State trade or commerce." Finally, under Section (3) of the same Article, a State Legislature was prohibited from imposing a tax on the sale or purchase of any goods declared by Parliament as essential to the life of the community, unless assent to such law was given by the President.

The operation of sales tax laws made by the States under these provisions, however, soon created practical difficulties; controversies which resulted from them reached the Supreme Court in appeals from the High Courts. But even the Supreme Court could not give an altogether satisfactory interpretation. The Court was sharply divided in its pronouncements. On one occasion the Court by a narrow majority reversed one of its own previous decisions on the subject.

The Court's divided decision as well as its reversal of its own earlier position, put the whole question of taxes on Inter-State sales by the States in a new perspective. The decision, as it stood, prohibited the States from imposing sales tax on any inter-State transaction until Parliament by law provided otherwise. The upshot of the divergent opinions of the judges was the Sixth Amendment of the Constitution. The Amendment retained clause (1) of Article 286 in the original form, but, for the rest, the following provisions were substituted:

"286 (2). Parliament may by law formulate principles for determining when a sale or purchase of goods takes place in any of the ways mentioned in clause (1).

"286 (3). Any law of a State shall, in so far as it imposes, or authorises the imposition of, a tax on the sale or purchase of goods declared by Parliament by law to be of special importance in inter-State trade or commerce, be subject to such restrictions and conditions in regard to the system of levy, rates and other incidents of the tax as Parliament may by law specify."

In accordance with these provisions, Parliament passed the Central Sales Tax Act, 1956, embodying the above-mentioned principles and that law now governs the different aspects of this rather complicated subject.

CHAPTER 33

EMERGENCY PROVISIONS

No CHAPTER of the Constitution has been the subject of more acrimonious attack by its critics than that dealing with the Emergency Provisions. The Constituent Assembly witnessed one of its most agitated scenes during the discussion on these provisions. Many prominent members of the Assembly opposed the inclusion of these provisions in the Constitution as they thought that they were inconsistent with the democratic provisions embodied elsewhere. The majority of the members, however, favoured the inclusion of these provisions, although reluctantly, as a precautionary measure against possible disruptive forces destroying the newly established Union.

The Constitution provides for three different categories of emergency and in each case the President is empowered to declare the emergency.

(1) *War Emergency* (Art. 352)

If the President is satisfied that a grave emergency exists whereby the security of India or any part of its territory is threatened by war, external aggression or internal disturbance, he may proclaim a State of emergency. The Proclamation may be revoked subsequently; if not, it should be laid before Parliament. If Parliament does not approve of it within two months, it will become ineffective.

It may be that at the time of the Proclamation, the House of the People has been dissolved or its dissolution takes place within two months after the Proclamation. In either case, it shall be laid before the Council of States. If the Council passes it, it must still be approved by the House within thirty days after the meeting of the new House of the People. If on the other hand, the Council itself has not approved the Proclamation, it will cease to be valid.

The power of the President to declare an Emergency may be made use of even before the actual occurrence of the aggression or disturbance, if the President is satisfied that there is imminent danger.

Effect of the Proclamation (Arts. 353 and 354)

As soon as the Emergency is proclaimed, the federal provisions of the Constitution cease to function in the area affected by the Proclamation. As a result, there is a two-fold expansion of the authority of the Union. First, the executive power of the Union will extend to the giving of any directions to any State Executive in the emergency area. Secondly, Parliament's law-making power will extend to the subjects enumerated in the State List. Further, the President is empowered to restrict or prohibit by order the distribution of revenues that are normally to be assigned entirely to the States under the financial provisions of the Constitution. However, all such orders have to be placed before each House of Parliament for its approval. The combined effect of the operation of these provisions is the emergence of a full-fledged unitary government.

(II) *Constitutional Emergency in the States* (Art. 356)

If the President is satisfied on receipt of a report from the Governor or otherwise that a situation has arisen in which the government of a State cannot be carried on in accordance with the provisions of the Constitution, he is empowered to proclaim an Emergency. As a result, (*i*) he may assume to himself all or any of the functions of the State or he may vest all or any of those functions in the Governor or any other executive authority; (*ii*) he may declare that the powers of the State Legislature shall be exercisable by Parliament; and (*iii*) he may make any other incidental or consequential provisions necessary to give effect to the objects of the Proclamation. The President, however, cannot assume to himself any of the powers vested in a High Court.

The Proclamation will have to be approved by the Houses of Parliament in the same manner in which a war-emergency Proclamation has to be approved. But even if Parliament has approved the Proclamation, it will normally cease to operate one year after the Parliamentary approval. The Proclamation can be repeated successively if necessary so as to allow the period of Emergency to continue for a maximum of three years.

If the Emergency Proclamation authorises Parliament to exercise the powers of the State Legislature, it is open to Parliament to adopt one or the other of two alternative courses. It may pass all legislative enactments for the State including financial legislation. But if Parliament does not find it convenient to do all this additional work, it may confer on the President the power of the State Legislature to make laws, or authorise the President to delegate this power to any suitable authority. Parliament is also empowered to authorise the President to sanction expenditure from the Consolidated Fund of the State, if the House of the People is not in session pending approval of such expenditure by Parliament. It is also provided that any law made by any of the authorities mentioned above will continue in force until repealed or altered by a competent legislative or other authority.

Suspension of Fundamental Rights (Arts. 358 and 359)

During the period of Emergency as declared under either of the two categories discussed above, the State is empowered to suspend the fundamental Rights guaranteed under Article 19 of the Constitution. The term "State" is used here in the same sense in which it has been used in the chapter on Fundamental Rights. It means that the power to suspend the operation of these Fundamental Rights is vested not only in Parliament but also in the Union Executive and even in a subordinate authority. Further, the Constitution empowers the President to suspend the right to move any court of law for the enforcement of any of the Fundamental Rights. It means that virtually the whole chapter on Fundamental Rights can be suspended during the operation of the Emergency. However, such orders are to be placed before Parliament as soon as possible for its approval.

(III)   Financial Emergency (Art. 360)

If the President is satisfied that a situation has arisen whereby the financial stability or credit of India or any part of it is threatened, he may declare a Financial Emergency. The Proclamation in this case also should be approved by Parliament as in the other two cases of Emergency.

During the Financial Emergency, "the executive authority of the Union shall extend to the giving of directions to any State to observe such canons of financial propriety as may be specified in the direction" or any other directions which the President may deem necessary for the purpose. Such directions may include those requiring the reduction of salaries and allowances of government servants and even those of the judges of the Supreme Court and the High Courts.

Criticism in the Constituent Assembly

Critics in the Constituent Assembly characterised these provisions as too sweeping and autocratic.

"Coming to this grand finale and the crowning glory of this chapter of reaction and retrogression," observed K. T. Shah, "I find one cannot but notice two distinct currents of thought underlying and influencing throughout the provisions of this chapter: (1) To arm the Centre with special powers against the units and (2) to arm the government against the people ....Looking at all the provisions of this chapter particularly and scrutinising the powers that have been given in almost every article, it seems to me, the name only of liberty or democracy will remain under the Constitution."

H. V. Kamath who was another severe critic said:

"I fear that by this single chapter we are seeking to lay the foundation of a totalitarian State, a police State, a State completely opposed to all the ideals and principles that we have held aloft during the last few decades, a State where the rights and liberties of millions of innocent men and women will be in continuous jeopardy, a State where if there be peace, it will be the peace of the grave and the void of the desert."

According to H. N. Kunzru, the emergency financial provisions were a serious threat to the financial autonomy of the States.

While the whole chapter on emergency provisions was the subject of severe attack, two articles in the chapter were its special target. These were Articles 358 and 359 which dealt with the suspension of the freedoms guaranteed under Article 19 and the suspension of the provision for the enforcement of Fundamental Rights through the courts including the Supreme Court.

All these criticisms are serious and they reflected the fears of many members of the Constituent Assembly as well as large sections of the public. Nevertheless, looking back after a lapse of over three decades, one feels that if one can forget what happened during the Internal Emergency that existed from June 1975 to January 1977 which was indeed a dark period in the history of constitutional government in India, much of it was the result of imaginary fears, an extreme sense of idealism, lack of appreciation of the general nature of the Constitution and the working of federal constitutions in general. The fierce attacks made against these provisions and the fears expressed about them in the Assembly and outside during the time of the framing of the Constitution seem to have lost their sharpness in the light of the experience of the last few years. An analysis of these criticisms becomes easier now since the working of the Constitution during the first twenty-five years has demonstrated certain reasonably clear trends. For such an analysis, it is proposed to classify these criticisms under the following heads:

(1) The federal character of the Constitution will be destroyed and the Union will become all-powerful.
(2) The powers of the State—both the Union and the Units—will entirely be concentrated in the hands of the Union Executive.
(3) The President will become a dictator.
(4) The financial autonomy of the States will be nullified.
(5) Fundamental Rights will become meaningless and, as a result, the democratic foundations of the Constitution will be destroyed.

These may be examined one by one. It is true that the federal character of the government will be transformed into a unitary one as a result of the Proclamation of Emergency. But this is more or less true of almost any federation during a period of grave national emergency. The safety and security of the nation is the responsibility of the Union. The claim for the maintenance of the federal character has not the same importance as the requirements of national security. In case of a conflict between the two, the latter should prevail. But such a situation is an exceptional one. Hence the provisions to meet any emergency are the result of abundant caution.

The specific circumstances under which the Centre may be called upon to take over the administration of a State may be detailed. There may be for example, a physical breakdown of the government in the State owing to widespread internal disturbance or external aggression and for some reason or other, law and order cannot be maintained. Naturally, without the Centre's intervention there will be nothing but chaos. Then there may be a political breakdown. This is a point which requires careful analysis. A political breakdown can happen when no ministry can be formed or the ministries that can be formed are so unstable that the government actually breaks down. Normally, according to the Constitution, when there is great instability in government, the proper procedure will be to dissolve the Lower House and reconstitute it. If after a dissolution also, the same factions are reproduced in the local legislature and they make a ministry impossible, it will then be inevitable for the Centre to step in. Then there is a third contingency of economic breakdown.

The necessity for a strong Union to meet any eventuality was widely accepted during the period when the Constitution was being framed. The war in Kashmir, the recalcitrant attitude of some Princely States against joining the Union, armed insurrection in the Telengana region of Hyderabad State, the circumstances that called for the 'police action' in Hyderabad and a number of other disruptive forces,—all these were shaking the very foundations of the newly founded Union. Critics of the emergency provisions seem to forget the fact that for the first time in centuries, India has established a single administration embracing the entire country. The Union was too precious an achievement and it could not be allowed to be destroyed under the impact of disruptive forces generated by linguism, regionalism or provincialism from within or aggressive forces from without. The States are incapable of successfully facing an external threat and are not always trustworthy in meeting an internal crisis. Diversity of authority in an emergency will spell disaster.

The very first decade of the working of the Constitution has vindicated the wisdom of these provisions. During this period there have been six occasions when the President had to proclaim an emergency as a result of the breakdown of constitutional machinery in some of the States. The first such proclamation was made in 1951 when in the Punjab, the Bhargava Ministry resigned and an alternative ministry could not be formed. The proclamation of emergency was made on the basis of a report of the then Governor of the Punjab, to whom was later delegated, by the President, the executive power to carry on the State's administration during the period of emergency. At the same time, the legislative power of the State was given over to Parliament. The emergency, however, was only for a short period and parliamentary government was re-established immediately after the termination of the emergency. Not only did the Centre show no eagerness to keep the State under its direct control longer than was absolutely necessary, but it also helped the local political conditions to stabilise in order that a ministry could soon be formed.

The second occasion for the proclamation of emergency arose in 1952 when after the first general elections the formation of a stable ministry was found impossible in the PEPSU State. There was first a Congress Ministry which soon lost its majority in the Legislature. A coalition ministry which followed it was incapable of functioning smoothly on account of dissensions within the coalition. As a result of the proclamation of emergency, the State Legislature was dissolved. The Union appointed one of its senior Civil Service officers as Adviser to the *Rajapramukh* to carry on the administration during the emergency. Within six months new elections were held and the Congress Party came back to power with a stable majority.

The third occasion arose in 1954 in the newly created Andhra State under rather unusual circumstances. The ruling Prakasam Ministry was supported by the Congress Party and a number of independents. But the Government had only a slender majority in the State Legislature. The defection of some of its supporters in a crucial vote of no-confidence, arising out of the implementation of the recommendations of the committee which reported on the working of prohibition in the State, brought about its downfall. The opposition members who joined hands to defeat the Ministry belonged to three parties besides independents and dissident Congress Members. Naturally, it was not easy for such disparate elements to join together for the formation of a new ministry.

Moreover, the members of the then State Assembly were elected in the first general elections to the Legislature of the former composite State of Madras from which Andhra was created in 1953. In the circumstances, public opinion within the State itself was in favour of a new election. But the defeated Prakasam Ministry was unwilling to carry on even as a care-taker government during the period required for holding the new election. The Governor's report had made these points clear and in the light of them the President proclaimed the emergency, and took over the administration. The President's rule, however, came to an end with the formation of a stable Government after the election to the State Assembly in 1954.

The fourth occasion which necessitated the proclamation of emergency arose in 1956 when the then Congress Ministry of the former State of Travancore-Cochin resigned as a result of its loss of majority in the Legislature. Since no other party was capable of forming an alternative ministry, taking over of the administration by the Union became inevitable. As in the case of PEPSU, an Adviser was appointed to assist the *Rajapramukh* to whom was delegated the executive power of the State. The emergency lasted for about a year during which the new State of Kerala was formed and the second general elections held. Although the election did not produce a stable majority for any party in the State Legislature, a coalition of the Communist members and some independents made the restoration of Parliamentary government possible in the State in 1957 immediately after the results of the election were declared.

The fifth occasion for a proclamation of emergency arose under unusual circumstances once again in the State of Kerala. These circumstances developed after the assumption of power in that State in 1957 by the Communist Party of India. A popular agitation in the State supported by the entire opposition began gathering momentum from the beginning of 1959. Soon it assumed formidable proportions and a State-wide civil disobedience movement took the law and order position in the State to a situation of utter collapse. In the circumstances the Governor of the State reported to the President in July 1959 that he had come to the conclusion that the administration of the State could not be carried on in accordance with the Constitution any more. On the basis of this report the proclamation of emergency was issued by the President on 31st July, 1959. The emergency lasted only for seven months at the end of which elections were conducted to constitute a new Assembly in the State. The election of February 1960 brought to an end the political uncertainty in the State and a new ministry with an overwhelming majority in support of it was installed in the State in February 1960.

The sixth occasion which necessitated the proclamation of emergency arose in 1961 when the coalition Ministry of the Congress Party and the Ganatantra Parishad in Orissa State which was functioning for over three years found it impossible to continue any longer. The Ministry submitted its resignation to the Governor on whose advice the proclamation of emergency was made by the President. The emergency did not last even six months. For, in the mid-term elections of June to the Orissa Assembly, the Congress Party was returned with a comfortable majority and as a result, a Congress Ministry was soon installed in office.

The constitutional machinery broke down again in Kerala, for a third time, necessitating the seventh proclamation of emergency by the President in 1964 as a result of a successful no-confidence motion against the Ministry. No alternative Ministry was possible and hence the President had to proclaim an emergency.

On July 5, 1966 President's rule was proclaimed in the Punjab making the number of such proclamations eight. The President's rule in the State was necessary to facilitate the smooth transfer of power to the two new States of Punjabi Suba and Haryana created by reorganising the Punjab.

Between 1967 and May 1977 there were in all 28 proclamations of emergency in the States.

These instances indicate the purpose and the manner in which in actual practice a proclamation of emergency will be made by the President. They may be summed up in the following terms:

(1) The essential condition for the intervention of the Centre is the political instability in the State, that is, the virtual breakdown of the Parliamentary system of government.

(2) The Union will watch the situation of instability with utmost caution and provide every opportunity for the formation of an alternative ministry.

(3) If a new election after the dissolution of the State Legislature is called for to remedy the situation, the defeated Ministry may be allowed to carry on the administration as a care-taker government pending the new election.

(4) The proclamation of emergency will only be the last resort when (*i*) the existing Ministry does not have the confidence of the Legislature, (*ii*) no alternative ministry can be formed, and (*iii*) the defeated Ministry is unwilling or unable to carry on as a care-taker government pending new elections.

(5) During the period of emergency, the legislative work of the State will be transferred to Parliament. Delegation of such work to any administrative body will be reduced to the minimum.

(6) As soon as the political situation within the State becomes conducive to responsible government, it will be restored.

In the cases detailed above, Central intervention almost invariably brought about the emergence of stable Ministries at the termination of the emergency. Thus, in practice, the emergency provisions for Central intervention in case of a breakdown of constitutional machinery in the States, have proved to be not only a protective device for responsible government in politically unstable States but also a blessing to political parties who were unwilling to shoulder responsibility for a time on account of group rivalries or any other unfavourable circumstances.

During a period of emergency, it is natural that the Executive becomes unusually powerful. This is a tendency of governments all over the world, federal or unitary. The experience of parliamentary democracies indicates that a Parliament is vigilant and through the members of the Opposition, particularly, it manages to compel the Executive to account for all its actions. Thus Parliament has the power to check the Executive whenever the latter goes beyond reasonable limits. Emergency provisions do not in any way cut Parliament out of the picture, and Parliament has always the right to call the Executive to order; and if they find that the Executive has exceeded their powers in regard to the operation of any of the provisions enacted under the emergency laws, they can always pull them up; they can even dismiss the Ministry and replace them.

Many critics have drawn attention to the position of the President during an emergency. They think that the President can become a dictator, if he so wishes during the emergency. But this is not quite so. We have already seen the real scope of the President's powers. The chances of his becoming a Caesar or a Tzar are practically nil. There is hardly an occasion when the President can rule the country without the assistance of a Council of Ministers. To think of the President and the Ministers combining in a conspiracy to flout the Constitution by maintaining a perpetual emergency and dissolving the House of the People every time it comes into being, is a fear arising more out of a basic mistrust in the strength of democracy and its institutions than an understanding of the working of democratic governments. No constitution can avoid such a situation if those who are charged upon to work it deliberately try to wreck it. It cannot be helped under any system of Government, whatever might be the constitutional provisions.

Even if the President is bent upon acting autocratically with or without the Ministry, by declaring emergencies, it is impossible for him to carry on the administration without the approval of Parliament. For, there is no provision in the constitution authorising the President to appropriate funds without Parliamentary sanction. Hence, at the most, the President may carry on his autocratic rule only until the end of the current financial year; to run the administration any further he would need the support of Parliament.

How effectively Parliament would and could function during a period of national emergency was a subject of speculation until 1962, when the President proclaimed emergency under Article 352. But the manner in which Parliament has dealt with the Emergency and functioned during the Emergency show that instead of the Executive arrogating to itself the powers of Parliament in the name of emergency, Parliament has subjected the Executive to greater control and scrutiny in all its actions vitally affecting the nation. In fact, the debates in Parliament demonstrated the eagerness with which the Executive sought the approval of Parliament not only with regard to the actions already taken by the Government but also those proposed for the future.

The only exception to this in practice was the Internal Emergency period of 1975-77. There was widespread abuse of executive power in many parts of the country in many forms during this period. The extent of abuse became clear only after the lifting of Emergency in 1977. Naturally, the new Parliament which came into being after the General Elections of March 1977, was interested in preventing the repetition of such a situation in future and hence initiated steps to amend the Constitution suitably to limit the powers of the Government to proclaim internal emergency.

The Amendment (Forty-fifth) adopted by Parliament in December 1978 ensures that proclamation of Emergency can be made only on the basis of written advice tendered to the President by the Cabinet. Internal disturbance not amounting to armed rebellion will no longer be a ground for declaration of emergency. Emergency can be proclaimed only when the security of the country is threatened by war, external aggression or armed rebellion. As an additional safeguard, proclamation of emergency will require approval within a month by resolution of Parliament by a majority of the total membership and not less than two-thirds of the members present and voting.

The provisions dealing with financial emergency were introduced at a time when the economic situation in India, soon after the coming of Independence, had become suddenly serious. Explaining the reasons for their incorporation in the Constitution, Ambedkar said: "This article more or less follows the pattern of what is called the National Recovery Act of the United States passed in 1933 which gave the President power to make similar provisions in order to remove the difficulties, both economical and financial that had overtaken the American people, as a result of the great depression."

The provisions for financial emergency, again, show how the framers of the Constitution have drawn upon the experience of the working of federalism elsewhere. There has, however, been no occasion so far to make use of these provisions.

Finally, one may consider the provision for the suspension of Fundamental Rights. Apparently this is by far the most unwholesome provision in the Constitution.

The provision for the suspension of constitutional rights does not mean however that with the proclamation of emergency, there will be an automatic suspension of Fundamental Rights. It may be quite possible to keep the enforcement of the Fundamental Rights intact and there need not be a universal suspension throughout the country merely by reason of the Proclamation. Further, the order of suspension should be placed before Parliament and it will be free to take whatever action it deems fit.

The working of the Constitution so far shows that the suspension of fundamental rights took place only rarely. That happened as a result of the proclamation of national emergencies in 1962, 1965, 1971 and 1975. The proclamation did not, however, affect all the fundamental rights embodied in the Constitution. Those affected were Articles 14, 19, 20, 21 and 22. The implications of such suspension have been dealt with in detail elsewhere earlier in this work.[1]

In contrast to the national emergencies mentioned above fundamental rights were never suspended during any of the emergencies proclaimed in the States. That remains a good precedent. Even during a national emergency, suspension of fundamental rights should be restricted to the absolute minimum. There have been no instances so far of the Union Executive behaving high-handedly towards the States or ignoring Parliament in the name of emergency. The apprehension that the President may act as a dictator is not one of the acute discomforts of our political thinking. On the other hand, the emergency provisions have been on the whole, justified when viewed from the experience of the past.

1 See Chapter 22.

PART VII

MISCELLANEOUS PROVISIONS

CHAPTER 34

THE COMPTROLLER AND AUDITOR-GENERAL OF INDIA

THE PROVISION for independent audit is an essential ingredient of parliamentary democracy. The fundamental basis of parliamentary system of government, as we have already seen, is the responsibility of the Executive to the Legislature for all its actions. The legislature will be able to enforce this executive responsibility only if it is competent to scrutinise the activities of the Executive, and exercise on each of them its judgment in an appropriate manner. There are certain activities of the Executive which can easily be scrutinised by any one, while others are difficult for a group of laymen to scrutinise. Checking of accounts and assessing the soundness or otherwise of the financial transactions of the Executive is a technical job which falls in the latter category and Parliament, composed as it is of laymen in general, is not a competent and suitable instrument for making such scrutiny. Yet, it is a function of Parliament to scrutinise the financial dealings of the government and to ensure that the tax-payer's money is properly spent. Parliament needs the assistance of an expert for this purpose and it is in this context that the office of the Comptroller and Auditor-General becomes an essential ingredient of parliamentary democracy. For, it is the Comptroller and Auditor-General who through his expert advice enables Parliament to discharge this function efficiently. By performing such an important function the Comptroller and Auditor-General makes himself an indispensable instrument in the proper working of a parliamentary government. It is this important role that makes his office one of the four pillars of our democratic Constitution, the other three being the Legislature, the Executive and the Judiciary.

There is nothing strikingly original in the provisions of the Constitution dealing with the office of the Comptroller and Auditor-General. Such an office (the Auditor-General of India) had already been in existence as an integral part of India's constitutional machinery since 1919. The idea of the office itself comes from England where it has a history of almost a century.

In India, the Auditor-General received statutory recognition for the first time under the Government of India Act of 1919. Such recognition, however, did not mean complete independence from the Executive. The Auditor-General was to conduct an audit subject to any general or special orders of the Secretary of State-in-Council and his reports on the Government Accounts were to be sent to that authority through the Governor-General. The Government of India Act of 1935 substantially increased the independence of the Auditor-General by abolishing the control of the Secretary of State and the Auditor-General was required to submit his annual Audit Reports to the respective legislatures through the Government of India and the Provincial Governments.

The framers of the Constitution, realising the importance of an independent agency for audit under parliamentary democracy, made the Comptroller and Auditor-General fully independent so that he could discharge his functions efficiently and fearlessly.

Independence of the Comptroller and Auditor-General

Under Article 148, the Comptroller and Auditor-General of India is to be appointed by the President by warrant under his hand and seal, just as a judge of the Supreme Court is appointed. He can be removed from office only in like manner and on the like grounds as a judge of the Supreme Court. Every person appointed to be the Comptroller and Auditor-General, before he enters upon his office, has to make and subscribe before the President an oath or affirmation in a form prescribed for the purpose. His salary and other conditions of service may be determined by Parliament. But once appointed, neither his salary nor his rights in respect of leave of absence, pension or age of retirement can be varied to his disadvantage. At present, the Comptroller and Auditor-General receives a salary of Rs. 4,000 per month, the same salary as that of a judge of the Supreme Court. After retirement or resignation from office, he is not eligible for any office of profit under the Government of India or any State Government. The administrative expenses of the office of the Comptroller and Auditor-General, including the salaries, etc. of the office staff, are charged upon the Consolidated Fund of India. It is also provided that the conditions of service of persons serving in the Indian Audit and Accounts Department and the administrative powers of the Comptroller and Auditor-General will be prescribed by rules made by the President after consultation with the Comptroller and Auditor-General. Such rules, however, are subject to the provisions of the Constitution as well as any law made by Parliament in this behalf. A comparison of these provisions with the corresponding provisions dealing with the judges of the Supreme Court will show that they are substantially the same in scope, and that the office of the Comptroller and Auditor-General, as far as its independence is concerned, has been modelled on the Supreme Court. As such, the Comptroller and Auditor-General can function, in the discharge of his responsibilities, as an authority established under the Constitution, whose independence is safeguarded by the express provisions of the Constitution.

Duties and Powers of the Comptroller and Auditor-General

Articles 149 and 150 deal with the powers and duties of the Comptroller and Auditor-General. According to Article 149, Parliament is empowered to prescribe the powers and duties of the Comptroller and Auditor-General in relation to the accounts of the Union and the States and any other authority or body established either by the Union or the State. Accordingly Parliament passed an Act in 1972 dealing with these matters. It upholds the independence of the Comptroller and Auditor-General of India and enables him to work effectively and efficiently. According to Article 150, the Comptroller and Auditor-General has the power to prescribe the form and manner in which the accounts of the Union and the States shall be kept, subject to the approval of the President.

The department of the Comptroller and Auditor-General is expected to discharge three main functions:

(1) to audit the Government's expenditure;
(2) to see that the financial rules and orders which have a bearing on governmental expenditure are obeyed; and
(3) to satisfy itself that those who sanction expenditure have the power to do so.

However, a most important function of the Comptroller and Auditor-General, though it is not one which forms part of his statutory obligations, is to examine the accounts from the standpoint of economy and to draw the attention of the Public Accounts Committee to cases of apparent waste and extravagance. Wherever a parliamentary system of government prevails this is considered to be the most important function of this office.

The Comptroller and Auditor-General and the Public Accounts Committee

It is the duty of the Public Accounts Committee to examine the appropriation accounts and the reports of the Comptroller and Auditor-General on them and such other accounts laid before Parliament as the Committee may think fit. The purpose of such examination is to ensure the accountability of the Executive to Parliament with respect to all its activities in the financial field. In carrying out its investigations, the Committee receives the expert advice of the Comptroller and Auditor-General who takes it through the intricacies of government accounts. The Committee examines departmental witnesses who are summoned to appear before it and to answer the criticism which the Comptroller and Auditor-General has brought against the working of their departments in his annual reports. It is widely accepted that the success or failure of the work of the Public Accounts Committee depends mainly on the quality of the reports of the Comptroller and Auditor-General. His reports will not only ensure that appropriations made by Parliament are not exceeded without supplementary grants but also that the expenditure conforms to the rules. In addition, he must also satisfy himself on behalf of Parliament about the wisdom, faithfulness and economy of the spending programme of the Government.

Under Article 151, the reports of the Comptroller and Auditor-General relating to the accounts of the Union are submitted to the President. Those relating to the accounts of the States are submitted to the Governors. These reports are laid before Parliament and the State Legislatures respectively.

The service rendered by the Comptroller and Auditor-General is of inestimable value to safeguard the interests of the taxpayer.

Audit is the watch-dog of the finances of the nation and the Comptroller and Auditor-General is the supreme overseer of the Government's financial activities on behalf of Parliament. In a country like India where public expenditure is increasing at a fast pace year after year, there is scope both for the widening and for the intensifying of the role of the Comptroller and Auditor-General for the better realisation of the democratic ideals embodied in the Constitution.

Chapter 35

PUBLIC SERVICES

THE STANDARD and efficiency of administration in any country depend ultimately on the calibre, training and integrity of the members of the Public Services. When the aim of a Constitution is the establishment of a welfare State, it is evident that the functions of such a State will embrace a wide range of activities. The successful operation of these activities depends upon the availability of men of vision, ability, honesty and loyalty to man the administrative apparatus of the State. The concern of the framers of the Constitution to ensure this is clear from the provisions dealing with the Constitution and functions of the Public Service Commissions. We have also seen the constitutional guarantee of equality of opportunity in matters of public employment. Not content with these, they went further and made certain special provisions dealing with the Public Services in India in order to make them feel contented and secure in their positions.

One of the major problems of a democratic government is the proper adjustment between the 'political wing' and the 'civil service wing' of the administrative machinery. The former is the representative of the people, and, as such, enter and leave office according to the will of the people. The latter, on the other hand are permanently in office and are often called upon to serve different masters at different times; to translate into action different policies at the behest of different masters. This they can do only if they maintain an attitude of political detachment and eschew a partisan approach. At the same time, they should be loyal to the government of the day. Let us examine the extent to which this ideal is embodied in the Constitution.

Article 309 empowers Parliament and the State Legislatures to regulate the recruitment and the conditions of service of the Public Services of the Union and the States respectively. Article 310 ensures that all persons who are members of the Defence Services or of the Civil Services of the Union or of All India Services hold office during the pleasure of the President. Similarly, members of the State Services hold office during the pleasure of the Governor. Since the President or the Governor is only the constitutional head of the State, the powers of the President or the Governor here are those which are exercised by the Union Cabinet or the State Cabinet. Hence, the Cabinet wields the real power of controlling all categories of services. This is in harmony with the democratic and responsible character of the Government which ensures the responsibility of the Executive to the Legislature.

"To hold office during the pleasure of the President or Governor" does not, however, mean that a member of the public services can be dismissed arbitrarily by the President or the Governor. There are certain constitutional safeguards against such an action. These are embodied in Article 311 in the following manner: (1) No member of a civil service of the Union or an All India Service or a State Service can be dismissed or removed by an authority subordinate to that by which he was appointed. (2) No such member shall be dismissed or removed or reduced in rank until he has been given a reasonable opportunity of showing cause against the action proposed to be taken in regard to him.

The object of this Article, as Ambedkar made it clear in the Constituent Assembly, is to lay down a general proposition that in every case of action which affects a member of the civil service adversely, notice shall be given. "I should have thought that that was probably the best provision that we have for the safety and security of the civil service, because it contains a fundamental limitation upon the authority to dismiss." There can hardly be any doubt that one of the most important aspects of the public services is 'permanence in office'. This is so closely associated with the 'security of service' that it is difficult to think of the one without at once associating it with the other. Continuity of personnel is of great importance. Constant change in the services is costly in money and more costly in effectiveness. Civil servants must be given such security of tenure as will give them confidence to deal forthrightly with their "masters". This is to a large extent obtained by the constitutional guarantees mentioned above.

There are, however, a few exceptions where the civil servants are not given all these facilities to defend themselves. These are:

(*i*) Where a person is dismissed or reduced in rank on the ground of conduct which has led to his conviction on a criminal charge;

(*ii*) Where in the interest of the security of the State, it is not expedient to give such an opportunity to the civil servants.

During the last three decades, the High Courts and the Supreme Court were, in a series of cases, called upon to declare the validity or otherwise of dismissals or removals of public servants from service by the Union or the States in the light of the protections provided by the Constitution. In Shyamlal *vs.* State of U.P. the Supreme Court held that "a compulsory retirement does not amount to dismissal or removal and, therefore, does not attract the provisions of Article 311." Similarly, termination of contractual service by notice under one of the provisions of the contract also does not amount to dismissal or removal contemplated under Article 311. In Mahesh Prasad *vs.* State of U.P., the Court held that Article 311(1) does not mean that the removal from service must be by the very same authority who made the appointment or by his direct superior. It is enough if the removing authority is of the same rank or grade. Giving reasonable opportunity of showing cause against the action proposed to be taken in regard to a civil servant does not imply giving more than one such opportunity. Further, if the civil servant concerned does not make use of such opportunity given to him, he does so at his own risk.

The question as to whether non-compliance with the provisions of Article 320, under which the Government is expected to consult the Public Service Commission in every case of disciplinary action, will affect an action properly taken against a civil servant under Article 311 came up for consideration before the Supreme Court in State of U.P. *vs.* M. L. Srivastava. The Court held that "Article 320 cannot be held to be mandatory and is not in the nature of a rider to Article 311 and Article 311 is not controlled by Article 320."

The Supreme Court had occasion to make an exhaustive analysis of the scope and ambit of the constitutional safeguards embodied in Article 311 in the light of all judicial decisions until 1958 in the case of Purushotam Lal Dhingra *vs.* Union

of India. The facts of this case, briefly, are as follows: Purushotam Lal joined the Railway service as a signaller in 1924.
As a result of successive selections to higher posts, he became
Chief Controller (a class III service post) in 1950. In March
1951 he was selected by a selection board for the post of Assistant
Superintendent, Railway Telegraphs, which was a gazetted post
in Class II Officers' cadre. He joined duty in the new post in
July 1951. In 1953 his superior officer made certain adverse
remarks against him in his confidential report for the year ending March 1953. The views expressed in this report were con-
firmed by another superior officer soon after. These remarks
were placed before the General Manager who wrote: "I am disappointed to read these reports. He should revert as a subordinate till he makes good the shortcomings noticed in this chance
of his as an officer. Portions underlined are to be communicated." The appellant made a representation against the remarks
made against him. But this did not produce any favourable
result. By August 1953 orders were issued reverting him to
class III. He appealed unsuccessfully first to the President of
India through a representation. In 1955 he filed a writ petition
in the Punjab High Court. The judge who heard the petition
declared that since Purushotam Lal was not given an opportunity to show cause against the action proposed to be taken in
regard to him, provisions of Article 311 were violated and hence
the action taken against him was invalid. On a Letters Patent
Appeal filed by the Union of India, a Division Bench of the
High Court consisting of two judges, reversed the above order
and dismissed the writ petition. Hence the appeal to the Supreme Court by the petitioner.

The Supreme Court was divided four to one in its decision.
Speaking on behalf of the majority, Chief Justice Das made the
following important observations:

"Subject to exceptions contemplated by the opening words
of Article 310(1), e.g. Articles 124, 148, 218 and 324, our
Constitution has adopted by the said Article 310(1) the
English Common Law Rule that public servants held office
during the pleasure of the President or the Governor as the
case may be and it has by Article 311 imposed two qualifica-

tions for the exercise of that pleasure; in other words, the provisions of Article 311 operate as a proviso to Article 310 (1). Upon Article 311 two questions arise namely, (1) who are entitled to protection and (2) the ambit and scope of protection.

"To limit the operation of the protective provisions of this Article to persons holding permanent civil posts or who are permanent members of the services will be to add qualifying words to the Article which will be contrary to sound principles of interpretation of the Constitution or a statute. There could also be no rational basis for the distinction. The Article makes no distinctions between the two classes, permanent and temporary (officiating, provisional and on probation included) both of which, therefore, are within its protections.

"The two protections under the Article are (1) against being dismissed or removed by an authority subordinate to that by which the appointment had been made, (2) against being dismissed, removed or reduced in rank without being heard. The words 'dismissed', 'removed' and 'reduced in rank' have acquired a special meaning at the time of the Constitution and it is only in those cases where the Government intends to inflict those three forms of punishment that the Government servant must be given reasonable opportunity of showing cause against the action proposed to be taken in regard to him. Therefore, if the termination of service is sought to be brought about otherwise than by way of punishment, then the Government servant whose service is so terminated cannot claim the protection of Article 311(2).

"The principle is that when a servant has a right to a post or to a rank either under the contract of employment, express or implied or under the Rules governing the conditions of service, the termination of service of such a servant or his reduction to a lower post is by itself and *prima facie* a punishment for it operates as a forfeiture of his rights to hold the post or the rank and to get the emoluments and other benefits attached thereto; but if the servant has no such right to the post or that rank as when he is appointed to a post permanent or temporary either on probation or on an officiating basis and whose temporary service has not ripened to a quasi-permanent service under the appropriate Rules, the termination of his employment does not deprive him of any right and cannot therefore by itself be a punishment. In other words if the Government has the right to terminate the employment at any time then such termination in the manner contemplated by the contract or by the Rules is *prima facie* and *per se* not a punishment and does not attract the protective provisions of Article 311.

"Even in such cases if the Government chose to proceed against the servant on the basis of misconduct, inefficiency and the like and inflict on him the punishment of dismissal, removal or reduction carrying with it penal consequences, the servant will be entitled to protection under Article 311(2).

"The two tests to be applied by Courts are (1) whether the servant had a right to the post or the rank or (2) whether he has been visited with evil consequences. If the case satisfied either of the two tests then it must be held that the servant had been punished and the termination of service must be taken as a dismissal or removal from service or the reversion to his substantive post must be regarded as a reduction in rank, attracting the provision in Article 311(2) and the provision thereof must have been complied with; otherwise the termination of service or reduction in rank must be held to be wrongful.

"The appellant was appointed to the higher post on an officiating basis and under the Railway Code and Fundamental Rules he had no right to continue in that post. Such appointment was terminable at any time, on reasonable notice, by Government and so his reversion did not operate as a forfeiture of any right and could not be described as 'reduction in rank' by way of punishment. It would not amount also to 'dismissal or removal' because of Note I to Rule 1729 of the Railway Code (applicable to the appellant). Further it did not entail the forfeiture of his future chances of promotion or affect his seniority in his substantive post. He cannot complain that the requirements of Article 311 (2) were not complied with."

In his dissent, Justice Vivian Bose agreed generally with the interpretation of Article 311 by the majority. But he said that the words 'dismissal, removal and reduction in rank' have special meaning and that Article 311(2) applies when penal consequence ensue, that the Article is attracted whenever a right is infringed thereby. He said:

"The test must always be whether evil consequences over and above those that would ensure from a 'contractual termination' are likely to follow and Article 311(2) cannot be confined to the penalties prescribed by the various rules or in other words the Article cannot be evaded by saying in a set of rules that a particular consequence is not a punishment or that a particular kind of action is not intended to operate as a penalty.

"In the instant case, though the order of reversion is non-committal, the General Manager's remarks or the otherwise irrelevant administrative notings which form the real foundation for the order, i.e. . . . till he makes good his shortcomings noticed in this chance of his as an officer cannot be ignored and Article 311(2) is attracted thereby.

"The real hurt does not lie in any of those things—the form of action or the procedure followed or what operated in the mind of a particular officer—but in the consequences that follow and, in my judgment, the protections of Article 311 are not against harsh words but against hard blows. It is the effect of the order alone that matters; and in my judgment, Article 311 applies whenever any substantial evil follows over and above a purely 'contractual one'. I do not think that the Article can be evaded by saying in a set of rules that a particular consequence is not a punishment or that a particular kind of action is not intended to operate as a penalty."

In Khem chand vs. the Union of India the Court said:

"The reasonable opportunity of showing cause against the action proposed includes:

(a)   an opportunity to deny his guilt and establish his innocence which he can do only if he is told on what the charges are based;

(*b*) an opportunity to defend himself by cross-examining the witnesses produced against him and by examining himself or any other witnesses in support of his defence; and finally,

(*c*) an opportunity to make his representation as to why the proposed punishment should not be inflicted on him which he can only do if the competent authority after the inquiry is over and after applying his mind to the gravity or otherwise of the charges proved against the government servant tentatively proposes to inflict one of the three punishments and communicates the same to him."

Can the services of a government servant be terminated on the ground of 'subversive activities'? This question arose in Balakotaiah *vs.* Union of India in which the appellant challenged the validity of the notices under Rule 3 of Railway Service (Safeguarding of National Security) Rules, 1949, and the orders of suspension and dismissal served on him. It was contended on behalf of the appellant that the Security Rules were void as they militated against the constitutional protections under Article 311 and the Fundamental Rights guaranteed under Articles 14 (equality before law and equal protection of laws) and 19 (1)(c) (right to form associations). The Court rejected these contentions and unanimously held:

1. It may be that the connotation of the words "subversive activities" in Rule 3 of the Security Rules is wide but that is not to say it is vague and indefinite. The object of the Rules as recited in the short title is safeguarding the national security which is emphasised in the provision to Rule 3. The words "subversive activities" in the context of national security is sufficiently precise to sustain a valid classification. The Security Rules, 1949, are not illegal as being repugnant to Article 14 of the Constitution.

2. The appellants have, no doubt, a fundamental right to associations under Article 19 (1) (c) (and to be members of the Communist Party and trade unions); but they have no fundamental right to be continued in employment by the State and when their services are terminated by the State they cannot complain of the infringement of any of their

constitutional rights when no question of violation of Article 311 arises.

3. The terms of employment (applicable to the appellants) provide for their services being terminated on a proper notice and so no question of premature termination arises. Rule 7 of the Security Rules preserves their right to all the benefits of pension, gratuities and the like they would be entitled to under the rules. The orders terminating their services stand on the same footing as an order of discharge under Rule 148 of the Railway Establishment Code and it is neither one of dismissal nor of removal so as to attract Article 311 of the Constitution.

4. The rules are clearly prospective in that action thereunder is to be taken in respect of subversive activities which either exist now or are likely to be indulged in, in future. That the materials for taking action in the latter case, as in the notices in the instant cases, are drawn from the conduct of the employees prior to the enactment does not render them retrospective.

Can a government servant join an association of civil servants which has not been recognised by the Government? The Supreme Court answered the question in the positive and declared Rule 4-B of the Central Services (Conduct) Rules, 1955, to be unconstitutional and void. It was unconstitutional because it contravened Article 19(1) (c) of the Constitution which guaranteed the right to form associations by prohibiting a government servant from joining or continuing to be a member of any association of government servants which has not been recognised or whose recognition has been withdrawn by the Government. By the same decision the Court declared that Rule 4-A, which prohibits any form of demonstration, was also violation of the government servants' rights. But in so far as the said rule prohibited a strike, it could not be struck down for the reason that there was no fundamental right to resort to strike.

Has the State the power under Article 310 to punish a government servant for acts unconnected with his official duties? This question was answered in the affirmative by the Allahabad High

Court in the case of L. N. Pande. Delivering the judgment of the Court, Justice Dhawan said that

"the action taken against the official would be justified if the Government was of the opinion that the act in question amounted to misconduct, unbecoming or unworthy of a Government official or violated the unwritten code of conduct, provided that the Government complied with the provisions of Article 311 and gave a reasonable opportunity to the accused official to show cause against the action proposed to be taken against him. He further pointed out that if the contention that a government servant was not answerable to the Government for misconduct committed in his private life was correct, the result would be that however reprehensible or abominable a government servant's conduct in his private life might be, the Government would be powerless to dispense with his services unless and until he committed a criminal offence or committed an act which was specifically prohibited by the Government Servants' Conduct Rules. This would clothe government servants with an impunity which would place the government in a position worse than that of an ordinary employer. It would be almost destructive of the principle laid down in Article 310 that every government servant held office during the pleasure of the President or Governor, as the case might be. The power of the State to dispense with the services of any government servant, though hedged with safeguards contained in Article 311 and other provisions of the Constitution, was real."

All India Services

Article 312 provides for the creation of All India Services. An All India Service is different from both the Central and the State Services. It has been pointed out earlier that under Article 309, the States are entitled to create their own civil services and lay down their own conditions of service just as the Centre is entitled to create its own services, make recruitment and lay down conditions of service. Thus, while Article 309 provides for separate jurisdictions for the Centre and the States, Article 312 takes away to some extent the autonomy of the States in this field by vesting in the Centre the authority to create All India Services. However, the framers were anxious to see that the vesting of such authority in the Centre should be with the consent of a substantial majority of the representatives of the States. This is why Article 312 provides that an All India Service can be created only if the Council of States declares by a resolution supported by not less than a two-thirds majority that it is necessary in the national interest to create one or more such All India Services. Such a resolution should be considered as tantamount to an authority given by the States. When once such a resolution is passed, Parliament is competent to constitute such an All India Service and lay down details connected with it.

All India Services, by their very nature, are instruments of national consolidation and unity. They ensure the maintenance of common standards all over the country in certain vital fields of administration. They facilitate the existence of a hard core of official in every State who, because of their membership in a service which falls, within the jurisdiction of the Centre, feel more free and independent to act with a national outlook and keeping in view the national interests. The framers of the Constitution had originally no intention of creating such All India Services. This was why the Draft Constitution did not make any provision in this regard. But the partition of the country and the creation of Pakistan, and the extremely unsettled conditions that prevailed in the country in the early days of Independence convinced those in authority of the necessity of such services as powerful instruments for the preservation of national unity. The example of the Indian Civil Service provided the necessary experience for the creation of such All India Services.

Originally, besides the old Indian Civil Service, there were only two All India Services, namely, the Indian Administrative Service and the Indian Police Service. Legislation was enacted in 1962 for the establishment of three more All India Services. These are: (1) The Indian Service of Engineers, (2) The Indian Forest Service, and (3) The Indian Medical and Health Service. The establishment of an Indian Agricultural Service has been accepted in principle and proposals for the establishment of an Indian Educational Service and an Indian Judicial Service are at present under active consideration. The Union has, however, created a number of Central Services. The more important of these are:

1. Indian Foreign Service
2. Indian Audit and Accounts Service
3. Indian Defence Accounts Service
4. Income-tax Officers (Class I) Grade II Service
5. Indian Railway Accounts Service
6. Indian Customs and Excise Service
7. Transportation (Traffic) and Commercial Departments of the Superior Revenue Establishment of Indian Railways
8. Military Lands and Cantonment Service
9. Indian Postal Service
10. Central Engineering Service
11. Indian Railway Service of Engineering
12. Superior Telegraph Engineering and Wireless Branches of the Posts and Telegraph Department
13. Central Secretariat Service
14. Central Information Service
15. Indian Ordnance Factories Service

The Constitution embodies also certain provisions aimed at safeguarding the interests of the members of the Indian Civil Service.

Public Services and the Welfare State

Viewing the constitutional provisions as a whole, there can be no doubt that they are intended to build up a Public Service that would fit in with the changed character of the State in India. Of course, a civil servant must possess the traditional service virtues of integrity, loyalty and efficiency. His honesty should be above reproach, his loyalty unquestioned and his efficiency in conformity with recognised standards. The British in India had artificially created a kind of self-styled dignity in the higher services which aimed at a deliberate aloofness from the general public. Such a position ceases when the Government of the Union and the States under the Constitution are dedicated to achieve mass welfare at a

24

fast pace.   The Public Services today are expected to have a growing passion for social service and to identify themselves with the people.   Efficiency today means something more than an efficient performance of routine duties.   It implies the active direction of the economic life of the people with the declared object of ultimately eliminating poverty, disease and ignorance.

In this task, the co-operation of the Public Services—the permanent wing of the Government—with the Ministers—the political wing—is of utmost importance.   Control of the adminis-tration is no more the responsibility of the Civil Service.   It is the responsibility of the representatives of the people.   The Services must devote themselves to the service of the people under the direction of the people's representatives.   It is the Minister's business to determine the policy.   Once a policy is determined, it is the business of the civil servant to carry it out with good will and devotion, whether he personally agrees with it or not.

At the same time, it is the traditional duty of the civil servant to make available to his political chief all the information and experience at his disposal in order to help him to arrive at a right decision.   The civil servant will not be able to do this, sometimes at the risk of displeasing his chief, unless he has security of tenure. The civil servant can, under the Constitution, give his advice without fear or favour in the interests of efficient administration.

One of the virtues of a parliamentary democracy is the ample opportunity that it affords for the harmonisation of two different and even conflicting parts in the same machinery.   By nature and training the permanent civil servant is conservative, narrow in outlook, and is often apt to exaggerate the importance of technicalities.   He looks at things with the eye of an expert and displays a bureaucratic attitude.   A politician on the other hand, by nature and experience, is well versed in human affairs.   His vision is broad, his attitude compromising and ideas progressive. He has got the qualities of initiative and judgment.   His broad outlook and strong common sense, born out of a long experience of human affairs, bring about a healthy and constructive outlook on all problems.   A combination of these two—the administrator and the politician, the civil servant and the Minister—should produce wholesome results.

While the permanent services maintain the continuity of the

administrative process, the Minister provides the basis of its popular character. The Minister serves as a link between the legislature and the administration and ensures the co-ordination of the two to the best advantage of the country. It is in the interest of efficient administration that these two wings of the Government should maintain their separate identity. The civil servant should maintain his rigid neutrality in politics and the Minister should scrupulously adhere to this principle and appreciate the attitude of the civil servant. Then only can the permanent services become a real link between successive Ministries and provide stability and continuity of administration.

There are, however, a number of obstacles in India which still hamper the harmonious collaboration of the service and ministerial wings in the Government. These are found more in the States than in the Centre. The Government at the Centre unlike most of the States, has had the unique advantage of political stability. Not only has the same party been in power for three decades but also the top leadership remained largely unchanged. One must add to this also the high calibre of the Ministerial wing in the Central Government. In contrast, most of the States have been suffering from many disadvantages. There have been frequent changes in the top leadership of several States, even when the same Party has continued to stay in power in most of them. The reorganisation of States brought about many changes, territorial and personnel. As a result, many new Ministers who lacked administrative experience joined the Government's top ranks. A high percentage of the older and more experienced officers left the States for positions of greater importance at the Centre. Those who replaced them had not the same experience as their predecessors. All these have adversely affected the efficiency of public administration in India.

Yet, there are factors obtained in the present context which are capable of creating harmony, amity and unity between the ministerial and the service wings of the administration. Of these, the most important seems to be the common objective to which both the Ministers and the civil services are committed. The Directive Principles embodied in the Constitution provide that common objective and it has become a common ideology that animates the economic and social foundations of independent

India and which permeates the mind of every educated Indian today. So long as there is unity in this basic objective, those who are charged with the responsibility of translating this objective into reality will have to work together with understanding and such understanding is bound to emerge in the natural course of events. On the political plane, with the emergence of a more and more democratic society resulting from successive general elections based upon adult suffrage, many of the old prejudices will disappear and greater tolerance and understanding will ensue. Finally, those who harboured ill-will and even animosity in pre-independence days—political as well as civil servants—are fast disappearing. A new generation is taking their place and members of this new generation are free from such ill-will or suspicion. With the building up of healthy traditions and conventions, there should be little difficulty for laying the sound foundations of a system where the members of the ministerial and service wings work hand in hand as inseparable limbs of the same organism.

CHAPTER 36

THE PUBLIC SERVICE COMMISSIONS

AT THE time of the framing of the present Constitution, India had had some experience of Public Service Commissions functioning as integral parts of the old Constitution. The Government of India Act of 1935 had provided for the establishment of Public Service Commissions both at the Centre and in the Provinces. When the present Constitution came into being the Federal Public Service Commission was already functioning. The experience of the working of these Commissions was of value to the framers of the Constitution in dealing with this part. Except for a few changes, they have in fact closely followed the provisions of the Government of India Act of 1935 in this regard.

Why Public Service Commissions

Experience in most democratic countries has shown that under the old system of private and political patronage the government used to be deprived of the services of the most able men. This was because their place was taken by those whose main qualification was the possession of influence. Civil servants actually in office were discouraged from giving of their best to their work, because advancement depended not on their ability and zeal, but on the chances of political and private favouritism. The civil service was unable to provide continuity of administrative experience for the benefit of successive governments, because the senior posts changed hands when governments changed. The number of civil servants was often unnecessarily enlarged in order to provide posts for the dependants of those who held the reins of political power. By drawing on the widest possible field for recruitment, the public service gets more able people than when it relied on a system of personal contacts. Moreover, it was able to divide the talent more evenly amongst all the government departments.

In a country like India the necessity and importance of Public Service Commission should be evident. The population of 480 million is multilingual and multi-racial. One must also take note of the existence of a number of religious minorities and socially and educationally backward classes and communities. If political considerations and favouritism dominate the recruitment to the public services under these conditions, the injury to the nation will be incalculable. It will certainly affect the efficiency and integrity of the public services. What the Royal Commission on the Indian Civil Service wrote in 1924 is true even today.

"Wherever democratic institutions exist, experience has shown that to secure an efficient Civil Service it is essential to protect it, so far as possible, from political and personal influences and to give it that position of stability and security which is vital to its successful working as the impartial and efficient instrument by which Governments, of whatever complexion, may give effect to their policies. In countries where this principle has been neglected, and where the 'spoils system' has taken its place, an inefficient and disorganised civil service has been the inevitable result and corruption has been rampant."

The function, therefore, of a Public Service Commission is two-fold: first, it must, to adapt a famous phrase in American history "keep the rascals out"; secondly, it must try to put the best men in. It is difficult to over-emphasise the importance of this function.

That the Constituent Assembly was fully aware of this vital role of the Public Service Commissions was made clear by the members who participated in the discussion on the subject.

Constitution of the Union Public Service Commission

Article 315 makes it obligatory for the Union to constitute a Public Service Commission. It is presided over by a Chairman who is designated as the Chairman, Union Public Service Commission. The Chairman and the members of the Commission are appointed by the President. They hold office for a period of six years from the date they join duty or until they attain the age of sixty-five years, whichever is earlier. It is provided that, at least one half of the members of the Commission should be persons with a minimum of ten years' experience in Government service. This is intended to ensure always the presence of men of experience in civil service on the Commission so that it may function as an expert body. The number of members on the Commission is determined by the President by regulations. At present there are eight members on the Commission.

A member of the Commission is ineligible for the same appointment for a second term. His further employment elsewhere also is severely restricted. The Chairman of the Union Public Service Commission is ineligible for further employment either under the Government of India or under the Government of a State. A member other than the Chairman is eligible to become either the Chairman of the U.P.S.C. or the Chairman of a State Public Service Commission. But for these two offices he is ineligible for appointment to any post under the Union Government or any State Government in India.

The President is empowered to determine by regulations the salary and other conditions of service of the members of the Commission. He may also make regulations with respect to the strength of the staff of the Commission and their conditions of service. It is provided that the conditions of service of a member of the Commission cannot be varied to his disadvantage after his appointment. The Chairman and members of the Commission are paid Rs. 4,000 and 3,500 per month respectively as salary. These amounts compare favourably with the salaries of comparable positions at the highest level in the Government. The entire expenses of the Commission, including the salaries and allowances of its members, are charged to the Consolidated Fund of India.

A member of the Union Public Service Commission can be removed from Office only by an order of the President on the ground of misbehaviour. The Constitution prescribes a procedure to prove such misbehaviour. According to this, the matter will be referred to the Supreme Court by the President and the Court will conduct an enquiry in accordance with the procedure prescribed under Article 145 of the Constitution and will submit a report to the President. Pending the enquiry by the Supreme Court, the President may suspend the member concerned. The President is empowered to remove by order a member of the Commission also on the following grounds:

(1) if he is adjudged an insolvent; or (2) if he engages

during his term of office in any paid employment outside the duties of his office; or (3) if he is, in the opinion of the President, unfit to continue in office by reason of infirmity of mind or body; or (4) if he becomes in any way concerned in any contract or agreement made by or on behalf of the Government of India or a State Government or in any way participate in its profit or benefits except as an ordinary member of an incorporated company. All these provisions are intended to make the Commission an independent and impartial body to discharge its responsibilities in an efficient manner.

Constitution of State Public Service Commissions

Under Article 315, each constituent State of the Union should have a Public Service Commission. There is however provision for setting up Joint Public Service Commissions each serving more than one State. But such Commissions may be set up only by the law of Parliament on a request for the same by the States concerned. The Constitution also permits the Union Public Service Commission to render its services to a State, for all or any of the needs of the State, with the approval of the President.

The members of a State Public Service Commission are appointed by the Governor, and those of a Joint Commission by the President. As in the case of the Union Commission, the appointment is for a maximum period of six years. But if a member attains the age of sixty-two years while in service, irrespective of his having completed six years he must retire from service. The members of State and Joint Public Service Commissions are not eligible for any appointment under the Union or the States except that a Chairman may become the Chairman or a member of the Union Public Service Commission or the Chairman of any other State or Joint Service Commission and a member may, in addition to the above-mentioned offices, become the Chairman of the Commission of which he is a member. The conditions of service of the members of the State Public Service Commissions are more or less the same as those of the Union Commission. The only significant point of difference is in salary which varies from State to State. The conditions of service of a member of a State Public Service Commission may not be varied to his disadvantage after his appointment. The number of members on the State Commissions also varies from State to State. The basis and the procedure for the removal of the members of the State or Joint Commissions are the same as for the members of the Union Public Service Commission.

Functions of the Commissions

Under Article 320, the Commissions have the following functions:

(1) To conduct examination for appointments to the services of the Union or the State;

(2) To assist the States in framing and operating schemes of joint recruitment if two or more States request the Union Commission in this behalf;

(3) To advise the Union or State Government:

    (*a*) on all matters relating to methods of recruitment to civil services and for civil posts;

    (*b*) on the principle to be followed in making appointment to civil services and civil posts and promotions, transfers, etc. from one service to another;

    (*c*) on all disciplinary matters affecting Government servants of the Union or the States;

    (*d*) on claims for costs of legal proceedings instituted against a Union Official or a State Official;

    (*e*) on claims for the award of pension in respect of injuries sustained by a Union official or a State official on duty; and

    (*f*) any other matter specifically referred to it by the President or the Governor.

Under Article 321, the functions of the Union Commission or a State Commission may be extended by an Act made by Parliament or the Legislature of the State concerned. Such an Act may also bring within the scope of the functions of the Commission matters connected with the services of public institutions such as local bodies or public corporations under the Union or

State Government. This is important in view of the fact that as the activities of both the Union and the State Governments increase, more and more of public corporations and such other institutions are bound to be established involving the employment of an ever increasing number of officials.

Report of the Commissions

The Union Public Service Commission has to submit to the President an annual report on the work done by the Commission. The report accompanied by a memorandum explaining the action taken by the Government on the recommendations of the Commission is to be placed before both the Houses of Parliament. Similarly, a State Commission has to submit to the Governor an annual report which with the memorandum explaining the action taken by the State Government on the Commission's recommendations is placed before the State Legislature. The memorandum should explain the reasons for the non-acceptance of the recommendations of the Commission by the Government if there are any such cases.

It must be observed here that the Public Service Commissions envisaged under the Constitution including the U.P.S.C. are only advisory bodies. It might be asked why the recommendations of such an important body as the Public Service Commission are not obligatory on the Government. The framers of the Constitution, in this respect, have followed the practice that obtained under the Constitution Act of 1935. Experience has shown that the recommendations of the Commission have more influence if they are advisory than mandatory in character. The danger is that if the Commission is given mandatory powers there is possibility of conflict between the Commission and the Government and there may arise situations when they behave as rival governments in the same territory, each trying to establish its will over the other. The real safeguard against the rejection of any recommendation of the Commission lies in the Parliamentary control that is provided for by the Constitution. The Government has to justify its action before the Legislature which has the power of repudiating the Government's action.

The Public Service Commissions in India are in a much

stronger position from a constitutional point of view than statutory bodies or Commissions set up in Britain or the United States. This is because these Commissions are set up by the same sovereign authority which sets up the Executive, the Legislature and the Judiciary. All of them are created by the Constitution itself. But in Britain, the United States and elsewhere Public Service Commissions are the creations of the Legislature and, as such, the British Parliament and the United States Congress have the power to modify them as they like. In other words, they are subordinate bodies. In India, the Public Service Commissions are in no way subordinate to the Legislature or the Executive. Thus, while a Public Service Commission would not ordinarily like to withhold information on any particular subject, its constitutional right to withhold any such information should be recognised.

Obviously, the Constitution-makers wanted to provide all reasonable safeguards to make the Public Service Commissions in India immune from all undue influence and to enable them to carry out their duties with impartiality, integrity and independence.

Magnitude of the Commissions' Work

A glance over the annual reports of the Public Service Commissions—Union as well as the State Commissions—will show the variety and volume of their work. Conducting of competitive examinations for recruiting personnel to the various services is one of the most arduous tasks undertaken by these Commissions. In one of its recent reports, the Union Public Service Commission gives the following details with regard to some of its functions:

(1) For the twenty-seven examinations conducted by the Commission, there was a total of some 56,956 applicants. Of these, the Commission interviewed over 2,800 candidates. Some of the more important of these examinations are the combined competitive examinations for the Indian Administrative and the Indian Police Services and the various Central Services. Some 8,000 candidates appeared for these examinations. Among others, those which attract large numbers are the Joint Services Wing Examination, the Engineering Service Examination and the Ministerial Service Examination.

(2) Direct recruitment by interview has become an important method of selection as a result of the increase of governmental activities after the attainment of Independence. Over 47,000 applications were handled in this connection and some 9,500 candidates interviewed with a view to filling up some 1,400 posts.

(3) Many of the superior posts, particularly in the regularly organised Services, are filled by promotion of officers who have acquired a certain standard of experience in junior posts in those Services. Recommendations for such promotions are made by the Departments concerned and the Commission is requested to ratify them. On an average, the Commission handles over 10,000 such cases annually.

(4) The Commission is consulted about certain minor forms of recruitment such as temporary appointments for periods exceeding one year but not exceeding three years, grant of extension of service and re-employment of certain retired Government servants. It handles about a thousand such cases a year.

(5) The Commission has to be consulted in disciplinary cases before the President imposes the penalty of censure or any more serious penalty, such as, suspension or dismissal. About two hundred such cases are annually handled by the Commission.

(6) The Commission also handles a good number of cases, such as those involving regularisation of appointments, claims for the award of pension, claims for re-imbursement of legal expenses incurred by Government servants in defending legal proceedings instituted against them in respect of acts done in the execution of their duties.

The Commission in its Reports has acknowledged that apart from a few isolated instances, the Ministries and Departments generally observed the provisions of the Constitution. It means that on the whole the recommendations of the Commission are accepted and acted upon by the Government. In fact, most of the reports show that there was not even one case where the Union Government had not accepted the recommendations of the Commission. No greater test is required to prove the effectiveness of the Commission as an independent body under the Constitution even though its recommendations are only of an advisory nature.

CHAPTER 37

OFFICIAL LANGUAGE

FEW CONSTITUTIONS have such elaborate provisions dealing with the official language as the Constitution of India. Ordinarily, official language is not a subject which requires any special treatment in a constitutional enactment. This is because, in most countries, a single language is employed as the common medium of expression of the entire population, or at least of an overwhelming majority. There are, of course, exceptions to this general pattern in some parts of the world, and some countries have made even special provisions to solve the problems arising out of bilingualism or multi-lingualism within their borders. India belongs to the latter category, hence a special chapter in the Constitution dealing with the official language.

The following table will throw light on the linguistic problem of India:[1]

TABLE 11

Language	Number of people speaking (in millions)			Percentage of total Population
	1951	1961	1971	
Assamese	5	6	9	1.4
Bengali	25	31	45	7.4
Gujarati	16	20	26	4.8
Hindi, Urdu, Hindustani and Punjabi	150	183	209	42.5
Kannada	14	17	22	3.5
Malayalam	13	16	21	3.4
Marathi	27	33	42	7.3
Oriya	13	16	22	3.5
Tamil	27	33	38	7.0
Telugu	33	40	45	7.4
Others	30	40	70	11.8
Total	356	435	549	100

[1] These figures are based on the 1951, 1961 and 1971 Census.

In the words of the Official Language Commission:

"The difficulty and complexity of the language problem that the country has to tackle are manifest. We seek to find a medium of expression for the strong elements of identity in the cultural life of the country and as a linguistic counterpart of the political unity which the country has rediscovered after many centuries. In doing so, we seek to replace a working system based on the English language which, albeit foreign to the people, is one of the world's richest and most widely spoken languages and has many general merits to recommend it. The languages we can replace English by are at present insufficiently developed for the multifarious occasions of official and non-official intercourse, that arise in a modern community. Several of these dozen or so languages are, however, spoken by numbers in excess of many current European languages claiming to be advanced means of communication and are thus, in point of the number of people who speak them, entitled to a high place in the world's roll of languages. Hindi has been chosen as the Union Language on the principle and, we think, sufficient ground that amongst the regional languages it is spoken by the largest number of people in the country."

During the course of the discussion on the official language, the Constituent Assembly witnessed some of the most agitated scenes, surcharged with emotion riding on the crest of linguistic fanaticism. Nevertheless, the Assembly produced a compromise formula after a long and heated discussion. The provisions dealing with official language are the product of this compromise formula.

Language of the Union (Arts. 343 and 344)

The main provisions dealing with the official language of the Union as embodied in Articles 343 and 344 are as follows:

(1) Hindi written in Devanagari script will be the official language of the Union.

(2) For a period of fifteen years from the commencement of the Constitution, however, the English language will continue to

be used for all official purposes of the Union. But during this period, the President may authorise the use of Hindi in addition to English.

(3) Even after fifteen years, Parliament may provide for the continued use of English for any specific purpose.

(4) At the end of five years from the commencement of the Constitution, the President shall appoint a Commission to make recommendations for the progressive use of the Hindi language and on the restrictions on the use of English and other allied matters. The President is obliged to appoint such a Commission at the end of ten years after the commencement of the Constitution for the same purpose. While making their recommendations the Commission should give due regard to the industrial, cultural and scientific advancement of India, and the just claims and the interests of persons belonging to the non-Hindi speaking areas in regard to the Public Services.

(5) The Commission's recommendations will be examined by a thirty-man Committee of Parliament (20 members from the *Lok Sabha* and 10 from *Rajya Sabha*) elected in accordance with the system of proportional representation and the Committee will make a report to the President. The President may issue directions on the basis of the report of the Committee.

In accordance with the constitutional provision, in June 1955, at the end of five years after the commencement of the Constitution, the President appointed a Commission consisting of twenty-one members with B. G. Kher as its Chairman.

The Commission submitted its report to the President by the middle of 1956. The report which runs into five hundred pages is an impressive document dealing with every one of the questions referred to the Commission in a thoroughgoing manner. The Report, however, set off one of the bitterest controversies in the country. One of the serious defects of the Report was the strong and utterly uncompromising minutes of dissent by two of its prominent members representing two major languages of the country, namely, Bengali and Tamil. Nevertheless, the Report is a very valuable document for understanding the immensity and complexity of the language problem of India.

As provided for in the Constitution a thirty-member Committee of Parliament with the Home Minister of the Union Government as its Chairman examined the recommendations of the Commission. The Report of the Committee was submitted to Parliament on 8 February 1958. While the Committee has expressed the definite opinion that adherence to the constitutional settlement which envisages the replacement of English by Hindi for Union purposes and by the regional languages for the official requirements of the States is the only safe and practicable course to adopt, the approach to the question of final change-over has to be flexible and practical. Thus, the Committee has in general endorsed the recommendations of the Official Language Commission except that it emphasises the necessity for flexibility in the change-over.

Regional Languages

Each State Legislature is empowered under Article 345 to adopt any one or more of the languages in use in the State for all or any of the official purposes of the State concerned. But so far as communication between a State and the Union or between one State and another is concerned, the official language of the Union will be the authorised language. In order to protect the linguistic interests of minorities in certain States, the Constitution has incorporated a special provision. This is in addition to the cultural rights that are guaranteed as Fundamental Rights under Article 29 of the Constitution. According to this, the President is empowered under Article 347 to direct a State Government to recognise a particular language for official purposes either for the whole or part of the State, if he is satisfied, on a representation made to him in this regard, that a substantial proportion of the population of the State desires such recognition. This power in the hands of the Centre will help to curb any tendency towards linguistic fanaticism and the domination of a majority over linguistic minorities in different States.

The Language in Courts

Under Article 348, the Constitution makes a special provision for the retention of the English language if Parliament so decides even after the fifteen-year period for the following purposes:

(1)   All proceedings in the Supreme Court and the High Courts.

(2)   Authoritative texts of Bills, Acts, Ordinances, Orders, Rules, regulations and bye-laws issued under the Constitution or under any law.

However, Parliament is empowered to stop the use of English even in the Courts whenever it likes, once the fifteen-year period is over. It is also provided that Hindi or any regional language may be used even earlier for conducting the proceedings in a High Court if the President gives his consent for the measure.

Special Directives

The Constitution embodies certain special directives with a view to safeguarding the interests of linguistic minorities. Thus, under Article 350 every person is entitled to submit a representation for the redress of any grievance to any officer or authority of the Union or a State in any of the languages used in the Union or in the State as the case may be. In addition, there are two special directives which have been incorporated as a result of the recommendations of the States Reorganisation Commission through the Seventh Amendment of the Constitution in 1956. According to these:

(1) It shall be the endeavour of every State and of every local authority within the State to provide adequate facilities for instruction in the mother-tongue at the primary stage of education to children belonging to linguistic minority groups. The President is empowered to issue such directions to any State as he considers necessary for securing the provision of such facilities.

(2) The President will appoint a Special Officer for linguistic minorities. It is the duty of this special officer to investigate all matters relating to the safeguards provided for linguistic minorities under the Constitution and report regularly to the President. The reports of the Special Officer are to be laid before each House of Parliament and sent to the Government of the States concerned.

25

The Constitution also embodies a directive for the development and enrichment of the Hindi language with a view to making it serve as a real medium of expression for all the elements of the composite culture of India.   Such enrichment may be secured by drawing primarily on Sankrit and secondarily on other languages. According to the Language Commission, 'other languages' means all other languages and not necessarily the languages of India specified in the Constitution.   Hence, in the process of development and enrichment of the Hindi language there is no inhibition as to drawing from any language including the English language.

The Eighth Schedule of the Constitution specifies fifteen languages.

EIGHTH SCHEDULE

(*ARTICLES* 344(1) *AND* 351)

LANGUAGES

1. Assamese.	8. Marathi.
2. Bengali.	9. Oriya.
3. Gujarati.	10. Punjabi.
4. Hindi.	11. Sanskrit.
5. Kannada.	12. Sindhi.
6. Kashmiri.	13. Tamil.
7. Malayalam.	14. Telugu.
	15. Urdu.

In spite of the controversies and bitterness that still exist in the country on the language problem, it must be admitted that the adoption of the provisions dealing with the official language by the Constituent Assembly marked a triumph of Indian nationalism and national unity.   It showed that even in the face of the most acute differences emanating from deep-seated sentiments, men of goodwill, who have the good of the nation at heart, can find a solution to the most baffling problem.   This realisation should augur well for the future of the country, and the urge for preserving the unity and integrity of the nation should help Indians to find solutions for every problem that threatens to divide them.

CHAPTER 38

ELECTIONS

THE CONSTITUTION of India has provided a separate chapter on elections. In this respect, it has made a departure from the usual practice of Constitutions to leave elections as a comparatively unimportant subject to be dealt with by the legislature. The fact that detailed provisions in this regard have been made in the Constitution shows how anxious the Constitution-makers had been to safeguard this political right as an integral part of the Constitution itself. With a view to ensuring this objective the Constituent Assembly entrusted its Committee on Fundamental Rights to deal with this problem also. The Committee recommended that the independence of elections and the avoidance of any interference by the Executive in the elections should be regarded as a Fundamental Right and necessary provisions should be made in this regard. But the Assembly decided that, although it was a matter of fundamental importance, its place was not in the chapter on Fundamental Rights but elsewhere. Accordingly, the Drafting Committee made special provisions of a detailed character and embodied them in a separate chapter of the Constitution.

The Legal Framework

Under the Constitution provision is made for an Election Commission which is entrusted to deal with the following matters:

 (*a*) election of the President of India;
 (*b*) election of the Vice-President of India;
 (*c*) the Union Parliament and the composition of its two Chambers;
 (*d*) qualifications of members of Parliament;
 (*e*) composition of State Legislatures;
 (*f*) qualifications of members of State Legislatures;
 (*g*) duration of Parliament and the State Legislatures;
 (*h*) elections—to Parliament and State Legislatures;
 (*i*) reservation of seats in the House of the People and the State Assemblies for the Scheduled Castes and Tribes; and
 (*j*) the determination of population for purposes of election.

Under Article 327, Parliament is vested with the supreme power to legislate on all matters relating to elections, including elections to State Legislatures. Under Article 328, the States have also been vested with certain limited powers of legislation with respect to elections. But such legislation should not be in conflict with any Parliamentary legislation in this matter.

Parliament passed two major measures laying down the detailed law under which elections are to be held. The first was the Representation of the People Act, 1950, which provided for qualifications of voters and matters connected with the preparation of electoral rolls. It also laid down the procedure for delimitation of constituencies, and allocated the number of seats in Parliament to the States and fixed the number of seats in the respective State Legislatures. The second, viz. the Representation of the People Act, 1951, provided for the actual conduct of elections and dealt in detail with subjects like administrative machinery for conducting elections, the poll, election disputes, by-elections, etc. Under these two Acts, statutory rules were made by the Central Government and these were respectively called the Representation of the People (Preparation of Electoral Rolls) Rules, 1950, and the Representation of the People (Conduct of Elections and Election Petitions) Rules, 1951. Subsequently the two Acts and the Rules were amended as and when changes became necessary. One of the most important of these amendments is with regard to the preparation of the electoral rolls. Originally it was provided that separate rolls should be prepared for the Parliamentary and Assembly Constituencies. The amendment has prevented a considerable amount of duplication of work by laying down that only one electoral roll need be prepared for all constituencies.

It is within this framework of law that the three General Elections have been held. The law seems to have come, as the occasion arose. Now it is high time that this mass of election law scattered over too many legislative enactments is codified into a simple comprehensive legislation on the subject.

One General Electoral Roll

At first, it may appear that the constitutional provision in this regard is superfluous. But it has a history behind it. During the

British rule, under the pressure of communal politics separate electorates were established in India. Accordingly, in every Constituency there were as many lists of electoral roll as there were Communities recognised for the purpose. Thus, the Muslims all over India had a separate electoral roll and voted only for candidates who stood for election from the Constituency reserved for the Muslims. How unnatural was this system of communal electorates needs no special emphasis. Article 325 is a declaration that separate electorates have been finally abandoned. As a result, the people of India, irrespective of their religion, race, caste, or sex will belong to one general electoral roll in every territorial constituency for election. In this way, an unnatural system that prevailed in India for a few decades has been removed and a composite political community has been established by the Constitution.

Universal Adult Suffrage

One of the outstanding features of the Constitution is adult suffrage. It means that every person—man or woman—who is not less than twenty-one years of age has the right to vote in the election to the House of the People and the State Legislative Assembly. The only grounds for disqualification are (*i*) non-residence, (*ii*) unsoundness of mind, (*iii*) crime, and (*iv*) corrupt or illegal practice. This provision has been hailed as the "fountainspring of India's democracy". For, it has swept away at one stroke all the antiquated and undemocratic qualifications prescribed to be eligible for voting—property, income, status, title, educational qualification and so on.

The cumulative effect of the above two provisions on democracy in India is indeed far-reaching. Under the Government of India Act, 1919, there were only three per cent of India's population who were entitled to exercise their franchise. Under the Act of 1935, with a more broad-based franchise, only ten per cent exercised this elementary right of citizenship. But now, every citizen is entitled to it. The principle of one man, one vote, one value has become a constitutional right. The removal of the notorious system of communal electorates which had broken up Indian society statutorily into religious and communal compartments is in perfect harmony with the establishment of adult suffrage. As a result, the citizens of India will now vote as individuals and not as Hindus, Muslims, Christians or Sikhs.

The Electoral Machinery

In one vitally important respect, the Indian Constitution is almost unique and has followed the example of Canada. The *sine qua non* for a true democracy is the holding of fair and free elections of the peoples' representatives to the legislative bodies. The elections, in other words, must be conducted in a completely non-partisan spirit and provision was accordingly made in the Constitution to ensure that the party in power, at no time, may be placed in a position to influence the conduct of the elections to its own benefit.

Article 324 enacts that the superintendence, direction and control of all elections in India are vested in an independent body called the Election Commission. The power of the Commission included the power of appointing Election Tribunals for the removal of doubts and settling of disputes in connection with the elections. According to an amendment of the Representation of People Act (1966), however, the provision for constituting election tribunals has been abolished. Election petitions hereafter will be heard by the High Courts. It also provides that the revision of electoral rolls will be made only according to the directions of the Election Commission and not otherwise.

The Election Commission consists of the Chief Election Commissioner and as many Election Commissioners as the President may from time to time fix. They are all appointed by the President. During the General Elections in 1951-52 two Regional Commissioners were temporarily appointed by the President to assist the Election Commission, with headquarters at Bombay and Patna respectively. In connection with the second General Elections, 1957, three Deputy Election Commissioners were temporarily appointed with headquarters at Delhi. No Regional Commissioners were appointed for the second elections. It is understood that one of these three Deputy Election Commissioners may have to continue on a permanent basis.

The Commission is an independent body. Its independence is

secured by Article 324(5) which provides that the Chief Election Commissioner shall not be removed from office except in like manner and on the like grounds as a judge of the Supreme Court and that any other election commissioner shall not be removed except on the recommendations of the Chief Election Commissioner. However, it must be pointed out that the independence of the Election Commissioners is not of the same nature as that of the judges of the Supreme Court. A Judge of the Supreme Court once appointed holds office upto the age of 65 years while the Chief Election Commissioner can be appointed for any limited period. The Constitution also provides for the availability of adequate staff facilities for the discharge of the functions of the Election Commission.

At the State level, during the General Elections of 1951-52, the Chief Electoral Officer of a State did not have any statutory status or functions. It was felt later that he should be given a legal status and vested with specific powers and duties. The term "Chief Electoral Officer" was accordingly defined in the Rules as an officer appointed by a State Government to perform the functions of the Chief Electoral Officer under the Rules. In the light of the experience gained so far, the Election Commission has come to the conclusion that the Chief Electoral Officer of a State should be a senior Officer of the State Government. The Commission is of the opinion that part-time officers seldom find time to make extensive tours of the districts and hence lose touch with the election officers at the district level which is of utmost importance. However, the Commission feels that in case a part-time officer is appointed as the Chief Electoral Officer, a junior whole-time officer should be made available to him as his Deputy.

At the district level, the machinery varies from State to State. In some States there is a whole-time District Election Officer in every district with a nucleus of his own which is strengthened during election time. In some others, an officer belonging to the normal administrative set-up in the district is placed in charge of election work with a nucleus of his own. In yet others, there is no definite scheme and the work is done haphazardly during the peak election time by the normal administrative machinery. It is, therefore, necessary that the machinery should be systematised and put on a permanent and satisfactory basis.

In regard to the preparation and maintenance of the electoral rolls of a constituency, the permanent machinery consists of the Election Commission, the Chief Electoral Officer and the Electoral Registration Officer of the constituency. There is an electoral Registration Officer for each Assembly Constituency and it is his responsibility to prepare and annually revise the electoral roll for the constituency as required by law. The law has also made provision for the appointment of one or more Assistant Electoral Registration officers to assist the Electoral Registration Officer in the performance of his functions.

For each Parliamentary or Assembly constituency, a Returning Officer is appointed by the Election Commission. He has to be an Officer of the Government. One or more persons who are also officers of the Government are appointed as Assistant Returning Officers to assist him in the performance of his functions.

The actual poll is conducted by a large number of Presiding and Polling Officers. For every polling-station, a Presiding Officer and a few polling officers are appointed in respect of each separate election, Parliament and Assembly. In case elections are held simultaneously for Parliament and the Assembly, some of these officers are appointed to take charge of both at a polling station. They are usually assisted by as many policemen and other staff as may be necessary.

The First General Elections (1951-52)

The First General Elections in India were a historic event and attracted widespread interest and attention in the country and abroad. The organisation and conduct of the elections on such a vast scale naturally presented many difficulties which had to be surmounted. It stands to the eternal credit of the political consciousness and orderliness of the Indian people, a large percentage of whom are illiterate, that a General Election of such a gigantic magnitude was held in the most successful manner.

A notable feature of the Elections was the whole-hearted participation of a number of political parties. It has been admitted by all that the Elections were free and fair and were held in a truly democratic atmosphere. There were in all some 175,000 candidates to fill 3,278 seats in State Assemblies and 1,823 to fill

493 seats in the House of the People. Not less than 75 parties, big and small, national and regional, moderate and extremist, participated. Of these many were new parties. Most of them have now faded away. All this is clear proof of the democratic atmosphere, the emergence of various points of view and the eagerness of a large number of men and women to serve the people through the legislatures.

By conducting the Elections in a peaceful, orderly and efficient manner, the Election Commission justified its position as an independent body. Elaborate arrangements had been made and every possible precaution taken by the Commission to see that during the elections, the independence of the voter and the secrecy of the ballot were fully maintained. Approximately a staff of 560,000 were engaged in handling 600 million ballot papers and they did a remarkable job.

An electorate of 171,747,300 voted the Congress Party to power at the Centre with a thumping majority. The Party gained 364 of the 489 elected seats and became the first party to organise the first Indian Government after Independence. This outstanding success was true to expectations in all the major circles of the public.

In the States, the Congress tally was on an average good, with thumping victories in some and marginal gains in a few. Thus in the Part 'A' States of Assam, Bihar, Bombay, Madhya Pradesh, Punjab, Uttar Pradesh and West Bengal, the electorate almost gave a *carte blanche* to the Congress to form the Government. With the Communists running second with 62 seats to their credit in the Madras Assembly and the Ganatantra Parishad with 31 seats in the Orissa Assembly, the Congress found itself in hot waters in the two States and had to seek the support of Independent members to form Ministries in these states.

Among the Part 'B' States, P.E.P.S.U. proved the problem State for Congress with the Akali Party securing just 7 seats less than the Congress Party and the Congress itself failing to secure an absolute majority. Rajasthan gave Congress just a marginal lead and in Travancore-Cochin the Congress had to resort to coalition in order that it might form the government. The mid-term election in Travancore-Cochin in 1954 and the events that followed proved that the Congress as a political party was never popular

in that State ever since the advent of Indian Independence and the
second General Elections of 1957 only completed the story by
reducing the Congress as representing only a minority there.

All the Part 'C' States gave the Congress unstinted support.
From an overall point of view, therefore, the Congress Party had
gained a good amount of electoral support.

The Second General Elections (1957)

Reporting on the Second General Elections, the Election
Commission states: "The second general elections were less of an
adventure or novelty as compared to the first when even the most
optimistic people had felt doubtful as to how far a large country
which had only just attained its independence and had yet to settle
down to a democratic form of government could successfully
carry through a country-wide programme of democratic elections
based on adult suffrage". However, the reorganisation of the states
in 1956 introduced a considerable amount of uncertainty and at
one stage it became doubtful as to whether it was possible to see
through the legal and administrative formalities to enable the
elections to be held according to the schedule. It was in fact
felt by some influential sections of the public that an amendment
to the Constitution to extend the life of the first Indian legislature
was an imperative necessity. But it stands to the credit of the
Election Commission that it set its face boldly against any such
contingency and achieved a seemingly impossible task, thereby
averting a very bad precedent in the annals of new India's
constitutional history.

Thus the Elections to the House of People and all the State
Assemblies excepting for the Union territory of Himachal Pradesh
and the Kangra district of Punjab, were completed by March 1957.
The streamlining of the election machinery in the light of the
experience gained during the first elections enabled the reduction
of the period of poll from 17 weeks in the General Elections of
1951-52 to just over a fortnight in 1957.

The Second General Elections created parliamentary history by
putting the Communist Party at the helm of affairs through the
ballot, in the southern State of Kerala. This event, more than
anything else, has brought into clear relief the truly federalist

character of India's democracy. An electorate of over 193 million, in the biggest democracy in the world, voted for Congress Government at the Centre and in eleven States. Although the Communists failed to gain an absolute majority in Kerala, they could muster enough support from the Independent ranks to form a stable ruling party in Kerala and were assured of non-interference from the Centre. (The Communists, however, lost their dominant position in the mid-term election of February, 1960 by winning only 28 out of a total of 128 seats in the Kerala Assembly). In the eastern coastal State of Orissa, neither the Congress Party nor its closest rival, the Ganatantra Parishad, could gain an absolute majority. However, the Congress Party managed to obtain the support of some minor parties and independents in the Assembly to enable it to form the ministry. Subsequently the Congress combined with the Ganatantra Parishad to establish a stable ministry in the State.

The magnitude of the elections surpassed even that of the First General Elections, which had to that date been acclaimed as the biggest democratic experiment in the world. The electorate increased by over 20 million and the number of votes polled jumped from 103.3 million to 112.3 million. The votes polled constituted 49.2 per cent of the voting capacity of the country as against the corresponding figure of 44.9 per cent for the 1951-52 elections.

From the point of view of the Election Commission, the task involved the preparation of 510 million ballot papers, deployment of a staff of over a million and the procurement of 2,960,000 steel ballot boxes.

To facilitate the smooth conduct of the elections, immediately after the reorganisation of States in 1956, the Commission revised the list of recognised State parties in terms of the newly constituted States. The position of the four all-India parties, viz. the Indian National Congress, the Praja Socialist Party, the Communist Party of India and the Bharatiya Jan Sangh, however, remained the same. In the case of State parties slight alterations had to be made according to the changed political map of India; but all the same the percentage minimum of 3 per cent of the votes polled in an area was observed as the standard for recognition as a State or regional party. In the Second Elections the electorate chose its representatives from as many as 26 parties, from the small Mizo Union, restricted in its activities to a part of Assam Hills, to the mighty Congress organisation.

The Congress Party swept the polls in the Parliamentary election by securing 371 of the 494 elected seats or roughly 75 per cent of the House. Thus it slightly improved on its record during the First General Elections. In the State Assemblies the Congressmen numbered roughly 65.1 per cent of the successful candidates. This percentage was also almost the same as the corresponding one for the First Elections. The figures for the rest of the parties in the Parliamentary elections are almost negligible.

In the Assembly elections the three all-India parties other than the Congress, viz. the Praja Socialist, the Communist and the Jan Sangh, registered a slight improvement over their performances in the 1951-52 elections. Among the other parties, Ganatantra Parishad in Orissa almost turned the table against the Congress.

Reviewing the Assembly election results state-wise, it is found that the Congress which had scored 90 per cent successes last time in the then Saurashtra State and Uttar Pradesh, failed to repeat its performance. But Madhya Pradesh came very near to giving the party that high percentage of success by choosing 232 Congress nominees in a House of 288. Almost the same level of achievement was recorded by the party in Madras, Mysore, Punjab and Rajasthan, the respective tallies being 151 (out of 205), 150 (out of 208), 118 (out of 154) and 119 (out of 176) seats. The percentage of Congress successes varied from 34 in Kerala to 81 in Madhya Pradesh. The Second Elections have considerably strengthened the Congress position in Rajasthan where in the First Elections it had secured only a marginal absolute majority of 82 in an Assembly of 160. But, perhaps, the biggest event of far-reaching importance, from the point of view of the Congress, was the success of the Congress in Andhra where it cut into some of the Communist strongholds and its reverses in Kerala where it ran a lame second to the Communist Party. While the Congress recorded a progressive victory in Rajasthan at the expense of the Jan Sangh, the Ram Rajya Parishad and the Independents most of whom were rulers of former Princely States, it failed to beat the challenge of the former rulers of Princely States merged in

Orissa, where the Ganatantra Parishad led by the Princes prevented the Congress from securing an absolute majority. In fact, the Parishad gained some seats in Congress strongholds. In the mid-term elections of 1961 in Orissa, however, the Congress retrieved its position and gained an absolute majority inflicting heavy losses on the Parishad. As against the outstanding successes of the Congress in Andhra and Rajasthan, the two big States of Uttar Pradesh and Bombay, which in 1952 had voted solidly for the Congress, registered a marked decline in the number of Congress candidates returned. Another safe Congress area, Bihar, also returned a smaller number of Congress nominees than it did in the First Elections.

In Madhya Pradesh and Mysore, the Communists could make little or no impression. The Jan Sangh had its highest poll in Uttar Pradesh. The Hindu Mahasabha lost much of its importance in the Second Elections.

Reporting after the conclusion of the Second General Elections, the Election Commission observed:

"If the first general elections served to teach the vast number of uneducated voters what the vote means, the second general elections familiarised them with the exercise thereof with discrimination and understanding. Another welcome and remarkable feature that has already emerged is the implicit and growing confidence which the Election Commission and the election machinery in the States have come to enjoy in the eyes of the political parties and the general public. Within the space of a few years, therefore, doubts which naturally existed as to the preparedness of the people for democratic self-government or the wisdom of extending universal adult franchise in a country with an overwhelmingly illiterate electorate have been completely dispelled. All observers agree now that an election is no longer a merely novel entertainment provided for the electorate in the cities or the countryside but has come to be a serious political struggle between the contending parties and candidates, the outcome of which ultimately depends on the deliberate choice made by the electorate between the contestants. The degree of political maturity displayed by the electorate even in many backward areas has indeed astonished many impartial observers and students of politics."

The subject of elections is a dynamic one. It grows according to the surroundings and contingencies. In India itself the pattern evolved for the first elections has undergone a remarkable change and so will it be in the coming years till it attains perfection.

The Third General Elections (1962)

The most outstanding aspect of the results of the Third General Elections was the clear mandate which the Congress Party, led by Prime Minister Nehru, received once again from the electorate to continue its uninterrupted rule of the country for another five years. An equally important but depressing aspect was that after sixteen years of parliamentary democracy, the Nation had not yet found an opposition party of national importance to provide an alternative to the Congress in the foreseeable future. On the national front, however, there were two significant developments: first, the decline of the Praja Socialist Party which until now held the position of the leading opposition and secondly, the emergence of the Swatantra Party as one of the two leading parties in the opposition.

The total strength of the electorate for the Third General Elections was over 216 million as against 193 million in 1957. Polling was held for 489 seats in the Lok Sabha embracing practically the entire country and 3,121 seats in the State Assemblies. The only two State Assemblies for which there was no general elections in 1962 were those of Kerala and Orissa as in the case of both these States mid-term elections were held in 1960 and 1961 respectively. A total of over 114 million votes were cast, approximately 53 per cent of the total electorate. This shows the unmistakable trend of the steadily increasing interest of the electorate to participate in the democratic process.

In the Third General Elections the Communist Party secured the second place with 9.96 per cent of the total votes polled. This was indeed an impressive performance in view of the fact that in 1952 the party had secured only 3.3 per cent of the total votes polled. On a closer examination, however, it would become clear that between 1957 and 1962 the Party had lost its momentum. For, in 1957 it had secured 8.92 per cent of the total votes polled, an almost three-fold increase on its figures of the First General Elections. In the Lok Sabha the Party won 29 seats, just two more than in 1957. In the State Assemblies its share was 184. The Communist strength was mainly confined to three States, namely, West Bengal, Andhra Pradesh and Kerala. The Party had, however, made some gains in Uttar Pradesh, Bihar and Punjab.

The Third General Elections had shown the decisive decline of the Praja Socialist Party which could secure only 6.84 per cent of the total votes, about 4 per cent less than what it secured in 1957. The Party could win only 12 seats in the Lok Sabha as against 19 in the earlier elections. A total of 179 seats were the Party's share in the State Assemblies as against 208 in 1957. It lost practically all its electoral support in Andhra Pradesh, Punjab, Madras and Rajasthan, halved its strength in Bihar, Maharashtra, Orissa and Uttar Pradesh and lost heavily in most of the other States.

As a new all-India Party, contesting General Elections for the first time, the record of the Swatantra Party in 1962 was quite impressive. The Party secured 6.85 per cent of the total votes polled and earned for it the second leading position among the opposition parties. In the Lok Sabha it secured 18 seats and in the State Assemblies a total of 166 seats. But more important than the 166 seats was the fact that the Swatantra became the leading opposition party in three State Assemblies, namely, Rajasthan, Gujarat and Bihar. With the merger of the Ganatantra Parishad in Swatantra, in Orissa too the party became the leading opposition.

Although the Jan Sangh had increased its percentage from 5.93 in 1957 to 6.44 in 1962 of the total votes polled, the Third General Elections conclusively proved that it was not really an all-India Party. For, its strength was confined only to the Hindi-speaking areas of Northern India. The Party secured 14 seats in the Lok Sabha as against 4 in 1957, an impressive increase when considered on a percentage basis. Similarly, its total in State Assemblies advanced from 46 in 1957 to 116 in 1962. But most of these were concentrated in three States only, namely, Uttar

Pradesh, 49, Madhya Pradesh, 41, and Rajasthan, 15.

Although the Third General Elections witnessed an increase in the number of all-India parties from four to five, the number of regional parties registered a substantial fall. There were only about a dozen such parties which deserve even a mention in this context. Of these, the only party which made a significant, even spectacular, gain was the Dravida Munnetra Kazhagam (D.M.K.) of Madras. Out of a total of 206 seats in the State Assembly, the Party captured 50 and out of a total 41 seats for the State in the Lok Sabha it secured 7. Thus the D.M.K. has established itself as the leading opposition party in Madras.

Communal parties like the Akali Dal, the Muslim League, the Hindu Mahasabha and the Ram Rajya Parishad have been steadily losing their appeal to the electorate. Each of them had been able to secure only a few seats. Similarly, parties like the Forward Bloc, Revolutionary Socialist Party, Republican Party, Peasants and Workers Party and the Jharkhand Party (of Bihar) also lost considerable ground between 1959 and 1962. The Socialist Party, a breakaway group of the P.S.P., had some successes in a few of the Northern States but not significant enough to create any new trend. Viewed in general the regional parties are certainly on the decline and their influence in years to come is destined to dwindle.

The number of Independents has also registered a significant decline both in the number of seats contested and the seats won. For example, in the Lok Sabha they held 36 seats in 1952 but the corresponding figures in 1957 and 1962 were 25 and 24 respectively.

In comparison with the two previous General Elections, there was substantial improvement in the manner in which the elections were conducted. The polling throughout the country (except a few constituencies in the snow-bound Himalayan regions) was completed in five days and the results were declared in the next three days. This in itself was a remarkable organisational feat in view of the elaborate arrangements required for the conduct of a colossal task involving over 200 million people. Apart from substantially reducing the period of polling, the Commission brought into effect another significant improvement by introducing the marking system. This system eliminated many of the corrupt practices which existed under the old system of a separate ballot box for each candidate. There was considerable anxiety that the marking system might prove a failure due to widespread illiteracy among the electorate. But on the whole, it proved a success. The Election Commission deserves also a tribute for the meticulous manner in which the arrangements connected with the Elections were worked out. And the Indian people have shown how they could conduct themselves in a peaceful and orderly manner in a nation-wide popular exercise like this which forms one of the foundations of democracy in India.

Fourth General Elections

In several ways the Fourth General Elections were remarkable. Jawaharlal Nehru was no more and the Congress Party was fighting a general election for the first time without him. The new leader of the Party was Indira Gandhi and this was the first general election under her leadership which itself was yet to be firmly established. The opposition parties were fully aware of the weaknesses of the ruling party and were bent upon exploiting them in their bid to capture power both at the Centre and in the States. There were, however, two developments which made the opposition less united and more divided than during the Third General Elections. First, the Communist Party of India was split into two, the C.P.I. and the Communist Party Marxist (C.P.M). Secondly, a number of new smaller parties had emerged in the States, mostly splinter groups taking their origin from the existing parties.

The results of the Fourth General Elections showed that the Congress Party was no more an impregnable fortress that it once was and as a consequence it lost heavily both at the Centre and in the States. For the first time since the inauguration of the Constitution the Party lost control of several States including the States of West Bengal and Madras.

As against 361 seats which the Congress had won in the Lok Sabha in 1962 with 44.73 per cent votes, it was able to secure only 284 seats with 40.82 per cent of the total votes polled. Among the opposition, the Swatantra Party got the leading position with 42 seats as against 18 in 1962 and 8.54 per cent votes. Swatantra was followed by the Jan Sangh with 35 seats and 9.29 per cent votes. In 1962 Jan Sangh had only 14 seats in the Lok Sabha. The split had far-reaching adverse effect on both Communist parties. While the C.P.I. got 23 seats as against 29 in 1962, the C.P.M. did rather well with 19 seats in their maiden contest. But together the Communist parties polled only 9.36 per cent (C.P.I. 4.90 and C.P.M. 4.46) votes as against 9.94 by the undivided party in 1962. The S.S.P. bagged 23 seats as against 6 in 1962 with 4.89 per cent of votes. The P.S.P. was able to secure only 13 seats and 3.08 per cent votes. The number of independents had gone up by more than a 100 per cent, from 20 in 1962 to 43 in 1967. They had polled a total of 14.39 per cent votes as against 9.63 in 1967.

The opposition parties, viewed as a whole, had done much better than ever before. From 133 seats in 1962 their strength had gone up to 236 in 1967, a remarkable increase indeed. But viewed from another point of view their performance was unsatisfactory. India's Parliament was still without an officially recognised opposition party. For that status a party required a minimum of one-tenth of the total membership of the Lok Sabha. The Swatantra Party which led the opposition had only 42 members which was 10 short of the required minimum.

The Fourth General Elections for the first time gave several opposition parties opportunity to assume power in the States either alone or in combination. Tamil Nadu provided the most shocking results for the Congress Party which had been ruling the State continuously for over two decades. A regional party, the Dravida Munnetra Kazhagam (D.M.K.), scored a comfortable victory over the Congress, with an absolute majority of seats in the Legislative Assembly, enabling it to form a new Government on its own strength. The most remarkable feature of the elections there was that every leader of standing in the Congress Party was defeated by a D.M.K. candidate. Even the President of the Congress Party, K. Kamaraj, a former Chief Minister of the State, was defeated in an Assembly constituency. The Congress had suffered heavy losses in several other States also. The most important among them were West Bengal, Bihar, Madhya Pradesh, Uttar Pradesh, Punjab and Rajasthan. The only State which continued to be as strong a fortress as ever before was

Maharashtra with a performance which was even better than that in 1962.

Fifth General Elections

Since the General Elections are normally held once in every five years, the Fifth General Elections should have taken place only in 1972. But the ruling party decided to go to the electorate and seek a new mandate a year ahead and hence the Fifth General Elections were held in 1971. From the political point of view the 1967-71 period was notable for unprecedented events. Of these, the most significant was the split in the Congress Party following the election of V. V. Giri as President of India consequent on the sudden death in office of President Zakir Husain in 1969. After the split, the ruling wing of the Party was known as Congress (R) and the organisation wing was known as Congress (O). Even before the split, the Party's strength in the Lok Sabha, as we have seen earlier, was not as formidable as in the past. But as a consequence of the split the ruling wing was reduced to a minority having only 228 seats out of a total of 522 in the House. The Congress (O) had 65 members.

Although the decision of the Government of India to hold elections in 1971 was related to parliamentary (Lok Sabha) elections only, some of the States also decided to hold elections to their Assemblies at the same time. Tamil Nadu (Madras) was a notable example among them. In the case of some States, mid-term elections to the Assemblies had taken place even earlier than 1971. Uttar Pradesh and Kerala are two examples of this category. In the case of the rest of the States, Assembly elections took place only in 1972. Hence a review of the Fifth General Elections should necessarily cover the results of the elections in 1971 and 1972.

The most striking feature of the 1971 Lok Sabha elections was the outstanding performance of the ruling Congress which captured 362 out of a total 520 elected seats in the House. In the dissolved House the Party had only a minority of 228 seats. That means a gain of 134 seats which enabled the party to command a clear two-thirds majority in the House. The Party was able to achieve this spectacular electoral triumph in spite of the fact that there was an electoral alliance among some of the opposition parties to forge a united front popularly known as 'grand alliance' against it. The Congress (O), Swatantra, Jan Sangh, S.S.P. and a few other smaller parties were members of this United Front.

In contrast to 1967 almost all the opposition parties suffered heavily in the elections of 1971. For example, Swatantra could secure only 7 seats, Jan Sangh 21, Congress (O) 13 and Socialist Party 5. Of the two Communist parties, C.P.I. which had electoral alliance with the ruling Congress secured 24 seats while C.P.M. gained 25 seats largely from West Bengal. Among the regional parties, D.M.K. alone which fought the elections in alliance with the ruling Congress was able to achieve signal success by bagging 23 seats from Tamil Nadu. The number of independents also had come down to 14 from a total of 43 in 1967.

The sweeping victory which the ruling Congress gained in the Lok Sabha elections was reflected in the State elections both in 1971 and later in 1972. The result was that the Party staged a spectacular come-back in every State except Tamil Nadu, Meghalaya and Manipur. In Tamil Nadu the victorious D.M.K. was in alliance with the Congress. Similarly in Meghalaya the All Party Hill Leaders' Conference (A.P.H.L.C.) which won a majority of seats in the State Assembly was in alliance with the Congress. It was only in Manipur that the Party was unable to gain a majority of seats; but even there it was the largest single party in the Assembly. On the whole, the Fifth General Elections marked the massive victory of the ruling Congress Party after the many reverses which the Party suffered during the 1967-71 period.

In its report on the Fifth General Elections (1971-72) the Election Commission pointed out that 354 successful candidates were elected to the Lok Sabha, each polling more than 50 per cent of the votes polled. Of the remaining candidates, six candidates obtained only between 20 and 30 per cent of the votes polled while 23 candidates between 30 and 40 per cent and the rest between 40 and 50 per cent.

The total number of votes polled was about 151.50 million

which was approximately 55.22 per cent of the total electorate
of 274 million; 3.24 per cent votes were rejected as invalid.

Sixth General Elections

The Sixth General Elections brought about a revolution through
the ballot. It proved to the whole world that India was politically still a democracy where the citizens freely choose their
rulers. In a truly dramatic manner, the ruling Congress Party
which held the reins of power for over thirty years, was swept
off the ground by the newly-formed Janata Party and its allies.

In the normal course the Sixth General Elections should have
been held in 1976. But the life of the Lok Sabha was first
extended for a year under the emergency and again through the
Forty-second Amendment of the Constitution which extended its
duration from five to six years. Thus legally the House could
continue until April 1978. But to the astonishment of not only
her countrymen but even the whole world, Prime Minister Mrs.
Indira Gandhi suddenly announced in January that the postponed
elections would be held in mid-March of 1977. Emergency regulations were relaxed and the process of parliamentary democracy was once again in full swing. A sudden political awareness electrified the 318 million voters of the country.

For the first time in the country's history the Congress Party
faced a strong opposition; united, determined and under a strong
leadership. The newly formed Janata Party was the leader of
the opposition. It consisted of the Old Congress, the Jana Sangh,
the Bharatiya Lok Dal (B.L.D.) and the Socialist Party. The
merger of all these all-India parties to form a new party was an
unprecedented event in India's political life. Jayaprakash Narayan
was the architect of the new political party and Morarji Desai
its Chairman. The Janata Party was supported by another new
party the Congress for Democracy (C.F.D.) which was led by
Jagjivan Ram who broke off from the ruling Congress immediately after the announcement of the election. The Marxist
Party and some regional parties like the Akali Dal also gave
their support to the Janata-C.F.D. combination.

The opposition parties took full advantage of the unpopular
measures of the Emergency period and denounced the dictatorial

tendencies which manifested themselves under Indira Gandhi's leadership during the period. They declared that the real issue in the election was 'Dictatorship *vs.* Democracy' whether India wanted democracy or dictatorship. The ruling Congress Party countered it by focussing attention on stability and progress and declared that the real issue was 'Democracy *vs.* Chaos'.

The Sixth General Election was gigantic in several respects. As many as 318 million voters were eligible to exercise their franchise. There were 2439 candidates for the 542 seats. The Congress Party had put up 493 candidates leaving the rest for its allies. The Janata Party and its allies contested 538 seats. The C.P.I. had 91 and the C.P.M. 53 candidates. Regional or State parties had 77 candidates while unrecognised parties had 80 candidates. There were also 1222 independents. In all 373,684 polling stations were set up.

The election was free, fair and decisive. The electorate was alert and discriminating too. The illiteracy of the Indian masses did not affect the election. They used their franchise effectively. In the northern parts of the country where the excesses of the emergency had their bitter effect, the voters supported the opposition. The result was dramatic. The Janata Party and its allies swept the poll and scored an overwhelming victory. Not only the Congress Party as a whole, but its leader, Indira Gandhi, and most of her cabinet colleagues were decisively defeated.

The only States where the ruling Congress Party was able to show its popularity were all in the south, Andhra Pradesh, Karnataka and Kerala. In Andhra Pradesh the Congress won 41 out of 42, Karnataka 26 out of 28 and Kerala 20 out of 20. In Tamil Nadu the Congress was in alliance with the All India Anna DMK and it had its salutary effect.

Maharashtra, the traditional stronghold of the Congress Party had been able to return only 20 Congress candidates out of a total of 48 seats. In Gujarat it could manage to win only 10 out of 26 seats. In Assam, again a traditional citadel of the Congress, the Party could capture only 10 out of 14 seats. The single seat in Sikkim went in favour of the Congress. In Kashmir the Party was able to get a majority of seats.

But the most amazing feature of the results was the almost

total rout of the Party in the most populous States in the country, namely, Uttar Pradesh and Bihar. The Party was not able to get even a single seat out of a combined total of 139 seats! The Party's position in the other northern states was no better. It won none in Haryana, Punjab, Himachal Pradesh and Delhi. In Rajasthan it managed to win just 1 out of 25 seats.

The only State where the elections to the State Assembly took place along with the Parliamentary election was Kerala. There the Congress-led united front scored a stunning victory over the opposition including the Janata Party by capturing 111 out of a total of 140 seats in the State Assembly.

Viewing the election results as a whole, it is a fact that the Janata Party with its allies could score a decisive victory over the Congress by capturing over two-thirds of the total membership of the Lok Sabha. At the same time it is clear that this victory is confined largely to the northern part of the country. The four southern states with a total population of 155 million have given an equally near unanimous verdict in favour of the Congress and its allies. Whether this will have any far-reaching consequences on the political future of the country and its federal system are too early to predict. To a large extent it will depend upon the manner in which the Janata-dominated Central Government's performance in administering the country during the next few years.

This chapter may be concluded with a brief mention of the admirable manner in which the Sixth General Election was conducted by the Election Commission of India. Conduct of an election involving some 318 million people is unprecedented in history, anywhere in the world. When we also consider that this gigantic exercise was to be conducted among a voting population which is largely illiterate, we get the true magnitude of the achievement. The Election Commission was able to handle it not only efficiently but in a record time. The polling was concluded in just four days and most of the results were declared within the next twenty-four hours. This in itself was a remarkable organisational feat in view of the elaborate arrangements required for the conduct of a colossal task involving some 318 million voters. The

Commission deserves a tribute for the meticulous manner in which the arrangements connected with the Elections were handled by it. And the people of India have shown how they could conduct themselves in a peaceful and orderly manner in a nation-wide popular exercise like this which forms one of the foundations of a democratic system of government.

CHAPTER 39

SPECIAL PROVISIONS RELATING TO
CERTAIN CLASSES

A SPECIAL feature of the political life in India under the British was the existence of communal electorates. Nationalist opinion was always opposed to it. Yet it continued, and in course of time established a pattern of communal politics unknown in any other country. According to this, almost every religious minority in India, the Muslims, the Sikhs, the Indian Christians and others, had a certain number of seats reserved for it in the legislatures. This privilege was extended to the Anglo-Indians and the Europeans also. Under the Constitution Act of 1935, the Scheduled Castes also were to be treated as a separate community and given separate representation. But the historic fast of Gandhiji at Poona in 1933 prevented it and the Scheduled Castes were given reservation in constituencies based upon joint electorates with other Hindus. In 1947 when India became independent, this was the situation.

Although the country was divided between India and Pakistan on a religious basis, the partition of the country did not by itself solve the problem of religious minorities. Pakistan became a 'Muslim' State, but all the Muslims of undivided India did not migrate to that State. Some forty million Muslims still remained in India. Besides, there were large groups of other religious minorities such as Christians, Sikhs, Jains, Parsees and others. The Scheduled Castes and Tribes were still treated on a par with religious minorities deserving special consideration. When the Constituent Assembly took up this question in 1947 there was nothing fundamentally different from the old ideas on the subject. The Assembly formed a Committee, the Advisory Committee on Fundamental Rights and Minorities, with Sardar Patel as its Chairman, to study the different aspects of the problem and make recommendations to the Assembly so that these recommendations could be given due recognition in the provisions of the new Constitution. The Committee took over two years to prepare a detailed report which was generally in favour of some form of reservations for the minority communities. In the meantime,

Independence and the problems created by partition brought about a new outlook, and a substantial change in the attitude of many members who belonged to the various minority communities in the Assembly. H. C. Mukherjee, an Indian Christian leader from Bengal, took the lead and appealed for the abandonment of the proposal for reservations in legislatures. This proposal soon found favourable response from many others and the Constituent Assembly decided not to embody the principle of communal reservation in the Constitution.

The decisions of the Constituent Assembly arising out of the discussions on the recommendations of the Advisory Committee opened a new trend in Indian politics. The main features of this new trend were (1) abolition of separate electorates, (2) abolition of reservation of seats in the legislatures, and (3) abolition of special safeguards to minorities.[1] The only exceptions made were with regard to the three communities, Scheduled Castes, Scheduled Tribes and Anglo-Indians, each of which had a special case. But even in these cases the special provisions were to exist only for a limited period of ten years from the commencement of the Constitution. These provisions are embodied in a separate chapter of the Constitution.

Representation of Anglo-Indians in the Legislatures

The Constitution empowers the President under Article 331 to nominate a maximum of two members of the Anglo-Indian community to the House of the People, if he is of the opinion that the community is not adequately represented. From a population point of view, the Anglo-Indian community is not entitled even to one seat in Parliament. The President will act on the basis of this constitutional provision only when no Anglo-Indian had been elected to the House of the People in the General Elections. Until 1977, there were two nominated Anglo-Indian members in the House of the People.

Just as the President is empowered to make these nominations,

---

[1] In 1978 the Government of India appointed the Minorities Commission with a view to continuously looking into the problems of Minorities and suggesting remedial measures. The Commission consists of a Chairman and four members.

the Governor of a State is empowered under Article 333, to nominate such number of Members of the Anglo-Indian community to the State Legislative Assembly as he considers appropriate, if in his opinion the community needs representation in the State Assembly and has not been adequately represented. At present, there is provision for four Anglo-Indian nominated members in the Legislative Assembly of West Bengal and one each in the Legislative Assemblies of Andhra Pradesh, Bihar, Maharashtra, Kerala, Madhya Pradesh, Madras, Mysore and Uttar Pradesh. Thus, the community has now been given representation in the Legislative Assemblies of all the States in which their population is over two thousand.

Reservation in Services

Under Article 336, the Anglo-Indian community was given special consideration with regard to appointments in certain services. Accordingly, during the first two years after the commencement of the Constitution, they would be appointed to posts in the railways, customs, postal and telegraph services on the same basis as immediately before the 15th of August, 1947. This reservation would be progressively reduced at the rate of ten per cent after every two years and was to completely cease at the end of ten years. Such reservation, however, was not to bar the members of the community from being appointed to any post under the Government if found qualified for appointment on merit as compared with the members of other communities. It may be mentioned here that the response from the Anglo-Indians for the posts reserved for them had been extremely poor.

Grants for Educational Benefits

The Anglo-Indian community was entitled to special educational grants under Article 337 of the Constitution for a period of ten years. During the first three years, this grant was to be equal to what the community had been receiving in 1947. Thereafter, it was to be progressively reduced at the rate of ten per cent at the end of every three years and it would completely cease as a special concession to the community at the end of ten years. It is further provided that at least forty per cent of the annual admissions in the Anglo-Indian educational institutions receiving such grants should be made available to members of other communities.

These provisions, on the whole show the genuine desire of the framers of the Constitution to accommodate the special interests of a small community like the Anglo-Indians and infuse confidence in them. When the British left India in 1947, the Anglo-Indians were apprehensive of their future in free India. But soon, the members of the community found that not only were their interests safe but the leaders of independent India were prepared to give them even special consideration so that they could continue as Indian citizens with hope and confidence.

The Scheduled Castes and Tribes

According to the 1961 Census, there were some 94.4 million people who were entitled to the benefits provided under the Special provisions of the Constitution. Of these, the Scheduled Castes alone number some 64.5 million. They are divided into several groups and are spread all over the country. The Scheduled Tribes number some 29.9 million. Most of them are in the States of Bihar, Assam and Madhya Pradesh. The Backward Classes which include the ex-criminal tribes, have not been precisely defined yet, but they are believed to number over 5 million.

Reservation in Legislatures

Under Article 330, a certain number of seats are reserved for the Scheduled Castes and Tribes in the House of the People. The number of these seats is in proportion to their population and is specified in the list of seats allotted to each State. As has been pointed out earlier, there are no separate electorates for these communities. They were returned through reservation in plural constituencies where each voter had two votes—one for the general seat and the other for the reserved seat.[2] At present, there are 114 seats reserved in the House of the People for these communities. Of these, 77 are reserved for the Scheduled Castes

[2] An amendment to the original law provides for the abolition of these double-member constituencies and the establishment of single-member constituencies for the Scheduled Castes and Tribes.

and the rest for the Scheduled Tribes. Table 12 will show the State-wise representation.

TABLE 12
THE HOUSE OF THE PEOPLE

Name of the State	Number of Members	Number of seats reserved for	
		Scheduled Castes	Scheduled Tribes
1. Andhra Pradesh	42	6	2
2. Assam	14	1	2
3. Bihar	54	6	5
4. Gujarat	26	1	3
5. Haryana	10	2	—
6. Himachal Pradesh	4	1	—
7. Jammu and Kashmir	6	—	—
8. Karnataka	28	4	—
9. Kerala	20	2	—
10. Madhya Pradesh	40	4	8
11. Maharashtra	48	3	3
12. Manipur	2	—	1
13. Meghalaya	2	—	2
14. Nagaland	1	—	—
15. Orissa	21	3	5
16. Punjab	13	3	—
17. Rajasthan	25	5	3
18. Sikkim	1	—	—
19. Tamil Nadu	39	7	—
20. Tripura	2	—	1
21. Uttar Pradesh	85	12	—
22. West Bengal	42	8	2
Union Territories			
1. Andamans	1		
2. Arunachal Pradesh	1		
3. Chandigarh	1		
4. Dadra and Nagar Haveli	1		
5. Delhi	7	1	—
6. Goa	2		
7. Lakshadweep	1		
8. Mizoram	1		
9. Pondicherry	1		
Special Representation			
Anglo Indians	2		
Total	544	78	38

Not only in Parliament but also in the State Legislatures, the political interests of the Scheduled Castes and Tribes are protected by reservation. Here again, the method adopted was the same, namely, that of reserved constituencies, joint electorates and representation proportionate to the population. Table 13 will show the number of seats reserved in each State Assembly.

TABLE 13

LEGISLATIVE ASSEMBLIES

State	Number of seats in the Assembly	Number of seats reserved for	
		Scheduled Castes	Scheduled Tribes
1. Andhra Pradesh	294	43	11
2. Assam	126	5	26
3. Bihar	324	40	32
4. Gujarat	182	10	17
5. Karnataka	224	28	1
6. Kerala	140	11	1
7. Madhya Pradesh	320	43	54
8. Maharashtra	288	33	14
9. Orissa	147	25	29
10. Punjab	117	33	Nil
11. Rajasthan	200	28	20
12. Tamil Nadu	234	37	1
13. Uttar Pradesh	425	89	Nil
14. West Bengal	294	45	15
Total	3,315	470	221

Reservation of prescribed number of seats in the House of the People and the State Legislative Assemblies does not mean that the maximum number of seats available to the Scheduled Castes and Tribes is limited to such reservation. On the contrary, members of these communities are free to contest as many additional seats as they choose to do. In fact, in the 1971 General Elections, in addition to the reserved seats, six members from the Scheduled Castes and three from the Scheduled Tribes were returned to the Lok Sabha against unreserved seats. Thus in a House of 494 elected seats, members of these two communities had a total of 116 seats. Similarly, in the State Assemblies too, representatives of these communities were elected against fifteen unreserved seats. Of these, eight were members of the Scheduled Castes and the rest from Scheduled Tribes. Thus, in a total of 3,315 seats in the State Assemblies 691 seats were held by members of these communities. It is also interesting to note in this connection that these figures are proportionately higher than those held by the members of these communities as a result of the earlier General Elections.

Special Consideration in Services

Under Article 335, a general direction to the Union and State Governments is given for giving special consideration to the members of these communities in the services consistent with the maintenance of efficiency in administration. This means that candidates from the Scheduled Castes or Tribes should satisfy at least the minimum educational and other qualifications prescribed for various posts of the different services under the State. It must be noted, however, that there is no fixation of a percentage of jobs in the Constitution for these communities. There is also no fixed period for the continuation of this preferential treatment. Naturally, the State is expected to continue such treatment until these communities make substantial progress educationally and economically and reach a certain level of equality with the rest of the Indian society.

In the light of the constitutional provisions, the Government of India reconsidered the position of the Scheduled Castes and Tribes in 1950. As a result, a new policy was laid down according to which their share of recruitment was fixed at twelve and a half per cent for All India Services on the basis of open competition and sixteen and two-thirds per cent for direct recruitments. The maximum age-limit prescribed for them for appointment was also raised by three years. In 1952, this rule was further relaxed raising their age-limit to five years above the maximum prescribed for others. All these provisions are also in conformity with the exception provided under Article 16(4) to the Fundamental Right of equality of opportunity in public appointments.

Further, there is a special provision in the Constitution under which in the States of Bihar, Madhya Pradesh and Orissa there will be a Minister in charge of Tribal Welfare who may, in addition, be in charge of the welfare of the Scheduled Castes and Backward Classes. At present, there are separate Ministries or Departments for the welfare of these communities in almost all the States. In 1966 there were no less than 17 Ministers and 12 Deputy Ministers in the State Governments belonging to these communities. Besides, there were six Ministers in the Union Government, two of whom were Cabinet Ministers, another two Ministers of State and the rest Deputy Ministers. The number has been increasing steadily in subsequent years.

Special Officer

Under Article 338, the President is empowered to appoint a Special Officer for the Scheduled Castes and Tribes to investigate on all matters relating to the safeguards provided for them under the Constitution, namely (i) representation in legislatures, (ii) claims to representation in services and (iii) the operation of the Fundamental Rights, and to report to him on these at regular intervals. Under this provision the Special Officer is also entrusted with the interests of the Backward Classes as well as the constitutional safeguards of the Anglo-Indian community.

The first Special Officer, designated as the 'Scheduled Castes Commissioner' was appointed under this provision in November, 1950. He was assisted by ten Assistant Regional Commissioners, each in charge of a region. The Commissioner submits to the President every year a report which is laid before each House of the Parliament.

Commissions of Investigation

Under Article 340 of the Constitution, there is provision for the appointment of two Commissions by the President, one to investigate and report on the administration of the Scheduled Areas and the welfare of the Scheduled Tribes and the other to investigate the conditions of socially and educationally backward classes and to make recommendations as to the steps that should be taken by the Union or any State to remove such difficulties. The reports shall be laid before both the Houses of Parliament together with statements explaining the Government's action on them. The appointment of the first Commission within ten years after the commencement of the Constitution was obligatory. Moreover, the Union Executive is empowered to issue directions to the States for the implementation of the recommendations of the Commission. The second Commission relating to Backward Classes, is optional, and the Union Executive can only advise the States to implement its recommendations. However, it must be emphasised that these are intended to provide the machinery for enquiring into the operation of those Fundamental Rights and the Directive Principles meant particularly for the advancement of the Backward Classes and the Scheduled Tribes.

Under Article 340 of the Constitution, the President appointed the Backward Classes Commission in January 1953. The Commission was charged with the main task of determining the criteria under which any sections of the people of India (in addition to the Scheduled Castes and Tribes) should be treated as socially and educationally backward classes; and in accordance with such criteria, prepare a list of such classes setting out also their approximate numbers and their territorial distribution. The Commission submitted its report after working for two years. But the Government after giving careful thought to the Report of the Commission found it impossible to accept its recommendations. The main drawback of the Report was that the Commission could not find objective tests and criteria for classifying socially and educationally backward classes. The result was a list containing as many as 2,399 communities out of which 913 alone accounted for an estimated population of 115 million.

In its bid to prepare a list of the Backward Classes, the Government of India sought the assistance of the State Governments to make *ad hoc* surveys for determining the precise criteria for the purpose. But the replies received from the State Governments were not satisfactory to the Centre which thereafter entrusted the task to the office of the Registrar-General of India. The Report prepared by that Office forms the basis for determining the list of

27

socially and educationally Backward Classes now for the purpose of extending to them governmental help for their progress.

The Constitution vests in the President the power to notify the castes, races and tribes to be included in the Scheduled Castes list of a State. But once the notification is issued, his power comes to an end and he cannot revise or modify the list. Any such revision or modification can be made only by Parliament. The same procedure is prescribed for the determination of the Tribes and tribal communities.

In the course of the last three decades the Scheduled Castes, Scheduled Tribes and Backward Classes have made remarkable progress. A few years back, they were some of the most backward peoples anywhere in the world. In subject India, most of them were the so-called 'Untouchables' with the lowest social status and living in abject poverty, ignorance and illiteracy. But today, many of them have climbed considerable heights on the social ladder and many more are fast following them. Every successive Report of the Commissioner registers the all-round increase in the tempo of the work relating to the welfare of these classes. Perhaps, the most original provision in the Constitution where it deals with these classes is the provision for the appointment of a Special Officer charged with the responsibility of watching the progress of these communities as envisaged under the Constitution.

The drive towards the rapid all-round progress of these communities is directed mainly through four channels, the political, the social, the economic and the educational. We have seen earlier the special constitutional provisions to safeguard their political interests. In the social field, the campaign for the removal of untouchability is gathering momentum and has already produced excellent results. The general awareness that the members of the Scheduled Castes are fellow citizens with equal rights and privileges and are entitled to the same courtesy and consideration is fast growing among the so-called upper castes. In the economic field, with the enactment of many labour welfare laws, minimum wage laws, co-operative and land distribution laws, they are making substantial progress. Many cottage industries such as weaving and leather industries are providing members of these communities an additional income. The greatest stress has been laid on the provisions for educational facilities and the progress in this field has been indeed remarkable. Thousands of fellowships, scholarships, studentships and freeships are given every year to the members of these communities by the Union and the State Governments. A sum of over Rs. 300 million was spent for the welfare of these communities under the First Five Year Plan with extremely encouraging results. Under the Second Plan the amount so spent was over double the above amount. The Third Plan provided for programmes estimated to cost about Rs. 1,140 million. The Fourth Plan placed the figure for the same purpose at Rs. 2,400 million. The Fifth Plan provided a much larger amount. Thus with the active interest of the State in the rapid advancement of these communities there is every reason to hope that they will soon catch up with the rest of Indian society and play an equally vital role in the all-round progress of the nation.

The ten-year period of safeguards, particularly the reservation of seats in the legislatures was later extended twice by constitutional amendments, each time by ten years, thus extending the period until 1980. This is likely to be further extended. It may now be hoped that the progress that these communities will make during the years 1960-80 will take the country to another milestone in its all-round progress enabling the abolition of reservations altogether in whatever form they exist today.

CHAPTER 40

AMENDMENT OF THE CONSTITUTION

FEDERAL CONSTITUTIONS as a rule are rigid as most of them have extremely difficult and even complicated procedures of amendment. Amending a federal constitution like that of the United States is perhaps the most difficult. Under the Australian Constitution too, the amending process is complex. In contrast, the Constitution of India presents a much simpler picture.

A constitution is a fundamental document. It is a document which defines the position and power of the three organs of the State, namely, the Executive, the Legislature and the Judiciary. It also defines the powers of the Executive and the Legislature as against the citizens. In fact, the purpose of a constitution is not merely to create the organs of the State but also to limit their authority, because if no limitation is imposed upon the authority of the organs, there will be tyranny and oppression. Naturally, such a fundamental document as a constitution should not undergo too frequent and easy changes, as that would undermine the confidence of the citizens in the abiding nature of the Constitution. Further, it would make it impossible to provide a reasonably ascertainable standard against which the conduct of the various organs of government can be measured. The case of a federal constitution is particularly significant in this context because it delimits not only the powers of the different organs of government but also achieves a balance which is often delicate between the Centre and the units of the federation. These considerations are powerful enough to preserve intact the original document which gives expression to the manner in which the governmental system is to be ordered into existence. As such, any amendment of the constitution should be justified by compelling reasons and circumstances.

It should be understood at the same time that a constitution is a dynamic document. It should grow with a growing nation and should suit the changing needs and circumstances of a growing and changing people. Sometimes under the impact of new powerful social and economic forces, the pattern of government will require major changes. If the constitution stands as a stumbling block to such desirable changes, it may, under extreme pressure, be destroyed. A constitution as such cannot have any claim to permanence; nor should it, because it has been adopted and has been working ever since, claim absolute sanctity.

As Ambedkar pointed out in the Constituent Assembly, the provisions for amendment while they embodied a certain measure of rigidity with regard to some parts of the Constitution, were flexible and afforded facilities for a simple process of amendment with regard to others. Pointing out the details of the scheme, he stated:

"We propose to divide the various articles of the Constitution into three categories. In one category we have placed certain articles which would be open to amendment by Parliament by simple majority. (Provisions such as those which deal with the establishment or abolition of Upper Houses in the States are examples of this type). The second set of articles (for amendment) require a two-thirds majority of Parliament. (Parts III and IV of the Constitution which deal with the Fundamental Rights and Directive Principles respectively belong to this category.) The third category requires a two-thirds majority of Parliament plus ratification by the States. The States are given an important voice in the amendment of these matters. These are fundamental matters where States have important powers under the Constitution and any unilateral amendment by Parliament may vitally affect the fundamental basis of the system built up by the Constitution. (Provisions dealing with the division of legislative power between the Union and the States fall in this category.)"

The procedure for amendment is detailed under Article 368 of the Constitution. According to this, an amendment may be initiated only by the introduction of a Bill for the purpose in either House of Parliament. When the Bill is passed in each House by a majority of the total membership of that House and by a majority of not less than two-thirds of the members of that House present and voting, it shall be presented to the President for his assent. When the President gives his assent, the Constitution stands amended in accordance with the terms of the Bill. But, as pointed out earlier, in the case of certain amendments, ratification by the Legislatures of not less than one half of the States by resolutions to that effect is required before the amending Bill is presented to the President for assent. The following provisions of the Constitution fall under this category:

(1) Articles 54 (Election of President), 55 (Manner of election of President), 73 (Extent of the executive power of the Union), 162 (Extent of the executive power of States), or 241 (High Courts for Union Territories);
(2) Chapter IV of Part V (Union Judiciary); Chapter V of Part VI (High Courts in the States); Chapter I of Part XI (Legislative relations between the Union and the States);
(3) Any of the Lists in the Seventh Schedule;
(4) The representation of States in Parliament; and
(5) Provisions dealing with amendment of the Constitution.

There is hardly another federal constitution which provides a comparable example, combining rigidity and flexibility in a manner exemplified in the above-mentioned provisions.

During the first sixteen years of the Constitution it was amended twenty times. Such rapid succession of amendments during such a short time in the life of the Constitution, has been attacked by many of its critics as a sign of weakness in the Constitution. Some of them thought that the Constitution should not be made so cheap as to admit of amendment so quickly and easily. There is an element of truth in this criticism. Yet, on close examination it will be seen that there were compelling circumstances which led to constitutional amendments during a momentous period of stabilisation and consolidation of the political freedom won just a decade earlier. While some of the amendments were a natural product of the eventual evolution of the new political system established under the Constitution in 1950, there were others necessitated by practical difficulties in the working of certain provisions of the Constitution. The reorganisation of States and the consequent constitutional amendment is the best example of the former type while the amendments dealing with the right to property provides a good example of the latter type. We have dealt with the various amendments earlier while discussing the relevant parts of the Constitution. Nevertheless, it seems appropriate here to recount them in the chronological order.

The First Amendment (1951) amended Articles 15, 19, 31, 85, 87, 174, 176, 341, 342, 372, and 376. It also added a new Schedule (Ninth Schedule) to the Constitution. The main purpose of the Amendment was the removal of certain practical difficulties experienced in the working of some of the Fundamental Rights, particularly rights under equality before law, freedom of speech, and the right to property.

The Second Amendment (1952) amended Article 81 in order to remove the prescribed limit of 750,000 of the population for one member to be elected to the House of the People. According to the original provision, at least one member was to be elected to the House of the People for every 750,000 of the population. It was further provided that the maximum number of elected members to the House should not exceed 500. But it was soon found that these limits could not be adhered to in practice in the light of the actual size of the country's growing population.

The Third Amendment (1954) brought about changes in the Seventh Schedule consisting of the three legislative lists. As a result, the scope of the Union's legislative power was enlarged by the inclusion of certain items, which were originally in the State List, in the Concurrent List.

The Fourth Amendment (1955) further amended Article 31 and 31A (Right to Property). It also amended article 305 and the Ninth Schedule.

The Fifth Amendment (1955) amended Article 3 and provided a new procedure for ascertaining the will of a State Legislature with respect to territorial or boundary changes that affect it.

The Sixth Amendment (1956) further amended the Seventh Schedule. It also amended Articles 269 and 286 dealing with inter-State Sales Tax.

The Seventh Amendment (1956) brought about the most comprehensive changes till then in the Constitution. The Amendment, as was stated earlier, was primarily concerned with the re-organisation of States. Along with such reorganisation, a large number of consequential changes had to be effected. Thus, the

Amendment affected substantially the First and the Fourth Schedules besides many articles of the Constitution.

The Eighth Amendment (1960) extended the period of reservation of seats in legislatures for the Scheduled Castes and Tribes by another ten years.

The Ninth Amendment (1960) provided for the transfer of certain territories of India to Pakistan under an agreement between India and Pakistan as a part of a comprehensive settlement of border disputes between the two countries.

Similarly, the Tenth Amendment (1961) integrates the areas of Free Dadra and Nagar Haveli with the Union of India and provides for their administration under the regulation-making powers of the President (Article 240).

The Eleventh Amendment (1961) obviates the necessity of a joint meeting of the two Houses of Parliament (Article 66) by constituting them into an electoral college for the election of the Vice-President. It also amends Article 71 so as to make it clear that the election of the President or the Vice-President shall not be challenged on the ground of any vacancy for whatever reason in the appropriate electoral college.

The Twelfth Amendment (1962) integrates Goa, Daman and Diu with the Union of India with effect from December 20, 1961, by adding them to the First Schedule as the eighth Union Territory and by providing for their administration under Article 240.

The Thirteenth Amendment (1962) provided, along with the creation of Nagaland as the sixteenth State of the Indian Union under the State of Nagaland Act (1962), for certain special protections to the Nagas. According to these, notwithstanding anything in the Constitution, no Act of Parliament in respect of religious or social practices of the Nagas, Naga customary law and procedure, administration of civil and criminal justice involving decisions according to Naga customary law, and ownership and transfer of land and its resources, shall apply to the State of Nagaland unless the Legislative Assembly of Nagaland by a resolution so decides. The Amendment provides also for the vesting of certain special responsibilities in the Governor of Nagaland.

The Fourteenth Amendment (1962) provided for the incorporation of the former French Establishments in India, under the name Pondicherry, as an integral part of the territory of the Indian Union. It also amended Article 81 to increase, from a maximum of twenty to twenty-five the number of seats assigned in the Lok Sabha for the Union Territories. Further it inserted a new Article 239A providing for the creation of local Legislatures or Council of Ministers or both in the Union Territories of Himachal Pradesh, Manipur, Tripura, Goa, Daman and Diu, and Pondicherry.

The Fifteenth Amendment (1963) seeks to raise the retiring age of High Court Judges from 60 to 62 years. It also empowered the various High Courts to hear cases against the Union Government. Another feature of this Amendment was that it restricted the scope of Government servants to appeal against government decisions in disciplinary matters. Accordingly they will have only one opportunity now as against two opportunities they enjoyed until 1963.

The Sixteenth Amendment (1963) seeks to enable Parliament to make laws providing penalty for any person questioning the sovereignty and integrity of India. Under the provisions of this Amendment, a person shall not be qualified to be chosen to fill a seat in Parliament or in the Legislature of a State unless, *inter alia,* he makes or subscribes before a person authorised by the Election Commission an oath or affirmation that he will bear true faith and allegiance to the Constitution and will uphold the sovereignty and integrity of India.

The Seventeenth Amendment (1964) amends the definition of the term "estate" in Article 31A to include lands held under *ryotwari settlement* and also other lands in respect of which provisions are normally made in land reform enactments. The Amendment has retrospective effect from January 26, 1950, the day on which the Constitution was inaugurated. It also amends the Ninth Schedule of the Constitution to include therein 44 State enactments relating to land reforms in order to remove any uncertainty or doubt that may arise in regard to their validity.

The Eighteenth Amendment (1966) provides for the creation of two new states, namely, Punjabi Suba and Hariyana as a result of the reorganisation of the former State of Punjab and the Union Territory of Himachal Pradesh.

The Nineteenth Amendment (1966) provides that Article 324, clause I, shall be amended by deleting the words "including the appointment of election tribunals for the decision of doubts and disputes arising out of or in connection with elections to Parliament and to the Legislatures of States shall be vested in a Commission".

The Twentieth Amendment (1966) introduced Article 233-A in the Constitution, validating the appointment, posting or promotion of a person as a District Judge, if such appointment was illegal or void by reason of its not being in accordance with Article 233 or 235 (dealing with control over subordinate courts by High Court etc.)

The Twenty-first Amendment (1969) provides for the recognition of Sindhi as one of the national languages of India by including it in the Eighth Schedule to the Constitution.

The Twenty-second Amendment (1969) created an autonomous hill State "Meghalaya" within the State of Assam.

The Twenty-third Amendment (1969) provides for the extension of the reservation of seats for Scheduled Castes and Tribes and the nomination of members of the Anglo-Indian community for another 10 years.

The Twenty-fourth Amendment (1971) affirms the Parliament's power to amend any part of the Constitution, including Fundamental Rights by amending Articles 368 and 13 of the Constitution. This neutralises the decision in the Golaknath case.

The Twenty-fifth Amendment (1971) bars the jurisdiction of courts over acquisition laws in regard to the adequacy of the amount paid in lieu of take over. The word "compensation" in the case of take over is deleted and the word "amount" is substituted.

A new clause provides that if any law is passed to give effect to the Directive Principles contained in clauses B and C of Article 39 and contains a declaration to that effect, it shall not be questioned on the ground that it takes away or abridges Fundamental Rights or on the ground that it does not give effect to the principles contained in the declaration.

The Twenty-sixth Amendment (1971) withdraws the recognition given to former rulers of Princely States and abolishes the privy purses granted to them. It deleted Articles 291 and 362 of the Constitution and inserted a new Article 360-A. In Article 366, a new clause was inserted in the place of clause 2.

The Twenty-seventh Amendment was passed in 1974. Under

this Act, two Union Territories, Mizoram and Arunachal Pradesh were set up.

The Twenty-eighth Amendment (1972) deletes Article 314 of the Constitution, which had given protection to the ICS officers' conditions of service and privileges and inserted a new Article 312-A.

The Twenty-ninth Amendment (1972) included the Kerala Land Reforms (Amendment) Act, 1969 and the Kerala Land Reforms (Amendment) Act, 1971, in the Ninth Schedule to the Constitution to protect these Acts from judicial review under Article 31-B and remove any uncertainty or doubt there could have arisen in regard to the validity of these Acts.

The Thirtieth-Amendment (1972) curtails the number of appeals to the Supreme Court. Formerly appeals to the Supreme Court were decided on the basis of the valuation of the subject matter. The Amendment makes only such cases which involve a substantial question of law, appealable to the Supreme Court.

The Thirty-first Amendment (1973) was passed by Parliament on May 8, 1973. The Act amends Art. 81 of the Constitution so as to increase the upper limit of elective seats in the Lok Sabha from 525 to 545.

The Thirty-second Amendment (1974) passed by the Parliament in May 1974 implements the 6 point programme for Andhra Pradesh.

The Thirty-third Amendment (1974) invalidates the acceptance of resignation by members of the State Legislatures and Parliament, which were made under duress or coercion or any other kind of involuntary resignation.

The Thirty-fourth Amendment (1974) provides constitutional protection to 20 Acts passed by the various States, as land reforms, by including them in the 9th Schedule to the Constitution.

The Thirty-fifth Amendment Act passed by Parliament in September, 1974 provided for Associate State status to Sikkim.

The Thirty-sixth Amendment Act, makes Sikkim a State of the Indian Union — the 22nd State.

The Thirty-seventh Amendment (1975) provides for a Legislative Assembly and a Council of Ministers for the Union Territory of Arunachal Pradesh.

The Thirty-eighth Amendment (1975) was passed by Parliament in July, 1975. This amends Arts. 113, 213, 289-B, 352, 356, 359 and 360 of the Constitution. It makes the declaration of Emergency by the President and the promulgation of Ordinances by the President, Governors and Administrative Heads of Union Territories non-justiciable (beyond the purview of the judiciary).

The Thirty-ninth Amendment (1975) amends Arts. 71 and 329 of the Constitution and the Ninth Schedule. It places the election of the President, Vice-President, Prime Minister and the Speaker beyond judicial scrutiny.

The Fortieth Amendment (1975) amends the Ninth Schedule to include 64 Central and State laws. The 64 laws thus included now remain beyond judicial scrutiny.

The Forty-first Amendment (1976) raises the retiring age of State Public Service Commission members from 60 to 62. This does not affect the members of the Union Public Service Commission who retire at the age of 65.

Forty-second Amendment (1976)

Of all the amendments of the Constitution during a period of twenty-six years since its inauguration, the Forty-second Amendment stands out as the most comprehensive. It also became the most controversial. No proposal for amendment of the Constitution had attracted so much attention and criticism in the past as this amendment.

The Union Law Minister, who piloted the Bill claimed on its behalf that "a Constitution to be living must be growing. If the impediments to the growth of the Constitution are not removed, it will suffer a virtual atrophy. The amendment was necessitated for removing the difficulties which had arisen in achieving the objective of socio-economic revolution which would end poverty and ignorance, disease and inequality of opportunity. The democratic institutions provided in the Constitution are basically sound and the path for progress does not lie in denigrating any of these institutions. However, there could be no denial that these institutions have been subjected to considerable stresses and strains and that vested interests have been trying to promote their selfish ends to the great detriment of the public good."

Those who criticised and opposed the amendments alleged that they were intended to destroy the democratic character of the Constitution as it was originally enacted and it was a determined attempt to pave the way for the eventual establishment of a dictatorial regime.

Briefly the Amendment brings about changes in the following provisions of the Constitution; Preamble; Fundamental Rights (Arts. 31 and 32); Directive Principles of State Policy (Arts. 32, 43 and 48); A new Part, Part IV A entitled "Fundamental Duties"; Union Executive (Arts. 55, 74 and 77); Parliament (Arts. 81, 82, 83, 100, 102, 103, 105 and 118); Union Judiciary (Arts. 131, 139, 144 and 145); Comptroller and Auditor-General of India (Art. 150); State Executive (Art. 166); State Legislature (Arts. 170, 172, 189, 191, 192, 194 and 208); High Courts (Arts. 217, 226, 227 and 228); Relations between the Union and the States (Art. 257); Service (Arts. 311 and 312); A new Part entitled "Tribnals" (Art. 323); Emergency Provisions (Arts. 352, 353, 356, 357, 358 and 366); Amendment of the Constitution (Art. 368); Seventh Schedule (Union List, State List and the Concurrent List).

Forty-third Amendment (1978)

The Forty-third Amendment deleted Article 31D, which was a part of the Forty-second Amendment and which had empowered Parliament to deal with anti-national activities. The Amendment also restored the power of the Supreme Court to decide on the constitutionality of State laws and that of the High Courts to go into the constitutional validity of Central laws which they had lost under the Forty-second Amendment. The Amendment also specifies that the duration of the House of the People and of the State Assemblies shall be five years and not six years as was made by the 42nd Amendment.

CHAPTER 41

CONCLUSION

A CONSTITUTION when written does not breathe. It comes to life and begins to grow only when human elements get together and work it. As time passes, it almost imperceptibly changes in form and content and assumes a new shape and even a new meaning. This comes of the nature and temper of those who work it. Time and circumstances do have their impact on it. Yet, it is men, more than anything else who shape and mould the destiny of a written constitution.

As Ambedkar observed:

"However good a constitution may be, it is sure to turn out bad because those who are called to work it happen to be a bad lot. However bad a constitution may be, it may turn out to be good if those who are called to work it happen to be a good lot. The working of a constitution does not depend wholly upon the nature of the constitution. The constitution can provide only the organs of State such as the Legislature, the Executive, and the Judiciary. The factors on which the working of these organs of the State depend are the people and the political parties they will set up as their instruments to carry out their wishes and their policies. Who can say how people of India and their parties will behave? Will they uphold constitutional methods for achieving their purposes or will they prefer revolutionary methods of achieving them? If they adopt the revolutionary methods, however good the constitution may be, it requires no prophet to say that it will fail. It is, therefore, futile to have any judgement upon the constitution without reference to the part which the people and their parties are likely to play."

No constitution is perfect and the Constitution of India is no exception to this general rule. But it goes to the credit of India that the urge for constitutional government was so deep-seated

430

in her that she devised a constitution of her own within three years after achieving political independence. The Constitution she adopted was intended to be not merely a means of establishing a governmental machinery but also an effective instrument for orderly social change. The strength and stability of a constitution depends largely on its ability to sustain a healthy and peaceful social system and when occasion demands, facilitate the peaceful transformation of its economic and social order. From this point of view the Constitution has set an ideal which not even its severest critic would characterise as outmoded or reactionary. Its basic objective is to establish a democratic, secular republic with a view to securing justice, liberty, equality and fraternity to all its citizens. It aims to translate into practice the noble concept of a co-operative commonwealth, a blending of political democracy with economic and social democracy. It embodies the most comprehensive policy directions to the State and its agencies to ensure the establishment of a Welfare State.

On the eve of the adoption of the Republican Constitution of India, many noble sentiments were expressed on the floor of the Constituent Assembly by its members. Some of them recalled the hoary past of India which was not unfamiliar with the concept of democracy and republicanism. It was, perhaps, true that the ideals of democratic government and republican institutions were first conceived and practised a thousand years before Christ when the people of Mithila established the world's first republic. Such thoughts about a great past have indeed a heart-warming effect. What is important, however, is not the consciousness of our ancient greatness but the ability to make democracy as envisaged under the Constitution a success in the present circumstances. Historical evidence indicates that in the days of the Buddha or even earlier certain types of democracy did flourish in parts of India. But the republics of those days were confined to small areas, tribes and clans and operated in a highly decentralised fashion. The system, however, could not withstand the pressure of monarchical ideas based on centralisation of power and the republican ideals became soon a memory of the past. Hence, references to glorious republican institutions in an obscure era can yield but poor comfort in the context of modern challenges. The challenge that faces the country today is whether a constitution embodying democratic principles and establishing republican institutions can withstand the pressures of a highly centralised administration embracing the entire country.

Ambedkar focussed the attention of not only the Constituent Assembly but the whole nation as early as 1949 on this aspect of the problem when he asked the following significant questions: "On the 26th January, 1950, India will be a democratic country and she will have a democratic Constitution. What would happen to her democratic Constitution? Will she lose it? What should we do to preserve our democracy?" These questions are not easy to answer. Yet it is the duty of everyone who is interested in the preservation of constitutional government and democracy in India to try to answer them.

A democratic system can endure only when the citizens as a whole hold fast to constitutional methods for achieving their social and economic objectives. Now that constitutional methods are open and available, they must abandon the bloody or coercive methods of revolution, of civil disobedience, of non-cooperation. For achieving social and economic objectives these methods should have no place in the country. Democracy cannot long survive among any people with whom the loudest voice counts as the voice of wisdom or when coercive pressures take the place of reason and persuasion.

Similarly, no country can remain democratic and no people can preserve a constitutional government, if the generality of the people are imbued with an immoderate sense of hero-worship. As John Stuart Mill said, people should not lay their liberties at the feet of even a great man or trust him with powers which enable him to subvert their institutions. There is nothing wrong in being grateful to a great man, but as Daniel O'Connel said, "No man can be grateful at the cost of his honour, no woman at the cost of her chastity, and no nation at the cost of its liberty."

Dealing with this matter Ambedkar said:

"This caution is far more necessary in the case of India than in the case of any other country. For, in India *Bhakti* or what may be called the path of devotion or hero-worship, plays a part in its politics unequalled in magnitude by the part it plays in the politics of any other country in the world. *Bhakti* in religion may be a road to the salvation of the soul. But in politics, *Bhakti* or hero-worship is a sure road to degradation and eventual dictatorship."

A political democracy without an economic and social democracy is an invitation to trouble and danger. Politics is more a result than a cause. Often this fact is forgotten in the external manifestations of the authority of the State. Political upheavals occur because of unsatisfactory economic and social conditions. The dictum of Aristotle, that extreme inequalities cause revolutions in a democracy, although expressed in the context of Greek politics of a remote past, holds good for all ages. Wherever living standards are satisfactory, political stability is normally assured. Where there is economic instability, upheavals are bound to occur. Hence in order to ensure lasting political stability, its base should be firmly planted in an economic and social democracy. While economic democracy emphasises the absence of extreme inequalities of wealth and adequate means of livelihood for everyone, social democracy stands for a way of life which recognises liberty, equality and fraternity as the principles of life. In the words of Ambedkar "these are not to be treated as separate items of a trinity. They form a union of a trinity."

One of the perils of constitutional government and democracy in Asian countries is that in these countries political changes have preceded social and economic changes. Europe presents a substantially different picture. There, by and large, political changes followed an economic and social revolution. In most of the European countries particularly of Western Europe, the Industrial Revolution preceded the emergence of political democracy. This is the reason why Europe is in a better position to preserve its political stability than Asia. Unless Asia can bring about rapid economic and social changes among her peoples, the measure of political democracy that she has introduced is bound to be destroyed sooner or later. India presents, perhaps, the most challenging test in this context, and she is struggling to realise rapidly an economic and social democracy, through democratic methods employed under a system of political democracy. If she does not achieve quick and wholesome results in this great experiment, she too, like several of her neighbours, is likely to lose

28

the initiative of a democratic political order and succumb to some form of dictatorship. Equality in politics and inequality in economic and social life is a life of contradiction. Such a life cannot last long. It is necessary that every effort should be made to remove this contradiction at the earliest possible opportunity.

The successful working of a democratic constitution requires in those who work it a willingness to respect the viewpoints of others, a capacity for compromise and accommodation and a real feeling of forbearance. Inflexibility and intolerance on the part of those who happen to be the rulers of the day will sow the seeds of hatred and vengeance. Constitutional government and democracy have no meaning if decisions are always taken on the strength of a numerical majority and the genuine feelings of the minority are bypassed and ignored. It is true that constitutional government would be brought into contempt if the people do not respect and abide by majority decision. Yet, wisdom demands the finding of a line of demarcation between the fields where majority opinion should of necessity prevail and where minorities, whether of opinion or of interest, ought to be allowed to prevail if the results do not militate against the security of the State. Persistence in courses of conduct alienating minorities, linguistic or religious, simply because of the strength of a 'brute' majority, is not the way to strengthen democracy. In this respect the developing of healthy conventions and strict adherence to them have an important role to play.

Elsewhere, we have pointed out the imperative necessity of developing a sound party system for the successful working of the parliamentary system of government adopted under the Constitution. But the success of a party system largely depends upon the availability of effective and efficient leadership to the parties. Fortunately for India, the national movement threw up in its onward march a set of leaders, able, devoted and trusted. They guided the country in the initial stages of her independence in settling some of the most vexed problems such as Partition, Integration of the Indian States and the framing of a new Constitution. They also gave a good start to the country in her economic and social transformation. But the old leadership is disappearing and its place is not being taken up by that of a new generation capable of fully shouldering the new responsibilities and inspiring the confidence of the masses. Prior to 1964 one heard often that vexed question, 'who will succeed Nehru'? The succession was smooth and orderly but the problem of effective top leadership still remains. But what the country needs today, and even more tomorrow, is not so much a top leader as a widespread under-standing of the facts and consideration which are relevant to the problem of leadership as such in a parliamentary democracy. No nation can expect to get an efficient top leadership without carefully building up a series of levels lower down of properly selected and trained leadership. Many years ago Walter Bagehot pointed out that nothing changes the face of politics as the change from one generation to another. While change is inevitable, it is essential to ensure that along with the changes of leadership, the qualities that must be common to leadership in every age are not destroyed.

Among such qualities are those of courage, character, integrity and social awareness. But among these, character and integrity are of even more importance under a democratic system. One often hears of a crisis of character in the country. In a country in which leadership becomes corrupt and character gets corroded, democracy cannot prosper. When a nation is engaged in mighty efforts of national consolidation and economic rehabilitation, it needs more and more leaders of great integrity and character. Only such leadership can inspire the masses and create in them the enthusiasm for producing better and richer results.

One of the most serious weaknesses of democracy in India is the widespread illiteracy and ignorance of the masses. The introduc-tion of adult franchise at one stroke among a predominantly illiterate people has its own inherent dangers. So long as they are unable to exercise the franchise in an intelligent manner after analysing the political issues in a rational way, democracy is not safe. For they may be stampeded through empty slogans and irresponsible promises into becoming camp followers of unscrupulous political adventurers. It is, therefore, of the utmost importance to educate the masses and instil in them a genuine sense of political consciousness and the right constitutional temper. As Edmund Burke said, 'let us educate our masters' for the sustenance of our democratic order.'

In a country so large in size and with a perplexing diversity in geography, language, race and culture as India, the stability of a democratic system depends largely on its ability to decentralise authority and build up self-governing institutions of an integrated nature at all levels of the administration. However, in view of the great and urgent need for rapid economic development of the country, as a whole, the fathers of the Constitution were compelled to assign a predominantly leading role to the Central Government in the affairs of the nation. They were justified in doing so in the context of economic and social development in India at the time they framed the Constitution. But if centralisation was dictated by the economic necessities of the present, decentralisation becomes imperative for the political stability of the future. The structure of Indian polity has ultimately to be one based on the solid foundations of self-governing local institutions at the village level which facilitate the building up of a hierarchy of well-knit and closely bound units of administration at every successive higher level. The progress of democracy in India is inseparably bound with the extent to which these local institutions are established and the manner in which they function in the years to come.

Whatever may be its imperfections, a constitution need not and should not stand in the way of a country's progress. Even if it is made only to suit the conditions and circumstances of one age, it need not fail in another. It is difficult to imagine of a constitution like that of the United States, written in the eighteenth century, suiting the altogether different conditions of the twentieth century. Yet it has worked and worked fairly well. In contrast, France has had no less than five constitutions within nearly the same period. Whether the latest one will help France to secure political strength and stability is yet to be seen. In post-war Europe, no constitution was hailed as more democratic than that of the Weimar Republic of Germany. Yet it could not prevent Hitler in his sinister march to power and the establishment of a totalitarian regime.

The fact that the Indian Constitution has been amended forty-five times in twenty-nine years since its inauguration has been a subject of severe criticism both in India and outside. The critics consider that the Constitution is a 'sacred document' which should not become the subject of too frequent amendments. There is some substance in this criticism. Yet there is another side to the

matter. A constitution is only a means to an end and not an end
in itself. It has no sanctity. It must conform to the needs and
conveniences of the country and of changing times. In an age
like the present, when science and technology have made
spectacular changes in the lives of human beings, no constitution
can claim rigid permanence and at the same time be able to adapt
itself to the changing conditions. It is better to have amendments
which will provide easy adaptability to altered conditions, rather
than an abrupt end under the weight of revolutionary social
changes.

A period of three decades is perhaps too short a period in the
life of a nation. As such, an evaluation of the working of the
constitution has only a limited significance. Many of the objectives
set before the nation are yet to be realised. But still the trend is
unmistakably clear. It was during this period that the initial tests
of the Constitution were conducted. The first to the sixth
General Elections on the basis of adult suffrage, the reorganisation
of the States, the establishment of a full-fledged cabinet system of
Government both at the Centre and in the States, the setting up
of an independent judicial system all over the country with the
Supreme Court of India at its apex, the testing of the value and
effect of the Fundamental Rights and the passing of a long list
of social and economic legislation to give effect to the Directive
Principles—all these have been done in accordance with the
provisions of the Constitution.

While steady progress has been thus maintained under the
Constitution, there have been stresses and strains both due to
internal difficulties and external factors. As many as over forty
times the emergency provisions had to be invoked to set aright the
breakdown of constitutional machinery in the States. In 1962 a
national emergency was proclaimed by the President as a result
of the Chinese Communist aggression on the territory of India
with far-reaching consequences. In 1965 the country faced
another threat to its security as a result of the aggressive designs
of Pakistan. In 1971 emergency was again proclaimed to meet
the Pakistani challenge following the civil war in East Pakistan.
In 1975, for the first time, internal emergency was proclaimed
resulting in the suspension of many fundamental rights and the
imposition of many restrictions on the operation of the democratic

system. The Constitution was also amended many times either to remove the difficulties experienced in its working or to facilitate greater mobility in the social change that it originally envisaged. So far there have been forty-five such amendments. These amendments, however, have not in any substantial manner modified the basic ideals for which the Constitution stood, or altered the framework of governmental machinery it sought to establish.[1]

The Sixth General Elections of 1977 have shown that the democratic urge is very deep-rooted in the people of India and their faith in the fundamentals of the Constitution and a constitutional system of government is firm and strong.

The complete and unqualified triumph of the rule of law under the Constitution may still be a far-away goal. Nevertheless, India can feel reasonably satisfied that she is well on the right path towards that goal. The Constitution, on the whole, has worked fairly well and remained an inspiring document for the citizens of this land.

[1] Critics of the Forty-second Amendment claim that it has substantially modified the basic framework of the Constitution. Those who support the Amendment claim, however, that the Amendment has not brought about any such basic change. To come to any firm conclusion on this question we have to carefully watch the working of the Constitution since the Amendment for a reasonably long period of time.

SELECTED BIBLIOGRAPHY

Section I: *Acts, Reports and other Documents*

All India Reporter (from 1950 to date)— *Constitutional Law Decisions*

Cabinet Mission Plan (1946)

Constitution of India (Draft—1949)

Constitution of India (Text—1950)

Constitution of India as Modified upto 1st September, 1951

Constitution of India as Modified upto 1st November, 1977

Constitutional Proposals of the Sapru Committee (1945)

Debates in the Central Assembly (India) 1921 *to* 1945

Debates in the Constituent Assembly of India (10 Vols.)

Debates in the House of Commons (relating to India, particularly 1934-35, 1942-43 and 1945-47)

Debates in the House of Lords (relating to India)

Debates in the Lok Sabha and Rajya Sabha of the Parliament of India (1950 to date)

Federal Court (of India) Reports from 1937 to 1950

Government of India Act, 1919

Government of India Act, 1935

Government of India's Despatch on Constitutional Reform

India (A Reference Annual) from 1955 to date

Indian Independence Act, 1947

Montagu-Chelmsford Report, 1918

Nehru Committee Report, 1928

Presidential Addresses of the Indian National Congress (particularly from 1922 to date)

Proceedings of the Round Table Conferences (2 Vols.)

Quit India Resolution (1942)

Report of the Reforms Enquiry Committee (1924)

Report of the All Parties' Conference (1928)

Report of the Simon Commission (1930)

Report of the Federal Structure Committee (1932)

Report of the Joint Parliamentary Committee (1934)

Report of the Joint Select Committee (1935)

Report of the Backward Classes Commission (1955)

Reports (Annual) of the Commissioner for Scheduled Castes and Tribes (from 1951 to date)

Report of the Election Commission of India—First General Elections, 1951-52

Report of the Election Commission of India—Second General Elections, 1957 and also subsequent reports

Report of the States Reorganisation Commission (1955)

Report of the First Finance Commission (1952)

Report of the Second Finance Commission (1957)

Report of the Third, Fourth, Fifth, Sixth and Seventh Finance Commissions
Report of the Official Language Commission (1956)
Report of the Committee of Parliament on Official Language (1953)
States Reorganisation Act, 1956
Supreme Court Reports (from 1950 to date)
White Paper on Indian States (Government of India, Ministry of States, 1950)

Section II: *Books*

AGGARWAL, R. N., *Financial Committees of the Indian Parliament*
AGGARWALA, OM PRAKASH, *Fundamental Rights and Constiutional Remedies* (3 Vols.) (1956)
AGGARWALA, OM PRAKASH, *Cases on the Constitution of India* (1959)
AIYAR, S. P., *Federalism and Social Change* (1961)
AIYER, ALLADI KRISHNASWAMI, *The Constitution and Fundamental Rights* (Srinivasa Sastri Memorial Lectures, 1955)
AIYER, ALLADI KRISHNASWAMY and AIYANGAR, N. R., *Government of India Act, 1935 with a Commentary, Critical and Explanatory* (1937)
AIYER, SIVASWAMY, *Indian Constitutional Problems* (1928)
ALEXANDER, H., *India since Cripps* (1944)
ALEXANDROWICZ, CHARLES H., *Constitutional Developments in India* (1957)
ALI, SADIQ, *The General Election 1957: A Survey* (1959)
ALTEKAR, A. S., *State and Government in Ancient India* (2nd revised and enlarged edn. 1955)
AMBEDKAR, B. R., *Ranade, Gandhi and Jinnah* (1943)
AMBEDKAR, B. R., *Thoughts on Linguistic States* (1955)
AMERY, L. S., *India and Freedom* (1942)
ANDREWS, C. F., *India and the Simon Report* (1930)
ARCHBALD, W. A. J., *Outline of Indian Constitutional History* (1926)
AZAD, MAULANA ABUL KALAM, *India Wins Freedom* (1959)

BAILEY, S. D., *Parliamentary Government in Southern Asia* (1953)
BAINS, J. S. (Editor), Studies in Political Science (1961)
BANERJEA, P., *Public Administration in Ancient India* (1916)
BANERJEE, A. C., *The Making of the Indian Constitution, 1939-47* (extracts from documents) (1948)
BANERJEE, A. C., *Indian Constitutional Documents, 1758-1945,* 3 Vols. (1946)
BANERJEE, A. C., *The Constituent Assembly of India* (1947)
BANERJEE, A. C. and BOSE, D. R., *The Cabinet Mission in India* (1946)
BANERJEE, BENODE BEHARI, *Outline of the Dominion Constitution for India* (1948)
BANERJEE, D. N., *Early Administrative System of the East India Company in Bengal* (1943)
BANERJEE, D. N., *Partition or Federation, a Study in Indian Constitutional Problems* (1946)

BANERJEE, D. N., *The Draft Constitution of India: A Critique* (1949)
BANERJEE, D. N., *Our Fundamental Rights, Their Nature and Extent* (1960)
BANERJEE, R. D., *The Age of the Imperial Guptas* (1933)
BANERJEE, SURENDRANATH, *A Nation in Making* (1925)
BASU, DURGA DAS, *Commentary on the Constitution of India*
BASU, DURGA DAS, *Cases on the Constitution of India* (2 Vols.)
BENI PRASAD, *A Few Suggestions on the Problem of the Indian Constitution* (1928)
BENI PRASAD, *The State in Ancient India* (1942)
BENI PRASAD, *Hindu-Muslim Questions* (1941)
BEOTRA, B. R., *The Two Indias* (1932)
BESANT, ANNIE, *How India Wrought for Freedom*
BEVERIDGE (LORD), *India Called Them* (1947)
BHALLA, R. P., *Elections in India*
BHANJDEO, P. C., *Financial Position of the Government of India* (1935)
BHARATAN KUMARAPPA and others, *Cultural Foundations of Indian Democracy* (1955)
BLUNT, SIR EDWARD, *The Indian Civil Service* (1937)
BOSE, SUBHASH CHANDRA, *The Indian Struggle* (1932)
BOWLES, CHESTER, *Ambassador's Report* (1954)
BRAILSFORD, H. N., *Rebel India* (1931)
BRECHER, MICHAEL, *Nehru, A Political Biography* (1959)
BRIGHT, J. S. (Editor), *Selected Writings of Jawaharlal Nehru* (1950)

Cambridge History of India, Vols. V and VI (1913)
CAMPBELL-JOHNSON, ALAN, *Mission with Mountbatten* (1951)
CHANDA, A. K., *Indian Public Administration* (1959)
CHANDA, A. K., *Aspects of Audit Control* (1960)
CHANDRAN, J. R., and THOMAS, M. M. (Editors), *Religious Freedom* (1956)
CHATTERJEE, BASANT, *The Congress Splits*
CHAUDHURI, A. S., *Constitutional Rights and Limitations* (1956)
CHAUDHURI, A. S., *Law of Writs and Fundamental Rights* (1959)
CHIROL, VALENTINE, *Indian Unrest*
COATMAN, JOHN, *The Indian Riddle* (1932)
COATMAN, JOHN, *India—The Road to Self-Government* (1941)
COUPLAND, R., *Cripps Mission* (1942)
COUPLAND, R., *The Indian Problem—1833-1935* (1942)
COUPLAND, R., *India, a Re-statement* (1945)
COUPLAND, R., *Constitutional Problem in India* (1949)
COWELL, HERBERT, *History and Constitution of the Courts and Legislative Authorities in India* (1936)
COX, PHILIP, *Beyond the White Paper: A Discussion of the Evidence Presented Before the Joint Select Committee on Indian Constitutional Reforms* (1934)
CUMMING (SIR), JOHN, *Modern India* (1932)

DAIN, C. M., *State Legislatures in India*
DAS, B. C., *The President of India*

DAS, G. N., *Concept of Equality in the Eye of Law* (1959)

DAS, M. N., *The Political Philosophy of Jawaharlal Nehru* (1960)

DAS, S. C., *The Constitution of India, A Comparative Study* (1960)

DESAI, A. R., *Social Background of Indian Nationalism* (1954)

DIVETIA, KUMUD, *The Nature of Inter-relations of Governments in India* (1957)

DODWELL, HENRY, *A Sketch of the History of India from 1858 to 1918* (1925)

DOUGLAS, W. O., *We the Judges* (1956)

DUBE, MAYA, *The Speaker in India*

DUFFETT, W. E., HICKS, A. R. and PARKIN, J. R., *India Today* (1942)

DUNCAN, ARTHUR, *India in Crisis* (1931)

DUTT, PALME, R., *India Today* (1946)

EDDY, J. P. and LAWTON, F. H., *India's New Constitution: A Survey of the Government of India Act,* 1935

FISHER, F. B., *India's Silent Revolution* (1920)

FORBES, ROSITA, *India of the Princes* (1939)

GADGIL, D. R., *Federating India* (1945)

GADGIL, D. R., *Some Observations on the Draft Constitution* (1949)

GANDHI, M. K., *The Removal of Untouchability*

GANDHI, M. K., *India's Struggle for Swaraj* (1921)

GANDHI, M. K., *Communal Unity* (1949)

GANGULEE, N., *The Making of Federal India* (1936)

GANGULEE, N., *Constituent Assembly for India* (1942)

GARRAT and THOMPSON, *Rise and Fulfilment of British Rule in India* (1935)

GLEDHILL, A., *Republic of India, the Development of Its Law and Constitution* (1951)

GOREY, V. K., *United States of India, a Constructive Federal Solution*

GOUR, SIR HARI SINGH, *Future Constitution of India* (1938)

GRIFFITHS, SIR PERCIVAL, *The British Impact on India* (1952)

HAKSAR and PANIKKAR, *Federal India*

HALAYYA, M., *Emergency: A War on Corruption*

HARRISON, SELIG, *India, the Dangerous Decades* (1960)

HARTOG, LADY, *India, New Pattern* (1955)

HORNE, E. A., *Political System of British India with Special Reference to the Recent Constitutional Changes* (1922)

HULL, WILLIAM I., *India's Political Crisis* (1930)

ILBERT, COURTNEY, *Government of India, a Brief Historical Survey of Parliamentary Legislation Relating to India* (1922)

INDIAN INSTITUTE OF PUBLIC ADMINISTRATION, *Organisation of the Government of India* (1958)

IRWIN, LORD, *Some Aspects of the Indian Problem* (1932)

ISWARI PRASAD, *Medieval India* (1943)

JAYASWAL, K. P., *Hindu Polity* (2nd ed. 1953)

JENNINGS, SIR IVOR, *Some Characteristics of the Indian Constitution* (1953)

KABIR, HUMAYUN, *Britain and India* (1961)

KALE, V. G., *Gokhale and Economic Reforms* (1916)

KEITH, ARTHUR BERRIEDALE, *Constitutional History of India*, 1600-1935 (1937)

KHAN, SIR S. AHMAD, *Indian Federation* (1937)

KHAN, SIR S. AHMAD, *Federal Finance* (1939)

KRISHNAN, K. B., *Problem of Minorities or Communal Representation in India* (1939)

LAJPAT RAI, *The Political Future of India* (1930)

LAL, A. B. (Editor), *The Indian Parliament* (1956)

LAL BAHADUR, *The Muslim League* (1954)

LEE-WARNER, *The Native States of India* (1933)

LEVI, WERNER, *Free India in Asia* (1954)

LUMBY, E. W. R., *The Transfer of Power in India 1945-47* (1954)

MACDONALD, J. RAMSAY, *Government of India*

MADHOK, BALRAJ, *Political Trends in India* (1959)

MAHARAJ, HEMINATH, *Is the Republic of India Secular?* (1956)

MAJUMDAR, B. B. (Editor), *Public Administration in India* (1953)

MAJUMDAR, R. C., *An Advanced History of India* (1948)

MAJUMDAR, R. C., *Three Phases of India's Struggle for Freedom* (1960)

MANSHARDT, CLIFFORD (Editor), *The First Decade, August 15, 1947-August 15, 1957*

MASALDAN, P. N., *Evolution of Provincial Autonomy in India—1858-1950* (1953)

MASANI, M. R., *The Communist Party of India* (1954)

MASANI, R. P., *Britain in India* (1960)

MASHRUWALA, K. G., *Some Particular Suggestions for the Constitution of Free India* (1946)

MASHRUWALA, K. G., *Gandhi and Marx* (1951)

MEHTA, ASOKA, *Inside Lok Sabha* (1955)

MEHTA, G. L., *Understanding India* (1959)

MENON, V. K. N., *India Since Independence—From the Preamble to the Present*

MENON, V. P., *The Integration of the Indian States* (1956)

MENON, V. P., *The Transfer of Power in India* (1957)

MINTO (COUNTESS OF), MARY, *India, Minto and Morley* (1934)

MISRA, B. R., *Economic Aspects of the Indian Constitution* (1952)

MITTER, B. L., *The Indian Constitution* (1945)

MONTAGU, E. S., *The Indian Diary* (1930)

MORRIS-JONES, W. H., *Parliament in India* (1957)

MOTI RAM, *Guide to Constituent Assembly*

MUDALIAR (SIR), A. R., *An Indian Federation* (1933)

MUKHERJEE, P., *Indian Constitutional Documents Containing Government of India Acts* (1915 and 1916)

MUNSHI, K. M., *Warnings of History, Trends in Modern India* (1959)

MURTI, A. S. N., *Free State for India with Regional Plan for a New Constitution*

MURTY, P. N. and PADMANABHAN, K. V., *Constitution of the Dominion of India* (1947)

NAIK, R. B., *Paramountcy in Indian Constitutional Law: Study of the Legal Aspects of the Relationship between the Indian States and the Government of India from the Days of the East India Company*

NANAKCHAND, PANDIT, *Law of Elections and Election Petitions in India* (1951)

NARASIMHAN, V. K., *Democracy Redeemed*

NARAYAN, I., *From Dyarchy to Self-government* (1950)

NARAYAN JAYAPRAKASH, *Towards a New Society* (1957)

NEHRU, JAWAHARLAL, *An Autobiography*

NEHRU, JAWAHARLAL, *The Unity of India* (Collected Writings) (1937-40)

NEHRU, JAWAHARLAL, *The Discovery of India* (1947)

NEHRU, JAWAHARLAL, *Independence and After* (Collection of Important Speeches from 1946 to 1949)

NEHRU, JAWAHARLAL, *Speeches 1949-53*

NEHRU, JAWAHARLAL, *A Bunch of Old Letters* (1959)

NIHAL SINGH, GURUMUKH, *Landmarks in Indian Constitutional Development* (1952)

O'DWYER, MICHAEL, *India As I Knew It* (1925)

PALMER, JULIAN, *Sovereignty and Paramountcy in India* (1930)

PANDIT, H. N., *The P.M.'s President*

PANIKKAR, K. M., *The Working of Dyarchy in India, 1919-1928*

PANIKKAR, K. M., *A Survey of Indian History* (1954)

PANIKKAR, K. M., *The State and the Citizen* (1956)

PUNNIAH, K. V., *Constitutional History of India* (1925)

PYLEE, M. V., *Constitutional Government in India* (1960)

PYLEE, M. V., *Constitutional History of India* (1977)

PYLEE, M. V., *The Federal Court of India* (1966)

RAJKUMAR, N. V., *Indian Political Parties* (1949)

RAMACHANDRAN, V. G., *Law of Preventive Detention* (1954)

RAMACHANDRAN, V. G., *Fundamental Rights and Constitutional Remedies* (1960)

RAMASWAMY, M., *Distribution of Legislative Powers in the Future of Indian Federation* (1944)

RAMASWAMY, M., *Fundamental Rights* (1946)

RAMASWAMY, M., *Law of the Constitution of India* (1938)

RAO, B. SHIVA and others, *The Challenge to Democracy* (1953)

RAO, K. SUBBA, *Conflicts in Indian Polity*

RAO, K. V., *Parliamentary Democracy of India* (1959)

RAO, RAMAKRISHNA, *Judicial Review and Elective Franchise* (1956)

RAO, VENKOBA K., *Fundamental Rights* (1953)

RAO, V. VENKATA, *The Prime Minister* (1954)

RAU, B. N. (Editor), *Constitutional Precedents* (2 Vols.) (1947)

RAU, B. N., *Indian Constitution in the Making* (1960)

RAY, S., *Democracy in India, The Discovery of Free India* (1959)

RUTHNASWAMY, M., *Revision of the Constitution* (1928)

SAMPURNANAND, *Indian Socialism* (1961)

SANDERSON, G. D., *India and British Imperialism* (1951)

SANTHANAM, K., *The Constitution of India* (1951)

SAPRE, B. G., *The Growth of the Indian Constitution and Administration* (1928)

SAPRU, TEJ BAHADUR, *Constitutional Proposals of the Sapru Committee* (1946)

SASTRY, K. R. R., *Indian States* (1941)

SCHUSTER, GEORGE and WINT, GUY, *India and Democracy* (1941)

SEN, GERTRUDE EMERSON, *Cultural Unity of India* (1956)

SETALVAD, M. C., *War and Civil Liberties* (1946)

SETALVAD, M. C., *The Common Law in India* (1961)

SHAH, K. T., *Provincial Autonomy under the Government of India Act, 1935* (1938)

SHAH, K. T. and BAHADURJI, GULESTAN J., *Governance of India: A Commentary on the Government of India Act of 1919 with Additional Chapters on the Indian Local Government, Indian Army, Indian Finance and the Native States* (1928)

SHARMA, S. R., *How India is Governed* (1954)

SHARMA, S. R., *Democracy in the Saddle* (1940)

SHARMA, SRI RAM, *The Supreme Court and Judicial Review in India* (1952)

SHARMA, SRI RAM, *Some Independent Government Agencies in the Indian Constitution* (1953)

SHARMA, SRI RAM, *The Supreme Court in Indian Constitution* (1960)

SHUKLA, V. N., *Constitution First Amendment Act, 1954*

SINHA, D. C., *Our Legislative Procedure* (1936)

SITARAMAYYA, PATTABHI, *History of the Indian National Congress*, 2 Vols. (1947)

SMITH, W. R., *Nationalism and Reform in India* (1938)

SPEAR, PERCIVAL, *India, Pakistan and the West* (1958)

SPRATT, PHILIP, *India and Constitution Making* (1948)

SRINIVASAN and MATHRUBUTHAM, *The Representation of the People Act* (XLIII of 1950) *As Amended by Acts LXXXIII of 1950 and XXVII of 1951* (1951)

SRINIVASAN, S. N., *Democratic Government in India* (1952)

STOKES, ERIC, *The English Unitarians and India* (1959)

SUNDA, E. S., *Federal Court of India, a Constitutional Study* (1936)

SUNDARAM, LANKA, *A Secular State for India* (1944)

THOMPSON, E., *The Other Side of the Medal* (1925)

THOMPSON, E., *Making of Indian Princes* (1944)

TYAGI, A. R., *Rights and Obligations of Civil Servants in India* (1959)

TYNE, C. H. V., *India in Ferment* (1923)

VARADARAJAN, M. K., *Indian States and the Federation* (1939)

VENKATARAMA, T. S., *A Treatise on Secular State* (1950)

VENKATARANGAIYA, M., *The Case for a Constitutional Assembly for India; a Historical and Comparative Study* (1946)

VENKATARANGAIYA, M., *Draft Constitution of India* (1949)

WATTAL, P. K., *Parliamentary Financial Control in India* (1953)

WHITE, SIR FREDERICK, *India—a Federation? being a Survey of the Principal Federal Constitutions of the World, with Special Reference to the Relations of the Central to the Local Government in India* (1936)

WILSON, PATRICK, *Government and Politics of India and Pakistan—1855-1955. A Bibliography of Works in Western Languages* (1955)

Y. M. C. A. Publishing House, Calcutta, *The Secular State in India, A Christian Point of View* (1954)

Y. M. C. A. Publishing House, Calcutta, *India's Quest for Democracy* (1958)

ZACHARIAS H., *Renascent India* (1933)

ZAIDI, A. M., *The Annual Register of Indian Political Parties*, Vols. I, II, III and IV (1972 to 1977)

POSTSCRIPT

As this goes to Press, the President of India has given his assent to the latest amendment to the Constitution, the Forty-Fourth Amendment Act, 1978, on 30th April 1979. This Amendment is of special importance as it modifies, removes or nullifies a number of provisions of the Forty-Second Amendment which were assailed as undemocratic and as undermining the spirit of the Constitution as originally envisaged by its framers.

The Constitution (Forty-Fourth Amendment) Act, 1978

The Act received the assent of the President on 30th April 1979. It has 45 sections and amends a large number of Articles of the Constitution. The main provisions are as follows:

1. *Article* 19: This Article deals with the seven freedoms as originally provided in the Constitution. Of these, *the right to acquire, hold and dispose of property* (19)(i)(f) has been taken away.

   This means, in effect, that property is no more a fundamental right.

2. *Article* 22 (4) provides for preventive detention. The amendment aims at making the conditions of preventive detention more rigorous in the interest of the individual. The amended provision, for instance, reduces the initial period of detention from three months to two months. Further, the conditions under which the period can be extended have been made more difficult.

   "No law providing for preventive detention shall authorise the detention of a person for a longer period than two months unless an Advisory Board constituted in accordance with the recommendations of the Chief Justice of the appropriate High Court has reported before the expiration of the said period of two months that there is in its opinion sufficient cause for such detention:

447

Provided that an Advisory Board shall consist of a Chairman and not less than two other members, and the Chairman shall be a serving Judge of the appropriate High Court and the other members shall be serving or retired Judges of any High Court:

Provided further that nothing in this clause shall authorise the detention of any person beyond the maximum period prescribed by any law made by Parliament under sub-clause (a) of clause (7)."

3. In *Article* 30, after clause (i) the following clause has been inserted:

"(IA) In making any law providing for the compulsory acquisition of any property of an educational institution established and administered by a minority, referred to in clause (1), the State shall ensure that the amount fixed by or determined under such law for the acquisition of such property is such as would not restrict or abrogate the right guaranteed under that clause."

4. The sub-heading "Right to Property" occurring after *Article* 30 has been omitted.

Article 31 of the Constitution which deals with the right to property has been altogether omitted. Consequential changes have been made in Articles 31A and 31C.

5. A new clause as follows has been added to *Article* 38:

"(2) The State shall, in particular, strive to minimise the inequalities in income, and endeavour to eliminate inequalities in status, facilities and opportunities, not only amongst individuals but also amongst groups of people residing in different areas or engaged in different vocations."

6. *Article* 71 which deals with matters connected with the election of a President or Vice-President is amended as follows:

"71. (1) All doubts and disputes arising out of or in connection with the election of a President or Vice-President shall be inquired into and decided by the Supreme Court whose decision shall be final.

(2) If the election of a person as President or Vice-President is declared void by the Supreme Court, acts done by him in the exercise and performance of the powers and duties of the office of President or Vice-President, as the case may be, on or before the date of the decision of the Supreme Court shall not be invalidated by reason of that declaration.

(3) Subject to the provisions of this Constitution, Parliament may by law regulate any matter relating to or connected with the election of a President or Vice-President.

(4) The election of a person as President or Vice-President shall not be called in question on the ground of the existence of any vacancy for whatever reason among the members of the electoral college electing him."

7. *Article* 74 is amended by adding the following proviso at the end:

"Provided that the President may require the Council of Ministers to reconsider such advice, either generally or otherwise, and the President shall act in accordance with the advice tendered after such reconsideration."

8. *Article* 77 is amended by taking away the following clause (4) from it:

"No court or other authority shall be entitled to require the production of any rules made under clause (3) for the more convenient transaction of the business of the Government of India."

This was inserted by the Constitution's Forty-Second Amendment Act, 1976.

9. *Article* 83 in the amended form restores the earlier position of the duration of the House of the People, namely,

29

five years. The Forty-Second Amendment had made it six years.

10. *Article* 103 has been substituted by a new Article which reads as follows:

"103. (1) If any question arises as to whether a member of either House of Parliament has become subject to any of the disqualifications mentioned in clause (1) of Article 102, the question shall be referred for the decision of the President and his decision shall be final.

(2) Before giving any decision on any such question, the President shall obtain the opinion of the Election Commission and shall act according to such opinion."

11. *Article* 105 has been amended as follows:

"In Article 105 of the Constitution, in clause (3) for the words "shall be those of the House of Commons of the Parliament of the United Kingdom, and of its members and committees, at the commencement of this Constitution", the words, figures and brackets "shall be those of that House and of its members and committees immediately before the coming into force of section 15 of the Constitution (Forty-Fourth Amendment) Act, 1978" shall be substituted.

12. *Article* 123 was amended by the Forty-Second Amendment Act by adding a new section (4) prohibiting any court of law questioning "the satisfaction of the President" in promulgating an Ordinance. This section has been removed by the Forty-Fourth Amendment.

13. *Article* 132 has been amended as follows:

(*a*) In clause (1), for the words "if the High Court certifies", the words, figures and letter "if the High Court certifies under Article 134A" shall be substituted;
(*b*) Clause (2) shall be omitted;
(*c*) In clause (3), the words "or such leave is granted",

and the words "and, with the leave of Supreme Court, on any other ground" shall be omitted.

14. *Articles* 133 *and* 134 have been amended as follows:

In Article 133 of the Constitution, in clause (1), for the words "if the High Court certifies—", the words, figures and letter "if the High Court certifies under Article 134A—" shall be substituted.

In Article 134 of the Constitution, in sub-clause (c) of clause (1), for the word "certifies", the words, figures and letter "certifies under Article 134A" shall be substituted.

After Article 134 of the Constitution, the following article shall be inserted, namely:

"134A. Every High Court, passing or making a judgment, decree, final order, or sentence, referred to in clause (1) of Article 132 or clause (1) of Article 133, or clause (1) of Article 134,

(*a*) may, if it deems fit so to do, on its own motion; and

(*b*) shall, if an oral application is made, by or on behalf of the party aggrieved, immediately after the passing or making of such judgment, decree, final order or sentence, determine, as soon may be after such passing or making, the question whether a certificate of the nature referred to in clause (1) of Article 132, or clause (1) of Article 133 or, as the case may be, sub-clause (c) of clause (1) of Article 134, may be given in respect of that case."

15. *Article* 139-A, clause (1) is amended as follows:

"(1) Where cases involving the same or substantially the same questions of law are pending before the Supreme Court and one or more High Courts or before two or more High Courts and the Supreme Court is satisfied on its own motion or on an application made by the Attorney-General of India or by a party to any such case that such questions are substantial questions of general importance, the Supreme Court may withdraw the case or cases pending before the High Court or the High Courts and dispose of all the cases itself:

Provided that the Supreme Court may after determining the said questions of law return any case so withdrawn together with a copy of its judgment on such questions to the High Court from which the case has been withdrawn, and the High Court shall on receipt thereof, proceed to dispose of the case in conformity with such judgment."

16. In *Article* 150, for the words "after consultation with", the words "on the advice of" shall be substituted.

17. In *Article* 166 clause (4) prohibiting Courts "requiring the production of any rules made for the more convenient transaction of the business of the Government of the State" has been omitted.

18. Amendment to *Article* 172 restores the original provision of five years regarding the duration of State Legislatures.

19. *Article* 192 has been substituted by the following:

"192. (1) If any question arises as to whether a member of a House of the Legislature of a State has become subject to any of the disqualifications mentioned in clause (1) of Article 191, the question shall be referred for the decision of the Governor and his decision shall be final.

(2) Before giving any decision on any such question, the Governor shall obtain the opinion of the Election Commission and shall act according to such opinion."

20. *Article* 194 is modified as follows:

In Article 194 of the Constitution, in clause (3), for the words "shall be those of the House of Commons of the Parliament of the United Kingdom, and of its members and committees, at the commencement of this Constitution", the words, figures and brackets "shall be those of that House and of its members and committees immediately before the coming into force of section 26 of the Constitution (Forty-Fourth Amendment) Act, 1978" shall be substituted.

21. *Article* 213 clause (4) dealing with "the satisfaction of the Governor in promulgating Ordinance" has been omitted.

22. *Articles* 217, 225, 226 *and* 227 all dealing with High Courts, have been amended. Of these, the most important are the amendments to Article 226 which remove the limitations imposed on the powers of the High Courts by the Forty-Second Amendment.

23. *Article* 239B which gives power to the Administrator to promulgate Ordinances during recess of Legislature of a Union Territory has been omitted.

24. *Article* 257A has been omitted. This was a new Article introduced by the Forty-Second Amendment to provide for the deployment of armed forces of the Union to deal with law and order in any State.

25. In Part XII of the Constitution after Chapter III, the following Chapter has been inserted:

"Chapter IV—Right to Property. 300A. No person shall be deprived of his property save by authority of law."

26. *Article* 329A which makes special provision as to elections to Parliament in the case of the Prime Minister and the Speaker has been omitted.

27. *Article* 352 has been amended as follows:

(*a*) in clause (1):
(*i*) for the words "internal disturbance", the words "armed rebellion" shall be substituted;
(*ii*) the following Explanation shall be inserted at the end, namely:
"Explanation: A Proclamation of Emergency declaring that the security of India or any part of the territory thereof is threatened by war or by external aggression or by armed rebellion may be made before the actual occurrence of war

or of any such aggression or rebellion, if the President is satisfied that there is imminent danger thereof."

(b) for clauses (2), (2A) and (3), the following clauses shall be substituted, namely:

"(2) A Proclamation issued under clause (1) may be varied or revoked by a subsequent Proclamation.

(3) The President shall not issue a Proclamation under clause (1) or a Proclamation varying such Proclamation unless the decision of the Union Cabinet (that is to say, the Council consisting of the Prime Minister and other Ministers of Cabinet rank appointed under Article 75) that such a Proclamation may be issued has been communicated to him in writing.

(4) Every Proclamation issued under this article shall be laid before each House of Parliament and shall, except where it is a Proclamation revoking a previous Proclamation, cease to operate at the expiration of one month unless before the expiration of that period it has been approved by resolutions of both Houses of Parliament:

Provided that if any such Proclamation (not being a Proclamation revoking a previous Proclamation) is issued at a time when the House of the People has been dissolved, or the dissolution of the House of the People takes place during the period of one month referred to in this clause, and if a resolution approving the Proclamation has been passed by the Council of States, but no resolution with respect to such Proclamation has been passed by the House of the People before the expiration of that period, the Proclamation shall cease to operate at the expiration of thirty days from the date on which the House of the People first sits after its reconstitution, unless before the expiration of the said period of thirty days a resolution approving the Proclamation has been also passed by the House of the People.

(5) A Proclamation so approved shall, unless revoked, cease to operate on the expiration of a period of six months from the date of the passing of the second of the resolutions approving the Proclamation under clause (4):

Provided that if and so often as a resolution approving the continuance in force of such a Proclamation is passed by both Houses of Parliament the Proclamation shall, unless revoked, continue in force for a further period of six months from the date on which it would otherwise have ceased to operate under this clause:

Provided further, that if the dissolution of the House of the People, takes place during any such period of six months and a resolution approving the continuance in force of such Proclamation has been passed by the Council of States but no resolution with respect to the continuance in force of such Proclamation has been passed by the House of the People, during the said period, the Proclamation shall cease to operate at the expiration of thirty days from the date on which the House of the People first sits after its reconstitution unless before the expiration of the said period of thirty days, a resolution approving the continuance in force of the Proclamation has been also passed by the House of the People.

(6) For the purposes of clauses (4) and (5), a resolution may be passed by either House of Parliament only by a majority of the total membership of that House and by a majority of not less than two-thirds of the members of that House present and voting.

(7) Notwithstanding anything contained in the foregoing clauses, the President shall revoke a Proclamation issued under clause (1) or a Proclamation varying such Proclamation if the House of the People passes a resolution disapproving, or, as the case may be, disapproving the continuance in force of, such Proclamation.

(8) Where a notice in writing signed by not less than one tenth of the total number of members of the House of the People has been given, of their intention to move a resolution for disapproving, or, as the case may be, for disapproving the continuance in force of, a Proclamation issued under clause (1) or a Proclamation varying such Proclamation:

(*a*) to the Speaker, if the House is in session; or

(*b*) to the President, if the House is not in session, a special sitting of the House shall be held within fourteen days from the date on which such notice is received by the Speaker, or, as the case may be, by the President, for the purpose of considering such resolution;

(*c*) clause (4) shall be renumbered as clause (9) and in

the clause as so numbered, for the words "internal disturbance" in both the places where they occur, the words "armed rebellion" shall be substituted;

(*d*) clause (5) shall be omitted.

28. *Article* 356 has been amended as follows:

(*a*) in clause (4)

(*i*) for the words, brackets and figure "one year from the date of the passing of the second of the resolutions approving the Proclamation under clause (3)" the words "six months from the date of issue of the Proclamation" shall be substituted;

(*ii*) in the first proviso, for the words "one year" the words "six months" shall be substituted;

(*iii*) in the second proviso, for the words "one year" the words "six months" shall be substituted;

(*b*) for clause (5), the following clause shall be substituted, namely:

"(5) Notwithstanding anything contained in clause (4), a resolution with respect to the continuance in force of a Proclamation approved under clause (3) for any period beyond the expiration of one year from the date of issue of such Proclamation shall not be passed by either House of Parliament unless:

(*a*) a Proclamation of Emergency is in operation, in the whole of India or, as the case may be, in the whole or any part of the State, at the time of the passing of such resolution, and

(*b*) the Election Commission certifies that the continuance in force of the Proclamation approved under clause (3) during the period specified in such resolution is necessary on account of difficulties in holding general elections to the Legislative Assembly of the State concerned."

29. *Articles* 358 *and* 359 are amended as follows:

Article 358 of the Constitution shall be renumbered as clause (1) of that article and

(*a*) in clause (1) as so renumbered:

(*i*) in the opening portion, for the words "while a Proclamation of Emergency is in operation", the words "while a Proclamation of Emergency declaring that the security of India or any part of the territory thereof is threatened by war or by external aggression is in operation" shall be substituted;

(*ii*) in the proviso, for the words "where a Proclamation of Emergency", the words "where such Proclamation of Emergency" shall be substituted;

(*b*) after clause (1) as so renumbered, the following clause shall be inserted, namely:

"(2) Nothing in clause (1) shall apply:

(*a*) to any law which does not contain a recital to the effect that such law is in relation to the Proclamation of Emergency in operation when it is made; or

(*b*) to any executive action taken otherwise than under a law containing such a recital."

In Article 359 of the Constitution:

(*a*) in clauses (1) and (1A), for the words and figures "the rights conferred by Part III", the words, figures and brackets "the rights conferred by Part III (except Articles 20 and 21)" shall be substituted;

(*b*) after clause (IA), the following clause shall be inserted, namely:

"(IB) Nothing in clause (IA) shall apply:

(*a*) to any law which does not contain a recital to the effect that such law is in relation to the Proclamation of Emergency in operation when it is made; or

(*b*) to any executive action taken otherwise than under a law containing such a recital."

30. *Articles* 360 *and* 361 have been amended as follows:

In *Article* 360 of the Constitution:

(*a*) for clause (2), the following clause shall be substituted, namely:

"(2) A Proclamation issued under clause (1)

(*a*) may be revoked or varied by a subsequent Proclamation;

(*b*) shall be laid before each House of Parliament;

(*c*) shall cease to operate at the expiration of two months, unless before the expiration of that period it has been approved by resolutions of both Houses of Parliament:

Provided that if any such Proclamation is issued at a time when the House of the People has been dissolved or the dissolution of the House of the People takes place during the period of two months referred to in sub-clause (*c*), and if a resolution approving the Proclamation has been passed by the Council of States, but no resolution with respect to such Proclamation has been passed by the House of the People before the expiration of that period, the Proclamation shall cease to operate at the expiration of thirty days from the date on which the House of the People first sits after its reconstitution, unless before the expiration of the said period of thirty days a resolution approving the Proclamation has been also passed by the House of the People";

(*b*) clause (5) shall be omitted.

After Article 361 of the Constitution, the following article shall be inserted, namely:

"361A.   (1) No person shall be liable to any proceedings, civil or criminal, in any court in respect of the publication in a newspaper of a substantially true report of any proceedings of either House of Parliament or the Legislative Assembly, or, as the case may be, either House of the Legislature, of a State, unless the publication is proved to have been made with malice:

Provided that nothing in this clause shall apply to the publication of any report of the proceedings of a secret sitting of either House of Parliament or the Legislative Assembly, or, as the case may be, either House of the Legislature, of a State.

(2) Clause (1) shall apply in relation to reports or matters broadcast by means of wireless telegraphy as part of any programme or service provided by means of a broadcasting station as it applies in relation to reports or matters published in a newspaper."

Explanation: In this article, "newspaper" includes a news agency report containing material for publication in a newspaper.

31. In the *Ninth Schedule of the Constitution*, entries 87 (The Representation of the People Act, 1951, the Representation of the People (Amendment) Act, 1974 and the Election Laws (Amendment) Act, 1975), 92 (The Maintenance of Internal Security Act, 1971, and 130 (The Prevention of Publication of Objectionable Matter Act, 1976) are omitted.

32. Finally, all those provisions which were included under sections 18, 19, 21, 22, 31, 32, 34, 35, 58 and 59 of the Constitution (Forty-Second Amendment) Act of 1976 have also been omitted.

INDEX

ACTON, LORD, 305

Acts: Administration of Evacuee Property (1950), 256; Ajmer-Merwara (Extension of Laws) (1947), 259; Bihar Land Reforms (1950), 144; British Parliament (1911), 282; Central Provinces and Berar Regulation of Manufacture of Bidis (Agricultural Purposes) (1948), 111; Central Sales Tax (1956), 337; Charter Acts, 33; Citizenship (1955), 75-78; Constitution (1935), 5, 35, 38; 40, 43, 58, 60, 87, 169, 378, 409; Defence of India, 163, 164; Delhi Laws (1912), 258; Government of India (1909), 35; Government of India (1919), 36, 37, 354, 389; Government of India (1935), 3, 5, 6, 38, 43, 143, 169, 257, 306, 313, 323, 354, 373; Hindu Marriage (1955), 175; Hindu Succession (1956), 175; Indian Councils (1861), 35; Indian Independence (1947), 45, 47, 54, 58; Maintenance of Internal Security (MISA), 118, 119, 120, 121, 163, 164; Pitt's India (1784), 33; Preventive Detention Act (1950), 117, 118, 164; Protection of Civil Rights, 101; Public Employment (Requirement as to Residence) Act (1957), 97, 98; Regulating (1773), 33; Representation of the People (1950), 215, 388; Representation of the People (1951), 388; State of Nagaland (1962), 424; States Reorganisation (1956), 67, 200, 206; Untouchability Offences (1955), 100, 101; Uttar Pradesh Zamindari Abolition and Land Reforms (1950), 144

Adult Suffrage, Universal, 19, 20, 21, 53

Advisory Committee, Fundamental Rights and Minorities, 409, 410

Advocate-General, 269, 274, 275

Ahmed, Rashid *vs.* Municipal Board, Kairana, 110, 111

Aiyar, Alladi Krishnaswamy, 48, 131, 255, 268

Akali Dal (Shiromani Akali Dal) *see under* Political Parties

Alexander, A. V., 43

Alexandrowicz, 321

Ali, Fazl, 63

All India Services, 225, 319, 358, 359, 367, 368, 415

Ambedkar, B. R., 6, 12, 13, 14, 15, 16, 17, 18, 27, 48, 54, 58, 105, 116, 117, 127, 155, 177, 196, 197, 213, 252, 254, 272, 282, 293, 303, 304, 313, 333, 335, 349, 359, 421, 430

American Constitution (U.S.A.), 3, 9, 10, 15

Anglo-Indian, 5, 195, 212, 409, 410, 411, 412, 416, 426

Anthony, Frank, 18

Appleby, Paul H., 321, 322

Aristotle, 20, 433

Armed Forces, 90, 194, 291

Asia, 433

Assembly, Constituent, *see under* Constituent Assembly

Atkin, Lord, 164

Attlee, C. R., 42

Attorney-General, 194, 209, 210

Auditor-General of India, 353, 354

August Revolution, 42

Australia, 10, 39, 84, 229, 311, 318; Constitution, 9, 306, 420; House of Representatives, 224, 225; High Court, 9; Senate, 224, 225

Autonomy, Provincial, 38, 40, 43

Ayyangar, Gopalaswamy, N., 48

Ayyar, Venkatrama, 158

461

30

Hirakud, 174
Hitler, 436
House of the People, 19, 198, 205, 221-26, 389, 393, 394, 414, 429
Human Rights Charter, Universal, 89
Human Rights, Declaration of, *see under* United Nations

IMMUNITY OF INSTRUMENTALITIES, DOCTRINE OF, 323
Independence, Judicial, 19, 28, 29, 30
India Act (1784), 31
Indian, Administrative Service, Audit and Accounts Service, Civil Services, *see under* Services
Indian Airlines Corporation, 245
Indian National Congress, *see under* Parties, Political
Indo-China, 41
Indradeo Singh *vs.* The State of Bihar, 106
Industrial Finance Corporation, 245
Inter-State Commission, 335
Inter-State Council, 194, 316, 320
Inter-State Rivers, 315, 316
Inter-State Trade and Commerce, 333-37
Interpretation, Judicial, 7-9
Instrument of Instructions, 169
Iran, 41
Iraq, 41
Irish Republic, 27, 76, 102, 168, 222; Constitution (1935), 27, 88, 109, 168; Ireland, Partition of, 17; Seanad Eireann, 221

JAGJIVAN RAM, 405
Jan Sangh, Bharatiya, *see under* Parties, Political
Japan, 40; Constitution of, 88, 113, 114
Jennings, Sir Ivor, 168
Joint Services Wing Examination, 379

Judicial Committee of Privy Council in London, 249
Judicial Independence, 19, 28, 29, 30
Judicial Service, State, 296
Judicial System, 437

KAMATH, H. V., 127, 341
Kamaraj, K., 402
Kania, Chief Justice, 113, 114
Kapur *vs.* The State of Punjab, 111
Kerala Land Reforms (Amendment) Act (1969), 427; Act (1971), 427
Keshava Singh, 286, 287
Khemchand *vs.* Union of India, 364
Kher, B. G., 383
Kisan Mazdoor Praja Party (The Party of Workers and Peasants), *see under* Parties, Poltical
Kochunni *vs.* State of Madras, 151
Krishnamachari, T. T., 48
Kunzru, H. N., 63, 341

LAND ACQUISITION ACT (1894), 147
Language (Official), 382, 383, 384, 386; Parliamentary Committee on, 383, 384; Report of the Official Language Commission, 383, 384; Regional, 384; In courts, 384, 385
Laski, Harold, 23, 24
Legislative Assembly, Central, 243; Provincial, 47; State, 19, 62, 159, 189, 190, 191, 211, 221, 271, 273, 276, 277, 278, 279, 280, 387, 389, 396, 398, 399, 402, 411, 414, 415; Bihar, 284; Kerala, 136; Nagaland, 424; Orissa, 284; Uttar Pradesh, 189, 284, 286; West Bengal, 287
Legislative Council, 276, 277, 278, 279, 280, 282, 283
Legislative Procedure, 229-37
Legislatures, State, 20, 54, 59, 66, 90, 143, 144, 151, 166, 188, 209, 214, 239, 249, 265, 266, 267, 269, 270, 271, 273, 274, 275, 276-87, 289, 293, 313, 319, 334, 335, 339,

219, 221, 223; of State, 277, 425
Uttar Pradesh Zamindari Abolition
and Land Reforms Act (1950),
see under Acts.

VENKATARAMANA, 97
Vice-President, 188, 193, 208-9, 216,
219, 224, 387, 424, 428
Viceroy, 34
Vizag (shipyard), 174

WAVELL, LORD, 42, 44

Webb, Sydney and Beatrice, 168
Weimar Republic of Germany, 436
Welfare State, 7, 89, 112, 172, 431
World War I, 36, 107
World War II, 39, 86
Writs, Prerogative, *Habeas Corpus,*
155, 157; *Mandamus,* 155, 157,
158; *Certiorari,* 155, 158, 159;
Quo Warranto, 155, 159, 160

ZAKIR HUSAIN, 403
Zamindari, Abolition, 144, 148, 179,
180